D0085349

Religion

and Radical

Politics

Religion

An Alternative

and Radical

Christian Tradition

Politics

in the United States

Robert H. Craig

Temple University Press
Philadelphia

Temple University Press, Philadelphia 19122
Copyright © 1992 by Temple University. All rights reserved
Published 1992
Printed in the United States of America

The paper used in this publication meets the minimum
requirements of American National Standard for Information
Sciences—Permanence of Paper for Printed Library Materials,
ANSI Z39.48-1984
∞
Library of Congress Cataloging-in-Publication Data
Craig, Robert H. (Robert Hedborg), 1942–
Religion and radical politics : an alternative Christian tradition in the
United States / Robert H. Craig.
p.   cm.
Includes bibliographical references and index.
ISBN 0-87722-973-2 (hard : alk. paper)
1. Christianity and politics—History.   2. United States—Social conditions.
3. United States—Politics and government.   I. Title.
BR115.P7C689   1992
261.7′0973—dc20   91-46652

Contents

Acknowledgments

Without the support of my wife, Gail, and my children, Andrew and Ian, this book could not have been written. I am particularly indebted to endless conversations, detailed written comments, and the moral support of David O'Brien, though whatever limitations there are to this book are entirely my own. I also appreciate the assistance I received from Carol DeGrange and Gail Peterson Craig.

I particularly want to thank the staffs of a number of research libraries that have made available a countless array of material and resources from collections at Catholic University, Department of Archives and Manuscripts (Washington, D.C.), State Historical Society of Wisconsin (Madison), Frances E. Willard Memorial Research Library (Evanston, Illinois), Payne Theological Seminary (Wilberforce, Ohio), Wilberforce University (Wilberforce, Ohio), Southern Historical Collection, Manuscripts Department, University of North Carolina (Chapel Hill), Archives of Labor and Urban Affairs, Wayne State University (Detroit, Michigan), Union Theological Seminary (New York, New York), and Yale Divinity School (New Haven, Connecticut).

This book has been in the making for a number of years, shaped by a belief in my accountability to those who have given their lives in the struggle for liberation and all those who seek to create a society in which neither race, class, nor gender set boundaries to realization of one's dreams and the exercise of human freedom. In many ways this book is a conversation with the past, both my own and that of those who have historically shared a belief in the liberative power of Christ's gospel as good news to the poor and oppressed.

Religion

and Radical

Politics

Introduction

Religion and radical politics are most often associated with the Third World, where the resurgence of Islam or a radicalized church in Latin America seems to characterize the role that religion plays in struggles for social change. By contrast, religion in the United States is viewed as linked either to the Right, notably to such figures as Pat Robertson and Jerry Falwell and other politically conscious Protestant evangelicals, or to mainstream liberal politics supported by Protestants and Catholics aligned with the Democratic Party. Part of the explanation lies in the fact that for decades the types of political choices that religious people have made have been shaped and limited by the religious and political liberalism advocated by progressive Catholics working out the implications of official Catholic social teachings or by Protestants whose political heritage is deeply rooted in an earlier social gospel tradition and the Christian realism of Reinhold Niebuhr and his followers.

For Protestants both the social gospel, from the post–Civil War period to the Great Depression, and Niebuhr's Christian realism had a tremendous influence on the choice of ethical issues that were addressed and answered over the course of the last one hundred years, and they have colored the evaluations of populist movements and radical individuals. Catholic ethical reflection and analysis has been shaped by official social teachings of the church; the clergy and hierarchy have selected the issues to address and have developed the church perspective on them. Not until the advent of the Catholic Worker movement did serious ethical reflection take place outside the official tradition. In both cases, among Protestants and Catholics, the historical memory that sets the context for Christian ethical reflection tends to center on the dominant religious institutions and organizations, on the clergy, and by the middle of the twentieth century, on academic ethicists doing their work in a Christian framework. Given this emphasis, it is more than possible that Christian ethics may, wittingly and unwittingly, have served the interest of the dominant classes in church and society.[1]

1

This book is an exploration of the history of Christians who discovered the convergence between radical politics and Christian faith and the implications this convergence has for movements for social change. The past, in the words of Karl Marx, "weighs like a nightmare on the brain of the living,"[2] and if the present is to be the place where creative possibilities for the future are made actual, the past needs to be seen not as a nightmare but as a source of hope. This book considers the dominant religious traditions but places more weight on individuals and social movements that, while not necessarily representative of mainstream politics or religious attitudes, provide resources, insights, and forms of empowerment for responding to the contradictions of American society in the present. These persons and groups have for the most part been ignored in the writing of American religious history and the practice of Christian social ethics. They have not fit easily into the schemes of Christian social thought and action usually represented as the most significant. At the very least, they offer important critical comments on the social gospel, Christian realism, and Catholic social teachings. Together, they suggest an alternative tradition, still alive, that may be able to help us address the problems of poverty, oppression, and violence that remain before us.

Concretely, I suggest that certain groups have been left out of our historical memory; they have been ignored, as blacks and women have, or in the case of the industrial working class, their experience was interpreted and their situation judged from the standpoint of outsiders who claimed to speak on their behalf. Recent work in American social history brings to light African Americans, women, and working-class people who spoke and acted for themselves, as well as priests, pastors, and laypeople who, out of their solidarity with the poor and oppressed, offered alternative readings of the Christian tradition.

Like Judaism, Christianity is, according to Eduardo Hoornaert, a memory religion based "on a fund of historical data engraved on the memory of the faithful throughout the course of their history." Consequently, a recovery of the memory, both individual and collective, of Americans who have sought to be faithful to the gospel as good news for the poor, believed in God's deliverance from bondage of all those who are oppressed, and struggled for social justice can bring hope, for as Hoornaert believes, "Hope is bound up with memory. The vehicle of Christian hope is Christian memory. Without it Christian hope simply would not be." We might discover that there is a relationship between historical knowledge and present action, that "we ourselves are shaped by the past," as Christopher Hill puts it, but at the same time "from our vantage point in the present we are continually reshaping the past which shapes us."[3]

Most important, this book recounts historical events that have transformed the life histories of some remarkable human beings who have found their own voices and ways of responding to the varying forms of domination that have conditioned their lives. They can teach us how to regain the critical capacity to think, act, and reflect on the economic, political, social, and cultural forces that have shaped our lives so that we might be able to create a juster and more equitable society. It means a willingness to acknowledge that we can learn from others, especially people most often dismissed as unimportant because they lack power, status, and prominence in the eyes of people who measure the world according to the standards of wealth and privilege.

There is something very moving about listening to the poor and the marginalized as they speak about this country, the role of the church, and the disquieting radicality of Christian faith. If there is one theme in this book, it is diversity, not only of opinion but of analysis of what constitutes an alternative vision of America and what we can be as a people. There seems to be a new realization that in spite of all that divides us we desperately need a viable community, what Wendell Berry calls "a place, a resource, and an economy . . . [that] answers the needs, practical as well as social and spiritual, of its members—among them the need to need one another. The answer to the present alignment of political power with wealth is the restoration of community and economy." Neither Berry nor any of the individuals and social movements that you will encounter in this book would argue that a rediscovery of community is easy, for although almost everyone agrees that community is a meaningful concept, as Berry says, "neither our economy, nor our government, nor our education system runs on the assumption that community has value—a value, that is, that *counts* in any practical or powerful way." [4] The aspirations for community have taken various forms throughout the history of the United States, ranging from the struggle for economic democracy and a participatory expression of socialism to the search for alternatives to violence, racial hatred, and a gender-based social system.

In many ways the individuals and movements described in this book are part of a long tradition that understands the Christian gospel as, above all else, good news to the poor and oppressed. From the beginning of Christianity to the present, certain Christians have held fast to a "Galilean vision," the view that the practice of love and justice, rather than the legitimation of wealth and power, are the hallmarks of Christian witness. Most often it has been the poor who have challenged the fidelity of the church to its founder and have denounced the glaring gap between word and deed. In the United States Christians themselves created a radical tradition. In the title of his classic work *The Making of the English Working Class*, E. P. Thompson uses the word *making* to convey the degree to which men and women are active agents in the process of social change. Similarly, the making of a radical Christian tradition in the United States was part of a historic process whereby certain Christians discovered that God was present where people struggled for social and economic justice, affirmed the inherent worth and dignity of all persons, and committed themselves to the liberation of the oppressed. [5]

Here we encounter people who have much in common with members of Christian communities in Latin America who, writes Penny Lernoux, "live

3

their theology through solidarity, charity, and self-sacrifice. Theology is not an ivory-tower science but the application of faith, and as such it can challenge the secular and religious authorities on many issues." [6] Faith is not an abstraction but what empowers people to act, to engage in social transformation of the world about them. At the same time, the political arena becomes a context in which the radicality of faith is disclosed. As commitment to those marginalized by the dominant order deepens so does an awareness of the radical demands of the gospel and of a God who has throughout history sided with the poor.

Those who advocate varying theologies of liberation place great importance on the verification of faith by recalling the emphasis of the biblical tradition on doing the truth—a recognition that one's knowledge of God is most vividly expressed in the practice of justice. For them, Christian practice becomes the locus of theological reflection and analysis by joining faith and life and, so, in the words of Susan Brooks Thistlethwaite and Mary Potter Engel, calling "into question the dominant understanding that relieved theology and religious life of all political decisions and responsibilities. No longer are faith and life, theology and politics split apart, nor are abstract principles imposed upon the life of faith. Instead, liberation theologies stress the obligation of the Christian community and Christian theology to reflect and act upon their responsibilities in history." [7]

Martin Duberman has emphasized how much "a particular personality intersects with a particular subject matter." In other words, there is a correlation between what we write and the material we select or ignore, who we are as individuals and how we perceive the world. This book is, of course, no exception. It is only a beginning, a preliminary attempt to examine our past in the belief that sociohistorical analysis is an important ingredient in the development of a liberative approach to Christian ethics. It is certainly not an exhaustive treatment of what should constitute the totality of our historical memory.[8]

The five chapters of this book cover over a hundred years of American history, from the end of the Civil War to the latter part of the twentieth century. Chapter One, "Nineteenth-Century Labor Radicalism," raises questions about economic justice and a democratic society as viewed by working-class people and their supporters active in the Christian Labor Union, the fight for an eight-hour day, and the Knights of Labor. The Christian Labor Union was one of the earliest manifestations of Christian solidarity with the struggles of working-class people against industrial capitalism, and the Knights of Labor was the largest working-class organization in American history prior to the emergence of the Congress of Industrial Organizations in the 1930s. During this period the conflict between labor and capital brought forth some remarkable prophets: Jesse H. Jones, Edward H. Rogers, and T. Wharton Collens. These men, as well as the Knights of Labor and the Christian Labor Union combined the insights of a working-class interpretation of Christianity with an earlier republican tradition. They sought to replace competition with cooperation, self-interest with mutual trust, and the good of the individual with the common good.

Chapter Two, "Religion, Women, and Politics," is an analysis of feminism, class, and gender during the late nineteenth and early twentieth centuries. The chapter focuses on the lives of Frances Willard and "Mother" Jones. No two women were more dissimilar in background, tastes, and experience, and yet they both raised profound questions about the role, status, and place of women in American society. Jones in many ways typified the experience of immigrant Catholic working-class people as they came into conflict with a predominately Protestant culture. Willard, though a product of the Protestant middle class, was to become an outspoken critic of Protestant dominance, especially in its denial of equal rights and opportunities for women, and came to share as fervently as Jones the desire for a juster and more equitable social order.

Chapter Three, "The Fractured Vision of Christians and Socialists," deals with Christian Socialists and Eugene V. Debs's Socialist Party during the early twentieth century. Particular attention is given to the American Socialists' problematic handling of the relationship between race and class. While white Christian Socialists were pointing out the incompatibility between the teachings of Jesus and the dictates of a market economy, black Christians such as George Washington Woodbey, George W. Slater, Jr., and Reverdy Ransom envisioned a socialism that took seriously the reality of race as a significant factor in the shaping of American history.

Chapter Four, "Radical Politics and Southern Prophets," is the story of the struggle for racial equality as exemplified by the history of the Southern Tenant Farmers' Union and the People's Institute of Applied Religion during the 1930s and 1940s. It is important to recall that decades before the civil rights movement countless poor black and white sharecroppers and their allies embodied a Christian commitment to racial justice. Central to the story are the lives of Howard Kester and Claude Williams, southern white preachers who attempted to understand the burden of color as they combatted a system of domination in which poverty and racism were inseparable.

The fifth and final chapter, "The Great Evasion," deals with Marxism and nonviolence within the context of a critique of American capitalism and an affirmation of our need for community. The chapter is a study of Reinhold Niebuhr, Harry F. Ward, A. J. Muste, and Dorothy Day, who represent differing streams of twentieth-century Christian thought and practice. Niebuhr's approach to social reality stressed politics as the art of the possible. By contrast, Ward, Muste, and Day saw politics as an exercise of human imagination able to conceive the world and human possibilities in new and challenging ways. They had a fundamental belief in the redemptive power of Christian faith and an understanding of the democratic process that spoke of the person-in-community and the need for a recovery of the public dimension of life.

Nineteenth-Century

Labor Radicalism

The Christian Labor Union and the

Knights of Labor

The U.S. Catholic bishops' pastoral letter "Economic Justice for All" renewed the public debate about economic justice. Central to the bishops' letter, as David Hollenbach points out, is the idea that justice requires that all people be able not only to satisfy their basic economic and social needs but to participate fully in the life of the community. The bishops, drawing on a biblical tradition that speaks on behalf of the poor and marginalized, ask us to rethink our economic priorities as a people and come to terms with an increasing gap between the rich and the poor, both at home and abroad. While one can rightly point to the economic policies of the Reagan administration and its legacy of a staggering deficit, misplaced military priorities, and rapid increase in the rate of deindustrialization, the basic realities of inequality are not new to the American historical experience. Samuel P. Hays stresses that inequality is in fact fundamental to an understanding of American history. Irrespective of steady, if uneven, economic growth, periodic movements for reform, creation of new institutions aimed at easing the maldistribution of wealth and power, and changes in the governing political party and political rhetoric, inequality has persisted. Unfortunately, we have not shown equal persistence in addressing its sources and meaning.[1]

This chapter focuses on issues of inequality and economic injustice as analyzed by late nineteenth-century workers, particularly through the Christian Labor Union and the Knights of Labor. Working-class people recognized that inequality was not limited to income distribution but had to do with the very structure of industrial capitalism. The new industrial capitalist order, as they saw it, deprived people of control over the conditions that shaped their lives, debased the meaning of community, and reduced human beings to interchangeable parts of the industrial machine. Combining the insights of Christian faith with an earlier republican tradition, workers demanded freedom and equality, not only in the political arena but in the marketplace, since they believed they had economic and social rights that were as inalienable as those proclaimed by the founders of the American Republic.

Workers' critiques of American capitalism, their differing visions of how society should be reorganized, and their theological and ethical assessments of the emerging industrial order have been overlooked. Historians, ethicists, and other scholars have studied the gospel of wealth, the social gospel, and the beginnings of Catholic social teaching. Of course radicalized social gospel proponents and progressive members of the Catholic hierarchy did attempt to speak on *behalf* of working class people, but the fact remains that when oppressed people speak *for themselves,* name *their own reality,* and give voice to *their own experience,* their discourse is not only qualitatively different but disquieting. We must listen to this discourse if we are to rediscover what makes authentic economic justice possible, especially a justice that, as the bishops insist, requires not only equity but full participation by all persons.

The point deserves careful consideration because it is central to the argument of this book. Otto Maduro, Venezuelan theologian and sociologist, writes that "exploited classes frequently find themselves related to a particular religion in such a way that, instead of finding it an obstacle to their emancipation, they find original, unexpected and fruitful perspectives in it for their revolutionary struggle." Although the situation facing late nineteenth-century workers was not necessarily revolutionary, many workers found in the Christian tradition symbols and stories that affirmed their effort to resist the dominant social order and legitimated their struggle for an alternative. In doing so, they risked becoming rebels, outsiders, in the church as well as in society. Capitalism, after all, was and is maintained not only by economic and political means but by ideological means as well. Karl Marx insisted that "the ideas of the ruling class in every epoch are the ruling ideas, and the reason for this is that every class which is the ruling material force in society is, at the same time, its ruling intellectual force." [2]

The Italian Marxist Antonio Gramsci exposed the subtleties of this ideological dominance. According to Gramsci, the ideology of the capitalist class not only justifies its power but gains the active consent of the oppressed in their own oppression. In other words, the ruling class establishes its hegemony, summarized succinctly by Gwynn Williams as "an order in which a certain way of life and thought is dominant, in which one concept of reality is diffused throughout society in all its institutional and private manifestations, informing with its spirit all taste, morality, customs, religious and political principles, and all social relations, particularly in their intellectual and moral connotations." John Cammett quotes this definition in his study of Gramsci and points out that hegemony is obtained by consent rather than force and "in a general sense . . . refers to the 'spontaneous' loyalty that any dominant social group obtains from the masses by virtue of its social and intellectual prestige and its supposedly superior function in the world of production." [3]

For our purposes, what is at issue is the religious legitimation of industrial capitalism and how so many came to accept its social values and goals as their own. In that context it is important to explore how a working-class understanding of Christianity challenged the hegemonic function of the religion of the Gilded Age, how at least some workers created alternative ways of understanding themselves, their religion, and their world. In addition, given the manner in which the churches were enlisted, directly or indirectly, to sanction the new industrial order, the religious dimension of workers' experience could not be limited to organizations that used Christian labels or to utterances clearly discernible as explicitly religious. Religion was a part of daily experience, manifested in alternative visions and in expressions of human solidarity and the burning aspirations of the human spirit. If Christian faith has to do with the wholeness of human life, if it sustains the striving for community, if it gives concrete shape to love and justice and makes irreducible the worth of the human person, then religious and Christian experience cannot be confined to "official" Christian organizations or "orthodox" religious symbols and language.

Herbert Gutman's "Protestantism and the American Labor Movement: The Christian Spirit in the Gilded Age" was one of the first attempts to probe the significance of working-class interpretations of Christianity. It is particularly striking how greatly Protestant workers' understanding of a prophetic Christianity differed from the dominant religious ethos of the period and from the social gospel of middle-class Protestants. In place of a Christ who comforted the rich (the gospel of wealth) and a Christ who asked only that people be kind to one another (the social gospel), workers found a Christ who was, in the words of *Railway Times*, "an agitator such as the world has never seen before nor since . . . despised and finally murdered to appease the wrath of the ruling class of His time." In this reading, common among members of the Knights of Labor and the Christian Labor Union, Moses and Aaron became union organizers, and Peter, James, and John were three common sailors. The lot of working-class people was thought to be analogous to the captivity of Hebrew slaves, and their struggle for freedom, another Exodus. Andrew Carnegie and especially Henry Clay Frick were seen as modern-day pharaohs. Such readings of Scripture, such renderings of the tradition, even if confined to a minority, are important. C. Vann Woodward once insisted that the system of racial segregation "didn't just happen; it was consciously constructed. There could have been other choices and other people made other choices. Not all of those who were subject to the dominant system were in accord with it; that is, they dissented from it." The same could be said of nineteenth-century industrial capitalism.[4]

For those who believe that the system needs change, it is extremely important to know that they have predecessors, even a tradition, with which they can identify as Christians and as Americans. To better understand the choices workers made and their contribution to the struggle for economic justice, we need to examine the socioeconomic context in which industrial expansion took place and the Catholic and Protestant assessments of that system in the setting of conflicts between labor and capital.

Workers and Industrial America

The United States, unlike Europe, did not undergo a long period of transition from feudalism to capitalism; private property and relatively open markets in land and capital were well established during the colonial era. At the end of the American Revolution, about four-fifths of the nonslave adult men were independent property owners or professionals. A century later, by contrast, only one-third of the adult working men operated independent enterprises. By then control over the instruments of production had passed to nonworkers, as the workshops of independent craftsmen were replaced by factories that depended on an adequate supply of cheap labor. The sources were the surplus population of rural areas, displaced craftsmen, and most important, European immigrants. The U.S. population rose from 31.5 million in 1860 to 63 million in 1890 to 106.4 million in 1920; during that period 29 million immigrants came to the United States. Most were members of the working class, and they concentrated in the urban industrial centers of the North and West. During the period 1870–1920, 40 percent of the working class was foreign-born. A working class of immigrants and a Catholic church of immigrants faced managers and owners who were disproportionately native-born and Protestant.[5]

Mark Twain labeled the late nineteenth century "the Gilded Age," when material success measured one's humanity. A Norwegian observer, Knut Hamsun, wrote in the late 1880s: "A way of life has evolved in America that turns exclusively upon . . . acquiring material goods, a fortune. Americans are so absorbed in the scramble for profit that all their faculties are devoted to it; all their interests revolve around it." Hamsun concluded that "America's morality is money." The scramble seemed to pay off. By the end of the century the United States led the world in production of consumer and capital goods, thanks to government support, availability of foreign and domestic capital, technological advances in manufacturing, communications, transportation, mining, agriculture, and the apparently limitless supply of cheap labor. Andrew Carnegie summed up the triumph of this material progress: "We may safely say that no nation has ever enjoyed such universal prosperity. . . . It is probable that in many future decades the citizen is to look back upon this as the golden age of the Republic and long for a return to its conditions."[6]

Capital's golden age was perceived quite differently by members of the working class. In their view entrepreneurs like Carnegie had destroyed established trade unions, gained control over the production process, and reduced skilled workers to dependent wage earners. In doing so, they had also severed the relationship between work and human meaning, for the sense of dignity and self-worth of American working people had always been related to control of the productive enterprise. Farmers, independent craftsmen, and mechanics had long believed, with such American heroes as Benjamin Franklin and Thomas Jefferson, that wealth derived from labor; when people lost control of

9

their labor, the wealth created by work was easily transferred into other hands. By 1880 this principle sounded radical in the extreme. Robert Bennett, master workman of the Illinois State Assembly of the Knights of Labor, contended that what was happening to workers was the submission of labor to capital. Entrepreneurs were taking "from the toiling millions an unjust share of wealth they create, by way of watered stock on railroads, our financial system, truck stores . . . [and] the result of improved machinery, the enactment of laws (State and National) in favor of corporations, and laying burdens grievous to be borne by the industrial people." [7]

To justify this transfer of wealth, Carnegie and other celebrants of progress had to overcome the labor theory of value. They also had to ignore the economic depressions of 1873–1878, 1883–1885, and 1893–1897 and overlook the living and working conditions of American workers. Because of long hours and the structure of the workplace, the United States had one of the world's highest industrial accident rates. Between 1880 and 1900 over 35,000 workers were killed annually; an additional 536,000 were injured in the same period. Statistics compiled by state bureaus of labor regularly pointed to unhealthy housing, inadequate diet, and dangerous work environments. In 1884, for example, an Illinois Bureau of Labor Statistics report described the living conditions of a Polish upholsterer and his family, living in Chicago, whose total income for the year was $360:

> Family numbers 4—parents and two children, two boys, aged five and nine years, and one of them attends school. They rent a house containing 3 rooms for $5 per month, which is dirty and in an unhealthy location, and consequently had considerable sickness during the past year. The children pick up coal on railway track, and while doing so, one of them was run over by the cars, thereby losing a leg. He now blacks boots and sells newspapers, but his earnings are not taken into consideration. Father carries no life insurance, and does not belong to a trade union.

In the 1880s almost 40 percent of working-class families lived in poverty, earning less than the five hundred dollars a year necessary to provide a family of five with such basic necessities as food and housing. One out of four of these poor families lived in utter destitution, often surviving by scavenging, begging, and stealing. About 45 percent of the working class lived just above the poverty line, ever fearful of sickness, accidents, unemployment, and death. Only about 15 percent of the American working class enjoyed relative security, and even this group faced the constant threat of downward mobility. [8]

Whatever Carnegie may have believed, American workers, immigrant or native-born, did not think that the contrast between poverty and progress was inevitable or just; they agreed with Knights of Labor leaders such as Robert Bennett that owners were robbing workers of the fruits of their labor. The response of workers took a variety of forms ranging from political protest through the organization of local and national unions to protracted and often bitter strikes. The list of major strikes for the period extends from the Great Railroad Strikes of 1877 to the Homestead, Pullman, and Coeur d'Alene strikes of the 1890s. Against these actions employers used strikebreakers, private armies (which labor editor John Swinton described as "kept for the service of such corporations or capitalists as may hire [them] . . . for the suppression of such strikes as may be stirred by the turning of monopoly screws"), state militias, and a court system that had, in Gerald Eggert's words, a "predilection for the corporate side." [9]

By the turn of the twentieth century mass production had become the norm in manufacturing, and entrepreneurs like Carnegie had given way to the more impersonal corporations. By 1929 consolidation made the corporation the single most characteristic feature of the American economy. The end result was the creation of a corporate state, which integrated the corporation and the government in a working alliance. Cultural institutions provided the necessary legitimation to blunt challenges from the Left, especially socialism, through modest reforms aimed at easing discontent without changing the distribution of wealth and power. In addition, the growth of the corporate state served the major function of assuring market and financial stability by government intervention. [10]

Religion in the Gilded Age

In the Gilded Age religion, Protestant or Catholic, was a powerful force in American life, shaping fundamental individual and social values, judgments about right and wrong, and perceptions of industrial America. The religious press, pulpits, and self-proclaimed friends and foes of labor conveyed mixed signals to working-class people about the role religion should play in daily life. Legitimators of the status quo assumed that religious institutions and their representatives believed in the benefits of material progress as God-given as the gulf that divided owners from workers. Others, more sympathetic to the plight of working-class people, attempted to come to terms with the effects of industrialization, urbanization, and rapid social change by urging Christians to be charitable and responsible. Neither group had much to offer angry spokespersons for laborers, who had their doubts about religious proposals and pious platitudes. Most labor leaders thought the Protestant churches ignored the needs of the working class. Joseph Buchanan, Socialist, labor editor, and leader in the Knights of Labor strike against Jay Gould's railroad system during the 1880s, contended that "with few exceptions the pulpit took no interest in the labor movement except to lecture it and abuse it." Buchanan's observation was supported by workers' answers to questionnaires collected by the Massachusetts Bureau of Statistics of Labor. A late nineteenth-century study by H. Francis Power for the *American Journal of Sociology* concluded that Protestant ministers and the churches in general had little interest in the problems facing working people. One anonymous worker commented to Power: "The Church has, as an organized body, no sympathy with the masses. It is a sort of fashionable club where the rich are entertained and amused, and where most of the ministers are muzzled by their masters and dare not preach the gospel of the carpenter of Nazareth. The unjust and inequitable manner in which the commercial class, which sustains and maintains the churches for its own selfish purposes, has treated them, causes the laboring men to have nothing to do with the churches." [11]

What workers observed was the easy identification religious leaders too often made between Christianity and the status quo. Protestants, in particular, celebrated laissez-faire capitalism as the natural order ordained by God; many gave a theological coating to Social Darwinism as the unfolding of God's grace in the world. The result was the sanctification of private property and belief in the inevitability of competition and, says Yehoshua Arieli, in the "fixed relation between godliness . . . and successes and between vice and poverty." The bishops of the Methodist Episcopal church, the largest and wealthiest Protestant denomination in the country, preached responsibility to the rich and patience to the poor. Protestant luminaries such as Henry Ward Beecher assessed America's progress as a nation in terms of its material prosperity; he tied progress to riches and took the accumulation of wealth as a sign of God's favor and as a positive influence that made "the community more refined, and the whole land more civilized." Russell Conwell, Baptist minister, popular lecturer, and founder of the Philadelphia Temple, later Temple University, blatantly championed the connection between wealth and Christianity in "Acres of Diamonds," a lecture he delivered over six thousand times. Conwell told his audience it was their "duty to get rich," indeed, "your Christian and godly duty to do so." Protestant leaders gave their blessings to other movements that accompanied material progress, from modern science and technology to the belief that the market was the measure by which justice was to be achieved in social relations. Many Protestants, in their role as legitimators of industrial capitalism, simply overlooked what Jackson Lears calls the "darker side" of modernity, excusing or evading the pain, conflict, violence, and social dislocation of industrial America.[12]

In the latter part of the nineteenth century, however, new advocates of a public Protestantism appeared, more alert than the previous generation to the social demands of the Christian tradition. The social gospel movement, as it came to be known, arose among middle-class Protestants, largely but not exclusively clergy. Gradually its participants developed a new theological framework from their experience with the contradictions of capitalism—the conflicts between labor and capital and the gulf between wealth and poverty. As pastors, social workers, and church extension workers, these men and women wanted to make the church more responsive to the needs of workers and immigrants. Yet, with few exceptions, they remained wedded to basic elements of industrial capitalism and modern culture. The social gospel movement drew upon liberal theology, whose principal tenet was progress, interpreted as the ongoing development of the Kingdom of God in history. In addition, liberal social gospel leaders believed that the teachings of Jesus provided the criteria for judging the individual and society, and therefore they often considered such abstract concepts as cooperation, mutuality, service, personality, and sentimental love to be adequate guides in the formulation of economic and social policy. In Charles Sheldon's enormously popular novel *In His Steps*, for example, the pastor, a disciple of the social gospel, asks his congregation to consider the challenges the life of Jesus presents to all those who deem themselves his followers. What would it mean, he asks, to shape one's conduct on the question "What would Jesus do?" Sheldon and other liberals saw the human person as primarily moral and rational, and thus susceptible to moral suasion. They believed not necessarily that human beings are perfectible but that human nature is sufficiently plastic to allow for the creation of a new social order through individual conversion and benevolent action. The result of integrating the experience of suffering and social conflict with a liberal theology was an emphasis on the social dimensions of sin and on the possibility of building the Kingdom of God through cooperation and love.[13]

At heart, the social gospel was an attempt to Christianize society by reshaping social attitudes and institutions. Those who preached the social gospel sought to prick the conscience of a complacent public by speaking on behalf of those who bore the burden of unrestrained capitalism, but they remained out of touch with working-class life and certainly with working-class readings of Christianity. Advocates for a social gospel, like so many progressives, at times appeared radical as compared to apologists for the status quo, but their principle constituency remained the middle class, and their viewpoint reflected their identification with that class. Believing themselves to be neutrals in the struggle between labor and capital, they thought they could judge the conflicts of their time impartially. They were fearful of taking sides, lest the church, in the words of Shailer Mathews, "be identified with one social class and so lose its grip upon all others." [14]

What they offered was less an analysis of capitalism or a sociopolitical means of transforming the existing system than exhortations to do good. The "father" of the social gospel movement, Washington Gladden, argued that if the capitalists would measure both profits and wages by the Golden Rule, "instant peace" would result. Josiah Strong also located the primary cause of societal ills in selfishness. The institutional expression of the social gospel, the Federal Council of Churches, suggested that conflicts between industry and labor could be solved through cooperation. In seeking support for such cooperation, the council extolled "the doctrine of stewardship," convinced that "if only the churches in the process of education and moral suasion get owners to hold their property as stewards of God, our industrial problems would be solved." Even Walter Rauschenbusch, the most articulate and representative leader of the social gospel movement, could not escape its moralistic cast. Rauschenbusch had a basic faith in the power of ideas; he believed that the hope for human progress originated in religion, which he identified with moral forces, not with politics or education. In very Ritschlian terms he stressed that "the religious idea alone had power to transform." To workers Rauschenbusch offered "Christian, human sympathy" as a fundamental "remedy" to their problems. Such sympathy, joined with a conversion of the wealthy and powerful, would bring about the needed changes in the socioeconomic order. Henry F. May concluded that the "Social Gospel of the American nineteenth century . . . did not grow out of actual suffering but rather out of moral and intellectual dissatisfaction with the sufferings of others. It originated not with the 'disinherited' but rather with the educated and pious middle class. It grew through argument not through agitation; it pleaded for conversion, not revolt or withdrawal." [15]

Middle-class Protestants, even the best intentioned, remained outside the working class, unlike Catholics, who made up a heavy proportion of America's ethnically diverse workers. The institutional response of the Catholic church to the needs of working people was filtered through a maze of varying problems. For one thing, the demands of contending ethnic groups threatened to fragment the church. In addition, the church had to deal with nativists who perceived the post–Civil War influx of Catholic immigrants as undermining the Protestant "character" of America. As the nineteenth-century Methodist historian Daniel Dorchester put it, "The Roman Catholic Church is inimical to the best progress of society, and in direct antagonism to the historical religion of the nation— the religion of the Holy Scriptures." Finally, there was Rome's fear of secret societies and socialism. The European church associated secret societies with anti-Catholic groups such as the Masons. In the United States, secrecy and secret initiation rituals were part of workers' fraternal and mutual aid organizations such as the Odd Fellows, the Knights Templar, the Ancient Order of United Workmen, and the Sovereigns of Industry as well as early trade unions including the Knights of Saint Crispin and the Knights of Labor. The issue of secret societies came to a head when the Vatican condemned the Knights of Labor in Canada in 1884. Cardinal James Gibbons, fearing the possible alienation of the working class from the church and sensitive to the reaction of nativists, supported the Knights of Labor and forestalled condemnation in the United States. Despite their defense of the Knights of Labor, the hierarchy remained fearful of radicalism as antithetical to Christian life and dangerous for the still-insecure U.S. church. Papal teachings, particularly Leo XIII's *Rerum*

Novarum, affirmed the rights of working people, including the right to a living wage, but at the same time sanctified private property. Deep hostility to socialism and fear of governmental intervention against the church, in the words of David O'Brien, "set a framework beyond which reformers were forbidden to go." [16]

As one analyzes the strategy bishops employed to deal with the pressing conflicts between labor and capital, Joseph M. McShane's characterization of "masterly inactivity" seems most apt. Poverty was perceived not as a structural problem but as related to personal vices and attitudes. Consequently, the response of the church was to support temperance and the charitable works of various ethnic organizations and religious orders. One does not find among the bishops the uncritical Protestant celebration of wealth and privilege, but neither does one find a clear understanding of labor's problems. Cardinal Gibbons, often cast as a "friend" of labor, considered strikes a "questionable remedy" to the problems facing working-class people. Instead, he advised hard work, sobriety, self-denial, godliness, and contentment with "your station in life." Similarly, while Archbishop John Ireland took Leo XIII's encyclical as evidence that the church was the champion of working people, he unquestioningly accepted the myth of rags to riches and was sure that capital accumulation was socially beneficial. The "toiler," he thought, realizes that "he lives in a land of opportunities, where he may be rich to-morrow, and he is glad to defend his right to possible future possessions, by defending to-day the rights of other men to their possessions." [17]

Moving from the statements of the hierarchy to the role the church actually played in the lives of working-class Catholics presents a multidimensional picture. Richard T. Ely, the social gospel economist, observed that the average Catholic priest, as compared to his Protestant counterpart, had a better grasp of the problems facing workers. But that understanding did not automatically mean that priests supported the workers' cause. Victor Greene's study of the Slavic community in the anthracite coal regions of Pennsylvania points to the pivotal role of the church in helping uprooted peasants deal with the harsh realities of the coal-mining industry. Some priests supported the union-organizing efforts of Slavic workers; others saw unions as disruptive of law and order. In other parts of the country, from Rutland, Vermont, to DeSoto, Missouri, priests were occasionally active supporters and leaders of the Knights of Labor.[18]

Community studies by labor historians find the role of the church in the lives of working-class Catholics at best problematic. Stephan Thernstrom's analysis of Newburyport, Massachusetts, stresses how a largely Irish working-class Catholic population contributed to the growth of both church property and Catholic voluntary organizations. While working-class people were responsible for developing the prestige the church acquired over the course of the late nineteenth century, effective control of the church remained in the hands of a business elite, supported by the clergy, who espoused the dominant ideology of industry and success. Hundreds of miles away, in Albany, New York, Irish workers also contributed to the growth and development of the Catholic church. Church-sponsored voluntary cultural and social organizations forged a strong common Catholic identity. Nevertheless, parish life was still shaped by a business elite, which, like its Newburyport counterpart, was committed to the values of hard work, self-restraint, private property, and the overall soundness of the capitalist social order. Finally, John T. Cumbler, in his study of Lynn, Massachusetts, concludes that the church of Lynn did not really understand the problems facing its Irish working-class constituency. By continually taking a conservative stance on labor and social issues, the church failed to provide a countervailing institutional force. It refused to support union activities or any form of political or social action not under church sponsorship. It "opposed . . . all principles of subversive human society whether they be known as liberalism, socialism, anarchism, or by any other term." [19]

Further evidence of Catholic ambivalence and caution can be found in the work of Catholic journalists. During the 1870s, for example, Patrick Ford, editor of the *Irish World*, supported trade unions and strikes as means of resisting "combined Capital" and obtaining justice, and he regularly condemned a class system based on the perpetuation of human misery and exploitation. Ford later modified his views; in the late 1880s and 1890s he struggled as hard to combat radical ideas among Irish workers as he had earlier done to make them acceptable. As the *Irish World* became increasingly conservative, the Boston *Pilot*, under the editorship of John Boyle O'Reilly, became the leading advocate for labor. Historian Aaron Abell contends that the *Pilot* "devoted more attention . . . to the working-class agitation than did any other journal not published under labor auspices." O'Reilly denounced all forms of injustice that debased human beings, made in the image of God, but unlike Ford in his radical phase, O'Reilly opposed the use of strikes to solve labor's problems and argued instead for arbitration. O'Reilly was a romantic idealist who hoped for the resolution of societal problems by the application of "spiritual values of generosity, kindness, truth, and sacrifice." [20]

What gained the *Pilot* its notoriety were not so much O'Reilly's editorials as the weekly commentaries of the paper's anonymous labor correspondent, "Phineas." Here, Aaron Abell notes, was one of the few mainstream Christian commentators to grasp the central idea that labor's hopes for the future lay in its own hands. Only if workers organized themselves, instead of relying on the "better classes," could they create labor organizations such as the Knights of Labor to give "courage and confidence to the hitherto hopeless masses" and thus regain their lost sense of dignity and worth. The Catholic *Quincy Monitor* went beyond Phineas in exposing the political and economic sources of labor's problems. One editorial, "Workingman's Friends," noted with feigned amazement that during election years textile manufacturers and coal and iron "kings," who "receive the wages of treason from Capitalists," had the "un-blushing effrontery" to pose as the friends of working people. It seemed to the *Quincy Monitor* the height of irony that those who most loudly proclaimed their sympathy for the problems facing working-class people were the same ones most responsible for their misery and exploitation. Workers should use their hard-gained political experience to discern the difference between election pledges and political practice and to separate the demagogue from the statesman.[21]

While some Catholic journalists and newspapers wrote about the needs of working people, Humphrey Desmond, editor of Milwaukee's *Catholic Citizen*, addressed the responsibility of the church to deal with the conflict between labor and capital. Desmond argued for a more active church role, which should begin with less concern for upholding the status quo and more for supporting labor by denouncing monopolies, poor working conditions, and less than living wages. Desmond believed that the key to social justice was not so much the positions of the hierarchy as the actions of the laity. Critical of any attempt to create Catholic political parties or trade unions, he agreed with Phineas and the Catholic *Quincy Monitor* that the emancipation of workers would come not from above but from below. Rejecting the bishops' emphasis on charity, Desmond contended that workers could deal more effectively with the problems of poverty by organizing trade unions. The church had to realize, Desmond maintained, that "labor may find its own Moses, that useful, practical expedients are apt to come, not from men trained in seminaries, but from men close to the working conditions." Phineas, Desmond and the *Quincy Monitor* at least addressed the necessity of sociopolitical change and placed their faith in working people's abilities to solve their own problems through their own organizations. They were isolated voices in the Catholic church, however, which remained preoccupied with its own pastoral problems. Most Catholic journalists, like the bishops, though they readily acknowledged the problems confronting working-class people, were reluctant to give their unqualified support to trade unions.[22]

The Christian Labor Union

Defenders, apologists, and critics of industrial capitalism more often than not wrote, lectured, preached, and argued far removed from the day-to-day realities facing American workers. Even those most attentive to the problems of a rapidly changing social order, such as proponents of a social gospel, wanted to reform the existing system, not transform it. While they spoke out against the ravages of unrestrained individualism and the excesses of wealth and power, they refused to take sides. Their reliance on moral suasion and an abstract ide-

17

alism did little to meet the pressing needs of working people or provide them with tools for understanding the world around them. However, there were a few exceptions.

James Dombrowski's study of the Christian Labor Union concludes that it was "one of the earliest efforts to bring religion into the class struggle on the side of the workers." The union was founded in Boston in 1872 by a group of wage-working laypersons and led by Henry T. Delano, a Congregationalist ship carpenter, Edward H. Rogers, a Methodist ship joiner, and Jesse H. Jones, a Congregational minister. The CLU, through its two short-lived publications, *Equity* (1874–1875) and *The Labor-Balance* (1877–1879), supported both the Boston Eight-Hour League and the Socialist Labor Party, and according to the noted labor reformer George E. McNeill, "commanded the respect of labor organizations." What distinguished the CLU was its accountability to working-class people and its radical interpretation of the Christian tradition. Its goals were best summed up by a cabinetmaker interviewed by the Massachusetts Bureau of Statistics of Labor in the late 1870s: "Abolition of the present unjust political and social conditions. Discontinuance of all class rule and privilege. Abolition of the workingman's dependence upon the capitalist, by the introduction of co-operative labor in the place of the wage system, so that every laborer will get the full value of his work." The CLU's expressions of accountability and solidarity with workers were deeply rooted in its reading of Scripture. In ways analogous to the experience of present-day Christian-based communities, the CLU maintained that the Bible was centrally concerned with the destructiveness of poverty, issues of land tenure, labor, usury, and profit. They called the Bible "the chief Labor Reform book of the world." By contrast, they perceived the existing churches as engrossed in programs—Sunday schools, revivals, or temperance and missionary societies—that had little to do with either the needs of working-class people or Scripture. Churches seemed to be more preoccupied with singing the praises of mammon, accompanied by a disembodied spirituality, than with establishing God's Kingdom of justice on behalf of the poor and marginalized.[23]

The contribution of the Christian Labor Union to the cause of working people and to our understanding of economic justice is revealed in the lives of those most responsible for developing its analysis of the conflict between labor and capital: Jesse H. Jones, Edward H. Rogers, and T. Wharton Collens. Historians Henry F. May and C. Howard Hopkins have characterized them as neglected prophets, the first of a series of reformers who blazed the unpopular path that other left-wing Christian social movements would follow.[24]

When the CLU was founded, Jesse Henry Jones was pastor of the Congregational church in Rockland, Massachusetts. Born in 1836 of well-established New England parents, Jones decided to follow in his father's footsteps as a Congregational minister. After graduating from Harvard College, he entered Andover Theological Seminary. Although Jones was critical of Calvinist orthodoxy, he never accepted the liberal Social Darwinism of Herbert Spencer, and he had reservations about those aspects of biblical criticism which he believed lessened fidelity to the demands of Scripture on individual and corporate behavior. During the Civil War, he served first as a chaplain and later as captain of an infantry company. Like other labor reformers, Jones supported the wartime alliance workers had made with Radical Republicans, who were allied with the manufacturing elites of the North. Jones believed the alliance called for a reconstruction of the North as well as the South. He reminded the Radicals that, whereas workers had sided with them in their struggle against slavery, they would resist the "masters of wealth" just as strongly as abolitionists had fought the slave masters.[25]

After the war Jones served a number of pastorates in New York and Massachusetts. He was active in the Boston Eight-Hour League, served the working-class constituency of North Abington in the Massachusetts legislature, and edited the Christian Labor Union's publications. Acknowledging that the "power of press is proverbial," he contended that the New England labor movement needed a paper not afraid of "speaking the plainest truth" from a Christian standpoint on issues of concern to working people. It was not the function of the press to be the instrument of reform, Jones argued, for that could only be accomplished face-to-face. Instead, the press should communicate facts, both past and present, and describe the relationship between those facts and the day-to-day realities of life. Labor reformers such as George McNeill, Ira Steward, E. M. Chamberlain, and George Gunton praised the CLU publications, but the response of the Christian community was limited, according to Jones: "Except for . . . a letter from a negro minister in Arkansas, there has never come from a Christian brother one word of cheer." Undaunted, Jones worked for the Massachusetts Bureau of Statistics of Labor and in 1884 helped establish the first local of the Knights of Labor in North Abington. He continued to write for a number of Massachusetts publications, among them the *Labor Standard* of Fall River, and he was active until his death in 1904 in the women's suffrage, labor, and temperance movements.[26]

May contends that Jones is best understood as a "come-outer," uncomfortable with official Protestantism. Clearly he was indeed uncomfortable with the established church, but there was more to his life than an inability to accept the status quo. In refusing to grant legitimacy to the supposed virtues of the Gilded Age, he was not unlike other, better-known advocates of the social gospel, but he went beyond them in his radical reading of the Christian tradition and his identification with the hopes and aspirations of working-class people. Jones contended that it was necessary to transform the productive process so that working people could have control over both the means of production and the fruits of their labor. He believed the existing system was an "order of despotism, whose end is *death* of person and *people, and that end for our land is now hastening on apace. Life* must be found, and put in the place of death.

To find *the* life, and put it in the place of *the* death; and develop therefrom a new order, which shall be the order of freedom and blessedness of human toil, instead of despotism and drudgery. . . . rather than the making of money, this is the Labor problem." [27]

Edward Henry Rogers was born in 1824 in Medford, Massachusetts, the son of a ship carpenter who worked his way from foreman to owner of a South Boston shipyard, then lost it during the depression of 1837. Rogers's religious upbringing, like Jesse Jones's, was Congregational, but at the age of sixteen, when he sought membership in the Winthrop Congregational Church in Charlestown, his critical attitude toward Calvinist orthodoxy was found unacceptable. In addition, he discovered that "the church was very unsocial" and that "poor people were not wanted" by the merchants and mill owners who controlled it. He later joined the Methodist church and in its class meetings gained the self-confidence to enter the public arena. Upon leaving school he worked first as a dry goods clerk and then, like his father and brothers, entered the shipbuilding trade. At the outbreak of the Civil War, he became a ship joiner in the Charlestown navy yard, then served briefly with the Massachusetts volunteers. Returning to the navy yard, he became increasingly radicalized by his association with ship caulkers and carpenters, who had a history of strikes calling for a shorter working day. He later recalled that they taught him the importance of working-class organization. One of his coworkers was Henry Delano, a ship carpenter and deacon of the First Congregational Church of Charlestown. Delano's developing class consciousness and radical appropriation of the Christian tradition transformed Rogers's previously vague and ill-defined inclinations toward social reform into convictions about working-class solidarity and the closed shop. Rogers became convinced that one of the chief obstacles to Christian support of working people was individualism, which left the church with "no authority over the social question." The end result was its permanent abandonment of workers and an inability to speak out against "mammon worship." [28]

In the fall of 1864 Rogers was elected to the state legislature. As a spokesperson for over four thousand shipbuilders Rogers served on an investigative committee on the apprentice system and the hours of labor. Rogers insisted that "laboring men had as much right to develop and expand [their] mental and material capabilities and surroundings as have those whom wealth has favored with its advantages." After his experience as a state legislator, Roger continued to work for the eight-hour day, particularly targeting churchpeople. In a lecture, "Eight Hours a Day's Work," before the Third Massachusetts Methodist State Convention in 1870, he stated bluntly that labor had "no industrial rights which capital is bound by statute to respect" and that the rights of workers could not be won by "moral means," preferred by most Protestants. "Our success lies in our own hands, and depends upon the discretion [and] energy [with] which we continue to press our claim." For his own part, Rogers joined Jones, Delano, and other workers in the Christian Labor Union, and he insisted as strongly as Jones on the necessity for labor to have its own vehicle for expressing its views since capitalists shaped public opinion by their control of the press.[29]

In an 1876 pamphlet based on sermons given as a Methodist lay preacher, Rogers argued that Christ, like Moses, had been concerned with the material needs of common people, but the church, in its privatization and spiritualization of the Christian message, had reduced faith to individual religious experience at the expense of God's demand for justice. Jesus' concern for the poor was transformed into schools, temperance reform, and above all, preoccupation with the conversion of individuals. Protestantism's obsession with the individual, particularly Martin Luther's doctrine of justification by faith, led to a failure to take on the "strongholds of Mammon." The end result was a "public economy . . . based on selfishness," which "arrogantly demanded that the law of the market shall set aside the law of God." Hence a community that was supposed to preach love and justice had allowed the "pride and vain pomp" of the business system to displace fidelity to Jesus of Nazareth. Naturally, this attitude had emptied the churches of working people. To recover its own integrity the church must once again preach love and justice, reestablish contact with working people, and spend less energy on moralizing and more on self-sacrificing action on behalf of the poor.[30]

In the decades that followed the demise of the Christian Labor Union, Rogers continued to champion the cause of working people. With the emergence of Christian Socialism in the late 1880s and early 1890s, Rogers joined the Boston Society of Christian Socialists. Soon after, believing that it was important to belong to an organization and a church that "would be more in touch with the sentiment of the masses," as he put it in his "Auto-biography," Rogers withdrew from the Methodist church, of which he had been a member for forty-four years. He had come to believe that its leaders listened less to the Holy Spirit and more to the "conservative utterances of the traders and money changers in opposition to reform. Claiming to be the church of the common people it closes its press to our just complaints." Rogers joined the Church of the Carpenter, which had evolved from an Episcopal mission, founded in 1890, to become a center for Fabian social reform in the Boston area. Until his death Rogers was an active pamphleteer on behalf of a more equitable social order. Shortly before his death, he berated a Congregational pastor in Chelsea, Massachusetts, for being inaccessible to the "distressed cry of Labor" and for reducing the poverty and pain of working-class life to complaints about intemperance. Throughout his life Rogers challenged the church to recover the very meaning of the gospel as good news for the poor. For the gospel to be in fact good news, Christians had to work for structural transformation of a capitalist economy, stand in solidarity with workers as they reestablished their dignity as human beings, and proclaim that wealth and power must take a backseat to the meeting of basic human needs. Rogers implied that the Christian community had much to learn from working people about the nature of faith and the meaning of community.[31]

T. Wharton Collens joined the crusade for working-class people in the early 1870s when he read the published version of Rogers's address to the Methodist State Convention. Until his death in 1879, Collens corresponded with Rogers and was not only the major financial backer of the Christian Labor Union's publications but one of their more prolific contributors. Thomas Wharton Collens was born in New Orleans, Louisiana, in 1812. After a limited education, Collens first apprenticed as a printer and later became an editor and, by the early 1830s, a lawyer. Thereafter he served as deputy clerk for the United States Circuit Court, district attorney for Orleans Parish, and judge of the City Court of New Orleans. When the Christian Labor Union was founded, he was a judge of the Seventh District Court. In his youth he was greatly influenced by the utopian socialism of Robert Dale Owen and Charles Fourier, evident in Collens's stress on models of society that were structured to serve the common good and in his attempts to explore the implications of cooperation rather than competition as the basis of human life. Collens had come of age in antebellum America, and he would always maintain, as had labor leaders of the Jacksonian period, that the good society was based on labor as the source of all wealth.[32]

Robert C. Reinders, Collens's biographer, contends that by the early 1860s, Collens had distanced himself from "youthful iconoclasm" and returned to the Catholic church. But his rediscovery of faith, far from moderating Collens's earlier concerns with social reform and "the rights of labor," grounded these convictions less in the power of reason and more, he wrote to Rogers, on what "Jesus Christ has determined shall be the form and substance of his Kingdom on Earth." In "Views of the Labor Movement," written for the *Catholic World* in 1870, Collens argued that Catholics should not close their eyes to the clamor of the poor. Existing public and private responses were insufficient; Christian responsibility was not limited to pointing out the inadequacies of the system or the pitfalls of sociopolitical answers deemed out of keeping with church teachings. Instead, Christians should heed the call of Jesus on behalf of the poor and take seriously the "real communism" of Jesus and the apostles. Collens insisted that this communism had originated in the Christian mandate that the community share its worldly goods and possessions. In addition, Christian charity was demonstrated not by service to the Christian community but by "the alleviation of the burden and pains of the poor in general."[33]

Unable to win a proper hearing in the South, Collens joined forces with Jones and Rogers to support the Christian Labor Union, whose publications gave him a vehicle for communicating what he believed to be a Catholic perspective on political economy and the labor movement. Collens's Catholicism was shaped by his admiration for the Jesuit "reductions" in Paraguay, his familiarity with developing social trends among European Catholics, and his own

reading of the biblical texts. In opposition to what he regarded as the paternalism of most Catholic social commentary, Collens insisted that Christians
must acknowledge workers' need to create their own political alternatives to
the dominate social order. Christians could contribute to the workers' cause
through a discipleship that took seriously Christ's preaching on the abandonment of wealth, self-sacrifice, voluntary poverty, and Christian community.
Much of Collens's writing dealt with the establishment of decentralized Christian communities that could serve as models for a society without extremes of
wealth and poverty. Such communities "produced by the poor for the poor,"
would illustrate what Collens labeled "proportionalism," a system of political
economy in which labor was understood to be the source of wealth and the
measure of exchange, so that all participated equally in the abundance labor
created. Reflecting his past utopian socialism, Collens, more than Jones or
Rogers, believed that the first step in establishing a juster, more equitable society was to envision alternatives to a world ruled by mammon. As Jones wrote
upon Collens's death, he strove unceasingly to put before the public the "new
order of ages" where "the wolf also shall dwell with the lamb." [34]

Christian Labor Union and the Eight-Hour Movement

In the early 1870s, a member of the Massachusetts clergy, having lived among
factory workers for over twenty years, concluded that the end result of industrialization was the improvement of machinery for the benefit of "the capitalist
and not the laborer." Technological changes had not enhanced human lives.
Instead, they had reduced men to "stooping forms and hopeless faces," and
women to "dispirited, slovenly and aimless" human beings. Even children had
become "the embryos of an emasculated adulthood," experiencing "the collapse" of "childish merriment" as they joined their mothers and fathers, exemplars of "overtasked, exhausted and despondent humanity—veritable mudsills
of society." Employers constantly reminded workers "that Labor is dependent
upon Capital. Labor must work. Capital may or may not—the presumption is
very strong that it need not." In addition, the relationship between employer
and employee, as established by the wage contract, implied "a certain amount
of deference to . . . the ruling or managing power of the concern. . . . When
workmen accept employment from such a person, they must be understood
as surrendering their individual freedom to the extent which is necessary for
enabling him to fulfill the responsibility of his position." [35]

To Jones, Rogers, and Collens such unfair, undemocratic, and unrelenting
dehumanization was unacceptable. They not only criticized the shortcomings
of industrial America and advocated the eight-hour day but, in contrast to social
gospel advocates, they argued for a reconceptualization of the nature of work
and gave a religious meaning to a labor theory of value. As the captains of
industry subjugated labor to capital, Jones, Rogers, and Collens proclaimed
in *The Labor-Balance* that "the value of a thing is its power to make for life.

The cost of a thing is the labor, or lapse of life, which goes to produce it. The price of a thing ought to be its labor cost." Jones and Collens, in particular, approached the issue of work as part of a still only half-developed theology of life that set Christianity over and against the forces and idols of death and in opposition to the gods of capitalism, such as power and wealth, through which the capitalist mode of production structured work. It was an indication of how little value a capitalist society placed on the lives of working-class people, Collens stressed, that capitalism as a system necessitated the death of workers at an early age. He contrasted the life expectancies of theologians, teachers, doctors, lawyers, and merchants to those of miners, glass workers, copper workers, and above all, working-class children. Instead of serving "to preserve life, renew life, save life," work under capitalism shortened life, demeaned life, and denied workers the very right to life itself.[36]

Since one of the signs of the Kingdom is the fullness of life in which human beings can enjoy the fruits of their labor, the Christian Labor Union supported the battle for the eight-hour day. As Jones put it, when "the real religion of Jesus prevails, and his real spirit rules among men, and when all work is done to establish the kingdom of God on the earth, then, in no place where men work in large companies, shut in from the sky, will they work more than eight hours a day." The push for a shorter workday began in Massachusetts among Boston carpenters, who struck for the ten-hour day in 1825. Seven years later, in 1832, the ship carpenters and caulkers of Boston and Charlestown challenged the traditional sunup-to-sundown working day, and the house carpenters, masons, painters, slaters, and other artisans joined them. In May, 1835, Boston ship carpenters, masons, and stonecutters struck again for the ten-hour day, and in a meeting held at Julien Hall, they charged that "Capital . . . is endeavoring to crush labor, the only source of wealth." They demanded their "Natural Right to dispose of our time in such quantities as we deem and believe to be the most conducive to our own happiness." By July they were supported by other workers, who marched with them through wealthy sections of Boston singing the "Marseillaise." The strikes of Boston workers on behalf of the ten-hour day spread in the 1840s to women textile workers in towns such as Lowell, where women operatives were among the leaders of the ten-hour movement through the Lowell Female Labor Reform Association. From the 1850s until the outbreak of the Civil War the ten-hour movement fell into the hands of middle-class reformers, who were more concerned about their own political agendas than responding to the needs of working people, but the end of the Civil War witnessed a renewed attempt on the part of workers themselves to obtain shorter working hours.[37]

Karl Marx observed that "the first fruit of the Civil War was the eight hours' agitation, that ran from the Atlantic to the Pacific, from New England to California." In New England the Grand Eight-Hour League of Massachusetts and its successor, the Boston Eight-Hour League, were founded by Ira Steward and

George McNeill. Born in 1831, Steward was a self-educated machinist who was dismissed from his job for advocating the eight-hour day. Like Jones, Steward was deeply indebted to Radical Republican principles and the antislavery movement. Believing that the struggle for equality did not end with the Civil War, he connected freedom for African-American people to freedom for wage laborers. For Steward "the *idea* of eight hours isn't eight hours; it is *less poverty!* Eight hours is never an IDEA or a panacea, but as a *first measure.*" This first step would focus the attention of workers on the exploitative nature of the capitalist system, Steward said, in which the wages workers received were never equal to the wealth they produced, for if workers were truly paid what they produced, they would be as wealthy as the Astors and Belmonts of the world. The call for an eight-hour day was also a call for working-class solidarity, part of the drive to end the system that pitted overworked and underpaid workers against one another by maintaining a reservoir of cheap labor in the form of the unemployed. Thus the fight for a shorter workday was in reality nothing less than a demand for a "share of what we produce." Steward reasoned further that an eight-hour day would provide time and leisure in which working people could reclaim a sense of pride in themselves and their accomplishments, could educate themselves and study their common political and social interests. He also reminded capitalists that an increase in wages would permit an increase in production, for workers would have enough income to buy the commodities merchants and manufacturers were so eager to sell. The goal of the eight-hour day was to consign capitalists to the dustbin of history, along with "kings and royalties of the past," by putting back into the hands of workers "the wealth of the world," which they produced, by splitting the world not into workers and owners but into producers and consumers who divided the profits of capital between them.[38]

Like Steward, George E. McNeill, cofounder of the Boston Eight-Hour League, was an ardent abolitionist and labor reformer. Born in 1837 in Amesbury, Massachusetts, he began working in the Amesbury woolen mills at the age of fifteen; later he became a shoemaker and then a printer in Boston. McNeill was, according to Kenneth Fones-Wolf, New England's most renowned labor agitator, and his organizational skills greatly aided the eight-hour movement and influenced Steward's analysis of the eight-hour cause. McNeill underscored the effects of "the physical and moral degradation of over-work" on working people and stressed that the reduction in hours would not only allow workers to regain their dignity and renew the human spirit but also create work for the unemployed. It was, he wrote, a "demand for a better distribution of work, as well as a demand for an increase of value on each hour's service."[39]

In his lectures for the Boston Eight-Hour League, Edward Rogers used both McNeill's and Steward's perspectives. Reducing the hours of labor would address the problem of unemployment and would permit workers to meet their material needs and develop their creative faculties. But the only remedy, Rogers believed, that would grant working-class people the benefits of their own toil would be the establishment of equity in material affairs by extending political democracy to the economic arena. "We cannot save the Republic unless our republicanism can be extended to our industry." Rogers differed from McNeill and Steward in stating that "Christ regarded excessive labor as a sin." When work and labor were viewed from the perspective of Christ's preaching about the Kingdom of God and the creation of justice, then the "cruel injustices . . . being done to the working classes" could be seen to be in direct violation of Christ's teachings. Rogers observed that one of the classic examples of capitalist violation of the teachings of Jesus could be seen in the life of Amos Lawrence, the leading antebellum textile magnate, director of the Salmon Falls Company, and opponent of the ten-hour day. On the twenty-fifth anniversary of his death, Rogers remarked how "esteemed preachers and laymen" clamored to proclaim as the lesson of his life that "the desire for wealth, and the acquisition of it . . . [are in] no wise incompatible with the best personal integrity and a truly Christian character." Rogers asked how Lawrence could have been following Christ when his accumulation of capital was "wrung out of the hard necessities of the laborer." Nothing was more disastrously erroneous for Rogers than the opinion that the millionaire's property was the result of his own labor. Wealth was the product of the blood, sweat, and tears of workers and not nonproducers such as Lawrence. The church, he concluded, was sadly in need of a "humble confession of error" on its part for rejecting the demands of the Kingdom of God.[40]

Jesse Jones joined Rogers, Steward, and McNeill as a member of the Boston Eight-Hour League. He argued in the *Equity* "Editorial Notes" for June 1875 that the existing system was neither just nor equal. It was "born of injustice, and feeds on that same bitter lie for the nourishment of its life." The birthplace of the injustices of capitalism, Jones maintained, was the reduction of workers to wage earners. As wage earners, he wrote in "Eternal Life," workers became dependent for their survival on the "lords of life," the "masters of wealth" who decided who would live or die. Since workers did not control the tools of production, they had only the option to submit or starve. Jones, in much the same way as Ira Steward, drew upon the antislavery tradition to analyze workers' struggles for labor reform. The wage relation was understood as wage slavery, and the tyranny of slave masters as analogous to the domination of the "autocratic money kings." Workers, like slaves, were under the control of others. In an article titled "Wage Slavery," Jones stated: "Whenever one man's bread is controlled by another, The man whose bread is controlled by another, *He is that other man's slave*." Since capitalism debased human beings, the only adequate response was for working people to organize and use their energies to "secure the complete control of our own industry." In theological language, Jones expressed the aspirations of working-class people as an attempt to transform selfishness into an other-directed love that would change both personal and property relations by the "embodiment of otherness in the whole structure of the work system of society."[41]

Jones's concern for the transformation of society, such that "workers shall eat the fruits of their own toil and live in tranquility, instead of being . . . [reduced] to a starvation limit without a day's warning," made its most lasting contribution in the music he composed for the eight-hour movement. Philip Foner has noted the significant body of songs and poems the movement inspired. The most popular of all the songs, "Eight Hours," was based on a poem written by I. G. Blanchard, which appeared in the *Workingman's Advocate* in 1866 and was scored by Jesse Jones. "Eight Hours" was first published in the Christian Labor Union's *Labor-Balance* in April, 1878, and then appeared again in July in the *Labor Standard*. Foner contends that "Eight Hours" soon became the official song of the eight-hour movement and may have been the most popular labor song before the appearance of "Solidarity Forever." The final chorus of "Eight Hours" affirmed:

> Hurrah, hurrah, for Labor! for it shall arise in might;
> It has filled the world with plenty, It shall fill the world with light!
> Hurrah, hurrah, for Labor! it is mustering all its powers,
> And shall march along to victory with the banner of Eight Hours!
> Shout, shout the echoing rally till all the welkin thrill.[42]

God and Mammon

Solidarity with workers against wage slavery and for a new social order placed the Christian Labor Union in direct conflict with the religious legitimators of the status quo. In March of 1875 the Christian Labor Union wrote a letter in protest to the New York City Young Men's Christian Association for furnishing scabs during a longshoremen's strike. The CLU, noting both Christ's concern for the poor and the American revolutionary tradition of resistance to tyranny, declared that the actions of the YMCA in taking the "side of the oppressor" illustrated "the sophistry of a mammonized Christian sentimentality." Given the natural solidarity of the working class, attempts like that of the YMCA to divide the labor movement and, in the process, ally with the rich were "not only unchristian but antichristian." Members of the Christian Labor Union saw this type of religious legitimation of the status quo as indicative of an ongoing historical struggle. Jones wondered how the church could lose sight of Jesus' teaching that "you cannot serve God and Mammon." The church had so "married God and Mammon," Jones wrote, that the God of life had been replaced by the "god of money-making." The church not only burned incense at the altar of mammon but created a new "Prayer Book of Mammon," which celebrated the litany of accumulation based on taking interest on money, profit in trade, paying of wages, and the extraction of rent. For Jones, serving God entailed concern for the poor and opposition to those who oppressed them. It meant love of justice and not wealth and power. But the church had so distorted the teachings of Jesus as to believe that it "is serving God by serving Mammon." And this the church had done by focusing its energies on a self-serving preoccupation with building churches and with religiously oriented programs to the disservice of God's poor. Far worse than this self-absorption was the blatant way in which the church rationalized the accumulation of wealth by the belief that, in giving money to the church, one was serving God. The church never hesitated to accept money from individuals who had obtained their wealth in "the most iniquitous service of Mammon," naming seminaries after them and appointing them to head church agencies. Likewise, the church had no reservations about selling its pews to the wealthy and turning out the poor.[43]

Jones maintained that the greatest example of the "mammonized" nature of American Christianity could be seen in the career of Henry Ward Beecher, probably the most celebrated Protestant cleric of the nineteenth century. His death on March 8, 1887, was front-page news; the London *Standard* described him as "one of the comparatively few Americans who enjoyed a world-wide reputation." Jones, however, believed Beecher had consecrated himself to the service of mammon. His very life-style was based on making God the sanctifier of wealth, power, and privilege. Jones concluded that the marriage of God and mammon was a problem not only for the church but for the whole of society. The legitimation of wealth and the celebration of property, by fostering inequality, would bring about the downfall of the Republic. He believed, like many labor reformers, that traditional republican values of liberty, equality, and justice were at stake; "the property system of America must die, or the Republic is doomed."[44]

Rogers and Collens, like Jones, insisted that devotion to mammon was idolatry. The very foundation of the church was Christ's preaching of the gospel to the poor. Why, then, did the church devote so much energy to "counseling energetic business men" rather than "shortening the labors of the worthy poor?" asked Rogers in "Gain or Godliness?" The Christian gospel, Rogers argued in "Labor Reform in the Church," had been transformed by Protestants into a "one-sided spirituality" that left the church unwilling to take "responsibility for the evils in the industrial world." It was no wonder, he noted in *"Like unto Me,"* that secular organizations such as trade unions were doing the work of the church. Collens added in "Philosophy and Communism" that the Catholic church, too, had been "essentially established for the poor." Both Collens and Rogers reminded Christians of the meaning of the gospel as good news for the poor and of the implications of Christian discipleship for the life of the Christian community. It was necessary, Collens wrote to Rogers, for the church to assume responsibility for the actions of its members, and with "all the force of religious sanctions. . . resist the exposures which have embodied themselves in Mammon-worship."[45]

Knights of Labor

The Knights of Labor was the "quintessential" embodiment of the labor movement of the Gilded Age and "the first mass organization of the American working class," according to Leon Fink. Not until the emergence of working-class militancy in the 1930s, which led to the formation of the Congress of Industrial Organizations (CIO), did rank-and-file insurgency reach the scale of the Noble and Holy Order of the Knights of Labor. Founded in 1869, the Knights of Labor had almost one million members by 1886; by 1896 the order had initiated some two million members and organized fifteen thousand local assemblies in rural communities and urban centers in every state in the country. David Montgomery notes that "perhaps no other voluntary institution in America, except churches, touched the lives of as many people as did the Knight of Labor." Local and regional labor histories have recently contributed to our understanding of the role the Knights played in state and local politics, their successes and failures in organizing southern workers, and their attempts to include both skilled and unskilled as well as female and black workers. The order also fostered a national debate over the meaning of industrial capitalism, creating what Gregory S. Kealey and Bryan D. Palmer have termed a "culture of solidarity and resistance" to the dominant order. Religion was part of that culture.[46]

History of the Knights of Labor, 1869–1896

The Noble and Holy Order of the Knights of Labor was founded as a secret organization in 1869 by Philadelphia garment cutters. Organizationally, the order grouped individual members into local assemblies (LAs), which were either mixed locals or trade locals. Mixed locals grouped many occupations, from carpenters and printers to day laborers. At times, they approximated the goals of later industrial unionism by workplace organizing, which brought together skilled and unskilled workers, blacks and whites, men and women. Some also functioned as central labor councils, uniting various trades from the community. By the mid-1880s, half of the local assemblies were mixed. The others were trade locals, which most closely matched traditional craft unions, whose members all worked in the same trade. A number of LAs were composed entirely of black or women workers; others were made up of workers of a specific ethnic group. Beyond the LAs were district and state assemblies, with overall power resting in the general assembly, which acted on behalf of the order as a whole. In theory the Knights of Labor was hierarchically structured, but in practice much of the daily life of the order revolved around the LAs, which had a great degree of autonomy.

In terms of membership, the Knights evolved slowly, based first among garment and metal trades workers in Philadelphia. The organization gathered strength and members during the Great Railroad Strikes of 1877. By the next year the order abandoned its secrecy and became a public organization. It gradually gained momentum, particularly after a successful strike in 1885 against Jay Gould's southwestern railroad system. By the mid-1880s the Knights had organized LAs among boot workers, transportation, agriculture, and food-processing workers, as well as those involved in various manufacturing trades, from glass and pottery to textiles.[47]

The LAs had various functions, one of which was the creation of working-class solidarity. Nicholas O. Thompson, Philadelphia Knight of Labor, expressed a central goal of the organization: "Our Noble and Holy Order [tries] . . . to persuade the toiler, the artisan, the skilled mechanic, the humblest hewer of wood and drawer of water, male and female, of whatever shade or color, to banish forever the spirit of selfishness from their minds . . . and to unite together, with the principle of mutual assistance organized effort and cooperation: to stand a solid compact body, a bulwark against the assaults of capital, ready to aid and assist the wronged and oppressed, and to feel that our brother's weal is our weal, and our brother's woe is our woe." LAs also functioned like trade unions on behalf of their members, waging strikes for better wages and working conditions. The Knights effectively used boycotts against employers, formed both producer and consumer cooperatives as self-governing economic alternatives for workers, and engaged in state and local politics. Traditional interpretations portray the meteoric rise and fall of the Knights of Labor between 1886 and 1888. Yet, more careful research indicates that in spite of internal factionalism in the late 1880s, the Knights of Labor remained an important labor organization until the mid-1890s, having organized over sixty-five hundred new local assemblies between 1887 and 1896.[48]

Knights of Labor and Industrial Capitalism

George E. McNeill, who became a key Knight of Labor in Massachusetts, proclaimed that "there is an inevitable and irresistible conflict between the wage-system of labor and the republican system of government—the wage-laborer attempting to save the government and the capitalist system ignorantly attempting to subvert it." McNeill thus summarized a basic assumption that governed the Knights' critique of industrial capitalism: the wage system was in conflict with inherited republican ideals, and workers, not capitalists, were the real defenders of American democracy. Studies of antebellum workers point out that they saw themselves as part of a revolutionary tradition. They articulated an equal rights creed that emphasized that the very legitimacy of the democratic process depended upon the degree to which the rights and liberties of all were respected and guaranteed. Also central to republican values was the long-standing belief that labor was the source of wealth. Suspicious of all nonproducers, workers maintained that, just as their ancestors had sought to overthrow all forms of privilege and hierarchy, so they must continue the struggle against corruption of the Republic by wealth and unaccountable power.[49]

The republican tradition, like Christianity, could serve many purposes. Bruce Laurie contends that republicanism was the accepted creed of all classes. Richard Oestreicher, in turn, believes that the republican tradition led some native workers to join with the middle class in opposition to "immigrant workers, whom they saw as tools of monopolistic corrupters plotting to undermine American liberty." Others used that same tradition as the basis for a radical critique of industrial society. The Knights' appropriation of the republican tradition emphasized egalitarianism. For example, one of its principles, as Terence Powderly notes, was "for both sexes equal pay for equal work." Some Knights argued that equality should not be limited to the workplace alone. Lydia Drake of Battle Creek, Michigan, believed the order should strive to transform the existing system of laws, which "favored the few and oppressed the many . . . [and] betrayed the people's trust, established the rights of caste, the sin of usury, the curse of monopoly, the chains of slavery, and clothed their crimes with legal authority, therefore it is to [the] end that all *shall have equal rights,* equal privileges, equal opportunities and equal responsibilities under the law that we should labor." Only then, Drake concluded, could men and women enjoy the "products of their own toil." Organizationally the Knights of Labor interpreted equal rights for women to mean support not only for equal pay but for women's suffrage and equality with men in the order as well as in the home and factory. Susan Levine's analysis of women and the Knights of Labor stresses how the order helped to shape a world beyond that established by the prevailing bourgeois ideology of women's sphere, of hearth and home. Nevertheless, Levine maintains, there were limits to the labor ideology of the Knights as it related to the role of women in society. The Knights still held to domestic notions of a woman's place. Although women were able to use the language of domesticity to critique the competitiveness of a capitalist system as destroying both the home and family, the Knights saw no need to overturn "the traditional gender-based division of labor." Whatever the limitations of the Knights' ideology of equality for women, however, the order "projected an alternative industrial future for both men and women." [50]

The Knights' egalitarian vision embraced black workers as well. The Knights of Labor was the first labor organization to take seriously the need to organize skilled and unskilled black workers, and the official organ of the Knights of Labor, the *Journal of United Labor*, stated: "We should be false to every principle of our Order should we exclude from membership any man who gains a living by honest toil, on account of his color or creed. Our platform is broad enough to take in all." Despite this principle, in the South blacks were more often than not part of segregated black local assemblies, and the leadership of the Knights did little to educate the membership on the need to struggle

31

against racism as part of the credo Sidney H. Kessler quotes: "An injury to one is the concern of all." Above the level of the local assemblies, there was some effort to integrate the organization. In fact, given the context of the times, Leon Fink considers the Knights of Labor "a beacon of racial enlightenment in a dark sea." In a letter to a black member of the order, Terence Powderly wrote: "In heavens [*sic*] name, let not our foolish prejudices keep us apart when our foolish enemies are so closely allied against us," for "does any man suppose that the universal Father will question our right to Heaven because of our color? If the color of the heart is right, no matter about the color of the skin." As the nineteenth century came to a close and white supremacy was fast becoming the law of the land in the South, the Knights were on the decline nationally. Nevertheless, in the South the Knights continued to organize black workers and to serve the needs of the black community. Organizers in Florida pointed out that, even though the "political tricksters" most responsible for oppressing the poor were desirous of their demise, they would nonetheless strive to see "oppressed people, especially the colored people of Florida . . . lifted to a better and more prosperous conditions [*sic*]." [51]

Knights claimed that equal rights for women, blacks, and other working-class people could be secured only by creating a new industrial order. Industrial capitalism, according to Powderly, had led to the aggregation of "wealth, which, unless checked, will invariably lead to the pauperization and hopeless degradation of the toiling masses." It was "imperative, if we desire to enjoy the blessings of life, that a check should be placed upon its power and upon unjust accumulation, and a system adopted which will secure to the laborer the fruits of his toil." Thus, an editorial in the *Journal of United Labor* railed against the deception and sophistry of political economists who tried to make the working class invisible by turning people into a commodity to be bought and sold in the marketplace. [52]

Joseph Labadie, printer, Socialist, and founder of the first assembly of the Knights of Labor in Detroit, insisted that a first step in the direction of altering the existing system was "to draw all the classes of labor together." He meant "all." The Knights of Labor, in keeping with the beliefs and attitudes of ante-bellum workers, divided the world between the producing classes, those who engaged "in productive work," and the nonproducing classes, "living by and on the labor of others," who were considered dishonest and simply labeled "parasites." The order therefore excluded from membership only those deemed to be nonproducers: lawyers, bankers, professional gamblers, stockbrokers, and liquor dealers. Neither manufacturers nor merchants were excluded from membership; rather, they were judged on an individual basis according to their respect for the rights and dignity of working people. Even though the Knights recognized the possibility of including members who were, strictly speaking, not part of the laboring classes it was determined that "at least three-fourths of every local assembly must be composed of wage-earners or farmers." The

Knights sought alliances with all those who recognized the rights of working people and understood the importance of maintaining a republican system of values. In point of fact, the Knights of Labor defended a vision of human community that cherished interdependence, especially the individual-in-community, respect for individual rights, freedom, and independence as rooted in human solidarity, which they believed to be part of America's revolutionary republican heritage. They did not think that the emerging industrial order was unalterable and drew on past republican values as a way of both resisting the status quo and maintaining that other options were not only possible but desirable.[53]

Thomas Bender and Michael Cassity assert that the Knights were critics of a social order intent upon displacing the community, with its stress on decentralization, cooperation, and social accountability, as the locus of meaning, replacing it with impersonal economic and political structures marked by centralization and competition. Whether one labels the critique a resistance to modernization or gemeinschaft, it was a recognition on the part of the Knights of Labor that weighing human worth by the dictates of the market would ultimately destroy the social fabric of the Republic. That is why Leon Fink's stress on the Knights' understanding of political power as "a reappropriation of the state by society" is so very important. For the Knights of Labor, the state, which ought to be the "government of the people," seemed to serve only to preserve the interests of the "monopolies of power." A. A. Beaton, secretary master workman of District 86, lamented that "mammon sits enthroned to-day in the temple, where the common people thought the goddess of Liberty was reigning queen."[54]

To create a political system in which common people ruled required not so much the capturing of state power as the restructuring of political life so that communities would have control over the political process and government would be reconstituted in the service of the producers rather than the nonproducers. Neither the state nor the individual was the repository of republican values; rather, they represented what Fink calls "repoliticized associationalism." The search of workers for a decentralized approach to politics was analogous, Fink notes, to their attempt to achieve control over the workplace. Herbert Gutman adds that the workers' ideological criticism of industrial capitalism, based on a working-class reading of the republican tradition, was shared by native- and foreign-born workers alike. J. P. McDonnell, Irish nationalist, Socialist, labor editor, and union organizer, wrote that the "American Republic founded only a century ago on many excellent principles of justice . . . has become . . . a system [that] destroys all generous and humane feelings, stifles the conscience, makes men avaricious, lustful after wealth, dead to reason, blind to the sufferings of others, deaf to the appeals of justice. Remember that you work for your Emancipation and to substitute the capitalist 4th of July by that of the workers—with a new Declaration of Independence."[55]

Labor historians, influenced by the English Marxist historian E. P. Thompson, have stressed that the formation of class identity and consciousness is a historical process that has not only economic, political, and social but cultural dimensions. The cultural component of the working-class experience has become the focus of scholars whose work centers, writes David Montgomery, on "the mental links between material conditions and action." Hence, a sense of being working-class, Thompson says, emerges when "some men, as a result of common experiences (inherited or shared), feel and articulate the identity of their interest as between themselves, and as against other men whose interest are different from (and usually opposed to) theirs." Part of that sense of common identity is shaped by shared values and traditions that create a working-class culture. The Knights of Labor drew on traditional cultural patterns, such as the ideology of republicanism, but they also forged an alternative culture that stood in opposition to the celebrated values of the Gilded Age: competition, individualism, and personal success.[56]

George McNeill aptly summarized the Knights' assessment of the dominant culture: "Civilization is measured not by wealth, power or culture of the few, but by the quantity and quality of the opportunities possessed by the many. Civilization is common property." Working-class people also had an understanding of the public dimension of daily life that resisted both privatization and reduction to a set of commodity relationships. Thus the conflict of labor and capital appeared fundamentally moral. The Knights of Labor from the beginning adapted the ritual and ceremonies of fraternal societies and earlier labor organizations to emphasize that "labor is noble and holy." Members entered an organization whose creed acknowledged that "to rescue the toiler from the grasp of the selfish is a work worthy of the noblest and best of our race." They were part of a fellowship "dedicated to the service of God, by serving humanity." To be a Knight ideally meant to uphold the ancient idea of chivalry, with its defense of the weak and readiness to "redress wrongs." In that spirit, the Knights were ready for battle: "Our warfare is a warfare of reason against prejudice, of knowledge against ignorance." Through cooperation and mutual trust, they would unite those "whose hearts beat purely and warmly the pulsations of hearty sympathy for the oppressed labor of the land." The watchwords of the Knights of Labor were *organize* and *educate*. Leonard M. Wheeler, a Massachusetts member, explained how important the Knights of Labor was to working-class people: "I am like hundreds of others who a few years ago could look ahead and see nothing but misery, hard work, and starvation, but what a change. . . . the Knights of Labor seemed as if the cloudy Heavens had opened and I could faintly see a little bright clear sky . . . [and] we now number over three hundred and a good field before us."[57]

Wilson Carey McWilliams, tracing the idea of fraternity throughout American history, believes that the Knights of Labor sought a fraternal citizenry who would embody brotherhood and measure individual worth by moral rather than material standards. This aspiration resulted in expressions of solidarity and mutual assistance that were evident in picket lines, boycotts, the informal practice of limiting output so that all workers would have jobs, and in strikes that moved beyond the simple issue of wages to working conditions and the length of the working day. For example, during a strike in the Cumberland coal region of Pennsylvania in the early 1880s, the national organization appealed on behalf of the striking Knights to every local assembly, reminding them of the necessity "to make sacrifices to maintain their principles, and in many places there are contests for right and justice . . . [and] the positions of our brothers of the Cumberland region are so appalling in the dire necessity to which our brothers have been reduced, and in the humiliating conditions attempted to be imposed upon them by the heartless combination of employers, that it seemed to the Executive Board a case which appealed to the sympathies of every true Knight of Labor, regardless of past sacrifices or present difficulties." [58]

The Knights of Labor also developed a host of alternative institutions that nurtured their belief in cooperation, mutuality, and working-class solidarity. An institutional network extended from the local assemblies to consumer and producer cooperatives, which varied from newspapers to boot and shoe manufacturing to social clubs and even opera companies. Jonathan Garlock notes that each of the local assemblies established its own court to deal with the behavior of wayward Knights and resolve differences without "recourse to civil courts. Members charged one another not only for such violations of obligation to the Order as scabbing or accepting substandard wages, but for such violations of domestic obligations as wife-beating and desertion, and for such violations of standards of social conduct as public intoxication or the failure to pay boarding bills." [59]

Perhaps the most vivid illustration of what the Knights hoped to accomplish by fostering shared values, supportive institutions, and informal practices that reaffirmed workers' solidarity could be seen during the celebration of the fifteenth anniversary of the founding of the Knights of Labor by District Assembly 49 of New York City. The program was drawn from the "brothers and sisters" of the order whose musicals, dramatic productions, speeches, and songs inspired one Knight to ask, "Can it be possible that these are only workingmen?" What most touched the assembled Knights was a powerful reading by a Lady Knight of the English poet Thomas Hood's poem "The Song of the Shirt," which movingly described the miserable conditions endured by women garment workers. Feelings of solidarity ran high when the audience joined in singing the following chorus of a workers' song:

> Tyrants quail, dawn is breaking
> Dawn of freedom's glorious day—
> Despots on their thrones are shaking,
> Iron bands are giving way.

Lo! from labor's sons and daughters,
In the depths of misery.
Like the sound of many waters,
Comes the cry, "We will be free!"
Comes the cry, "We will be free!" [60]

Knights of Labor and Religion

The founders of the Knights of Labor were mostly Protestants, but the order grew to include a considerable number of Catholics—more than half the members by 1884, according to Terence Powderly, who led the organization from 1879 to 1893. Uriah Stephens, cofounder of the Knights of Labor and the first grand master workman of the order, intended to enter the Baptist ministry, but because of economic reversals his family suffered during the 1837 depression, he was indentured as a tailor instead. He subsequently became an active labor reformer, abolitionist, and organizer of the Garment Cutters' Association of Philadelphia, and he brought to the founding of the Knights of Labor a Christian perspective that shaped its development. When the first district assembly was being formed, Stephens set forth the purpose of the Knights of Labor. Like other members, Stephens drew upon the equal rights tradition and spoke of the order as a fraternity, a "universal brotherhood" of workers, not divided by ethnic background, skill, race, or gender. This tradition had always had a Christian dimension, for most Americans, even irregular churchgoers, professed a belief in basic Christian values. Stephens was not unusual in contrasting the republican tradition to the irreligious and unchristian ideology of industrial capitalism. Thus he could maintain that God affirmed the human worth and dignity of all workers in contrast to an "atheistic . . . idolatry" that, if left unchecked, would destroy not only the love of God but humanity as well. The task of the Knights was the "complete emancipation of wealth-producers from the thraldom and loss of wage-slavery, the entire redemption of the world's toilers from the political tyranny of unjust laws, and the annihilation of the great anti-Christ of civilization in the idolatry of wealth, and the consequent degradation and social ostracism of all else not possessing it, and its baneful effects upon heaven-ordained labor." [61]

Stephens's depiction of the exaltation of wealth as anti-Christian echoed the critique offered by the Christian Labor Union, but Stephens expanded on the CLU's analysis. He argued that it was not just the idolatry of wealth that was the problem but the capitalist system as a whole. The human person was made in the image of God, he said, and capitalism was a denial of what God intended for working people. Instead of creating a social order in which working people could develop their God-given capacities, capitalism produced a system in which capital dictated and labor submitted, in which capital was superior and labor inferior. Instead of taking pride in themselves, workers had come to "defer to wealth, to respect [its] . . . pretensions instead of boldly stripping it of its masks and exposing its hideousness." The only way workers could regain what capitalism took from them was to organize themselves, to become Knights in the struggle for justice.[62]

Other Knights, agreeing that capitalism belittled what God had created, contended that its religious apologists had betrayed Christian teachings. An editorial in the Knights of Labor's *Labor Enquirer* maintained that professed Christians "don't know what Christ himself did as a Socialist and politician." They had seen Christ's "picture somewhere and heard His name used by some fellow when he stubbed his toe," but they knew little else of the Christian message. The *Enquirer* wondered how it was possible that "the wealthy landlords in New York City dare sit on Sundays with their families in gay attire on their fine velvet cushioned seats in those fashionable churches, to mock their Divine Master, the meek and lowly Nazarene with their impious prayers." The clergy seemed to behave no differently, for they had placed "the pulpit in the service of capital," and like the beadle from Charles Dickens's *Oliver Twist*, they "raised a howl of horror because they (the working people) dared to ask for 'more.' "[63]

For the Knights of Labor, as for the Christian Labor Union, Henry Ward Beecher symbolized "the servant of mammon, the tool of the capitalist." The Knights found particularly reprehensible Beecher's distortion of the Christian tradition, which rendered it "so barren of all that can be called human dignity, human sentiment or human feeling." This seemed to be epitomized in a lecture to workers in which he asked, "Is not a dollar a day enough to buy bread? Water costs nothing, and a man who cannot live on bread is not fit to live." Knights believed that Beecher had replaced Christ's teachings of love and fraternity with "brutal heartlessness" and "the coarsest egotism." In marked contrast to Beecher's interpretation of Christianity, the Knights proclaimed that "its founder was a carpenter, that its chief apostle was a tent maker, and its leading spirits in the Apostolic day were fishermen, that its adherents were the poor and miserable." For George McNeill, the importance of Christianity to the "movement of the laborers toward equity" was that, properly understood, it challenged all those of wealth and power who sought to impose the rule of mammon. Christ, McNeill and other members of the order believed, had stood in solidarity with the poor and oppressed, "despised by the wealthy," feeling "hatred by the powerful."[64]

In fact, members of the Left, be they Knights, Socialists, or anarchists, all shared an image of Christ as a radical agitator who defended the rights of working-class people. For anarchists, Paul Avrich writes, Jesus was "the great socialist of Judea," who taught the same form of socialism as the Haymarket martyr August Spies. For Socialists, such as Eugene V. Debs, Christ was "the inspired evangel of the downtrodden masses, the world's supreme revolutionary leader." The implications of Jesus' teachings for workers, McNeill maintained, were to be found in fulfilling the demands of the Kingdom by creating a social order in which peace would prevail, human domination would cease, and "every man shall have according to his needs." [65]

Most workers looked upon the clergy as domestic servants of the status quo, but not all ministers shared the attitudes and views of the religious apologists for the Gilded Age. There were those, both Catholic and Protestant, who were sympathetic to the demands of workers, especially the advocates of a social gospel and the progressive-minded Catholics. And there were others who played a more active role on behalf of the working class. Cornelius O'Leary was an Irish-born priest who moved beyond simple moral suasion in his support for the Knights of Labor. Father O'Leary served as pastor of a railroad parish in DeSoto, Missouri, during the late 1870s and 1880s. The railroad shop workers, members of the Knights of Labor, had waged a successful strike in 1885 against the attempt of Jay Gould's Missouri-Pacific Railroad to cut wages. A year later, in 1886, the Knights struck again; this time the central issue was union recognition. Three thousand railroad workers intended to stop all freight movement in a five-state area and hoped for a brief strike, like the one the year before.

In DeSoto workers sidetracked trains, and the Missouri-Pacific moved its trains only by resorting to the protection of federal marshals. In the midst of the strike, O'Leary organized relief for the families of striking workers and criticized both the Missouri-Pacific and the courts for their treatment of strikers. He asserted that some of the strikebreakers were "fit for the penitentiary." As the strike continued, violence erupted. Tracks were torn up in Texas, strikers were killed in Illinois, and some six hundred people were jailed from western Illinois to western Texas. Eventually the strike was defeated, and few of the strikers were rehired. Congress convened hearings to investigate the causes of the upheaval. Of the five hundred witnesses called before the congressional committee, only one Catholic priest, Cornelius O'Leary, testified on behalf of the striking Knights of Labor. O'Leary defended the Knights and stressed that the violence had resulted from the policies of the railroad. The "railroad officials generally are unscrupulous and arbitrary," he said, and "boycotting [was] . . . only a legitimate reply to blacklisting." He maintained that if Jay Gould could buy legislatures to carry out his will, then ordinary people surely had the right to take the law in their own hands. Beyond his testimony to the congressional committee, O'Leary worked to gain support for the Knights of Labor from other clergy and spoke on behalf of the order to Monsignor Germano Staniero, papal delegate, during his visit to St. Louis as part of a tour of the United States. O'Leary was soon transferred from his parish in DeSoto, mainly, he believed, because of his support for the Knights of Labor. Terence Powderly said of Father O'Leary that he was a "true priest of the people." [66]

Terence V. Powderly

When Terence V. Powderly died in 1924, the *Philadelphia Inquirer* wrote, "The thing for which Powderly will probably be most remembered was the long and successful battle by which he prevented the Knights of Labor from coming under the ban of the Catholic Church." Subsequently interest in Powderly has almost entirely revolved around the role he played in struggles with the church hierarchy over the legitimacy of the Knights of Labor. Those who have touched on Powderly's religious life have judged him at best "a nominal Catholic," to use the words of Henry J. Browne. In addition, some have raised questions about his working-class credentials and his contribution to the Knights of Labor. Some suggest that he was less a visionary leader, more a hardworking labor bureaucrat, "more enthusiastic about keeping records, answering letters, drafting constitutions, or writing pronouncements," writes Richard Oestreicher, "than about addressing crowds or socializing with his supporters." Others contend that Powderly early in life came face-to-face with working-class realities. For all his personal reserve, self-preoccupation, and less than dynamic leadership style, according to Edward T. James, he did "have a genuine sympathy for the workingman; on occasion he depicted labor's injustices with eloquent voice." In this debate, little attention has been given to his radical reading of the Christian tradition.[67]

Terence Vincent Powderly was born in 1849 in Carbondale, Pennsylvania, one of twelve children of Irish immigrant parents. His father was in succession a coal miner, small mine operator, and railroad mechanic, part of what Oestreicher calls the "relatively fluid social structures" of Carbondale and "other small northeastern industrial communities" at midcentury. He grew up in a world that stressed self-improvement and drew its strength from the republican system that valued hard work and industry over privilege and power. Powderly began working at the age of thirteen as a switch tender for the Delaware and Hudson Railroad, which carted the anthracite coal of the region. By the age of seventeen, in 1866, he was apprenticed as a machinist, and he followed that trade for eleven years. He joined the International Union of Machinists and Blacksmiths in 1871 and later was president of his local. Machinists in the period following the Civil War, David Montgomery notes, were considered the "best minds" in the struggle for labor reform.[68]

During the panic of 1873, which brought unemployment, wage cuts, and destruction of many of the national trade unions, Powderly was fired and blacklisted as a union leader. He joined the ranks of the unemployed and experienced separation from wife and family and the constant search for a steady job. A decade later, Powderly would write that the responsibility for the unemployed, that "army of the discontented," lay with those "who turned a deaf ear to the supplications of suffering humanity, and gave the screw of oppression an extra turn because they had the power." He himself was unable to find permanent employment as a machinist until the end of 1875. In 1876 he joined the Knights of Labor, which had absorbed many of the trade union locals that had survived the depression, including the machinists and blacksmiths' union. Powderly was instrumental in forming a machinists local into a local assembly of the Knights, of which he was quickly elected master workman. The following year he was elected secretary of the Scranton District Assembly, and by 1879 became grand master workman of the Knights of Labor, an office he would hold until 1893.[69]

Any assessment of Powderly must ultimately confront the degree of Powderly's candor about his own life. Richard Oestreicher concludes that he was "never one to let the facts stand in the way of improving a story." In his autobiography Powderly claimed that the turning point in his life came in 1869 as a result of a mine disaster in Avondale, Pennsylvania. In September of that year a fire broke out in a mine shaft, and 110 men and boys died of suffocation. Powderly described the horror of seeing the "blackened, charred bodies of over one hundred men and boys as they were brought to the surface. When I saw a mother kneel in silent grief to hold the cold, still face of her boy to hers, and saw her fall lifeless on his dead body, I experienced a sensation that I have never forgotten." Avondale was to many miners a potent symbol of the dangerous working conditions anthracite coal miners faced. Just that spring the Workingmen's Benevolent Association, the first industrywide union of anthracite miners, had waged its first strike. Moved by his experience of the Avondale disaster and by an address by a respected WBA organizer, John Siney, on the meaning of Avondale, Powderly dedicated himself to improving "the conditions of those who worked for a living." Or so he said. Oestreicher takes issue with the accuracy of these recollections, noting that Powderly's own diaries contain no reference to the Avondale incident.[70]

Separating out what Powderly wished had happened from what actually happened is a task for a biographer. Here I want to note only that his letters, writings, and personal memoirs make it clear that Powderly had some important insights into the role religion should play in a critique of the dominant industrial order. In fairness to Powderly, it is perhaps appropriate to quote two sympathetic judgments from his own time. A biographical sketch that appeared in the Knights' *Journal of United Labor*, for example, simply stated that he possessed "a heart that feels for others' woes" and noted that "labor has today no more faithful friend than Terence V. Powderly, and our Order is indeed fortunate to have him at its head." A second appraisal comes from Mother Jones, Powderly's longtime friend and a tireless advocate for the rights of working people. In a letter to Powderly she remarked that "the world needs more like you . . . [for] you are the same honest T. V. Powderly of years ago, when the present Labor Lords were not heard of. . . . Some day the unwritten history will be given to the children yet unborn, and it is possible that they will make pilgrimages to your grave and plant flowers there on."[71]

Powderly never claimed to be a good Catholic, and if the good Catholic is defined solely by faithful church attendance, then that is a legitimate judgment. Yet, throughout much of his life, he thought of himself as a Catholic. His understanding of Catholicism was shaped by an experience he had when he was a young boy. A devout Irish aunt gave him a religious medal, telling him that it would protect him from harm and danger. That very afternoon he went swimming and would have drowned if he had not been saved by a friend. When he returned home, he gave back the medal and told his aunt what had just happened. She argued that God had sent his friend to save him, but Powderly concluded that belief in God made life more human, but belief in miracles, he later wrote to his niece, "didn't save me and had it not been for Whit Chamberlain I'd have drowned." [72]

While Powderly acknowledged that some individual priests, pastors, and members of the hierarchy were sympathetic to the workers' cause, he felt, overall, that labor had to contend with two forces: capital and clergy. Powderly had reservations about permitting members of the clergy to join the Knights. "A clergymen of any denomination is eligible to membership provided he practices what he preaches, and provided he preaches in the interest of humanity instead of Mammon," he wrote. But too many looked upon their ministry as a "profession or a trade" that was more concerned with amassing of wealth and teaching working people to obey their "masters" than with love of neighbor and Timothy's admonishment that "love of money is the root of all evil." Powderly's approach to the institutional church was to label it "Churchianity." He believed that the church was more concerned with defending the rich against the poor than with preaching the gospel of Jesus Christ. [73]

His critique of the church had more in common with the Protestant working-class critique of the status quo, drawing its insights from Scripture, than with the Catholic appeal to natural law and the social teaching of the church. Over against the wealth and power of the church stood Jesus as an agitator, crucified for his struggle on behalf of poor people. Christ, Powderly wrote, "lived and worked for the industrious poor, for them He agitated, for them He died." Thus, during the controversy that arose in the 1880s over the relationship of the Knights of Labor to the Catholic church, Powderly considered his position clear. Inasmuch as "the church [is] always herself on the side of wealth, usury, monopoly and oppression," he wrote to Daniel O'Donoghue, "I will array myself where I now stand, on the side of God's poor along side of those for whom Christ died. I prefer to stand at the foot of the cross . . . to forming hands with those who in this day and generation crucify over and over again the suffering patient image of the living God." [74]

Powderly's Christocentric reading of the Christian tradition grounded his belief in the Knights of Labor affirmation of the holiness and nobility of labor. In an unpublished poem titled "Christ or Pilate, Which?" he reflected that Jesus, in siding with the poor, made toil noble. In giving his life for the oppressed, Jesus told the poor that never again "to wealthy you must bend the

knee; he never intended that rage and dirt should . . . the lot of the toiler be."
Like many other members of the order, Powderly contended that the Knights
of Labor were more faithful to the demands of the gospel than the institutional church and the wealthy and powerful Christians who betrayed Christ in
both word and deed. Powderly summed up the conflict between Jesus and the
religious apologists of the Gilded Age:

Christ taught humility.
He taught no favoritism should be shown.
He loved the poor.
He walked among the poor.
He denounced the unjust rich.
He took the side of the laborer in the unequal struggle of life.
Christ preached absolute, undeviating justice.
Christ was merciful to the sinner.
He despised riches for himself.
He had not whereon to lay His head.
He not only gave to the poor but commanded others to do so.
He sternly forbade man to bear false witness.

They do not practice humility.
They play favorites.
They do not love the poor.
They do not walk among the poor.
They do not denounce the rich.
They do not take the side of the laborer in the struggle of life.
They do not preach, teach, or practice absolute, undeviating justice.
They are not merciful.
They do not despise riches.
They live in palaces, when they can, instead of not having
    whereon to lay their heads.
They do not give to the poor.
They bear false witness.[75]

In many ways Powderly embodied the critique of the working class against
the church and the dominant social order. It seemed all too apparent to him that
Jesus spoke on behalf of working people and stood in solidarity with them in
their attempts to establish a juster and more equitable society. He was genuinely
saddened by how easily the church had turned its back on the poor. Whereas
Jesus had condemned wealth, privilege, and power, the church had amassed
wealth, legitimated privilege, and protected the powerful. Thus, working-class
people, rather than the church, must become the bearers of Jesus' good news
to the poor.

The End of the Knights of Labor

In the decades after the demise of the Knights of Labor the labor movement would follow two divergent paths: socialism and so-called pure and simple trade unionism. In the formation of the Socialist Party in 1901, workers joined reformists, agrarian radicals, Christian Socialists, revolutionary syndicalists, and Marxists in a united effort to make the debate between socialism and capitalism the central issue of the American political agenda. The party focused on union organizing and electoral politics. Meanwhile, the trade unionism of the American Federation of Labor would evolve into a narrowly conceived business unionism. Thus, the AFL would focus primarily on white male skilled workers in craft rather than industrial unions and would contest not who controlled the workplace or defined the very meaning of work but "bread and butter" issues. The AFL, in other words, would accommodate itself to a market mentality and the separation of economic issues from moral, political, and social considerations.[76]

The Working Class Legacy

John Swinton, labor editor, wrote that the organized efforts of working people gave millions a new sense of their rights as labor was "becoming a public force" in the political process. "It is entering into legislation. It is piercing the press. It has become a formidable menace to the all-enslaving Money-Power, and is checking the insolence of our plutocracy. . . . Let us all and always so act to hasten the time when the rights of man, the practice of justice, the organization of industry, and the proper order of society shall be realized in this, our American Republic." In light of Swinton's observations it is important to acknowledge that the Christian Labor Union, the eight-hour movement, and especially the Knights of Labor helped make it possible for working people to envision their world, themselves, and the institutions that impinged on their lives in new ways. The Knights of Labor did not succeed in creating their cooperative commonwealth, but workers, by their own education, alternative institutions, and consciousness of themselves as workers, laid the basis for what might have been a different industrial America. Workers took issue with a ruthless individualism that debased all it touched, substituting egoism for mutuality and competition for cooperation. For the Knights of Labor the measure of economic justice was the quality of human life rather than material prosperity for the few. At the heart of their vision was a fundamental belief in a working-class solidarity that could overcome all that divided workers by skill, race, gender, and ethnic background. By means of local assemblies and the array of alternative institutional structures, the Knights forged a new sense of community, becoming what Sara Evans and Harry Boyte have labeled "schools for citizenship." Together, workers fostered fraternity and brotherhood and attempted to infuse into what they increasingly saw as a waning Republic, a true, rather than rhetorical, accountability to the people.[77]

As a legacy, late nineteenth-century workers can remind those who have succumbed to fatalistic and pessimistic notions about how institutions function, an economy is run, and a government is formed that things can be different and social change is possible. There is nothing inevitable about history when working-class people have a new sense of themselves and create vehicles for their own emancipation.

Jerome Davis, a radical professor of Christian ethics dismissed from Yale during the 1930s, wrote that "the capitalist system seems to have had a corrosive effect on the ideals and practices of Christianity."[78] This seemed most apparent to workers in the late nineteenth century as they struggled to come to terms with industrial capitalism. Their understanding of Christianity convinced them that the church ought to be serving the Kingdom rather than legitimating the amassing of wealth. It should be unmasking privilege and power rather than demeaning the poor and marginalized, and it should preach the disquieting gospel of the Nazarene rather than baptize the status quo. All this seemed self-evident because Christianity was a part of the workers' daily life and part of the fabric of public affirmations that people had worth and dignity simply because they were human. They should not be bought or sold or accumulated. In place of ethical reflections based on the application of norms or principles, so typical of advocates of a social gospel, the trade union fostered other-directed behavior, a living out of cooperation, mutual trust, sacrifice for the good of one's fellow toilers, and authentic expressions of community. That Christian faith informed such social practice is obvious, but only if faith is understood as integral to daily life. It was Christian faith outside the "corrosive effect" of capitalism, Christian life not yet compartmentalized and still refusing to sing pious songs in praise of the dominant order.

Workers active in the Christian Labor Union, the eight-hour movement, and the Knights of Labor were increasingly aware that all was not well with the new American Republic, founded only a century before. On one level, the religion of the Republic, be it Robert Bellah's "civil religion" or that of the established churches, was becoming identified with the dominant people, reinforcing the values, cognitions, and symbols of the capitalist social order and rejecting any alternative. William Hayes Ward, writing in 1883, noted that belonging to the religious community was "a step toward respectability"; church members, he thought, were more moral and wealthy, and conversely, "the classes which are eminently non-intelligent or non-respectable . . . are non-church-goers." Tension between the goals of Christianity and capitalism, between loyalty to God and loyalty to mammon, was resolved by the proper use of wealth, at times even called *Christian* wealth. How was the church to wrestle with the meaning of economic justice if it so identified with power and money? In the words of R. Heber Newton, an Episcopal minister and early advocate of a social gospel, it had "forgotten its Master's gospel, and . . . become the church of respectability and 'society' . . . the upholder of civilization as it is; now it has accepted the anti-Christian dogmas of the older political economists, and in so doing really turned traitor to the ethics of Jesus Christ." One could ask to what degree the uncritical attachment of the American people to a capitalist economy can be explained by the role the religion of the Republic has played in legitimating the capitalist system and accepting its social values and goals as its own.[79]

Beyond the issue of religion and capitalism both the Christian Labor Union and the Knights of Labor raised the question of the compatibility of democracy and capitalism. Can the republican valuation of cooperation over competition, of mutual trust over self-interest, of the common good over the good of the individual be practiced when a political economy is so structured as to determine justice by the dictates of the market and to force representative government to abide by the rules of the corporation? The creation of both an alternative set of values and the cultural institutions to sustain those values was a lasting contribution of the Knights of Labor. An economic system is part of an interdependent world, and moral questions are not personal issues alone but have to do with the quality of human life and a value system that makes it possible for life either to flourish or to die. At the heart of such a critique was a God who affirmed that human life was possible only when people had control over the productive process, when concrete human needs—from economic organization to control of their own lives—replaced what Franz Hinkelammert rightly calls the "entrepreneurial metaphysics" of "market, money, and capital."[80]

2

Religion, Women, and Politics

Feminism, Class, and Labor

Historian Linda Gordon maintains that one of the most difficult problems in writing women's history is to include both domination and resistance. "Sometimes we feel impelled to document oppression, diagram the structures of domination, specify the agents and authors of domination, mourn the damages," Gordon writes. At other times "we feel impelled to defend our honor and raise our spirits by documenting our struggles and identifying success in mitigating the tyranny." Women have been victims but not simply victims; agents but never fully agents. This duality seems to parallel Marxist debates over structure and human agency, and it finds expression in histories that focus on minorities, outsiders, and victims. In each case, the domination and resistance must be located explicitly in the larger historical process. "Women's history," writes Donald Matthews, is not exclusively "in retaliation for the tradition of male-oriented history." It is not women's history alone "but aims for inclusiveness through the introduction of women into the historical consciousness of both sexes." On the other hand, it is not simply a matter of adjusting the balance sheet by enlarging the historiographic framework, a history of redress. There must also be an understanding of the history of women in light of the "sex/gender system," recognizing that American society has been structured so that "duties, rewards, functions, and values" are allotted according to sex.[1]

Resistance and domination, development of women's historical consciousness and the exposure and analysis of the sex/gender system together generate the questions this chapter addresses. The subject matter is the interplay between women and American Christianity within the context of struggles for social change in the late nineteenth and early twentieth centuries. The life histories of people provide a window on the past, and no two women better exemplify the different insights into the dynamics of women's history than Frances Willard and Mother Jones. By temperament, background, religious upbringing, and experience, Willard, native-born middle-class Protestant, and Jones, Catholic working-class immigrant, were very different. Nevertheless they agreed with the working-class critique of the exploitative nature of a capitalist economy. Yet though they shared a vision of an alternative America, they differed on suffrage, temperance, and the meaning of women's emancipation.[2]

Janet Wilson James begins her exploration of women and religion from an acknowledgment that in American churches "women usually outnumber men; men exercise authority." Men do theology and ethics, and therefore categories, experiences, and modes of thought and forms of action are defined as if women are invisible, part of human discourse only as objects, never as subjects.[3]

This oppression has been resisted: some women have not been hesitant to speak about the "proper" role they should play within the church and the larger society in light of the liberative nature of the gospel. Many have seen the Christian faith as a way of perceiving and acting in the world to overcome the artificial distinctions created by the notion that only human beings of the male gender are made in the image of God. A century ago some remarkable women believed, to use Beverly Harrison's words, that "feminism is not for women only because we all need a recovery of our full, integrated humanity and the power of theological language to engage in our genuine struggle. . . . Feminism is a call to genuine strength in women *and* men, a strength born of the power of relationship. Active love and passion for justice sends our roots deep, to discover our connection with all that is. Such shared strength does enable us to keep faith, and we need that strength, for our faith calls us to ongoing, difficult, and challenging work."[4]

Frances Elizabeth Caroline Willard

Frances Willard, according to one of her contemporaries, did more to "widen [women's] outlook, and develop our gifts, than any man, or any other women of her time. Every movement for the uplifting of humanity has found in her a cordial friend and active helper. Every field of inquiry or investigation has shared in her quick, intelligent sympathy, and she has been essentially American in this, that she is always receptive to new ideas, without being frightened at their newness." In her own time many considered her one of the most important women of the nineteenth century. Now, her name is almost forgotten, perhaps because much of Willard's public recognition was due to her association with the temperance crusade, which during her lifetime became a broad-based movement for social reform. After her death in 1898, temperance became more and more a single-issue campaign focused on the legal prohibition of alcohol, an episode in American history that many would like to forget, along with those who participated in the temperance movement.[5]

Born on September 28, 1839, in Churchville, New York, a small community west of Rochester, Willard was one of five children, two of whom died at an early age. She grew up in Ohio and Wisconsin, reared in relative comfort and privilege. Her family was part of a growing and prosperous middle class of successful merchants, businesspeople, and professionals, Willard came of age in a period in which the expectations for daughters of middle-class families were defined by a cult of domesticity and women's sphere.[6]

The changes that accompanied the transformation of a colonial, household-based economy, in which the sexual division of labor was often blurred, into the burgeoning commercial capitalism of late eighteenth- and early nineteenth-century America not only altered the relationship between home and workplace but increasingly confined women to the home, to economic dependence on men, and to their role as wives and mothers. An ideology of domesticity justified separate spheres for men and women; men were to control the economy and politics, and women were to be caretakers of the family, with responsibility for the moral and religious upbringing of the children. From pulpit to press, from sermons to printed books, middle-class women were instructed in what was expected of them. Mrs. A. J. Graves, writing in the early 1840s, cautioned women:

> If man's duties lie abroad, women's duties are within the quiet seclusion of home. If his greatness and power are most strikingly exhibited in associated action upon associated masses, her true greatness and her highest efficiency consists in individual effort upon individual beings. The religion and politics of man have their widest sphere in the world without; but the religious zeal and patriotism of women are most beneficially and powerful exerted upon the members of her household. It is in her home that her strength lies; it is here that gentle influence, which is the secret of might, is most successfully employed; and this she loses as soon as she descends from her calm height into the world's arena.

Young women in particular were taught patterns of behavior and self-understanding and notions about the very meaning of their femininity that would allay resistance to or doubts about their subordinate station in life. According to the tenets of gender differentiation, women were marked by their maternal and nurturing characteristics, their needs, goals, and sense of fulfillment as women to be met by husband and children. Moreover, women were portrayed as gentle, meek, and delicate and, implicitly, as necessarily subservient and dependent.[7]

During her childhood, Frances Willard found it difficult to play the passive and deferential little girl, preferring to be known as "Frank." She found great pleasure in carpentry, the outdoors, and hunting with her brother Oliver. Willard recalled that her mother talked to her and her sister not "as girls, but simply as human beings, and it never occurred to me that I ought to 'know house-work' and do it." It came as a shock to her when, at eighteen years of age, she found herself forced to assume roles that conflicted with her freedom and independence; all of a sudden she was expected to wear certain types of clothes, endure supposedly fashionable hair styles, and adopt attitudes in conflict with her own sense of self. She wrote in her journal: "This is my birthday and the date of my martyrdom. Mother insists that at last I *must* have my hair done up woman-fashion. She says she can hardly forgive herself for letting me run wild so long. . . . My back hair is twisted up like a corkscrew; I carry eighteen hair-pins; my head aches miserably; my feet are entangled in the skirt of my hateful new gown. I can never jump over a fence again, so long as I live." She also resented the fact that when her brother turned twenty-one he could vote, but she could not, but for advocating the right to vote she was labeled "strong-minded." Then, as always, Willard listened to her own conscience, clinging to her belief in the inherent equality of women with men and their God-given right to live lives in which their childhood dreams might be realized.[8]

In spite of the resistance of her father, who agreed with his contemporaries that education was unnecessary for women, Willard finished her advanced education at North Western Female College in Evanston, Illinois, a community she was to be a part of for the remainder of her life. In college she was drawn to the writings of Margaret Fuller, seeing her as a model of what women could achieve, "a cultivated intellect, right judgment, self-knowledge, self-happiness," to which she added, "If she, why not we, by steady toil?" Graduating in 1859, she spent the next twelve years teaching and traveling abroad, coming to the conclusion that through education women could come to understand the forces that shaped their lives and learn to take control over their own future. Her decision to teach was influenced by her experiences with the exploitative conditions facing women in various parts of the world, and by the limited professional opportunities open to her. Throughout the nineteenth century, middle-class women were most often limited to teaching and nursing, though later in the century some were also working in libraries and settlement houses.[9]

In 1871 Willard was appointed president of the new Evanston College for Ladies, a women's school affiliated with Northwestern University. Evanston, like Northwestern, was a Methodist institution. It was the brainchild of Mary F. Haskin, who was, Willard said, committed to making women "felt as a force in higher education, not only as students, but professors and trustees," for "to have men only in these positions, was to shut up one of humanity's eyes." Willard's hopes for women's education were short-lived. Not long after assuming her post, she came in conflict with the newly named president of Northwestern, Charles Fowler, a Methodist minister, head of a large urban congregation in Chicago and well known in Methodist circles. The two had different perceptions of the relation of Evanston to Northwestern, the nature of women's education, and Willard's role in the University. These professional conflicts were exacerbated by personal tensions, Fowler having once been Frances Willard's fiancé. By June of 1874 Willard felt forced to resign her position and not long thereafter found herself drawn into the world of temperance reform and politics. Of this change in her life she commented: "I was to become a wanderer on the face of the earth; instead of libraries I was to frequent public halls and railway cars; instead of scholarly and cultured men I was to see the dregs of saloon and gambling house and haunt of shame." [10]

The Woman's Christian Temperance Union

The role of women in the temperance crusade, particularly through the Woman's Christian Temperance Union under the leadership of Frances Willard, has recently captured the attention of a number of historians. Barbara Epstein identifies in the activities of the WCTU a "campaign against . . . masculine culture," a grass-roots women's movement that helped women make the transition from the private sphere of the home and domesticity to the public sphere of politics and social change. At the same time, according to Ellen DuBois, the very success of the WCTU was due to its ability to utilize the language of home and family in such a way as to create a mass-based organization through which women could become active in political struggle. By contrast, says DuBois, the suffrage movement remained a minority movement throughout the nineteenth century precisely because it "focused on the public sphere and on a nonfamilial role for women" in a period in which most women were still "limited to the private realities of wifehood and motherhood." Given the importance of language and experience, one added dimension to the radicalizing role of the WCTU in the lives of middle-class women was that, as a Christian organization, the union raised questions not only about the place of women in society but about a male-centered interpretation of Christianity. [11]

The Woman's Christian Temperance Union was the outgrowth of what has been called the "women's crusade" of 1873–1874, which began in Ohio and spread through the Midwest and to sections of the East. It all began with a temperance address by Diocletian Lewis, "The Duty of Christian Women in the Cause of Temperance," in Hillsboro, Ohio, on December 23, 1873. Lewis was a well-known temperance lecturer, and he had often given this talk, sharing with his audience the story of his family's own battle with a drunken father and the success his mother and other women had obtained as they prayed in front of the local saloon to stop the selling of liquor. He exhorted women to follow the example set by his mother and to organize and take action. Quite soon a group of women did just that, forming the first of hundreds of "praying bands" of women who would confront saloon owners and those who supported intemperance in their local communities. The Hillsboro lecture was to start middle-class women literally taking to the streets in protest against what they considered the evils of drink and its corrupting effect on men, women, and children. [12]

Frances Willard believed that the importance of the crusade was multifold. It exposed women from privileged backgrounds to realities of life that many could not have imagined. For the first time they learned something about poverty and the conditions in which millions of people were forced to live. The crusade taught these women "their power to transact business, to mould opinion by public utterance, to influence the decisions of voters, and opened the eyes of scores and hundreds to the need of the Republic for the suffrage of women, and made them willing to take up for their homes and country's sake the burden of that citizenship they would never have sought for their own." The crusade took organizational form through the founding of the national WCTU in November of 1874. It would become the largest women's organization of the nineteenth century.[13]

Willard was active in the WCTU from its beginnings. In the fall of 1874 she was elected president of the Chicago union; later she became secretary of the state organization and correspondence secretary for the national organization. By 1879 Willard was president of the national WCTU, a position she would hold until her death in 1898. Ruth Bordin, author of the most recent biographical treatment of Frances Willard, stresses that she was politically very astute. Willard understood the need for women to empower themselves, to discover the artificiality of the constraints the dominant social order had placed on them and how these influenced their perception of themselves and their abilities. As noted earlier, the strength of the WCTU derived from the way in which it utilized the language of domesticity, women's sphere, and "womanhood" to help women move from the restrictions of the private realm to the public world. This strategy can best be illustrated by Frances Willard's approach to the issue of women's suffrage.[14]

The membership of the WCTU was drawn largely from native-born middle-class women, members of mainline Protestant denominations. In the beginning some members opposed women's suffrage, reflecting the attitudes and beliefs not only of the dominant culture but of the churches from which they came. Opposition to women's suffrage was argued on various grounds—from the belief that women's involvement in the political process would destroy the home and family to the belief in an inherent mental and physical inferiority that supposedly makes women emotionally and intellectually incapable of dealing with the harsh realities of political decision making. Edward D. Cope, writing for the influential *Popular Science Monthly*, maintained that those who advocated the franchise for women did so without taking into consideration the consequences of their actions. To press for women's suffrage, Cope argued, was not only to overlook the natural differences between men and women—that is, the rational versus the emotional approach to life—but to force women to relinquish their maternal and moral responsibilities for the preservation of civilization, producing detrimental effects on the relationship between the sexes. The institution of marriage would be threatened, and "home affection" would be weakened; the end result would be a decline in the civilizing influence of women and the creation of a race of "moral barbarians." Cope concluded that women's suffrage was "more dangerous than any form of absolutism." His fears were shared by

Senator George G. Vest of Missouri, who stated that "woman as she is to-day, the queen of the home and of hearts, is above the political collisions of this world and should be kept above them."[15]

Frances Willard's approach to her conservative sisters was to work for a limited form of the franchise by linking women's ballot to temperance reform. As early as 1875, as a delegate to the Illinois state WCTU convention, Willard was instrumental in the passing of a resolution that stated, "Since woman is the greatest sufferer from the rum curse, she ought to have the power to close the dramshop over against her home." Women's suffrage was presented not as a threat to home and family but as the very means by which they could be preserved. Borrowing the notion of "home protection" from the Canadian WCTU activist Lettia Yeomans, Willard became an advocate for the home protection ballot, which would give women the right to vote on state and local issues involving control of the liquor interests, from saloon licensing to outright prohibition. In her first home protection address, in the summer of 1876, she spoke about her experience as a young woman when her brother first voted with her father and how she and her sister were prevented from expressing their love of country. She could be silent no more, for women's only hope, as "the born conservator of the home," as the "Nemesis of home's arch enemy, King Alcohol," was in suffrage for women. Five years later, during the 1881 national meeting, Frances Willard witnessed the passage of a resolution declaring that the WCTU stood for " 'Home Protection' [that is, the vote for women on the temperance question only], where Home Protection is the strongest rallying cry; Equal Franchise, where the votes of women joined to those of men alone give stability to temperance legislation."[16]

The language of home protection became an important vehicle through which Willard could address such issues as rape, the treatment of women as if they were toys or dolls, their lack of self-respect either in the marriage relationship or as single women, and the conditions women faced in prisons, workplaces, and society. She asked why it was that "in Massachusetts and Vermont it is a greater crime to steal a cow than to abduct and ruin a girl" and why the legal system seemed to be so structured that it allowed men to exploit women with impunity.[17]

In addition, Willard helped members of the WCTU to understand that suffrage could not be limited just to temperance, and gradually the union assumed an important role in the suffrage movement. In Willard's 1892 presidential address she asked the members of the WCTU to reflect that "the right to vote in a democratic age is an acknowledgement by the States of the right of the citizen to have an opinion and a right to tender it for the guidance of her fellow citizens. . . . The voteless adult is nowhere, whose rights, whose individuality, whose common nature, even, are all held by sufferance, permitted rather than recognized, and as a consequence minimized beyond endurance." By 1894 the WCTU was cooperating with the work of the National American

Woman Suffrage Association, and Ruth Bordin concludes that the "WCTU made woman suffrage respectable in many white Protestant middle-class circles by the late 1890s." [18]

For Willard, as for many of her contemporaries, suffrage was not only about the enfranchisement of women; it had to do with women's consciousness of themselves as active agents in shaping their personal and collective lives. Willard looked upon the WCTU as a concrete manifestation of the "organizing power" of women, of what "comradeship among women" could accomplish. In an address before the National Council of Women she stressed that the "highest power of organization for women is that it brings them out; it translates them from the passive into the active voice; the dear, modest clinging things didn't think they could do anything, and lo and behold! they found out they could." Sisterhood was also a visible sign of women engaged in political struggle to transform society, women who understood themselves as part of a tradition established by their "Revolutionary Foremothers," as Willard called them. Just as important was women's discovery of their individuality, that "the ultimate object of every conceivable reform is to give . . . each individual of the human mass more completely back to himself; to restore to all the clear, perceiving brain, the strong, firm hand, the steadfast beating heart." [19]

Christianity and Feminism

For most of her life Frances Willard was a devout member of the Methodist Episcopal church. She is best understood as an evangelical Christian, but her evangelical sympathies had a good tinge of Methodist Arminianism and were thus in no way in conflict with the developing liberal currents of her day. Many liberal evangelicals saw no inherent threat to faith in the discoveries of science; in fact these women and men took a critical approach to Scripture, believing in the compatibility of reason and revelation and in the importance of one's experience of God's grace and the power of prayer. Like other nineteenth-century Methodists, Willard came under the influence of Phoebe Palmer, a preacher of Methodist perfectionism and leader in the Holiness movement, who stressed not only sanctification through faith but an active church role for women. Willard's religious experiences were also in keeping with a belief in the organic relationship between revivalism and social reform, that to be moved by the spirit of God led to action on behalf of others, not to self-absorption. Timothy Smith in his noted work *Revivalism and Social Reform* underscores the relationship between antebellum Protestant revivalism and movements for social change, from abolitionism to the development of social consciousness among evangelical Christians on issues of peace, women's suffrage, and the social dimension of sin. Similarly, in the post–Civil War period Willard maintained the inseparability of the experience of conversion, equality for women, and labor reform.[20]

To believe that in Christ all things were made new was for Willard an affirmation that distinctions based on gender, which denied women the full expression of their personhood, had no place in the church: "Woman, like man, should be freely permitted to do whatever she can do well." Unfortunately the Christian church, one of the first religious traditions to "recognize and nurture woman's spiritual powers, [was] one of the most difficult centers to reach with the sense of justice toward her." The source of the problem was "the white male dynasty reigning undisputed until our own day; lording it over every heritage, and constituting the only unquestioned apostolic succession." [21]

Willard had difficulty working with men who failed to recognize the contradiction between the gospel and sexism. Not long after she resigned from Northwestern University, when she was beginning her work with the WCTU, she joined the revivalistic campaigns of Dwight L. Moody. Businessman turned lay evangelist, Moody was the best known evangelist of the late nineteenth century. Willard's work with Moody was short-lived, for it quickly became apparent to her that Moody's saving of souls had little to do with social reform, especially as it related to temperance and women's issues. She was particularly bothered by meetings in which only the "brethren" were called forth, as if the Pentecost had not broken down everything that divided people: "There is neither bond nor free, male nor female, but all are one." Later, when Willard and the WCTU brought the issues of temperance and women's suffrage together, Moody commented that it was "a master stroke of the devil," for it focused attention on questions he believed had little to do with winning people for Christ.[22]

Years later, Willard again experienced the indifference of the male church leaders. In 1880 the WCTU proposed sending representatives to the national meetings of various Protestant denominations. The churches acted as if "something revolutionary had been proposed" when they were asked to agree. Willard's own Methodists came out against the receiving of "fraternal" delegates, stating they only recognized "ecclesiastical visitors." The irony was that women within the Methodist church had worked for lay representation at the general conference. Yet, when this was accepted for the first time in 1882, male laity joined the male clergy to oppose the seating of women delegates.[23]

As Willard gradually transformed the WCTU into an advocacy organization on behalf of women, she pressed the church establishment to come to terms with the problems posed by male dominance and sexist distortions of the Christian tradition. "By what righteous principle of law or logic are we excluded from church councils when we so largely make up the church's membership?" she asked. The male leadership of the church quoted the Bible and in the process proved that exegesis was the most "man-made of all sciences." If women were responsible for handling the biblical tradition they would give a different interpretation of Scripture and would remind men that the source of authority for the church was Christ, not Paul, who, as Willard saw it, simply legitimated what men wanted to hear. Why was it, Willard asked, that male exegetes could argue that the Sermon on the Mount or other parts of Scripture that seemed repugnant to modern people need not be taken seriously but dared anyone to question those portions of the Bible that spoke about the subjection of women? Willard believed that a female reading of the biblical texts would recover the liberative nature of the Christian message, Jesus as "emancipator" of women, "no less than humanity's Savior." Were not women, Willard asked, the first witnesses to Jesus' resurrection and among his earliest followers? Prophets of the early church witnessed that "no utterance" of Jesus marked "woman as ineligible to any position in the church He came to found; but his gracious words and deeds, His impartation of His purposes and plans to women; His stern reproofs to men who did them wrong, His chosen companionships, and the tenor of His whole life and teaching" were opposed to domination and oppression of women.[24]

Frances Willard contended that the distorted biblical exegesis of male theologians and their control of the church had led to sacerdotalism and dogmatism, accompanied by the "invention of hierarchies." They had even "made the Prince of peace a mighty man of war." Perhaps women could restore life to Christianity. Rather than discuss abstract theology, women would speak about the facts of life and the impact of a market-oriented economy by stressing the reality of "greed of gain, passion for power," and "the complicity of the church." Willard advocated the ordination of women as "preachers of the Word of God," for "men have always tithed mint and rue and cumin in their ecclesiasticism, while the world's heart has cried out for compassion, forgiveness and sympathy." Women knew what it meant to be "prostrate under society's pitiless and crushing pyramid." They understood the gospel as the good news of liberation from all that sought to diminish women as well as men. She concluded: "My creed on the whole question of woman's preaching . . . is summed up by Whatever is fit to be done at all may be done by anyone who can do it well." [25]

Willard's advocacy of women's equality was not confined to the church. "The free using of one's gifts of brain, and hand, and heart," she wrote, would break the bonds that limited both women and men. She tried to convince men of the aptness of a line from Tennyson, "the woman's cause is man's," and she rejected conventional ideas about masculine and feminine virtues, as if courage, intellect, hardihood were manly, and patience, gentleness, and compassion feminine. Men and women should "add to those already won virtues of the other" and develop a sense of their humanity that encompassed the capacities deemed male and female. Such an attitude would renew the institution of marriage, which in its present form was a manifestation of a man's power to abuse and misuse a woman's love, to have "control over her property; and in the state, to make all laws under which she is to live, adjudicate all her penalties, try her before juries of men, conduct her to prison under the care of men, cast the ballot for her, and in general hold her in the estate of a perpetual minor." When such laws and customs had been abolished, marriage might finally become a means by which two people could express love for each other, a relationship in which there was "an undivided half apiece for wife and husband; co-education to mate them on the plane of mind, equal property rights to make her God's own free woman, not coerced into marriage for the sake of a support, not a bond-slave after she is married . . . [and] in that day the wife shall surrender at marriage no right not equally surrendered by her husband—not even her own name." Thus for Willard the existing institution of marriage mirrored the distorted relationship between men and women that resulted from a gender-based misinterpretation of the Christian tradition and a fundamental denial of our God-given equality as human beings.[26]

Women, Labor, and Socialism

Increasingly radical as the years passed, Willard came to believe that temperance, equality for women, and a Christian reform of society were not possible unless the structural causes of the ills that plagued humankind were addressed. She told members of the WCTU that they must study political economy and realize that "the time has long passed when Christians can wrap themselves in a cloak of sanctity and sit and sing psalms, unheeding the great, struggling, toiling, suffering masses around them." [27]

One of the most important factors shaping Willard's increasing sympathy for radical solutions to social problems was her relationship to the Knights of Labor. Initially, she was drawn to the Knights in the hope of uniting the temperance agenda of the WCTU with the upsurge of the working class. As early as 1878 the order established that "no person who either sells or makes his living by the sale of intoxicating drink" could be admitted. Terence Powderly, in his annual address to the Knights of Labor in 1882, stated that temperance was an important question, even, perhaps, "the main issue." Those who drank demeaned not only themselves but all they touched. In words reminiscent of the temperance evangelist, he called rum the curse of humankind, for "its life on earth has been one of ruin to the bright hopes of youth, and the peace of old age. It has robbed childhood of its delights. It has stolen the laugh from the lips of the innocent, and the bloom from the cheek of manhood." Nevertheless, Powderly, himself a model of sobriety, tried not to impose his standards on the Knights' membership. He viewed drinking more as a negative influence on public perceptions of the order; furthermore, drunkenness seemed to Powderly indicative of a lack of responsibility toward other Knights, oneself, and one's family.[28]

Beginning in 1886, the WCTU and the Knights of Labor exchanged delegates at their annual meetings. What impressed Frances Willard was not simply the stance the Knights of Labor took on temperance at its national gatherings but the fact that the order, through its local assemblies, provided an alternative culture that "in every town and village draws young men away from the saloon, [while] its debates help to make them better citizens." She greatly admired Powderly, describing him to members of the WCTU as "ordained as the Moses

56

of his people to bring labor out of the wilderness by the peaceful means of co-operation, arbitration, and the ballot box." [29]

Willard was equally enthusiastic about the Knights' commitment to equal pay for women, the leadership role of women in the organization, and what seemed to her a fundamental belief in equality. In a November, 1886, WCTU circular, Willard told WCTU members that Knights were allies who shared a belief in the nature of cooperation, arbitration, and the power of the ballot box. The WCTU rejoiced "in your broad platform of mutual help, which recognizes neither sex, race, nor creed. Especially do we appreciate the tendency of your great movement to elevate women industrially to their rightful place by claiming that they have equal pay for equal work; recognizing them as officers and members of your societies, and advocating the ballot in their hands as their rightful weapon of self-help in our representative government." [30]

Contact with the Knights of Labor brought Willard face-to-face with the daily lives of working-class women. She began to speak about "over-worked and under-paid sister women" who needed justice, not charity, and to rail against the working conditions in sweatshops, factories, mills, and department stores. These occupations "killed," for they failed to "give employment to both body and mind," failed to give women any "reasonable hope for advancement," and allowed "few opportunities for air and sunshine." Privileged women, she noted, sat "in their clubs . . . saying what a wonderful country this was" because they could supposedly dress so cheaply and had "so much more time and money to improve" their minds. They were the very ones, Willard argued, who needed to "look into the wan faces of the women who make these garments and receive these prices for their work." Perhaps then they might understand the inequality of the economic system in which they lived and look more deeply into what the glories of sisterhood might require.[31]

In 1887 Willard was initiated into the Noble and Holy Order of the Knights of Labor. She confessed to Richard Ely that she was at first hesitant to join because she feared that her more conservative sisters would take offense and thus "hinder my helpfulness to the working people." But a hindrance she was not, for she came to believe that poverty was the cause of intemperance rather than the effect. If women within the WCTU knew what working-class women had to endure, they would realize that intemperance had more to do with being "ill-housed, ill-fed, and ill-clad" than anything else. Poverty fostered intemperance by robbing women and men of their humanity. What a country does for the poor, Willard said, "determines the decency, not to say the civilization, of a country." The women of the WCTU often viewed the world through the rose-tinted glasses of comfort, and some regarded the aspirations of working-class people as threats to "life and property." Willard informed them that the real menace to society was those who controlled "seven-eighths of the property," were indifferent to the unemployed, and failed to recognize the inherent dignity of labor. By the same token, those who were horrified by the notion of strikes needed to consider that they might be a defense against the "spectre of hunger and houselessness." Willard advocated the eight-hour day and claimed that it would mean that the value of labor would be measured not by money or one's "balance at the bank" but by a "day's work with brain or hand, honestly done and fairly measured." [32]

What particularly struck Willard about the working-class movements were the questions they raised about the Christian tradition. When working people read the Scriptures they questioned the use of the Bible to instill blind acceptance of authority, be it the submission of women to men or the subjection of workers to employers. Indeed, an understanding of the teachings of Jesus should bring a better life here and now, not in "a Heaven out of this world." [33]

Willard lectured the women of the temperance movement for their shortsightedness in reducing all the world's problems to intemperance, as though if "men and women were temperate all other material good would follow in the train of greater grace." Still, her position on drinking would not allow any sympathy for Eugene Debs as leader of the Pullman Strike of 1894. She wrote to Henry Demarest Lloyd that she had heard Debs was "under the dominion of whiskey to such an extent that in the very height of that awful strike . . . he had to be locked up because he was utterly out of his mind through drink. No such leader can ever command any small influence that the White Ribbon women may have." Her attitude toward Debs reflected a deeper problem in her defense of labor. In the massive conflicts between labor and capital, such as the Homestead Strike of 1892 and the Pullman Strike of 1894, she argued for peaceful arbitration, overlooking how intently the power of capital was bent upon crushing working-class organizations and the right of workers to organize. In the midst of these battles, the WCTU remained neutral, hoping to serve, says Mary Earhart, as a "mediator between capital and labor" and to maintain "peace with honor founded upon justice to both parties." By "pen and voice" the WCTU would "create well-informed public opinion." As much as Willard tried to identify with the labor movement and to understand the lives of working-class people, particularly women, she failed to comprehend that impartiality was of little use to labor when employers had on their side the courts and the government, and capital had about as much respect for the rights of workers as did men for the rights of women. [34]

In the same period in which Willard was forging an alliance between the Knights of Labor and the WCTU, she came under the influence of Laurence Gronlund and Edward Bellamy. Danish-American Laurence Gronlund served as an important interpreter of European socialism to Americans. In *The Cooperative Commonwealth* (1884) he presented socialism "digested by a mind, Anglo-Saxon in its dislike of all extravagances, in its freedom from any vindictive feeling against persons, who are from circumstances what they are." He Americanized socialism to make it palatable to reformists of the late nineteenth century. To Willard he communicated an understanding of socialism that was ethical and moralistic; in a mixture of religious and political language, he propounded a vision of the "future social order—the natural heir of the present one—in which all important instruments of production have been taken under collective control; in which the citizens are consciously public functionaries, and in which labors are rewarded according to results." The new social order was to be the product of a gradual evolutionary development guided by both education and reason. Gronlund rejected both class conflict and a materialist interpretation of history, relying upon the power of ideas, not the agency of a class-conscious working class, as the motor of historical change. Socialism, in his view, was evolving as an unfolding of God's purposes, and Willard thus came to see it as the gradual establishment of the Kingdom of God created by the force of ethical and moral ideas.[35]

On the advice of Gronlund, who noted that people found his own work dry, Willard turned to Edward Bellamy's *Looking Backward*, a popular presentation of Gronlund's ideas. Published in 1888, *Looking Backward* quickly became one of the best sellers of the nineteenth century, surpassing in sales "any other American novel since Harriet Beecher Stowe's *Uncle Tom's Cabin*." Written as a piece of utopian fiction, *Looking Backward* addressed the fear and uncertainty the Haymarket tragedy of 1886 and the ensuing labor strife engendered among middle-class Americans. It vividly described the problems besetting late nineteenth-century industrial America, from the detrimental effects of competition to the implications of a growing concentration of wealth and power. The story centers on Julian West, an upper-class Bostonian put into a hypnotic sleep in 1887. When he awakes, in the year 2000, he finds America transformed. He learns through conversations with a Dr. Leete and his daughter how American society had been reorganized by replacing competition with cooperation. Without conflict or violence the economy had been nationalized, leading to the eradication of inequalities based on class and gender. Technology and central planning were important and beneficial parts of West's new world.

The book inspired the formation of Nationalist clubs, which sought to propagate the ideas set forth there. Nationalists stressed brotherhood, solidarity, mutuality, affirmation—"the doctrine," according to Bellamy, "of those who hold that the principle of popular government by equal voice of all for the equal benefit of all . . . should extend to the economic organization as well; and that the entire capital and labor of the nations should be nationalized and administered by their people through their chosen agents, for the equal benefit of all, under an equal law of industrial service." [36]

In Frances Willard's 1889 presidential address to the national meeting of the WCTU, she asked the assembled women to consider the Nationalist platform in light of the constant struggle of people for food, clothing, and shelter. They should study the goals of the Nationalist clubs with an eye toward the "day when all men's weal is made the care of all by the very construction of society and constitution of government." While there is no indication that the membership of the WCTU was as drawn to these ideas as Willard was, she nevertheless insisted that "women take to Nationalism like a duck to water." [37]

It was true, in fact, that women made up a large percentage of the membership of the Nationalist clubs and played an important role in the spread of Nationalism. Both Mari Jo Buhle and William Leach point to the Nationalists' involvement in women's issues and their proclamation that a new social order was possible only if there was equality between women and men. In an address to the Woman's National Council, Frances Willard approvingly quoted Bellamy's statement that Nationalism would mean the elimination of the dependency of women on men. No longer reduced to an economic commodity, women could lead their own lives, enjoying, Bellamy said, as much "dignity and independence" as any man. Women were drawn to a vision of a society in which domestic life was transformed, and women would be employed outside the home. Technological innovations would dramatically change household work, and cooking and child care would be provided by the state. Bellamy influenced household reform by advocating cooperative laundries and kitchens, and Willard agreed with his ideas, calling for "cooperative housekeeping," which, coupled with "scientific rectification of household duties," would free women from the drudgery of housework. The collectivization of household work, she believed, would lessen daily toil for all women, irrespective of class. [38]

Willard's experiences with the Knights of Labor, her reading of Gronlund and Bellamy, and her involvement with the Nationalist movement came together in her championing of Christian Socialism. In the pages of the official organ of the WCTU, the *Union Signal*, she advocated socialism as "applied Christianity." Christians had come to a crossroads: either they must stand up for radical changes in the governing structures of society, or if they turned their backs on the existing state of affairs, they must take full responsibility for "a further concentration of wealth and power in the hands of a few and more grinding oppression for the many." To heed the clarion call of Christian socialism was, for Willard, to acknowledge that one had started down a path toward change, albeit evolutionary rather than revolutionary. There were those who shunned anything to do with incremental change, but Willard shared with other evolutionary Socialists a belief that one modified human society, like human character, slowly, by "investing the little increment of power that we possess to render, this heavenly dram a little more likely to be realized." Hence, like Bellamy and Gronlund, she believed in what today would be called consciousness raising—that education, agitation, and the gradual politicalization of people would eventually achieve desirable social ends. To argue for Christian socialism was to believe in the collective ownership of transportation and utilities, profit sharing, the eight-hour day, and the basic right of workers to collective bargaining. If asked for a Christian Socialist definition of socialism, Willard endorsed that offered by the British Trade Union Congress, "the principle of collective ownership and control of all the means of production and distribution."[39]

Through Christian socialism Willard could express her commitment to the necessity for structural transformation of American society while communicating to members of the Christian community that there was something fundamentally disturbing, disquieting, and perhaps threatening about the Christian faith. She asked whether in "every Christian there exists a socialist; and in every socialist a Christian," formulating the question in such a way as to make people think for a moment about what was at the heart of socialism and Christianity. Socialists were those who spoke about community, solidarity, cooperation, and brotherhood, who affirmed what human beings held in common rather than what separated them, who spoke of "we" and "our" rather than "I" and "mine." Words that affirmed the fundamental nature of the individual-in-community appealed to Willard because they pointed to a "working together of brothers and sisters under a system which makes the weal of each the care of all." The world view based on self-interest and competition, which pitted human beings against each other and conveyed a picture of the world as an arena of antagonistic forces, was difficult for Willard to comprehend, for it seemed to deny a relational understanding of human sociality. She believed deeply in the social nature of the human self and that conversion was a sign of people's ability to change.[40]

For her understanding of Christianity she believed herself indebted to the English Christian Socialists Charles Kingsley and Frederick Maurice and their American counterparts George D. Herron and W.D.P. Bliss, all of whom wrestled with an articulation of the social dimension of Christianity. Perhaps that is why she stressed that "the resurrection of Christ is the need of our day. He has dwelt behind a curtain of mysticism; He has been buried in the grave of ecclesiastical formulae," which have wrapped the truth of Christianity in a veil of superstition so that people no longer knew Christ. They "would hear Him gladly if He were permitted to speak the language of their common life." Christian socialism spoke to Willard in words that touched life, not evaded it. It spoke of a Christ not confined to the past but actively present where justice was a lived expression of Christian faith and people struggled to make "every-day living" reflect "the ethics of Christ's Gospel." To embrace life, she maintained, was to realize that Christian faith had to do with all that which made life possible, that mammon destroyed life and "competition corrodes men's character as rust spoils steel."[41]

As the nineteenth century came to an end, Frances Willard was at the height of her influence. Her work had inseparably united the struggle for temperance, equality for women, labor reform, and socialism. As a tribute to Willard's radicalism a cooperative colony founded in North Carolina took her name. In declaring their principles the colonists echoed Willard's beliefs: "Our religious motto shall be: In essential things, unity; in nonessential things, liberty; in all things, charity. Our business motto shall be, Manhood before money, cooperation vs. competition. Our political creed shall be the Prohibition of trusts, natural monopolies and the liquor traffic." Willard died in 1898, but the questions she raised and the issues she addressed remain. At the time of her death, another Socialist, Mother Jones, was raising hell of another order.[42]

Mother Mary Harris Jones

Debra Campbell claims that in "popular Catholic imagination" of an earlier day women were either nuns or mothers with large families, and hence "female Catholic reformers and activists" were an anomaly before Vatican II. Recent historical scholarship has done much to dispel such myths, and no one liked defying conventional wisdom more than Mother Jones. She was a labor organizer but above all an agitator. Once introduced by a college professor as a "great humanitarian," she quickly corrected him: "I'm not a humanitarian. I'm a hell-raiser." The hell she raised was always on behalf of working-class people. When asked where her home was, she responded, "Wherever there is a fight against oppression." Her life in many ways was an embodiment of the Knights of Labor slogan "Agitate, Educate, Organize!"[43]

The role of the agitator, the troubler of the peace of the powerful, is in need of rediscovery. So often in dealing with movements for social change undue attention is given to reformists, those we so often dub "realists" because they seem to have worked within the system. Aileen Kraditor in *Means and Ends in American Abolitionism* describes the abolitionists as agitators, people with little "reverence" for established institutions and values, who pressed demands that the general public perceived as unrealistic and extreme. Yet, as Kraditor points out, "if politics is the art of the possible, agitation is the art of the desirable." Compromise, practicality, and attainability were not part of the abolitionists' vocabulary, not because they were so much more "unrealistic" than the reformers but because they stood for a set of principles, believed in certain ethical values, and adopted a tactical style that insisted to the American public that they make freedom possible for African Americans, that they live up to their professed faith in the democratic ideals of freedom, equality, and justice. For example, William Lloyd Garrison was more concerned about the degree to which he "forced people to think" than about political expediency. Speaking to a later generation, Saul Alinsky noted that the world was made up of "two kinds of changers, the social changers and the money changers—the social changers go by many names: agitators, revolutionaries, catalysts, and 'outside' trouble makers." More important, they become "social changers" because they are able to "communicate and convince people that, if they find a way to join together, they need not fatalistically accept their plights but will have the power to affect the shape of their world."[44]

No one was better able to stir people up, bind them together, and infuse them with hope and courage for the future than Mary Harris Jones. Fred Mooney, coal miner, union organizer, and secretary-treasurer of District 17, United Mine Workers of America, described Mother Jones as the "white haired angel of the miners," whose "brand of oratorical fire . . . could permeate a group of strikers with more fight than could any living human being. She fired them with enthusiasm, she burned them with criticisms, then cried with them because of their abuses. The miners loved, worshipped, and adored her. And well they might, because there was no night too dark, no danger too great for her to face, if in her judgment 'her boys' needed her." [45]

As a public speaker, Mother Jones had an ability to captivate her audiences with vivid and colorful stories centered around the struggles of working-class people, in all their sufferings and joys, successes and failures. When she came to write her own autobiography, she sketched only those parts of her life "shared in common with the anonymous immigrants who made up much of the American labor force," denying the importance of "her personal suffering, struggle, and resistance." Remembering, we are told, is a selective process. In the case of Mother Jones, her strength was not in recalling the precise details of her life, for she often embellished on certain aspects of her career and was less than candid in her self-appraisal. On various occasions she stated that she was born anywhere between 1830 and 1844. Toward the end of her life she felt most comfortable with the birth date May 1, 1830, though parish records indicate that she was actually born in 1837.[46]

Mary was one of three children born to Richard and Mary Harris in County Cork, Ireland. She contended that she "was born in revolution," part of a family of Irish revolutionaries who had fought and died for a free and independent Ireland. County Cork in the 1830s, like much of Ireland, was predominantly agrarian and poor, with people eking out a subsistence living on small plots of land or as rural laborers confronted, says James Donnelly, with "serious underemployment, abysmally low wages, and high conacre rents"—in stark contrast to a landowning elite who served the interest of English imperial policy. This was the period when Irish nationalism spread among the poor. Rebellion took root in rural Ireland, and every decade from 1760 to 1840 witnessed at least one uprising. Indeed, young Mary Harris's grandfather was hanged for his defiance of English rule, and her father was forced to flee Ireland for his life with English soldiers on his tail.[47]

Mary Harris's father arrived in the United States in 1835, and like many Irish immigrants, he found work as a laborer digging canals and later working on the railroads. Although he obtained U.S. citizenship, he found work as a member of a railroad crew more readily available in Canada; so he settled in Toronto and in 1838 sent for his wife and children. In Toronto, as in other developing cities of Upper and Lower Canada, Irish immigrants made up a significant percentage of the early nineteenth-century working class—37 percent in Toronto in 1851.

Between 47 and 85 percent of the immigrants who arrived in Quebec and Montreal each year between 1817 and 1847 were Irish. In the years in which Mary Harris came of age, Toronto witnessed not only an influx of Irish immigrants but the beginning of the rise of industrial capitalism. Gregory S. Kealey describes how "between the late 1840s and the early 1890s Canada experienced its own industrial revolution. Toronto, Canada's second largest city, played a major role in this transformation. Its capitalists led the strategic drive for protective tariffs, enabling native industries to thrive and prosper; its working class provided the leadership for organized labour in central Canada."[48]

We know very little about Mary's early life, except that she learned dressmaking from her mother and was able to obtain enough education to enter the newly established Toronto Normal School, founded in 1847 as a teacher-training institution. The development of public schools was slow, coming only through a series of common school acts in the 1840s and 1850s, prior to which most poor children received what education they could through schools created by private and religious organizations mostly interested in the perpetuation of a submissive labor force. Options for women of this period, especially daughters of working-class families, were largely limited to the service sector of society—teaching, nursing, clerical work, and domestic service—or to overworked and underpaid factory employment.

While teaching might seem preferable to other types of work, nineteenth-century teachers were confronted with large classes, poor working conditions, and responsibility not only for the behavior of their students both in and out of the classroom but "physical maintenance of the school," notes Elizabeth Graham. She stresses that graduates of the Toronto Normal School were supposed to instill in their students the values of an expanding capitalist economy: "industriousness, thrift, duty, and self-discipline." Though Mary never graduated, her one year of training was more than most teachers had. Even so, she was not hired by the Toronto common schools because she was Catholic and public education in Toronto was still Protestant education. After a brief period as a private tutor with a family in Maine, in August, 1851, she assumed a post as a lay teacher at Saint Mary Convent, Monroe, Michigan. She stayed less than a year, confessing years later that she "preferred sewing to bossing little children." Nevertheless, she maintained that teaching had taught her "a hatred of injustice and a vast inquisitiveness," and that perhaps the best teacher was personal experience, from which she learned "that there is an irrepressible conflict that will never end between the working-class and the capitalist-class, until these two classes disappear and the worker alone remains the producer and owner of the capital produced."[49]

The year 1860 found Mary Harris in Chicago, Illinois, where she opened a dressmaking shop but found it difficult to earn a living. Deciding to give teaching another try, she moved to Memphis, Tennessee, where she had heard teachers were needed. Not long afterward, in 1861, she met and married

George E. Jones, iron molder and labor organizer. Iron molders created their first national labor organization, the National Union of Iron Moulders, in a founding convention in 1860. Prior to the outbreak of the Civil War no union was more militant in its struggle against capital. Membership grew rapidly, and locals were formed in New York, Detroit, Richmond, and Memphis. But the quick rise of the union was followed by its sudden decline as the Civil War gave foundry owners the leverage, Jonathan Grossman writes, for the "reduction of wages, the destruction of the molders' union, and the subjugation of labor to a passive acquiescence in all foundry regulations." Not until 1863 was the union reestablished under the banner of the Iron Moulders' International Union. The new president William H. Sylvis worked tirelessly on behalf of the iron workers, dealing with everything from strike relief to the demands of shop committees, whatever the workers needed. Sylvis staunchly affirmed the inherent dignity of labor and the right of workers to control the productive process. He asked what the good of "railway networks, canals, mineral resources, and internal improvements was if the wealth is controlled by and for the benefit of a few individuals while the great mass, the 'producing classes' are reduced to poverty?" Meanwhile, in Memphis George Jones was the local's full-time organizer. Like Sylvis, he worked to build a stronger union both in Tennessee and throughout the South.[50]

In 1867 a yellow fever epidemic struck the city of Memphis, where sanitary conditions were deplorable—the water supply contaminated, milk uninspected, and garbage and other waste uncollected. Conditions were worst in the poorer sections of town, where most Irish Catholics, including George and Mary Jones and their four children, lived. Moreover, the rich and well-to-do were able to flee the city, but the poor had no escape. The death toll from the 1867 epidemic is unknown, but the series of yellow fever epidemics that devastated Memphis in the 1870s left in its wake almost eight thousand dead. This outbreak took Mary Jones's husband and children. "All about my house I could hear weeping and the cries of delirium," she wrote. "One by one, my four little children sickened and died. I washed their little bodies and got them ready for burial. My husband caught the fever and died. I sat alone through nights of grief. No one came to me. No one could. Other homes were stricken as was mine. All day long, all night long, I heard the grating of the wheels of the death cart."[51]

The union buried her husband, and Mary Jones stayed on in Memphis to work with the victims of the epidemic. Later she returned to Chicago, where she and a partner established a dressmaking business. Chicago in 1870 had an Irish population of about forty thousand; by the turn of the century, it was the fourth largest Irish urban center in the United States, and this Irish influx evoked a nativistic reaction more hostile than in other midwestern cities. From 1870 to 1890 the overwhelming majority of Irish immigrants were part of Chicago's diverse working class. According to Michael F. Funchion, "Half of the men were unskilled laborers . . . [and] about three-fourths of the women were domestic servants." Furthermore in this era there was a sharp contrast between the lives of rich and poor. As a dressmaker for the "aristocrats of Chicago" Jones observed that "the lords and barons . . . lived in magnificent homes on the Lake Shore Drive . . . [while] I would look out of the plate glass windows and see the poor, shivering wretches, jobless and hungry, walking along the frozen lake front. The contrasts of their condition with that of the tropical comfort of the people . . . [for] whom I sewed was painful to me. My employers seemed neither to notice nor to care." [52]

The transformation of Mary Jones, sympathetic observer of the conditions in which the poor were forced to live and die, into "Mother" Jones, labor organizer and agitator on behalf of working-class people, was gradual. Her livelihood as a dressmaker ended with the Great Chicago Fire, October 7–9, 1871, which destroyed an area James W. Sheahan and George P. Upton describe as "one mile in width . . . and four miles in length, thus as large as half of New York City from the Battery to the Central Park, or as the whole peninsula of Boston." Almost one hundred thousand people were left homeless, among them Mary Jones, who took refuge with hundreds of others in old Saint Mary's Church, where she "camped until I could find a place to go." [53]

The Chicago fire was the event from which Jones dated the beginnings of a more active part in bettering the lives of working-class people. Her first recorded involvement in the labor movement came with the Great Railroad Strikes of 1877, which, Philip Foner argues, "brought the country closer to a social revolution than at any other time in its century of existence except for the Civil War." The strike followed on the heels of the Panic of 1873 and an economic depression that put millions of people out of work. The railroads, the largest employers of the era, had steadily cut wages, only reinforcing in the minds of the general public how capitalists could wantonly disregard human needs—an image railroad magnate Jay Gould reinforced with his remark that he could "hire one half of the working class to kill the other half." [54]

On June 1, 1877, the Pennsylvania Railroad cut wages by 10 percent, and it became clear that other railroads would soon follow suit. Indeed, on July 11, 1877, the president of the Baltimore and Ohio stated that starting on July 16, wages were to be cut by 10 percent, even though wages had been cut eight months earlier. B & O railroad workers in Martinsburg, West Virginia, responded with a strike. On July 16 firemen and later brakemen left their trains, vowing to "refuse to allow any freight trains to move." The vice-president of the B & O persuaded the governor to send in the militia, but the soldiers joined the striking railroad workers, who had the support of the community. The *Baltimore Sun* observed, "There is no disguising the fact that the strikers in all their lawful acts have the fullest sympathy of the community. . . . The singular part of the disturbances is in the active part taken by women, who are the wives and mothers of the firemen. They look famished and wild, and declare for starvation rather than have their people work for the reduction of wages. Better to starve outright, they say, than to die by slow starvation." Finally federal troops were called in and they got the trains moving.[55]

As the strike was broken in Martinsburg it began to spread from one rail line to another. In Baltimore, Chicago, and St. Louis, as well as other cities and towns along thousands of miles of track, strikers and their supporters confronted the military and the conflicts resulted in death and bloodshed for hundreds of people. In Pittsburgh the strike bordered on civil insurrection as striking railroad workers abandoned their trains and stood ready to battle the Pennsylvania Railroad. Fearing possible sympathy between the local Pittsburgh militia and the strikers, the governor called in the militia from Philadelphia, who arrived with an artillery battery. Railroad workers had gained control of the switchyard, and they were joined by factory workers, mechanics, unemployed men, and wives and children. Altogether about six thousand people met the Philadelphia militia. In the ensuing confrontation, twenty people were killed and many others injured. Word spread throughout the city, and a crowd estimated at twenty thousand, composed of strikers, workers, and their supporters, forced the Philadelphia militia into the railroad roundhouse, "put the railroad's property to the torch," and looted freight cars. The roundhouse caught fire and the militia was forced to flee the city.[56]

Into this setting came Mother Jones, invited by striking railroad workers. She later claimed that she was a member of the Knights of Labor at the time, but since women were not admitted into the order until 1881, it is highly unlikely. She felt she learned from the strike something about the nature of violence, both the violence of a burgeoning industrial order and the violence that can result from pent-up anger and frustration at the structural injustice of a system that denied working people their basic needs.[57]

What happened in Pittsburgh also demonstrated that the tremendous dissatisfaction was not limited to striking railroad workers but included factory workers and other segments of the working class and the unemployed. In some areas, such as St. Louis, Buffalo, New York, and Chicago, the upheaval became a general strike against declining living standards, an attempt by workers to gain control of a society that seemed to them, writes Philip Foner, to be governed by "the power of money." Workers' demands were best reflected in a manifesto that appeared everywhere the B & O line had laid track: "Strike and live! Bread we must have! Remain and perish! Our determination may seem frail, but let it come. . . . [The] community at large along the whole line in the Union are in our favor; and we feel confident that the God of the poor and the oppressed of the earth is with us. Therefore let the clashing of arms be heard; let the fiery elements be poured out if they think it right, but in heed of our right and in defense of our families, we shall conquer or we shall die." [58]

In the decades that followed, Mary Jones became Mother Jones, active in the movement for the eight-hour day, the Knights of Labor, socialism, and the unionizing efforts of American workers. Mother Jones's commitment to socialism dates from the 1890s, when she helped J. A. Wayland establish the *Appeal to Reason*. Jones had known Wayland since 1893 when he and others had tried to create a cooperative community in Tennessee known as the Ruskin Colony. Not long afterward, Mother Jones and a group of friends persuaded Wayland to start a paper dedicated to the education of workers. According to Elliott Shore, the *Appeal to Reason* "was the most successful institution of the socialist movement in the United States and the one national weekly newspaper that unified the movement from coast to coast." Jones asserted that she was responsible for getting the first subscribers to the *Appeal to Reason*. Wayland and his associate Fred G. Warren became her close friends. She remembered arguing with Wayland into the night about Voltaire and Victor Hugo and recalled of Warren's home, "If any place in America could be called my home, his home was mine." [59]

Jones became a member of the Kansas City local of the Socialist Labor Party in 1895. Later that decade she joined with those who bolted the Socialist Labor Party and founded the Socialist Party of America. Never much interested in ideological debates, Jones took a simple and direct approach to socialism. In an interview for the *Appeal to Reason*, Mother Jones stated that the issue of the day was an industrial battle between labor and capital and that workers would no longer beg "their masters to give them a day's work or a loaf of bread. They will simply take that which is theirs by rights. They produce it, and in producing it, they should own it. We are after the machinery of production, distribution and exchange." Jones's power as an advocate for socialism was most clearly captured in an article by Kate Richards O'Hare, one of the most noted American Socialists of her time. O'Hare said she owed her own conversion to socialism to Mother Jones and a speech she delivered at a Cigar Makers International Union ball in Kansas City. She recalled that Jones spoke "like a mother talking to her errant boys," explaining to working people that they "must support the political party of their class and that the only place for a sincere union man was in the Socialist Party." [60]

What gave credibility to Mother Jones as a spokesperson for socialism was her experience as a labor agitator and organizer. It sometimes seems that she participated in almost every major conflict between labor and capital from the latter part of the nineteenth century through the early decades of the twentieth century. Her name was synonymous with people's aspirations for justice, however expressed—in the battles of the International Workers of the World (IWW) for industrial unionism, the politics of the Socialist Party, the Great Steel Strike of 1919, or the endless smaller strikes by which workers sought to create a better life for themselves.

It is for her biographers to trace every labor-capital conflict in which Mother Jones was involved. Here we might pursue just a single strand, her work among miners, for if she ever felt at home, and most alive, it was there. Appropriately,

Dale Fetherling has titled his biographical study *Mother Jones, the Miners' Angel*. Certainly, her work with miners in West Virginia illustrates her organizing tactics, oratorical gifts, and hell-raising abilities. She once wrote to William B. Wilson, one of the founders of the United Mine Workers of America (UMWA) and later a member of Congress and the first secretary of the Department of Labor, that in West Virginia she had tramped in "the dead of night counting the rails on the RR track at walking many miles after a meeting with those slaves of the dismal caves that meeting has compensated for all I would not exchange that meeting for all the palaces or millions earth has." [61]

Mother Jones did not become an official organizer for the UMWA until 1900, but she was actively organizing coal miners as early as 1891 in Norton, Virginia. The UMWA, founded in 1890 as a new national union for bituminous and anthracite coal miners, built on the organizing efforts of the Workingmen's Benevolent Association, the Knights of Labor, and the National Progressive Union. Among its stated goals were the eight-hour day, the abolition of child labor, an end to the use of private armies during strikes and lockouts, and the establishment of working and living conditions that would allow those "whose lot is to toil daily in the recesses of the earth" to share in the "just fruits of our toil." [62]

During the early years of the new union, coal production and employment were on the rise, accompanied by an increase in mine disasters. Between 1891 and 1900 over a thousand miners were killed; the numbers climbed to over two thousand in the short period from 1906 to 1910, mainly because of gas and dust explosions. One accident, on March 20, 1895, was typical:

> Sixty-two men perished in a terrific explosion which occurred about 5:45 p.m. in mine No. 5, at Red Canyon, Wyo. . . . Just before the explosion a number of men had reached the surface, and those who started at once for home escaped injury in the flying debris resulting from the wreck of the hoisting works. The shock of the explosion was felt for miles around and was heard 7 miles away. The explosion blew out or loosened all the timbering and supports and cracked and shattered the walls and roof, so that the search for the dead was attempted at great peril.

Such accounts are common in the records of the state mine inspectors and the Bureau of Mines. The fatality rate for coal miners in the United States was higher than in any European country, three times greater than in Great Britain. Beyond the danger from mine explosions, conditions were terrible. An ordinary miner worked up to fourteen hours a day, and A. T. Shurick concludes, "there was seldom any special interest evidenced in his safety—a life being valued at only so many dollars, as a rule—and no interest whatever as to his welfare . . . [for] he was but a cog in the big machine which absorbed him mentally and physically, excluding all other interests in life." [63]

The coalfields of Appalachia, where Mother Jones began as a labor organizer, were rural areas, made accessible for exploitation by the development of a rail system that could get the coal to market. By 1930 Appalachia was the largest coal-producing region in the United States, generating almost 80 percent of the nation's production. Coal barons were more concerned about capital accumulation than the living conditions of workers and their families, be they what Homer Morris characterizes as "grimy mining camps" or "company owned houses, which were little better than cow stables in many camps." Coal companies owned not only houses but stores and churches, and there were, says Morris, "no local political officials, no mayor, no city council, no ward boss to attend to the immediate interests of the miners—there was only the coal operator." [64]

Company guards and company bosses didn't frighten Mother Jones, even when her life was in danger. When she was not allowed to speak on company property, she spoke on street corners. One reporter who accompanied Mother Jones during a strike in West Virginia in 1897 described how she moved from one mining camp to the next, "sleeping under any sort of shelter, eating the coarsest food, stripping herself of clothing to give away right and left." Between 1901 and 1902 Mother Jones was part of a UMWA organizing drive in the Kanawha and Fairmont regions of West Virginia. Union organizers who had been sent to Kanawha had their lives threatened and were often beaten or jailed by officials of the coal companies. Nevertheless, by train or more often on foot, Mother Jones traveled eight to ten miles a day, meeting with miners, giving speeches, and organizing locals of the UMWA so that miners could have a voice with which to demand better working conditions, a living wage, and shorter hours. Usually she was denied lodging in company towns and took shelter with miners. She recalled how she spent Easter with a group of unorganized miners and their families. After hearing about "their blasted hopes, and lives with no ray of sunshine," she noted, "one is not surprised that they all have a disheartened appearance, as if there was nothing on earth to live for." What maddened her most was that it was miners "who produce the wealth of the nation," and yet in return they received only legalized injustice.[65]

Coal production in northern West Virginia was controlled by the Fairmont Coal Company, and it resisted any attempt on the part of the UMWA to organize miners on land it considered its own. In response, Mother Jones and other UMWA organizers staged a thirty-mile march to Monongah, West Virginia, which stood in the center of the Fairmont Coal Company's territory. Edward M. Steel describes the column of hundreds of marchers, at the end of which came Mother Jones, with "a band and a color guard with American and Italian flags." Fairmont had no difficulty persuading Judge John C. Jackson to issue an injunction to prevent Mother Jones and other UMWA organizers from marching and assembling near company property, but Jones ignored the injunction. She was served with another while addressing a crowd in Clarksburg, and this time she was arrested, along with other UMWA organizers, and taken to the Parkersburg jail. Judge Jackson considered the UMWA organizers "vampires that live and fatten on the honest labor of coal miners of the country." As for Mother Jones, "It would have been better far for her to follow the lines and paths which the Allwise Being intended for her sex to pursue. There are many charities in life which are open to her in which she could contribute largely to mankind's distress . . . pursuits that she could engage in of a lawful character that would be more in keeping with what we have been taught and what experience has shown to be the true sphere of womanhood." Mother Jones was given a suspended sentence and the other strike leaders were given between two and three months in jail.[66]

Mother Jones did not return to West Virginia until the 1912 Cabin Creek and Paint Creek strike, which became, in the words of David Corbin, "one of the most protracted and bloody labor-management conflicts in American history." Cabin Creek and Paint Creek are two streams that flow into the Kanawha River through a mountainous region in southern West Virginia. Here, in 1902 Mother Jones had been successful in establishing unions as part of a UMWA organizing drive. In April, 1912, largely because of the intransigence of coal operators, contract negotiations broke down, and union and nonunion coal miners joined in a strike. The coal operators responded by bringing in strikebreakers and hiring three hundred Baldwin-Felts detectives, armed with Winchester rifles and machine guns, who forcibly, and often violently, evicted coal miners' families from coal company houses. On property not controlled by the coal companies, tent colonies sprang up. For company guards "it became a pastime . . . to fire on these tent colonies from ambush in the hills." Violence escalated when the coal barons brought in what came to be called the "Bull Moose Special," an armor-plated train mounted with machine guns and carrying "crack riflemen of the coal companies." Ralph Chaplin, later a noted Wobbly poet and song writer, was working at the time for a local Socialist newspaper. He described how "in the dead of night . . . the armored train drew up over the sleeping tent colony and opened fire with rifles and machine guns." Days later a battle between armed strikers and company guards left twelve miners and four guards dead. The governor declared martial law and sent in six companies of the state militia.[67]

Striking coal miners were not given the support they needed from UMWA officials, but Mother Jones and organizers from the Socialist Party of West Virginia came to help. Jones traveled from one section of the region to the other "holding meetings . . . [and] rousing the tired spirits of the miners." She was not afraid to confront those who held the power of life and death in their hands. Fred Mooney told the story of how Frank Keeney, a local strike leader, sought union help to organize miners in the Cabin Creek area; after being "met with a blunt refusal," he approached Mother Jones. In the heart of the Cabin Creek coalfields was a small mining town called Eskdale, part of what was termed "forbidden territory." It was an armed camp, said Mooney, full of guards with

71

rifles and machine guns. Nevertheless, Mother Jones drove into town. Getting out of her buggy, "she surveyed the scene with a critical eye and walked straight up to the muzzle of one of the machine guns, and patting the muzzle of the gun, said to the gunman behind it, 'Listen here you, you fire one shot here today and there are 800 men in those hills . . . who will not leave one of your gang alive.' " Her bluff worked, and she inspired such courage in local coal miners that Eskdale became a center for organizing the whole of the Cabin Creek coalfields.[68]

Throughout the strike Mother Jones did everything she could to explain to the people of West Virginia, and the nation at large, how badly coal miners needed better working conditions, decent wages, and the right to collective bargaining, while the coal companies and their hirelings continued to employ violence. As a public speaker Mother Jones was exceptional. Ralph Chaplin remarked:

> No words of mine . . . could compare with the vitriolic wrath of "Mother" Jones on the same subject. She might have been any coal miner's wife ablaze with righteous fury when her brood was in danger. Her voice shrilled as she shook her fist at the coal operators, the mine guards, the union officials, and all others responsible for the situation. She prayed and cursed and pleaded, raising her clenched and trembling hands, asking heaven to witness. She wore long, very full skirts and a black shawl, and her tiny bonnet bobbed up and down as she harangued the crowd. The miners loved it and laughed, cheered, hooted, and even cried as she spoke to them.[69]

On August 15, 1912, Mother Jones presented a petition to the governor of West Virginia on behalf of the striking miners, protesting that neither the courts nor the local officials had done anything to stop "the most cruel, inhuman treatment of the United Mine Workers." She then addressed a mass meeting on the steps of the capital where she held out a vision of what workers wanted: the death of slavery and oppression and the birth of a new world for working people and their children in which their homes would be built on the ruins of the "dog kennels" they had been forced to live in. Three weeks later, in an address to six thousand coal miners who had marched with her to the capital, she again criticized state officials and the "plunderers of the State" who had ignored the plight of striking miners. The miners cheered when she spoke about the whole machinery of "capitalism being rotten to the core." She concluded by insisting that marches and public mass meetings indicated "a milestone of progress of the miners and workers of the State of West Virginia. I will be with you, and the Baldwin guards will go. You will not be serfs, you will march, march, march from milestone to milestone of human freedom, you will rise like men in the new day and slavery will get its death blow." Not long afterward, as she was attempting to read the Declaration of Independence to a group of striking miners, she was arrested.[70]

Following her arrest, Mother Jones was handed over to state military authorities in Pratt, West Virginia, and incarcerated with hundreds of miners and strike leaders. The military charged her with stealing a machine gun from the militia, inciting a riot, and planning to dynamite the tracks of the Chesapeake and Ohio Railroad. Using the power they had under martial law, the authorities disregarded due process and established military tribunals that handed down arbitrary sentences to imprisoned miners. Outraged by this flagrant miscarriage of justice, Mother Jones wrote to Terence Powderly from what she called her "Military Bastille" that the Spanish Inquisition was alive and well in West Virginia. Her own prison was a two-room shack near a temporary "bull pen" created by the military for its prisoners. There she was guarded by a soldier with a loaded rifle and a fixed bayonet. The only comfort allowed her was a straw tick on the floor. Jones was found guilty of the charges leveled against her and given a sentence of twenty years in the state penitentiary. Aided by "sympathetic guards," however, she was able to smuggle out letters to friends. The Socialist press took up her cause, decrying her imprisonment, and its coverage led to a U.S. Senate committee investigation. Finally, Mother Jones was released, after eighty-five days of imprisonment, as part of a compromise among the leadership of the UMWA, the new governor of West Virginia, Henry D. Hatfield, and the coal companies. The settlement arranged by leaders of the UMWA ignored some of the major grievances of the striking coal miners dealing with union recognition and the private armies employed by the coal operators. David Corbin's study of the Paint Creek and Cabin Creek strike concludes that "the betrayal of the strike by the national union caused miners to rely more heavily on the cadre of rank-and-file leaders" who had struggled with them for principles of "justice, fraternity and liberty" that were born out of local experience.[71]

Although Mother Jones's work with the coal miners of West Virginia is only one window on her life, it illustrates a pattern of outrage at a system of domination that institutionalized oppression and made injustice its watchword. She believed that the wealth of this world was the product of the blood, sweat, and tears of workers and that capitalism, based on "a money aristocracy" robbed workers of every aspect of their humanity. More important, she had faith in the power of working people to create for themselves a more humane, just, and democratic social order. In a speech before the Pan-American Federation of Labor in Mexico City in January, 1921, she spoke of the need for workers themselves, not self-appointed leaders but those from "below," to make the "cause of human freedom" their own. That is perhaps why the life of Mary Harris Jones, in her own words, was not "spent in the parlors of tea parties or of midnight dinners and revellers, but in the trenches, with my boys, facing the machine guns. And I expect to close my eyes in these battles." John Brophy, a coal miner and later one of the founders of the CIO, who had opposed John Lewis's leadership of the UMWA, said it best: "She had a complete disregard for danger or hardship and would go in wherever she thought she was needed. And she cared no more about approval from union leaders than operators; wherever people were in trouble, she showed up to lead the fight with tireless devotion." [72]

Mother Jones on Religion

Mother Jones was raised and died a Catholic, though for many years of her life, if one gauges religious commitment in terms of its practice in the conventional sense of the word, her Catholicism was more evident by its absence. But if, as Mary Jo Weaver rightly observes, we take note of "her prodding antagonism toward Catholicism rather than a clear representation of its beliefs," then there is much we can learn from Mary Harris Jones. The legitimation of capitalism by religious institutions and their representatives seemed to Mother Jones a prostitution of "Christ's holy doctrine," as she expressed it to Terrence Powderly. She was particularly wrathful toward Catholic bishops in the service of the status quo. In a letter she wrote to William B. Wilson in 1902 she excoriated Michael Hoban, bishop of Scranton, for accepting without question the supposed service to the church of Charles Schwab, president of U.S. Steel Corporation; the bishop and the capitalist, she said, had "wined and dined on the backs of the robbed of Homestead all in the name of *Christ the Parasite*." During the Paint Creek and Cabin Creek strike she again deplored the "hypocrisy" of church officials. In the midst of the strike, the governor had appointed a commission to investigate and report its findings to the state legislature. The commission, headed by Patrick James Donahue, bishop of Wheeling, condemned the action of the coal operators but had little sympathy for the striking miners and the attempts to organize the coalfields. Bishop Donahue, Mother Jones fumed to Powderly, had been "fed and entertained by the exploiters of labor." His understanding of the strike was shaped by his conversations not with the coal miners themselves but with Charles Cabell, president of the Carbon Coal Company, to her mind the biggest exploiter of all the coal barons, noted for making a 200 percent profit on the food he sold miners at his company store. [73]

Her experience from 1913 to 1914 in Trinidad, Colorado, during a UMWA strike against the Colorado Fuel and Iron Company, controlled by the Rockefeller empire, drove home her doubts about the function of religious institutions. Not unlike the miners of Paint and Cabin creeks, coal miners in southern Colorado found themselves pitted against not only the coal company and its private armies but the state government and the militia. Mother Jones, a thorn in the side of both the coal operators and the military authorities, was deported from the strike region under armed guard on a number of occasions. In one particular instance, during January of 1914, she was arrested by the military and held for nine weeks in San Raphael Hospital, run by a group of Catholic sisters. It disturbed Mother Jones that the sisters had allowed "their religious institution to be turned into a military prison." She called them a group of "moral cowards" who were "owned body and soul by the Rockefeller interests." It was a "cold blooded" kind of religion, she thought, that would make the priests who worked at the hospital unwilling to challenge the ways in which the "uniformed murderers" of the military were used in a war against working-class people.[74]

Mother Jones perceived the use of religion in the service of domination as distortion of what was fundamental to Christian faith. Priests and ministers, whom she loved to call "sky pilots," preached a form of Christianity that had nothing to do with the real world. Protestants, especially, deceived people by identifying Christianity with the "machine of capitalism . . . while the chains of slavery were woven around them." Instead of raising their voices on "behalf of truth and justice," they only helped perpetuate a system in which "we rob each other and say it is right; we rent each other out to the ruling class to beat us." She wondered how the clergy could ask for money for foreign missions when people starved at home, or how they could deny that their own institutions were built on the "bleached bones of . . . people" who had been exploited, robbed, and cheated of the goods of this life so that the ruling class could accumulate wealth and power. It seemed to her ironic that those who most loudly sang "All for Jesus" and prayed "Our Father in Heaven" were the same individuals who asked, "Oh, Lord Jesus fix it so I can get three and four fellows' bread." For was it not the same institutions, she argued, that held the likes of a John D. Rockefeller, Jr., in such high esteem, holding up as a model Christian the very person who "has murdered, shot, starved, sent to an untimely grave men, women and children by the thousands." Here she was alluding to the Ludlow Massacre of April 19, 1914. During a strike against Rockefeller's Colorado Fuel and Iron Company in Ludlow, Colorado, soldiers of the state militia attacked a miners' tent colony, composed mainly of women and children, firing on it for hours with rifles and machine guns and then, toward evening, setting it on fire and burning it to the ground. The next morning the bodies were counted. Some estimate that thirty-two persons died from either gun wounds or the fire. In one tent thirteen people, two mothers and eleven children, died. Mother Jones concluded that if Rockefeller was the type of person that modern Christianity praised, if those who "dictate what we will eat and drink and wear, and where we will live," those who own "the nation," are the exemplars of religion, then "save me from getting any of it into my system."[75]

Mother Jones offered a different interpretation of Christianity, rooted in the struggles of the working class for a new dawn of freedom. For her Christ was an agitator, a rebel, and a "humble carpenter," a "fighter" who sought justice for poor people. Working people needed to remember that the foundation of Christianity was laid by twelve laborers, with "no college graduates among them," who "revolutionized the society amid which it rose." Likewise, God was more concerned about the quality of life before death than after; wherever "we are breaking the chains" of oppression, God was to be found. She maintained that she stood "for the teachings of Christ put into practice, not the teachings of capitalism and graft and murder. I stand for the day when this rotten structure will totter of its own vileness. I stand for the day when the baby child will live in God's fair land and enjoy its air, its food and its pleasures, when every mother will caress it warmly, where there are no parasites, no slaves." [76]

She coupled her prophetic insights into the radical nature of the Christian faith with a class-oriented reading of Scripture. At a mass meeting in Charleston, West Virginia, during the Paint Creek and Cabin Creek strike, she told strikers to remember that the labor movement was "a command by God Almighty." Moses himself had begun the first labor union when he organized workers to fight against those who exploited them. Eventually he "led them out of the land of bondage and robbery and plunder and into the land of freedom. And when the army of the pirates followed them the Dead Sea opened and swallowed them up, and for the first time the workers were free." People needed to remember that what occurred thousands of years ago was once again taking place in West Virginia. In fact it was workers and not capitalists who were more faithful to the radicality of the Christian tradition. Furthermore, it was workers and not the churches, or such organizations as the Salvation Army and the YMCA, who had suffered imprisonment and slander for the betterment of humankind. The test of labor's fidelity was that it counted itself among the "enemies of capitalism" and was dedicated to "the uprighting of the human race." [77]

After years of working with oppressed and exploited people, perhaps what Mother Jones drew on most strongly was what has come to be called a preferential option for the poor. It is an option Gregory Baum has defined as a "double commitment, implicit in Christian discipleship, to look upon society from the perspective of the marginalized . . . and . . . stand in solidarity with their struggle against oppression." Our sense of what it is to be human develops to the degree that we "feel the pains of our fellow beings in the great struggles" and come to terms with the importance of an active solidarity with them. Mother Jones maintained that "it has ever been the humble that have done the world's enlightening." She gave voice to the oppressed, those who had been victimized and sought justice. If we are to stand in solidarity with the oppressed, then we are to suffer what they suffer and experience what they experience and that means seeing the world very differently from those who would use Christianity as a means of legitimating privilege, of so distorting the Christian message that the word *Christian* becomes synonymous with the "blood-suckers" of this world. Mother Jones knew what it was to view the world from the bottom up and to have a basic, almost visceral, faith in working people, not bosses or even elected union officials. Because of that faith she believed in what working people could create for themselves, even though she had no romantic or idealistic illusions about what it meant to be poor and marginalized. [78]

Mother Jones on Women and Feminism

Philip Foner has underscored the degree to which feminist scholars have crit-
ized Mother Jones for trivializing women's issues and ignoring the problems
facing working-class women. To understand Mother Jones's relationship to the
women's movement and her perspective on class and gender, it is necessary to
come to terms with her own Irish-Catholic background.[79]

In a study of nineteenth-century Irish immigrant women, Hasia Diner argues that Irish family and social life reinforced "gender-based spheres." Just as
home and hearth demarcated a set role for women, so was public life reserved
for men only. Irish women tended to marry late, and they were "reared in a
culture that defined the worth of women in highly economic terms, and as such
women often had to choose between economic aspirations and marriage. . . . a
marketplace Irish culture allowed women to be assertive and, if need be, to defy
Victorian standards of respectable feminine behavior." While they never "accepted the subordinate and submissive role that the culture assigned to them,"
Irish women shared with men the "notion that separate spheres for men and
women operated for everyone's benefit." In an American context, the questions
and issues raised by American feminists seemed foreign, not only because they
were often couched in terms that bore a middle-class stamp but because there
was a strong anti-Irish and especially anti-Catholic tone to the feminism of the
period. Irish women often "found offensive" feminist advocacy of divorce,
abortion, birth control, and sexual freedom. Diner's analysis in part explains
the attitudes and responses of Mother Jones to gender-based issues raised by
feminists, but we need to look elsewhere if we are to fully understand her own
ideas about the place and role of women in American society.[80]

Mother Jones took pride in being "a workman's daughter" and in having
spent the bulk of her life battling "the authority of the capitalist class." For
Jones, sisterhood among women would remain only an ideal, removed from
human history, as long as the oppression and domination that marked the lives
of women who worked for a living was not altered. Furthermore, her experience persuaded her that just as there were two classes of men, so were there
two groups of women: "A lady, you know, was created by the parasitical
class; women, God Almighty made them." Her attitude toward "fashionable
women" bordered on contempt and loathing. Where others saw "the high ideals
of womanhood," concern for human betterment, and expressions of charity
toward others, she saw only vanity and indifference to the hungry and poverty-
stricken. Feelings of sisterhood existed among the poor "because the poor
know what suffering is and means, and sympathize with others."[81]

Mother Jones felt outrage toward upper-class women because she believed
herself a class-conscious Socialist and, as such, saw feminism and suffrage as
"fads" that "plutocrats" had created to occupy "women of leisure." She be-

lieved that she understood the needs, hurts, and pains of working-class women from her experience as an union organizer, on the shop floor, and in the coal-fields. Yet, for all her concern about working-class women, she never decried the domestic violence women suffered, nor did she make any concerted effort to relate her Socialist vision to gender-based issues. Nevertheless, simply to classify Jones as antifeminist, insensitive to the needs of women, and there-fore unimportant to our understanding of women's history is to do her a great disservice.[82]

Feminist though she was not, Mother Jones still spoke about women in ways that reminded working-class males that the world should not be structured so as to serve only the wants of men. Speaking to a convention of United Mine Workers of America at the turn of the century, Jones asked those assembled to consider why fathers took less pride in the birth of a daughter than a son and why they feared women both in the labor movement and in the workplace and tried to exclude them. Had not women, she later asked, also battled the same forces of domination, also been clubbed, jailed, and insulted, and thereby won the right to join with men as workers in the "industrial field"? She held up to men the image of women as mothers, wives, and workers, not with Victorian halos of sweetness and light, not with a self-effacing femininity, but as militant, defiant, and rebellious human beings.[83]

As an early organizer in the anthracite coalfields of northeastern Pennsylvania, Mother Jones first developed tactics for organizing among women, which she would employ during later strikes across the country. Working with a local UMWA district organizer, Thomas Haggerty, during a strike in Arnot, Pennsylvania in 1899, Mother Jones organized women to fight coal company scabs. She demanded that men take care of the children for a change and formed the women of the community into an "army"; armed with mops and brooms, they guarded the mines from scabs and chased them away. Years later during a strike in Greensburgh, Pennsylvania she again organized women to take on company scabs, and this time they and their children were arrested. Sentenced to thirty days in jail, the miners' wives and children put up such resistance that the sheriff remarked to Mother Jones, "I would rather you brought me a hundred men than those women. Women are fierce!" In jail Mother Jones encouraged them to sing, and they sang with such enthusiasm and collective force that after five days the judge ordered them released, to which Mother Jones responded, "No one could muzzle those women!"[84]

Above all else Mother Jones held out a vision of a world in which women could raise their children in safety, where fundamental needs of food, clothing, and shelter could be provided, and where women and men would no longer have to see "children with their hands taken off for profit," living in a society populated by "profit mongers with their flashing diamonds bought by the blood of children they have wrecked." If it can be rightly said that she was enamored of the role of "mother," it is because she believed that the capitalist system robbed children of their childhood and women of their ability to protect their young from exploitation. Speaking to a United Mine Worker's convention about her experience organizing women brewery workers in Wisconsin, she stressed the necessity of creating a country that gave back to "womanhood the economic rights that they have stolen from them" and the right of children to be "well born and well cared for." [85]

Mother Jones concluded that there were neither women's rights nor men's rights but "human rights." The suffrage movement misplaced its energy, she believed, for the central issue was not the right of women to vote but the overthrow of the whole political system. It seemed to Mother Jones that "the ballot will not bring us anything. I have watched the reform movement for the last fifty years. I have come to the final conclusion that there is only one thing [that] will bring us relief, and that is for us to stand on both feet . . . [and] get out in the fight! Organize; stop talking!" She believed her reservations about women's suffrage were confirmed by what happened in Colorado, where women did gain the right to vote, but nothing changed. Women and children still died and nothing was done during a strike to prevent "two hundred men [from being] bridled like dogs, put into box cars, sent out of the State, and landed in the desert, [where they] walked twenty miles without a drink of water." Voting rights for women had not prevented fifteen children from being murdered in Ludlow by the Rockefeller interests.[86]

The Legacy of Mother Jones

Mother Jones died on November 30, 1930, supposedly at one hundred years of age. Her death was followed by a requiem mass in Washington, D.C., and she was buried in a union miners' cemetery in Mount Olive, Illinois, where the bodies of fourteen miners who had been killed in a battle with sheriff's deputies in 1898 were also buried. Not long after her death a song was written called "The Death of Mother Jones": Its closing stanza evokes some of the determination she inspired:

> With a spirit strong and fearless
> She hated that which was wrong;
> She never gave up fighting
> Until her breath was gone.
> May the workers all get together
> To carry out her plan,
> And bring back better conditions
> To every laboring man.[87]

Her longtime friend Terence Powderly believed that her life was important because it was shaped by service to others and embodied a witness to Jesus' command that we feed the hungry, house the homeless, and free the captives. Of how many, Powderly asked, could it be truly said that they heard the cry of the oppressed and with determination and courage dedicated their lives to the struggle for justice, speaking the truth "even though it may not be palatable to others or helpful to herself"?[88]

Feminism, Class, and Religion

Given the differences in the lives of Frances Willard and Mother Jones it might be asked what can be learned from such very different women, one a middle-class Christian feminist and the other a working-class radical. Willard reminds us of the importance of the link between Christian faith and feminism; for Christians the central feminist questions about the role, place, and perception of women in American society are organically related to the ability to comprehend the liberative nature of the gospel's affirmation of the absolute equality of women and men. Equality has to do not just with economic and political mechanisms, with a just society, but with dreams and imagination, with the ability of women to live out their lives in ways of their own choosing. Frances Willard came to realize toward the end of her life that economic, social, political, and cultural realities were inseparable. A restructured social order was a prerequisite for the emancipation of women, but significant changes in the social and political arena were not possible without the support that the bonds of sisterhood, institutional and organizational power, and liberated imagination gave to women.

What particularly disturbed Willard was how male Christians could selectively read their Bibles, do theology, and speak of the church in ways that excluded women. It seemed there was a parallel between how men dealt with women and how they interpreted the conflict between labor and capital. The paternalism of men powerful in the economic arena did not differ fundamentally from the language of home and hearth—to protect women, to provide for women, just as working people were to be provided for—all in ways that clearly created dependency and submission. To build a society in which women were to be free, independent, and self-determining, the economy must be organized so as to guarantee the rights of working people to live productive, meaningful, and dignified lives.

Frances Willard and Mother Jones never met, but it is interesting to speculate on what they would have said to each other. Frances Willard would probably have told Mother Jones that she could learn from other women if only she would listen to them. Feminism was not just a middle-class phenomenon; it had much to say about the aspirations of all women for a fuller realization of their God-given humanity. In turn, Mother Jones would ask Frances Willard to try to comprehend the extent to which the realities of class shaped the world in which she lived. In the struggle of oppressed people for liberation there was no neutral ground, no place in which women or men could construct reasonable compromises. It was necessary to choose sides and live and work with the consequences of such choices.

Rosalyn Baxandall has described Elizabeth Gurley Flynn, noted Irish working-class radical, IWW organizer, and formative member of the American Communist Party, as a woman who "led a long, illustrious, and stormy life." These words also aptly summarize the life of Mary Harris Jones. Flynn believed Mother Jones to be one of the greatest agitators of her times, her name inextricably linked to the struggle for justice.[89] She fearlessly prodded the establishment of her day, and her life reaffirms the important role of agitators in American history. They have held out a vision of what should be, instead of accommodating themselves to what must be. To self-appointed leaders, including political and union leaders, who had little faith in the people's ability to determine their own needs, she was a constant reminder that socialism and democracy were alive in the hearts and minds of people only insofar as they were realities of their own making.

Those who would dismiss Mother Jones as antifeminist should realize that she understood the realities of class as they related to women struggling to feed and cloth their children, trying in whatever ways they could to protect them from the ravages of an exploitative and dehumanizing system. She wondered about the authenticity of feminism as articulated by women of privilege when nothing was done on behalf of their working-class sisters. Even when they recognized the bonds of sisterhood, she doubted whether such women realized that nothing would ever change unless there was a radical reorganization of the means of production. While she seemed to reduce the problems of her era to economics, and in this she differed little from other Socialists, she did capture the tension between class and gender, a tension that in our own time seems most closely related to issues of race and gender.

To Catholics in particular, she represents many things, from the role of women as troublers of the peace of the powerful to an alternative interpretation of Christianity. She broke the mold of the quiet and obedient woman who knows her place and keeps it. Her critique of the Catholic church was not unlike that offered by other working-class radicals, but it was deeply embedded in a class reading of militant Christ and gospel. It affirmed that the Christian message has to do with a visible and concrete sociopolitical economic restructuring of society and the relationship of people to each other. To what extent she can be regarded as a precursor of a Catholic form of feminism is another question. She did not specifically criticize the church for its treatment of women, but she did ask how the church, in its quest for acceptance, might be led down a path of power over others, most often in the name of law and order for the few. If feminism has to do with challenging the role and place of women in society and with new perceptions of what it means to be woman and Catholic, then Mother Jones is a possible starting point. She exemplified a different role for women, as agitator and organizer. Although she did not directly seek to undermine the separate spheres allotted to men and women, she did blur the distinctions in a way that planted doubts among those who sought to exclude women from the public arena. To claim Mother Jones is at the same time to come to terms with the history of working-class women and what it says about the Catholic church's agenda for the future.

3

The Fractured Vision of
Christians and Socialists

The Realities of Class and the

Invisibility of Race

The early part of the twentieth century marked the high point of the American Socialist Party and Christian socialism. Socialists endeared themselves to many, especially members of the working class, by exposing the realities of class struggle, emphasizing the economic sources of inequality, and demanding radical social change through a class-conscious trade union movement and electoral politics. Christians who joined the Socialist Party were eager to expose the bankruptcy of the existing system but also uneasy about the degree to which American Christianity was part of an ideological apparatus of domination and control, inseparable in its fundamental values, institutional structures, and corporate life from the rest of capitalist America.

While Socialists debated conservative trade unionists and representatives of the established order about the future of American society, Christian Socialists had to contend with antireligious Socialists and social gospel advocates. Whether Christian or not, Socialists agreed on the importance of class and class conflict but paid little attention to the links between class relations and racial oppression. Debsian Socialists were part of a long tradition of inattentiveness to race and racism. Indeed, Mario Barrera has observed that there is "no *tradition* of Marxist writings in America on race." Socialists have usually explained racism in terms of class and thus reduced it to secondary importance. The language, the way of interpreting social reality that has developed on the Left speaks about exploitation, dehumanization, and the contradictions of capitalism as if racism were not a crucial factor.[1]

This refusal to lend cognizance to race has shaped a society George Rawick has described as "born nearly free and racist." White Americans could talk about themselves, their freedom or lack of freedom, without reference to the suffering and death of Native Americans, Asian-Americans, African Americans, and Hispanics. Capitalism transformed generations into "dependent fodder for concentration in factories" and humbled "workers by force and cultural hegemony," writes Cedric J. Robinson. As a result, "the points of contact between Europeans and Blacks were enveloped by violence." Although racial conflicts cannot be understood apart from the economic and social contexts in which they developed, racism must be understood as a historical phenomenon in its own right, not just a dependent variable in the emergence of modern capitalism.[2]

Here, we can hardly resolve the complex issue of exactly how racism and class conflict are related. Instead, I want to explore questions of race and class as they were addressed by American Socialists, especially Christian Socialists. In so doing, this chapter touches on both the successes and the failures of Debsian socialism. As limited as words such as *success* and *failure* are, they are important to apply, for it was the task of socialism to embody the aspirations of not just some but all people who envisioned a different kind of American society for themselves and their children. In the course of this story we encounter a number of remarkable Socialists, black and white. George Washington Woodbey and George W. Slater spread the Socialist message through the black community. Reverdy Ransom, too, was attracted to socialism, though he shared some of the reservations of W. E. B. Du Bois and he could not tolerate a socialism that ignored the fundamental reality of race.[3]

Reinhold Niebuhr once observed that "a Christian espousal of socialism raises many problems which cry for an answer." A black Christian espousal of socialism raises even more questions, not only about the compatibility of Christianity and socialism but also about the relevance of socialism to the African-American experience. Du Bois noted how difficult it is to be black and American, for black people are born with a "veil" of consciousness mediated by a society that demeans the very essence of their humanity. Black Americans live with a "double-consciousness"—

> two souls, two thoughts, two unreconciled strivings; two warring ideals in one dark body, whose dogged strength alone keeps it from being torn asunder. The history of the American Negro is the history of this strife, —this longing to attain self-conscious manhood, to merge his double self into a better and truer self. In this merging he wishes neither of the older selves to be lost. He would not Africanize America, for America has too much to teach the world and Africa. He would not bleach his Negro soul in a flood of white Americanism, for he knows that Negro blood has a message for the world.[4]

The relationship between socialism and black Christianity was also double-sided. There were questions about whether American Socialists understood the struggle of African Americans; there was the unique contribution of black radicals and black Christian Socialists to a liberative interpretation of the Christian tradition and its relationship to American society. What emerges is that dimension of black Christianity which Manning Marable terms "blackwater," the drawing together of "the consciousness of oppression, a cultural search for self-affirmation and authenticity . . . [and] the realization that human beings have the capacity through struggle to remake their worldly conditions." [5]

Marable's "blackwater" points to a black Christian tradition of resistance to domination, which extends from Nat Turner, Harriet Tubman, and Denmark Vesey to Dr. Martin Luther King, Jr. It is a tradition that black theologians have uncovered, a tradition that understands how the lives of African Americans have been marked by poverty and economic oppression. But the consciousness of oppression for black Americans is joined with the search for self-affirmation *as a people,* their need to realize a world *of their own making.* Woodbey, Slater, and Ransom were an integral part of that same tradition; they provide a bridge to a dialogue Cornel West has called for, in which black theologians, Socialists, and Marxists would share their common concerns about "the plight of the exploited, oppressed, and degraded peoples of the world, their relative powerlessness and possible empowerment." Such a dialogue requires Christians to understand that American racism is rooted in the exploitative nature of capitalism, and it also requires them to explore the linkages between race and class as they relate to questions of Christian faith. [6]

Woodbey, Slater, and Ransom contributed to the development of the blackwater dimension of Christian faith and did so in the heyday of Debsian and Christian socialism. What we discover is that blackwater not only provides insights into questions of race and class and the distinctive nature of black Christian socialism but raises questions about any form of socialism that ceases to affirm the struggle for self-determination and human dignity. It means that socialism has as much to do with the cultural dimension of our existence, that which is connected with the ongoing struggle of the human spirit for liberation, as it does with the economic and political realities of life.

Debsian Socialism and the Race Question

Eugene V. Debs, writing at the turn of the twentieth century, declared: "Promising, indeed, is the outlook for Socialism in the United States. The very contemplation of the prospect is a well-spring of inspiration." In 1912 Debs received 6 percent of the presidential vote, and the Socialist Party elected twelve hundred of its members to public offices in 340 municipalities, including seventy-nine mayors in twenty-four states. The party's membership stood at 118,000 and its 323 English and foreign-language publications reached over two million people. The Socialist Party, formed in 1901, united reformists, trade unionists, agrarian radicals, Christian Socialists, revolutionary syndicalists, and orthodox Marxists. Diffused geographically, its greatest strength came from the mining, lumbering, and tenant-farming states of the West and Southwest. Diverse as the party was, it was united by a single strategy: to make the choice between socialism and capitalism the central issue in all its campaigns.

Ideologically, the party emphasized the revolutionary role of the proletariat and the importance of class struggle. Union organizing and electoral politics were its vehicles for making socialism part of the American political agenda.[7]

Recently, scholars have raised fundamental questions about the effectiveness of the Socialist Party's analysis of capitalism and its strategies for achieving socialism. Some argue that the Socialist Party was weakened by internal conflicts between skilled craft unionists and unskilled workers, between natives and immigrants, reformists and revolutionaries, those concerned with order, rationality, and hierarchy and those concerned with workers' control of the means of production. But preoccupation with such divisions obscures the response socialism offered to the contradictions people felt in their personal and public lives.[8]

James Green's study of rank-and-file "socialist agitators" provides excellent insight into why people became Socialists. In some regions, their trade union experience taught people that socialism was simply justice—in the words of an *Appeal to Reason* editorial, "giving the toiler the full product of his toil." The Socialist Party attracted union organizers such as "Big Bill" Haywood, leader of the Western Federation of Miners and an advocate of a revolutionary form of industrial unionism in which workers would take direct control of the industrial process. Like Debs, Haywood, best remembered for his role in the formation of the Industrial Workers of the World, wanted to make industrial unionism the basis of a political party that would unite all workers, be they skilled or unskilled, male or female, black or white. Industrial unions and a working-class political party would put "the working-class in possession of the economic power, the means of life, in control of the machinery of production and distribution, without regard to capitalist masters." Haywood, like most American Socialists, was not interested in socialism as an abstract ideal or utopian vision; he saw it as a concrete alternative arising from the realities of the working-class experience.[9]

Haywood and Debs would have nothing to do with what Hal Draper has called "socialism-from-above," that is, socialism as the elitist historical project of intellectuals, technocrats, and professional revolutionaries, which "made working class people the objects of social change, led, manipulated, or liberated by others." "Socialism-from-below," by contrast, could "be realized only through the self-emancipation of activitized masses in motion, reaching out for freedom with their own hands, mobilized 'from below' in a struggle to take charge of their own destiny." It was the energy and genius of working-class people, after all, that made the factories run and produced the wealth and whatever advances there were in the modern world. This radically democratic socialism was a realistic, tough-minded response to working-class life; to the class struggle between those who "produce all and have little or none" and "those who produce none and have all."[10]

On both sides of the Atlantic, the criterion of adherence to the essentials of socialism was acceptance of the reality of class struggle. Class struggle, Haywood argued, might seem unreal to the owners of capital, who saw the world through the "stained-glass windows of a cathedral," but in the factories, on the rails, or in the mills the struggle was apparent. As Haywood put it, "You must look through the dirty windows of the working shop. You must go with me down into the bowels of the earth. . . . there by the uncertain flicker of a safety lamp, there by the rays of a tallow candle you will understand something of class struggle." In some sections of the country, tenant farmers came to socialism out of their bondage to the landlords; in the Southwest, they were joined by miners, timber workers, and railroad workers. And some Socialists were skilled workers who had not forgotten the earlier artisan tradition of resistance to domination.[11]

In addition, a small number of radicalized middle-class professionals, such as Charles Edward Russell, saw in socialism an answer to "the social question." When Russell joined the Socialist Party, he was not simply voting for another political party. Applicants for membership were screened by a committee that questioned their motivation and commitment. Russell remarked that it was "like joining a church. One must have had experience in grace, one must show that one has come out from the tents of the wicked and capitalism." Kate Richards O'Hare, well-known Socialist agitator and organizer, spoke for a generation of Socialists: "I have no regrets for all the years and the grilling labors I gave the Socialist movement. It was well worth while. The Party served a valuable purpose in American life. We took light into dark places; we became the nation's conscience and prodded lawmakers into tardy action on many social problems; we were in the vanguard of all movements for social betterment and decent human relations. We were educators, 'the voices crying in the wilderness' for a quarter of a century, and we left our mark on America." [12]

Socialism and Racism

Still, there was a dark side to the Socialist Party. Russell observed that "it is odd that the people that have made in the world the loudest boast of their devotion to liberty and humanity are the people that have made the worst showing of race prejudice and race injustice." It was even more odd that Socialists, who voiced their opposition to all forms of dehumanization, failed to understand the insidious nature of racism. Laurence Moore captured this incongruity when he titled his analysis of Socialists and blacks "flawed fraternity." The "malign spirit of race hatred" permeated the country, said Eugene Debs, and Socialists were not immune to "race hostility against the negro." They tended either to avoid the issue or to bury it in slogans about class struggle. Debs knew that the Socialist position had more to do with regional and ideological factors than any consistent attempt to come to terms with racism.[13]

Some Socialists recognized the contradiction. Ernest Untermann, a well-known orthodox Marxist, argued that "sometimes the party, in acting for the immediate interests of the working-class, must come into apparent conflict with its ultimate ideals. This is unavoidable; we work toward our ultimate ideals through and despite these immediate contradictions." The "immediate interests" of which Untermann spoke were those of white workers, who believed in the necessity of excluding "definite races or nations" from entry into the United States. Other Socialists reminded Untermann that such compromises with racism were incompatible with Socialist ideals. The International Socialist Congress, meeting in Stuttgart, Germany, in 1907, affirmed the Socialist commitment to working-class solidarity and insisted that "exclusion along racial lines" was thus "in conflict with the principles of proletarian solidarity." [14]

Regional and ideological differences on the race question are illustrated by debates within the Socialist Party over the status of African Americans, the problem of immigration restriction, and the nature of southern socialism. All these issues were present from the beginning. The 1901 Unity Convention resolution on "the negro question" was the only official statement of the Socialist Party; it was "never reaffirmed at any other party convention," says Philip Foner. An early form of the resolution specifically decried "lynching, burning and disenfranchisement" of black Americans, but because of pressure from southern delegates, the condemnation was conspicuously absent from its final wording. Nonetheless, the resolution was significant given the racist climate of the times. The Socialist Party acknowledged that because of slavery and "recent emancipation therefrom," blacks "occupy a peculiar position in the working-class and in society at large." Racial prejudice was viewed as a tool with which capitalists divided the working class, pitting black and white workers against each other. The resolution declared that the black worker's "interests and struggles" were identical "with the interests and struggles of the workers of all lands without regard to race or color or sectional lines," and the party invited "the negro to membership and fellowship with us in the world movement for economic emancipation by which equal liberty and opportunity shall be secured to every man and fraternity become the order of the world." [15]

Some Socialists, such as Charles Dobbs, thought passage of the "Negro Resolution" was a mistake. The party should not "shut the door in the face of the black man," said Dobbs, but neither should it make any special appeal to black workers. Dobbs based his argument on the racist assumption that as "a race, the negro worker of the South lacks the brain and the backbone necessary to make a Socialist." Delegate Clarence Meily responded that socialism was based on "human solidarity." How, he asked, could Socialists, who embraced "all the despised and rejected of the earth," recognize "any distinctions of race, or color, or birth, or faith among its children?" Socialists must combat the racial prejudice of white workers: "Absolute economic equality for white and black, covering perfect uniformity not only in opportunities for labor, but also in all those public services, such as education, transportation (including, let it be added, hotel accommodations), entertainment, etc., which may be collectively rendered, together with complete recognition of political rights, must be insisted on more strenuously by the socialist than ever they could have been by any abolitionist agitator." [16]

Such open debate regarding the role of African Americans can be contrasted to the position of the American Federation of Labor. W.E.B. Du Bois, in his 1902 Atlanta University study *The Negro Artisan*, traced the AFL's attitudes toward black workers from its pronouncement that "working people must unite and organize irrespective of creed, color, sex, nationality or politics" to the acceptance of segregated unions and amendments to the constitutions of AFL-affiliated unions to "exclude Negroes." Most of the unions affiliated with the AFL at the turn of the century "had either few or no Negro members." Du Bois viewed the history of the labor movement from the Knights of Labor to the AFL as "a gradual receding from the righteous declarations of earlier years," accommodation to the racial prejudice of its membership and the country at large. The shift was most evident in the changing views of Samuel Gompers. In the 1880s and 1890s Gompers argued that the future of the trade union movement depended on organizing black workers and eliminating "consideration of a color line." Gradually, Gompers, like the AFL, modified his commitments. At first he maintained that in cases were it was impossible to organize integrated unions because of hostility to black workers, the formation of separate black unions was permissible, with the understanding that they were to be only temporary. But predictably, these temporary solutions became permanent. Gompers eventually became as racist as those he had once criticized. He contended that blacks were unorganizable and a threat to white workers, for they did not share "those peculiarities of temperament such as patriotism, sympathy, sacrifice, etc., which are peculiar to most of the Caucasian race." [17]

One important exception to the AFL's rather bleak history was the United Mine Workers, which actively recruited blacks. In 1900 the UMW had twenty thousand black members and ten years later, forty thousand. They "held local and district offices [and] helped organize both white and Negro miners." Indeed, in 1900, according to Herbert Gutman, the UMW was probably the "most important thoroughly integrated voluntary association in the United States." Another example of an integrated union was the Brotherhood of Timber Workers, an industrial union in western Louisiana and east Texas in the period from 1911 to 1913. Thousands of workers were organized by native southerners who rejected the segregationist and craft orientation of the AFL and tried to forge an interracial union to speak for a traditionally divided people. Gutman comments that far more work is needed on the experience of black and white workers in the period between 1880 and the outbreak of the First World War. Focusing only on the attitudes and practices of the AFL, composed largely of skilled craft unions, does little justice to other types of working-class experience. [18]

Factions of the Socialist Party close to the AFL shared many of its racist assumptions, particularly with regard to immigration restriction. The 1907 meeting of the Socialist International, which affirmed the importance of "proletarian solidarity," also condemned any form of restriction on immigration based on race or nationality. But some American Socialists, such as Robert Hunter, argued that "immigration presents for our serious consideration a formidable array of dangers," including "the likelihood of race annihilation and the possible degeneration of . . . the American type." Ernest Untermann characterized people of color as so "far behind the general modern development of industry, psychologically as well as economically, that they constitute a drawback, an obstacle and menace to the progress of the most aggressive, militant, and intelligent elements of our working-class population." One of the most outspoken racists was Socialist congressperson Victor Berger, leader of the powerful Milwaukee Socialist organization, who stated frankly: "I believe that our civilization, the European or Caucasian or whatever name you choose to call it, I believe that our civilization is in question." Confronted by such hysterics, Barney Berlyn gave the most appropriate response: "If we permit ourselves to go to work and tack on amendments to the proposition of 'Workingmen of all countries, unite'—if you tack on amendments to that, then tack on a clause to the name of the Socialist Party, the words, 'A damn lie.' " [19]

Before the Great Migration of 1910–1930, when 1.2 million black people moved north, the vast majority of African Americans lived in the South. The response of white, southern Socialists to the problems confronting black Americans varied. Many shared the dominant racism of the region. Ida M. Raymond, state secretary of the Socialist Party of Mississippi, remarked that it was impossible for white and black Socialists to "meet on equal terms and organize mixed locals." She celebrated the "heroic" deeds of the Ku Klux Klan in protecting white people, especially white women, from the "terrible outrages that were perpetrated by the Negroes." Other southerners were more paternalistic and condescending but equally segregationist. In contrast, there were those like Texas Socialist E. A. Brenholtz who actively fought the creation of separate locals. A. H. Dennett, a Virginia Socialist, declared that if "the local refuses comradeship to the black man because he is black," it should have its charter revoked. "If any individual member of the Socialist party refuses comradeship to the black man because of his color, let him be expelled from the party, for they are guilty of cowardice and treason." [20]

The differences among southern Socialists were exemplified by the state parties of Louisiana and Oklahoma. The Louisiana Socialist Party in its original state charter provided for "the separation of the black and white races into separate communities, each race to have charge of its own affairs." The national committee of the Socialist Party, because of publicity over the issue, withheld the Louisiana party's charter until it removed the offensive plank. Nevertheless, once granted a state charter, Louisiana Socialists set about organizing separate locals because they believed that this was the only "method by which black comrades can be assimilated into the movement." The end result was that the Socialist Party in Louisiana, with the exception of one black local in Lutcher, was lily-white.[21]

The Oklahoma Socialist Party was the most important state organization next to that of New York. In 1914 the people of Oklahoma elected five Socialist state representatives and one senator, and the party's gubernatorial candidate polled 21 percent of the vote. The leadership of the Socialist Party of Oklahoma "took a far more progressive position on the race question" than most Socialists, in the South or elsewhere in the country. Oscar Ameringer, an Austrian-born immigrant, labor organizer, and editor of the Socialist *Oklahoma Pioneer*, along with Patrick S. Nagle, lawyer and Oklahoma Socialist candidate for the U.S. Senate, Otto Branstetter, state party secretary, and John G. Willis, a Scottish immigrant blacklisted for his work with Debs's American Railroad Union in the 1890s and later candidate for lieutenant governor—all battled against the use of a grandfather clause in the state constitution to disenfranchise African Americans. They fought for economic and political equality for blacks and stood in the forefront of those who believed in the total incompatibility of socialism and any form of racism. Ameringer and Nagle argued that "the negro is entitled to equal opportunity for access to the means of life and to the full social value of his own labor." White workers should realize that "the negro belongs to the working class, and the working class must stand by the negro." Ameringer learned from his early experience in New Orleans as a Socialist working with the brewery and dock workers the "true nature" of the "race problem." As blacks and whites worked together, he believed whites would realize "that black men were men even as you and I. Beneath their black skins beat the same hearts, gnawed the same hunger, circulated the same blood. Below their kinky hair lodged the same dreams, longings and aspirations. Like you and me, they sought pleasure and evaded pain. What they asked from life was living. Happiness within four walls, a loving mate, children, and the chance to rear them better than they had been reared. Health, laughter, beauty, peace, plenty, a modest degree of security in sickness and age." Nevertheless, although the leadership of the Oklahoma state party had support for their defense of the rights of black people, they also knew that for many Oklahoma Socialists, particularly in the southwestern part of the state, racial prejudice was deeply embedded and stronger than class consciousness. Even in Oklahoma, party practice rarely corresponded with the idealism of party rhetoric.[22]

Biographer Nick Salvatore argues that Debs "shared a class analysis of racial prejudice but had shorn it of much of the violent racism that motivated other comrades." Debs refused to speak before segregated audiences on speaking tours in the South; he publicly condemned racism and was critical of those in the Socialist Party and the labor movement who refused to organize black workers. Like so many well-meaning radicals before and since, however, Debs tried to subsume the race question in the class question, and in the process he moderated his radicalism and failed to come to terms with the unique quality of the African-American experience. The end result was that Debs's understanding of the problems facing African Americans was one-dimensional. "There is no negro question outside of the labor question—the working class struggle," Debs maintained. "We have nothing special to offer the negro, and we cannot make separate appeals to all the races." [23]

Debs considered racism a product of class division and believed that the only solution to racism was to eliminate classes. Like many other Socialists then and now, Debs believed that socialism was primarily economic; all socialism could offer black Americans was economic equality. Most Socialists realized that economic equality was not possible without full political equality, but they recoiled from any notion of social equality. Debs made the analogy between social relations and religion that each was an individual matter and therefore not the proper concern of Socialists. Unable to understand that racism was more than a personal matter, Debs acted as if the differences between an Ida Raymond of Mississippi and an Oscar Ameringer of Oklahoma were comparable to those between Baptists and Methodists. Without significant black participation, and without a deeper understanding of racism, the Socialist Party's economic and political categories could not do justice to the African-American experience. Debsian socialism remained, therefore, largely a white phenomenon, and African Americans had little role in defining its character, its goals, its strategies, or its purposes. [24]

W.E.B. Du Bois and Hubert H. Harrison

The first response to the critique of the American Socialists' perception of race and class is to argue that we cannot transcend the limits of history, that American Socialists were a product of their times and cannot be held accountable for failing to develop forms of analysis and a general awareness of race relations that supposedly emerged only later. This view, however, is less tenable if we listen to the witness of W.E.B. Du Bois and Hubert H. Harrison. Both Du Bois and Harrison were Debs's contemporaries, Socialists who understood the interrelationship of race and class and the problems inherent in forms of Socialist analysis and practice that failed to respond to the needs of black workers, overlooked the racism of fellow Socialists, and reduced the realities of race to economic variables.

Martin Luther King, Jr., once said of W.E.B. Du Bois that "he was a radical all of his life"; it is often forgotten that he was for a brief period also a member of Debs's Socialist Party. Although Du Bois did not join the party until 1911, he had previously been sympathetic to socialism and held a number of beliefs he deemed "socialistic." In his *Autobiography* he declared that socialism was the "one great hope of the Negro American," and the Socialist Party was the "only party today which treats the Negroes as men, North and South." Much of his positive feeling toward the Socialist Party arose from his association with Socialists such as William English Walling, Mary White Ovington, and Charles Edward Russell—all founding members of the National Association for the Advancement of Colored People. Du Bois and others contended that the NAACP was born with Walling's investigation of a lynching and race riot in Abraham Lincoln's birthplace, Springfield, Illinois, during the summer of 1908. Walling, a white southerner, and his wife had just returned from czarist Russia, where they had been temporarily imprisoned for supposed revolutionary activity. It seemed to them that the pogroms against Jews in Russia had an American counterpart in the treatment of blacks. Out of Walling's experience in Springfield came a series of articles, correspondence, and meetings that led to the formation of the NAACP.[25]

Du Bois was also among the founders of the NAACP, editor for decades of its official organ *The Crisis*, and director of publicity and research for the organization. The NAACP was considered a radical organization, for it advocated equal rights for black Americans and condemned all forms of racial injustice. Yet even here it was difficult for blacks and whites to work as equals. Du Bois admitted to Mary White Ovington his frustration with certain white members of the NAACP and asked if "white and black folk cannot work together as equals; if this Association is unable to treat its black officials with the same lease of power as white, can we fight a successful battle against race prejudice in the world?" Nevertheless, although he questioned the ability of whites in the NAACP to understand the aspirations of African-American people, the overall position of the NAACP on issues and problems facing the black community was well beyond the comprehension of most Socialists, and Du Bois knew it.[26]

Du Bois contended that "the Negro Problem" was "the great test of the American Socialist." How could Socialists, he wondered, talk about class domination and the exploitation of working people and exclude from their analysis millions of black workers? He surmised that for most Socialists, class was a category meant for whites only. They "excluded Negroes and Asiatics from their scheme" and spoke about the triumph of socialism while ten million African Americans remained "serfs" in their own country. Many Socialists were unwilling to combat the racist attitudes and practices of white workers, which made the black worker feel that the "greatest enemy [was] not the employer who robs him, but his white fellow workingman." All of this was possible because "the average modern Socialists can scarcely grasp the extent of . . . hatred; even murder and torture of human beings," that characterized race relations in the United States. Even more, Du Bois believed, Socialists misunderstood the nature of democracy, for "the essence of Social Democracy is that there shall be no excluded or exploited classes in the Socialistic state; that there shall be no man or woman so poor, ignorant or black" who does not count. What did workers' control of industry or other Socialist programs matter if they did not mean to provide "a method of realizing the broadest measure of justice to all human beings." [27]

In the end, W.E.B. Du Bois was an active member of the Socialist Party for only one year. He resigned in 1912 to support the candidacy of Woodrow Wilson. Although Wilson's presidency only intensified the burden of color and even though Du Bois continued to think of himself as a Socialist and to believe that socialism could be a viable political alternative for African Americans, it was apparent to him that the American Socialist Party was not a vehicle for change. Du Bois questioned whether anything could be gained by joining with Socialists who discriminated against "black folk." Before class divisions and unequal distribution of wealth and resources could be addressed, it seemed to him, white working-class people would first have to understand that working-class people of color suffered from the same exploitation they did. He noted that although blacks "are mainly an exploited class of cheap laborers . . . we are not a part of the white proletariat and are not recognized by that proletariat to any great extent. We are the victims of their physical oppression, social ostracism, economic exclusion and personal hatred; and when in self-defense we seek sheer subsistence we are howled down as scabs." Understanding would be possible only if Socialists came to terms with the linkages between race and class. Racism was a fundamental part of a capitalist economy that pitted black and white workers against each other, thus destroying any sense of working-class solidarity. For Du Bois, bringing about a new social order had as much to do with culture as it did with economics and politics. It required self-transcending double consciousness, liberation in which African Americans could participate in shaping a society truly their own.[28]

One of Du Bois's most remarkable contemporaries was Hubert Henry Harrison, whom Joel A. Rogers describes as the foremost African-American intellectual of his time, although only "a very small proportion of the Negro intelligentsia has ever heard of him." When he died in 1927, at the age of forty-four, Harrison was a well-known black nationalist who had established a reputation for keenness of mind, public presence, and depth of insight into both African and African-American history. His life touched such diverse personalities as Marcus Garvey, A. Philip Randolph, and Chandler Owen. Born in St. Croix, Virgin Islands, on April 27, 1883, Harrison migrated to the United States at the turn of the century, settling in New York City, where he worked during the day at various jobs and completed his high school education at night. His teachers recognized him as a brilliant student, and he won prizes for his abilities in Latin and history, but he did not have the financial resources for further formal education. Harrison joined the Socialist Party and by 1909 was one of the best known black Socialists in the New York area. As a public speaker, he was unmatched, and his writings appeared in the *New York Call*, the *Modern Quarterly*, and the *New York Times*. Harrison worked within the black community to create support for the Socialist Party, and he was active with Elizabeth Gurley Flynn and Big Bill Haywood in the 1913 silk mills strike in Paterson, New Jersey. With Debs and Haywood, he repudiated the AFL as reactionary and believed that industrial unionism was the wave of the future.[29]

Like Du Bois, Harrison argued that the crucial test for Socialists was how they came to terms with the needs of African-American people. Initially, his own analysis of race and class foreshadowed the arguments of the noted sociologist Oliver C. Cox in his classic work *Caste, Class, and Race* (1948). Racism, Harrison maintained, was rooted in a capitalist economy and "race prejudice [was] the fruit of economic subjection and a fixed inferior economic status." Various segments of the working class—Irish, Jewish, and Italian—had suffered from racial prejudice. Yet there was a difference, for even as blacks rose in social status the issue of color remained. The function of racism was to divide the working class by pitting workers against each other, rather than against their common enemy: capitalism. Workers needed to realize that racism was an ideology of domination that only served the interests of the ruling class, and because "the economic necessities of a system of vicarious production led to the creation of a racial labor-caste," the only remedy was the overthrow of capitalism. Since socialism was ostensibly a working-class movement, it seemed incomprehensible to Harrison that Socialists would not organize the most ruthlessly exploited sector of the working class, African Americans. Given that conservative black leaders, such as Booker T. Washington, were not reluctant to serve the interests of capitalists, it seemed to Harrison that "on the grounds of common sense and enlightened self-interest it would be well for the Socialist Party to begin to organize the Negroes of America in reference to the class struggle." Part of the challenge to Socialists, then, was to respond to the needs of all working-class people. Socialists should take a stand against the disenfranchisement of African Americans, realizing the potential political strength of an organized black constituency. If Socialists, in their desire to gain support in the South, acceded to the demands of white southerners, they would pit "the white half of the working class against the black half" in a formula for defeat. "Can we hope to triumph over capitalism with one half of the working class against us?"[30]

By the end of 1914, Harrison was disillusioned by the Socialist Party's failure to come to terms with racism within its own ranks, its insensitivity to the needs of black people, and its lack of attention to the rising tide of racial hatred. He resigned from the party in 1915, but continued, like Du Bois, to think of himself as a Socialist. He refused "to put either Socialism or party above the call of his race." Harrison's experience with the Socialist Party, coupled with the impact of the First World War and especially the race riots in East St. Louis in 1917, led to a shift in his analysis. He concluded that race consciousness had to take priority over class consciousness.[31]

It seemed to Harrison that the human carnage of a world at war had resulted from a conflict among a white minority over "possession of the lands and destinies of the colored majority in Asia, Africa, and the islands of the sea." All the rhetoric about patriotism, justice, and democracy was designed to make the world safe for so-called white civilization. In this context, African Americans needed to see themselves as part of an international community in which the key issue was "not the exploitation of laborers by capitalists; but the social, political and economic subjection of colored peoples by whites." [32]

Harrison's views were solidified by what he termed the "East St. Louis Horror." In the months preceding the outbreak of racial violence in East St. Louis, the packing plants and the Aluminum Company of America brought in black workers from the South as strikebreakers. For weeks there was tension between whites and blacks as AFL trade union leaders complained of the tide of "cheap Negro labor." Finally, just before July 4, 1917, a riot erupted against blacks.

> For the great part of thirty-six hours, Negroes were hunted throughout the streets like wild animals. A black skin became a death warrant. Man after man, with hands upraised, pleading for his life, was surrounded by groups of men who had never seen him before and who knew nothing about him except that he was Black, and stoned to death. A Negro girl, seeking safety from a band of White men, was attacked by White women, and despite her pleas for mercy had her face smashed by a club wielded by one of the White women. An aged Negro, tottering from a weakness, was seized and hanged from a pole. Three million dollars' worth of property was destroyed. State guardsmen were called out and did nothing. The police seemed helpless or acquiescent.

When it was over, some estimated that forty to fifty African Americans had been killed and hundreds injured. Reflecting on these horrifying events, Harrison wondered about the meaning of working-class solidarity; white trade unionists were obviously "a collection of doddering jackasses which can publicly palliate such atrocities as that of East St. Louis and publicly assume, as Gompers did, responsibility for it." It became obvious to Harrison that for black Americans their "first duty . . . [was] to the Negro race." [33]

In the years that followed, Harrison lectured, wrote, and organized on behalf of race consciousness among African Americans. While he acknowledged that it was impossible to explain racism without an analysis of capitalism, he contended that racism was not reducible to economic factors alone. A far more significant explanation for Harrison was "a revulsion of racial feelings." These "feelings" were bolstered by whites' belief in the superiority of white civilization and their concomitant assumption that they had the "right and power to dictate to the darker millions what their way of life and of allegiance shall be." Black Americans needed to take pride in themselves, their history, and their accomplishments. The watchwords should be "courage, fortitude, heroism," based on an international consciousness of people of color.[34]

Harrison challenged Socialists to grapple with the reasons for the rise of black nationalism, with its accompanying critique of the Socialist Party. It appeared to him that few Socialists were attentive to a changing world, a world in which the struggle for African-American self-determination was less interested in accommodation to "white values," no matter how radical, than in expressing the aspirations of an oppressed people. Socialism would never appeal to black Americans as long as it was a language, a form of analysis, and way of acting in the world devoid of relevance to the black experience, to black people's efforts to forge a sense of identity, solidarity, and peoplehood within the context of a society governed by, shaped by, and accountable to whites only. Likewise, Socialists could learn something about their own shortcomings as committed radicals if they studied the reasons for the appeal of black nationalism to black workers and the extent to which it was part of an African-American cultural tradition of resistance to domination. Only then would socialism "have a chance to be heard by Negroes on its merits." [35]

Christians and Socialism

Christian Socialists were no more likely to heed Harrison's challenge than other Socialists. Like other Socialists, they spoke about capitalism, the exploitative nature of class relations, and the need for a Socialist alternative as if people of color were invisible. The qualifier "Christian" did not distinguish them from other Socialists when it came to questions of race and racism. Yet, although it is important to stress the shortcomings of Christian Socialists in failing to understand the centrality of race in American society, there is a dimension of Christian Socialism that must not be lost. For here was a movement that took seriously the fundamental reality of class and the importance of socialism as a political option for Christians.

The relationship between religion and socialism has been neglected. Most Socialists have agreed with Eric Hobsbawm that "the modern working class socialist movement has developed with an overwhelmingly secular, indeed often a militantly antireligious, ideology . . . [and] conversely, religio-political versions of socialism and communism have always been marginal and generally not very important phenomena." Hobsbawm's generalization has a ring of truth, especially in Europe, but it is also clear that in England, Canada, and the United States, Christianity did offer a set of values by which working-class people could come to terms with the violence and social dislocation that accompanied the rise of industrial capitalism. Just as industrial capitalism sought to mold society in its own image, a working-class interpretation of the Christian tradition forged a link between the struggle against the prevailing order and an alternative vision of a democratically structured society. Christians were active members of Debs's Socialist Party, and Christian Socialist organizations taught socialism in the name of Jesus and Marx. Christian Socialists sensed no incompatibility between their Christian beliefs and their espousal of socialism. As class-conscious Socialists, they actively strove to convert their fellow Christians.[36]

The Christian Socialist Fellowship

Christian Socialism originated in the late 1880s as the left wing of the social gospel movement, part of what Martin Marty has so aptly called "public" Protestantism. It found expression in a series of organizations such as the Society of Christian Socialists, whose members saw socialism as an instrument for furthering the aims of Christianity, thus subordinating political socialism to the lordship of Christ. The Society of Christian Socialists was not affiliated with the major Socialist party of the period, Daniel DeLeon's Socialist Labor Party. In fact, its members were more interested in the conversion of Socialists to Christianity than in advocating any form of socialism. Many Christian Socialists of the period, like Frances Willard, were influenced by the writings of Laurence Gronlund. They were drawn to Gronlund's interpretation of socialism as a cooperative commonwealth, the product of a gradual evolution guided by education and reason, and they were especially attracted by Gronlund's contention that the cooperative commonwealth was the unfolding of the Kingdom of God in history: "As Jesus divided the old world from the new by proclaiming the Kingdom of Heaven, the brotherhood of man, so Socialism is destined to realize it." [37]

The most important popularizer of late nineteenth-century Christian socialism was W.D.P. Bliss, Episcopal minister and founder of the Church of the Carpenter in Boston. Like Gronlund, Bliss rejected any notion of class conflict. Through the Fabian Society of Boston (later to become the Social Reform League), Bliss agitated for what he considered a nonpartisan socialism, "broad enough to include all that is of value, no matter whence it comes, and replace jealousy between reformers by cooperation for the general good." Socialism would come about through education, he thought; evolution, not revolution, was the key to the coming of socialism as a Christianized Kingdom of God.[38]

The decisive transformation among Christian Socialists occurred in the late 1890s, when Christian socialism became less a belief in evolutionary development through moral suasion and education and more an advocacy of class struggle and the political participation of Christians, as Socialists, in the public arena. This change can largely be traced to the influence of George D. Herron, one of the most controversial religious figures of the 1890s. His flamboyant public speeches on the Christian response to social injustice attracted large crowds. Herron hammered away at what he perceived to be the cultural captivity of the churches by capitalism. Christians had ceased to obey Christ and instead paid homage to capital. "If I were to stand before any representative religious gathering in the land, and there preach actual obedience to the Sermon on the Mount, declaring that we must actually do what Jesus said, I should commit a religious scandal," Herron declared, but "if the head of some great oil combination, though it had violated every law of God or man . . . were to stand before any representative religious gathering with an endowment check in his hand, he would be greeted with an applause so vociferous as to partake of the morally idiotic." Herron soon realized that it was not sufficient merely to denounce the evils of capitalism; justice required nothing less than a radically restructured society. He first supported the Socialist Labor Party and then Debs's Social Democratic Party, predecessor of the American Socialist Party.[39]

Indicative of Herron's changing attitudes was an address titled "Why I Am a Socialist," delivered before a mass meeting of the Social Democratic Party in Chicago's Central Music Hall on September 29, 1900. He stressed the need to create among workers a class consciousness that they were "the rightful owners and real producers of the earth." Socialism, he claimed, upheld the worth and dignity of the individual and was sensitive to the religious aspirations of the American people. Whether Socialists acknowledged it or not, socialism was a means by which Jesus' message of the Kingdom of God might be realized. The Socialist Party, rather than Christianity or the church, was the concretized Logos that expressed people's striving for spiritual ends. Socialism was in keeping with the goal usually sought by religion, cooperation. Socialism affirmed "that cooperation . . . is more practicable and liberating, more productive of the common good and of great individuality, than a competitive and individualistic organization. Jesus would call this the law of love. In modern economic terms, it is socialism." Since cooperation could be accomplished only through the training socialism provided in mutuality, responsibility, and service, then socialism was in essence religious. As such socialism would win the battle with capitalism, set the human spirit free, and provide an "atmosphere of freedom in which religious spirituality could best exist." [40]

Herron played a particularly important role in helping to merge the Social Democratic Party and the "kangaroos" of the Socialist Labor Party into the Socialist Party of America. Moreover, his entry into the Socialist camp opened the way for others. One of his more noted disciples was J. Stitt Wilson, who later became the first Socialist mayor of Berkeley, California. In the late 1890s, Wilson organized the Social Crusade and its publication, the *Social Crusader*, to spread Herron's message. When Herron converted to political socialism and endorsed the Social Democratic Party, the *Social Crusader* followed suit. Wilson, like Herron, changed roles from minister to Socialist evangelist, preaching the message of his newfound faith. Other Christian Socialists who made the same transfer from pulpit to Socialist politics included William T. Brown, Franklin H. Wentworth, and Carl D. Thompson, who became a leading Wisconsin Socialist and served as a Socialist member of the Wisconsin House of Representatives. Unfortunately, Herron's personal life weakened his effectiveness. Within the span of one year, 1901, his wife divorced him, he married Carrie Rand, he was deposed from the Congregational ministry, and he renounced Christianity. These events did much to retard the further movement of Christians into the ranks of the Socialist Party in the first few years of the twentieth century.[41]

Herron became disillusioned with the church and Christianity, but others continued to relate Christianity to socialism. In 1904 the *Christian Socialist*, edited by Edward Ellis Carr and Oscar Donaldson, began publication to provide a forum for Christians seeking to relate their faith to their developing commitment to socialism. The *Christian Socialist* was instrumental in the formation of the most active and influential of the prewar Christian Socialist organizations, the Christian Socialist Fellowship, which met for the first time at a national conference of Christian Socialists held in 1906 in Louisville, Kentucky. Unlike other groups, the CSF was designed to "win religious people to Socialism and not socialists to Christianity." Carr, in particular, insisted that the task ahead was to capture and revolutionize the churches. It would be possible to do so, he believed, because "all the Christian churches belong to Socialism by virtue of their faith in Jesus. Let us claim our own." At the Louisville meeting the *Christian Socialist* was designated as the official organ and support was unanimously given to the Socialist Party. According to the constitution adopted on June 18, 1906, the object of the CSF was "to permeate the churches, denominations and other religious institutions, with the Social Message of the Bible; to show that Socialism is the economic expression of the religious life; to end the class struggle by establishing industrial democracy, and to hasten the reign of justice and brotherhood upon earth." [42]

The Christian Socialist Fellowship was made up of pastors, seminary professors, social workers, and lay people, mostly from mainline Protestant denominations. At its peak the CSF had five hundred active members and five hundred associate members, with district organizing secretaries in twenty-six states, mostly in the North and Northeast. The *Christian Socialist* had a readership of over nineteen thousand. The CSF maintained that "as active members of the Socialist Party we thoroughly accept the economic interpretation of social and political issues, and have no desire to qualify it by a revisionist demand; and we are fully convinced that, as a matter of policy, the party ought to avoid every form of religious and anti-religious theory or dogma." Jesus was portrayed as a revolutionary who sided with the oppressed and, in the words of Edward Ellis Carr, engaged in the "historic struggle of the class-conscious proletariat toward the co-operative commonwealth." The teachings of Jesus demanded not only a rejection of capitalism but a new social order in which "men and women, outcast, maimed and weak" could live in a just and equitable society.[43]

As to the relationship of Christianity and socialism, J. O. Bentall, who was both an active member of the Socialist Party and a leading figure in the CSF, believed that the ideals propounded by Christianity were incompatible with capitalism and that socialism offered a modus operandi through which Christian ideals could be attained. In Bentall's mind, the relationship between socialism and Christianity was complementary, for "socialism is the material side of that of which Christianity is the religious." Rufus W. Weeks, like many others, insisted that Christian socialism was not a distinctive form of socialism. Properly speaking, he argued, there "is no Christian Socialism," since Christians who were Socialists agreed with Marxists about the role of economic forces in determining historical development and the working class as the agency for societal transformation. The main distinction between Christian Socialists and their secular comrades, he said, was their love of the church, their experience of Christ's presence, and their belief in the Kingdom of God and its power to transform human life.[44]

Christian Socialists also sought to distance themselves from the more reformist approach of the social gospel. One clear illustration of the difference between Christian Socialists and their social gospel contemporaries was their differing assessments of what became known as the Men and Religion Forward movement, 1911–1912. This was a social-gospel–informed interdenominational Protestant evangelistic campaign to "secure the personal acceptance of Jesus Christ by the individual manhood and boyhood of our times, and their permanent enlistment in the program of Jesus Christ as the world program of daily living." The sponsors and leaders of the campaign were well-known progressives and social gospel proponents, from Jane Addams and Raymond Robins to Graham Taylor and Charles Stelzle. With the intention of increasing public awareness of the need for a dedicated commitment to social service as part of one's religious self-understanding, intensive eight-day campaigns were held in seventy targeted cities, reaching an estimated million and a half people. The organizers, drawing on the developing social sciences, discussed the problems of urban life, poverty, and the need for social reform. Walter Rauschenbusch contended that the Men and Religion Forward movement "has done probably more than any single agency to lodge the social gospel in the common mind of the Church." Christian Socialists thought otherwise. They asked why the movement was so "heralded" by the press and why it was funded by "notorious capitalists magnates." In reality, they said, the movement was nothing more than "capitalist propaganda" designed under "the cloak of religion" to undermine socialism.[45]

Christian Socialists were particularly critical of Raymond Robins, an active municipal reformer, friend of Samuel Gompers and supporter of the American Federation of Labor against its more radical opponents. Robins worked with Charles Stelzle and others in what was called the Social Service Department of the campaign. Christian Socialist critics noted that a conservative audience might perceive Robins as something of a radical for exposing the social evils of the day, indicting those who fostered conditions in which numerous men, women, and children lived in want, and arguing on behalf of the right of workers to organize. But Robins's apparent radicalism was deceptive, for he concluded that social change was possible without any fundamental alteration of the capitalist system. Indeed, Robins thought the real menace to religion and society was socialism, not capitalism. What particularly infuriated Christian Socialists was Robins's contention that if one accepted socialism, one was "compelled to give up God, Christ, the Bible and religion; that the adoption of Socialism would mean the destruction of the best in Christian civilization, and . . . anyone . . . who believed in Socialism was an intellectual ass." Christian Socialists protested that this was a misreading of the prophetic tradition and showed an inability on Robins's part to understand that "capitalism, not the capitalists, is the creator of class divisions and class struggles." One of the major limitations of Robins's analysis was his unwillingness to acknowledge that the chief beneficiaries of programs of "social betterment" were not "workers and toilers" but those who profited from "a government of Business, by Business and for Business." Florence Kelley, Robins's fellow worker in the settlement house movement, demonstrated greater clarity of insight when she wrote to Robins: "Can anything short of the socialist reorganization of industry do anything more than use rosewater for the plague?" [46]

One of the many problems confronting the Christian Socialist Fellowship in spreading the message of socialism among Christians was the alienation of working-class people from the Protestant churches. They discovered that working-class people were far more attentive to the contradictions between Christianity and capitalism than most of the clergy. J. O. Bentall commented on how they perceived that "the teachings of Jesus are outraged and perverted every time they are accommodated to the competitive economic system and that the preacher who stands for the capitalist class in its iniquitous exploitation of the laborer has no conception of the fundamental principles of the Christian religion." In response to needs of Christians who rejected a capitalistic interpretation of Christianity, the CSF established centers where Christian Socialists could come together to celebrate their faith and commitment. Beginning in Chicago, centers appeared in major urban areas, including New York, Boston, Detroit, and Denver, as well as rural communities from Elkins, West Virginia, to Batavia, New York. The importance of alternative support structures for Christian Socialists extended to the creation of Socialist Sunday schools, as part of the work of CSF centers. Where there were no centers, other programs were developed, so that "the mind of the children need not be polluted with the slime of capitalistic doctrines." One Socialist Sunday school in Rochester, New York, asked children to pray:

O God of Life and Light, we yearn to be nobler, kinder, more genuine, more complete. We are hungry; fill us with knowledge and wisdom. We are thirsty; give us to drink deep draughts from the wells of justice. We are weak; make us strong to help in the sacred war of manhood and civilization against tyranny, inhumanity, exploitation and greed. Dedicate us anew to the service of our fellowmen, and heighten within us the sense of universal brotherhood, unselfish and international. Help us to be hard haters of unfairness and live lovers of equal rights for all; friends of real worth and enemies of sham; champions of liberty and opponents of slavery in all its forms. May we ever place the soul above gold, human comfort above selfish profit, the home above the market and right above all gain![47]

Where CSF centers did not exist Christian Socialists were held together through annual meetings, the work of CSF national and district secretaries, the *Christian Socialist*, and the efforts of individual members. The organizing strategies of Christian Socialists varied. In some cases they adapted the long-standing tradition of revivalism to their own end; Edward Ellis Carr, for example, led a series of Christian Socialist revivals in McKeesport, Pennsylvania. One minister commented that "Brother and Comrade Carr" had "quickened" among people the ability to "forgive and to love and work as never before." Listeners heard "a vital message of vital Christianity, applied to both the individual and the social life."[48]

On other occasions, Christian Socialists used Socialist camp meetings to propagate their newfound faith. A moving example was a series of camp meetings conducted in Graves County, Kentucky. At one weeklong meeting in Viola, Kentucky, during the summer of 1911, up to nine hundred people from the surrounding communities gathered to listen to Edward Ellis Carr and Paul H. Castle expound on the nature of socialism, the Bible, and Christian faith, accompanied by fellowship and the singing of Socialist songs, many composed by the Christian Socialist Harvey Moyer. While Castle took the stance of a teacher, with lectures that were described as "quiet, beautiful, pleasant and illuminating," Carr was the prophet, "like a thunderstorm, sweeping obstructions aside, shooting terrific thunderbolts at error and wrong." The camp meeting was financed by local Socialists, people who gave what they could, mostly farmers and workers who had devoted their lives to the cause. Most were converted through the reading of Socialist tracts and books and Socialist newspapers like the *Appeal to Reason*. One comrade, Lafe Nance, had helped to organize a lecture by Debs. After the lecture he and Debs had talked, Nance said, and on saying good-bye, they had "prayed that we might meet again in the grand and glorious Co-Operative Commonwealth."[49]

To reach a range of audiences, the editors of the *Christian Socialist* published special editions directed at various Protestant denominations, such as Methodists, Baptists, and Lutherans, and others for Catholics, African Americans, women, and businesspeople. In addition, the *Christian Socialist* ran a women's column, albeit somewhat irregularly. Women within the CSF agreed that the fellowship was something larger than the concept of "brotherhood," limited only to men. As Socialist women, they were committed to women's suffrage but critical of suffragettes who ignored the needs of working-class women. Furthermore, it appeared to them that many male Socialists paid only lip service to the equality of men and women. One writer identified a "masculinism" that reinforced male dominance under the guise of Socialist rhetoric. Socialists need not fear feminism, said the columnist, for it "stands for cooperation. Isn't the world suffering to-day, through all its evils, from its opposite, Masculinism, or competition? Surely no one need be frightened by this cry. The world has nothing to fear from Feminism, for it is the very thing that Socialism is emphasizing." Just as Socialist women had to combat sexism within their own ranks, so Christian Socialists had to acknowledge the problem of sexism within the church. It seemed to women that the church had too quickly forgotten that "all his life long Jesus was as deeply in conflict with the anti-woman element in contemporary life as . . . [with] the money-lenders." [50]

Beyond organizational and historical questions, the creation of the CSF raises the more important issue of how and why Christians became Socialists. Part of the answer can be found by examining the lives of various leaders of the fellowship. In many ways the quintessential Christian Socialist was Edward Ellis Carr. He was one of the founding members of the Socialist Party, editor of the *Christian Socialist*, and for a while, national secretary of the CSF. Carr insisted that he "was born a Socialist," having developed his convictions in childhood. Edward Bellamy's *Looking Backward* opened his mind to socialism, but it only made sense to him after he read Edward Averling's translation of Marx's *Capital*. The discovery that he was indeed a "class-consciousness Socialist" led to involvement in Socialist politics. He soon learned that such commitments had their penalty. As an ordained Methodist minister, Carr had developed a fairly successful church in Danville, Illinois, but it became apparent to the leaders of his church that Carr's Socialist convictions, and particularly his Socialist politics, were incompatible with the church's traditional emphasis on stability, order, and the maintenance of the status quo. Forced to leave his pulpit, Carr founded a "People's Church" to serve the working class. He and his family struggled to earn a living for a number of years, believing that the establishment of socialism took priority over a more comfortable life-style. [51]

Like many other Christian Socialists, Carr maintained that his political commitment intensified his awareness of the radicality of his religious tradition. From his perspective, Christianity appeared to have been "cursed, crippled, prostituted and trampled under foot by capitalism" until it became a privatized religion and lost sight of Jesus' preaching of the Kingdom of God. Christians had forgotten their heritage of prophets who sided "with the outraged poor in their class-struggle. They rebuked the princes and plutocrats continually, at the risk of their lives, and demanded the rights of the common people." Similarly, the modern church could not be neutral in the struggle for social change. Socialism, rather than competitive capitalism, offered Christians the possibility of living out their faith. They should join "the proletarian revolution, proceeding upon the class-struggle, until all injustice and inequality is destroyed and the human race is fully redeemed from oppression, want, ignorance and sin." [52]

J. O. Bentall agreed with Carr that only socialism could free Christianity from its captivity to capitalism. Bentall added that the real tragedy was that capitalism had made Jesus into a legitimator of wealth, power, and privilege; this was "the most blasphemous act that capitalism has yet committed." It was clear that "Jesus does not belong to the kingdom of robbery and oppression and can never become a peaceable and docile member of that royal household. . . . But the working-class will not let their Comrade languish in the confinement of the enemy. . . . Jesus belongs to labor and the religion of Jesus can find its home only in a system where justice and love are the foundation stones. Socialism will redeem the church and make her the power for good which she was intended to be." [53]

Bentall, the son of Swedish immigrants, was raised on a farm in rural Minnesota. He worked his way through Carleton College as a day laborer and farmhand and sustained himself through graduate studies at the University of Chicago as a lecturer and preacher. Converted at a young age, he became a Baptist and served for six years as an ordained minister at a church in St. Anne, Illinois, where he established what was considered a successful ministry, building an impressive church edifice with a new gymnasium, library, and classrooms. He soon became more interested in the world outside the church and purchased a local newspaper, which he turned into an instrument of social reform in the community. Newspaper writing led to his involvement in the temperance movement as lecturer and editor for the Anti-Saloon League of Illinois. He soon realized that the "liquor traffic" was related to poverty and that the contradictions of the existing system would never be solved as long as the rich exploited the poor, political corruption was rampant, and the clergy continued to pervert the very nature of the Christian gospel. He confessed that he had been a Socialist most of his life without realizing it. For him socialism was a cooperative system dedicated to the promise that "all the people shall own all the earth, instead of having a few people own all the earth. Socialism means an equal opportunity for all and that the worker shall enjoy the full benefit of his labor. . . . It means the removal of political corruption and industrial oppression, the end of child labor and white slavery. It means the establishment of the home and the family, of morality, of justice, of freedom of thought, of universal education, of brotherhood and comradeship. It means freedom in religion and opportunity to proclaim unhampered the gospel of the Carpenter of Nazareth." Bentall joined both the CSF and the Socialist Party. Later he became an editor of the *Christian Socialist* and state secretary of the Socialist Party of Illinois.[54]

While some questioned the compatibility of Christianity and socialism, others, such as Rufus W. Weeks, asked whether one could be a Christian and a businessperson. Weeks was a well-known CSF speaker and lecturer and vice-president of the New York Life Insurance Company. Charles Edward Russell commented on the incongruity: "Here was the vice-president of this most typical capitalist corporation not only an ardent Socialist but testifying to his faith with ponderable works. Year in and year out, his was the largest individual gift of money to the Socialist party. Never was altruism of purer strain; he had from it nothing but the acrid criticism of his fellows, social ostracism . . . and [he] endured all this as calmly as the taunts and spurns of his own class, and gradually he won the unbounded respect and confidence of the despised agitators to whom he had joined himself." As a Christian Socialist, Weeks maintained, he believed as fervently as any Marxist in economic determinism and class struggle: "Religiously we are with the churches, and politically with the militant Socialists." Still, it is difficult to understand why a businessperson would want to become a Socialist, especially given the profitability of the status quo. Weeks thought a society should be judged not by its profits but by its impact on the common good. As a businessperson, he understood that corporate capitalism produced structural unemployment and the exploitation of the working class through the extraction of surplus capital. Far more humane and Christian was the social ownership of the productive process, whereby all human beings would be guaranteed "the right to work and the living wage." Socialists were those who sought to transform industry from "the ownership of corporations to the ownership of the people. To join the Socialist movement seems therefore the most direct way in which a man can throw what force he has towards that transformation." [55]

One of the most intriguing Christian Socialists was Irwin St. John Tucker. Born on January 10, 1886, in Mobile, Alabama, he spent most of his early career as a roaming newspaper reporter. He was radicalized by his experience with a strike in 1908 in the coalfields of Birmingham, Alabama. Prior to the strike, as something of a lark, he had joined the Alabama National Guard to re-enact the Civil War battle of Chickamauga. Instead, his company was shipped to the Birmingham coal district. He and other soldiers soon discovered they had a lot more in common with the miners and their families than with the paid "special deputies." Tucker had a chance to witness the collaboration between the state government and the mine owners against the miners and their union, the United Mine Workers. It seemed to him that this "combination of industrial and political overlords" simply "herded" people around "like cattle" for its own ends, and the miners' struggle against systemic injustice won his sympathy. In the fall presidential election of 1908, he voted for Debs and took his first step down the path toward socialism. The next year he entered the Episcopal General Theological Seminary in New York City, where he was influenced by radical faculty members and his own reading of the early church fathers, who, he felt, "were radicals and revolutionaries to the last degree." He also learned of an Anglican protest tradition that extended from John Ball to the English Christian Socialists. What finally convinced him that he was a Socialist was his reading of a book by Charles Edward Russell, *Why I Am a Socialist*. Two weeks after he was ordained an Episcopal minister, he joined the Socialist Party. For the next few years he served as a minister at Saint Mark-in-the-Bowery. In 1914 he became managing editor of the *Christian Socialist*.[56]

Tucker agreed with Carr and Bentall that real Christianity could not exist under capitalism and that socialism would allow for the expression of Christian faith as "life, seeking life in fellowship and love." In 1916 he left the *Christian Socialist* to devote his energies to the work of the Socialist Party. With the entry of America into the First World War, the Socialist Party position of "unalterable opposition to the war" led to a general anti-Socialist hysteria created in large part by a governmental policy of suppressing any form of dissent. Irwin St. John Tucker, along with four other Socialists, was convicted under the Espionage Act for "conspiracy to obstruct the draft." Tucker received a twenty-year sentence in Leavenworth, which was later set aside by the Supreme Court on the grounds that the trial judge, Kenesaw Mountain Landis, was prejudicial during the trial. As a result of his trial, Tucker became even more critical of the church for its wartime religious idolatry; in rendering to Caesar what belonged to God, the church had forgotten its mission as messenger of the Prince of Peace. J. O. Bentall was also convicted under the Espionage Act for supposedly influencing a man in his employ not to register for the draft. He served eighteen months in Fort Leavenworth penitentiary.[57]

Few Protestant ministers agreed with Tucker and Bentall. The general attitude of the American Protestant community was that the Great War was a glorious crusade for God and country. Henry Churchill King, president of Oberlin College and noted Protestant liberal, stated "It is neither a travesty nor exaggeration to call this war on the part of America, a truly Holy War." Many Christian Socialists, such as J. Stitt Wilson, Carl D. Thompson, and Edward Ellis Carr, joined the ranks of prowar Socialists who embraced the ideals of a just war aimed at an honorable peace. Socialism now seemed alien to them, out of keeping with the forces supposedly making the world safe for democracy. Carr's Christian Socialist portrayal of the Christ who sided with the oppressed was all too easily made over into the image of a soldier in a khaki uniform.[58]

No analysis of the CSF is complete without some mention of its understanding of race and class. James Weinstein has contended that the Christian Socialist Fellowship took a more progressive stand on "the Negro question" than most members of the Socialist Party, but an examination of the *Christian Socialist* indicates otherwise. Christian Socialists were perhaps not such blatant racists as Socialists close to the AFL (the strong exception being J. Stitt Wilson); yet any acknowledgment of the realities facing African Americans, from the institutionalized violence of lynchings and race riots to political disenfranchisement and segregation, was conspicuously absent. Edward Ellis Carr, for example, argued that the real issue for black Americans was "suffering on account of economic robbery and economic slavery." Socialism would offer the black worker "the full product of his labor," the full economic product, that is. Carr saw no need for social equality or any form of "social intercourse between whites and blacks." It seemed to many Christian Socialists that racism arose from economic factors alone and that it was not up to Socialists to solve "the race problem"; that task had to be left to future generations. Carr resisted any implication that Socialists promoted equality between whites and blacks. When George W. Slater was appointed secretary of the CSF, the fellowship did a fund-raising drive to support Slater's outreach to the black community. An advertisement in the *Christian Socialist* declared: "There is more in Socialism for Negroes than they can find anywhere else. We do not teach social equality, but we do give the Negro a square deal—we deal with him justly. The Negroes might better be voting the Socialist ticket than the tickets of the parties that enslaved and robbed them in the past and mislead and misrule them in the present."[59]

Christian Socialism from the Bottom Up

Christian socialism, as represented by the CSF, expressed the aspirations of the left wing of mainline Protestant Christianity. Some sought to be the spokespersons for the dispossessed, while others sought to empower the dispossessed to speak for themselves. The disinherited themselves espoused a form of Christian socialism embedded in a revivalistic and evangelical understanding of the meaning of the Christian tradition.

The studies of James Green, *Grass-Roots Socialism: Radical Movements in the Southwest, 1895–1943*, and Garin Burbank, *When Farmers Voted Red: The Gospel of Socialism in the Oklahoma Countryside, 1910–1924*, focus on the southwestern section of the United States, especially Texas and Oklahoma. The Socialist movement there was organized by former populists, militant miners, railroad workers, and scores of Socialist agitators, some of the most effective of whom were evangelical preachers. Out of Texas and Oklahoma came the Socialist revivalists M. A. Smith, Stanley J. Clark, W. L. Thurman, and George G. Hamilton, who spoke in the language of the people about capitalist exploitation, Socialist alternatives, and a God who sided with poor and oppressed people. This form of grass-roots socialism was most clearly evident in the state of Oklahoma, where the social basis of the party resided not in the towns or cities but in the rural countryside, populated by evangelical Protestants. Socialism for these evangelicals was not something abstract or theoretical but an immediate and concrete answer to the problem of poverty. They were not reformists or gradualists, and they knew that conflict and struggle were necessary. The experiences of conversion, religious revivals, prayer and Bible study, so central to their understanding of Christianity, also shaped their understanding of socialism as an agency for the creation of a kingdom of justice, equality, and cooperation. The Kingdom of God was historical and not otherworldly. They believed, as Socialist preacher Andrew Spratt put it, that while "men are underpaid, while women are overworked. While children grow up in squalor, while exploiting and social injustice remain, the Kingdom . . . can never come on earth and never will."[60]

The same intensity that characterized church revivals marked the Socialist revivals. During one week in 1912, twenty thousand people flocked to Snyder, Oklahoma, a small town of 250, to listen to Socialist speakers. Usually Socialist preachers and national leaders such as Gene Debs or Kate Richards O'Hare would speak at these gatherings, and people would sing old familiar songs with new Socialist words, discuss Socialist literature, or argue about the Bible and socialism. The spirit of this popular socialism was most eloquently captured by a prayer that appeared in the Oklahoma Socialist publication *Sword of Truth*:

> Permeate our souls with divine discontent and righteous rebellion. Strengthen within us the spirit of revolt; and may we continue to favor that which is fair and rise in anger against the wrong, until the Great Revolution shall come to free men and women from their fetters and enable them to be kind and noble and human!
>
> O Lord, hasten the day!

George G. Hamilton described socialist preachers as "the kind of preachers who till the soil, pound iron, and build houses." Most were lay preachers, evaluated in local Socialist newspapers as much for their Christian beliefs as for their Socialist commitment. For example, "brother" G. A. Lambert was described as "a noble Christian preacher and an ardent Socialist"; another preacher was said to be "a red card Socialist as well as a consistent Christian." Socialist preaching denounced not only the sins of capitalist-minded clergy and their cohorts but also Darwinism and demon rum.[61]

George G. Hamilton himself was one such preacher, a Methodist out of the Red River valley of Texas. He had a well-earned reputation as a "vigorous and uncompromising" opponent of socialism, charging Socialists with being "antireligious and subversive of true morality." Yet beginning in April, 1910, in a debate with W. L. Thurman, a well-respected Socialist preacher from southern Oklahoma, Hamilton began to have doubts about his own position. His debate with Thurman was followed by further debates with other Socialist clergy such as M. A. Smith, Redden Andrews, and above all Stanley J. Clark, the "master debater of the Socialist movement." His opponents challenged him to read not just the literature of those opposed to socialism, or the few Socialists who had been interpreted as antireligious, but the vast array of Socialist books and publications. They particularly pressed him to read Walter Rauschenbusch's *Christianity and the Social Crisis*. Here was a book that literally changed Hamilton's life, a book that "entered into my very soul . . . and reveals a Christ-like compassion for the toiling, suffering millions of earth." It forced Hamilton to reread the Bible; he was especially moved by Rauschenbusch's rendering of the prophet Isaiah's attack on an individualistic understanding of sin and salvation. He discovered a prophetic tradition he had never known. Rauschenbusch made Hamilton see that Frances E. Willard had been right all along: "Socialism is the very marrow of Christ's gospel."[62]

Converted to the cause of socialism, Hamilton rode the lecture circuit on behalf of the Socialist Party, sharing his newfound insights into the injustices of the present socioeconomic order, which set human greed over human need. It was capitalism, not socialism, that was antireligious and immoral, "a monster of iniquity blighting human lives, wrecking human hopes, and damning human souls." The Texas Socialist J. L. Hicks likened Hamilton's conversion to that of Saul of Tarsus: it led to a new vision of the world whereby "the burdens and wrongs imposed upon the workers of the world are imposed upon him, his sympathies are expanded and he sees how those wrongs may be righted, and the same earnest voice [with] which he formerly warned the working class against what he thought before investigation was Socialism, will henceforth be heard in still louder tones appealing to the working class to accept what he now knows to be Socialism." Hamilton preached that socialism stood for the cause of justice, human liberty, and the realization of all the principles of human solidarity and love that Christianity had taught down the ages. He believed that socialism was "fundamentally right" because it was "a people's movement," rooted in a basic faith in people's ability to determine the shape and character of their own lives and institutions. The triumph of socialism would be the advent of the Kingdom of God, a "day when the workers of the world shall come into their own and inaugurate the era of Liberty, Equality, Fraternity, Justice, and Brotherhood."[63]

Religion and the Socialist Party

The reaction of secular Socialists to Christian Socialists varied. In one exchange, a Socialist who assumed the pseudonym "Julian" remarked that the theories of Christian socialism were attempts to Christianize the Socialist movement. Trying to reconcile the "earthly doctrines of revolutionary socialism with the teachings of the meek and lowly Nazarene" only led to a situation in which "both socialism and Christianity fare but indifferently." By contrast, Robert Rives LaMonte stressed that the message of Jesus was compatible with socialism's emphasis on human solidarity, brotherhood, and fellowship. Nevertheless, he insisted, "organized Christianity . . . is a capitalist institution . . . just as the State is. It draws its revenues from the capitalist class [and is expected] to do its bidding. As an institution it is and will be against us, but none the less in Christianity itself, it may be, there is lying dormant the germ of the Religion that is to be." This new religion of the future might come about through the transformation of Christianity, but LaMonte believed that it was a fanciful dream to hope that Christianity "may grow into the Religion of Socialism." He concluded his analysis of the relationship of socialism and Christianity with a tactical suggestion. Given the nature of American society, it would be suicidal to attack Christianity; it was far better simply to demonstrate that socialism provided the necessary basis for living by the ethics of Jesus.[64]

Other Socialists shared LaMonte's belief that it was necessary to separate Jesus from institutionalized Christianity. Kate Richards O'Hare lambasted the clergy for defending capitalism, contending, as did LaMonte, that socialism was in reality applied Christianity. Into the fray came self-proclaimed Marxists such as John Spargo and Ernest Untermann. Spargo, before immigrating to the United States, had been a Protestant minister and an important figure in the British Social Democratic Federation. In America, he noted, Christian Socialists had cooperated closely with secular members of the Socialist Party, in sharp contrast to their European and British Christian counterparts. He pointed out that members of the Christian Socialist Fellowship "did not begin a propaganda to christianize the socialists, but confined themselves to doing socialist propaganda among Christians—not the propaganda of a diluted socialism, but the same straight, uncompromising socialism for which the socialist party stood." [65]

By contrast, Ernest Untermann questioned the comparison Christian Socialists made between Jesus and Marx. To link the two, he believed, one had first to demonstrate that Jesus had advocated class struggle as the means of realizing his ethical ideals. This was not the case, as Untermann saw it, for Jesus had obviously appealed to all classes. More important, Marx's conclusions about economics and politics could not be separated from Marx's method of dialectical materialism, as he felt Christian Socialists had done: "You cannot accept some of Marx's theories and reject others. They stand and fall together. If you reject one, you reject them all. You cannot be a Marxist Socialist in economics and politics, and a theist and metaphysical idealist in philosophy, and still claim to be at one with Marx." [66]

Edward Ellis Carr took issue with Untermann's Marxist fundamentalism. Carr did not believe that everything Marx said was infallible. He admitted that Christian Socialists separated Marx's economic theories from his "antireligious dogmas," but socialism, after all, was an "economic science," not "sectarian dogmatism." There was a natural relationship between Jesus and Marx: Jesus provided the ideal of "the historic struggle of the class-conscious proletariat toward the co-operative commonwealth," whereas Marx discovered the method for fulfilling this ideal. Untermann needed to understand, said Carr, that "he who creates the ideal is the greater . . . for the ideal must precede and is a constant spur and aid toward mastering the method. . . . The ideal is comparatively useless without the method of its achievement; but the method is forever impossible without the ideal. Jesus was necessary to Marx, while Marx showed how Christianity may be made practical." [67]

Most Christian Socialists had no problems with debates between themselves and other Socialists about the relationship between religion and socialism, but they were more disturbed by Socialists who took a hostile, often dogmatic approach to the issue. They advocated religious pluralism, embracing the theist and the atheist, the religious and the nonreligious, and they bridled whenever Socialists attempted to "represent atheism or any other form of religion or antireligion as an essential part of the Socialist philosophy." In fact, many argued that Christians were unsympathetic to socialism largely because some Socialists professed it to be "an atheist, anti-religious movement." If Socialists had been more sensitive to the role of religion in American life, Christian Socialists maintained, there would have been no need for either the *Christian Socialist* or the CSF.[68]

On an official level, the only attempt of the Socialist Party to address religion came at its 1908 national convention. The Platform Committee proposed a plank calling for religion to be "treated as a private matter—question of individual conscience." In response, some delegates contended that religion was not a private matter but a social question and that the plank was an attempt to placate "the religionists and those whose only ambition is to pray to God and crush mankind." Others, such as James Carey, a member of the Platform Committee, wanted all mention of religion to be stricken from the record. He considered his religious views irrelevant to the economic struggle of the proletariat, and besides, he said, "I don't want to force upon the public, or upon the working class, a discussion of some abstract philosophy that will obscure the question of emancipation." Eliot White, district secretary of the CSF for Massachusetts, agreed with Carey on the need to leave out any reference to religion. Others, such as A. M. Simons and Christian Socialist Frederick Strickland upheld the necessity of the plank. Simons maintained that "if Lord Kelvin (a late nineteenth century British scientist) . . . could reconcile his scientific knowledge with religion, it is not for me to rise to such a tremendous height as to say that he is a fakir, or deceived." Finally, J. Mahlon Barnes, national secretary of the Socialist Party, declared that the convention had to decide one way or the other on the issue of religion since it would be quoted by the press and would become part of the official record of the party. In the end the convention adopted the phrasing proposed by Morris Hillquit, which stated: "The Socialist movement is primarily an economic and political movement. It is not concerned with matters of religious belief." Hillquit's motion became part of the declaration of principles of the Socialist Party but was not incorporated in the platform.[69]

Beyond official statements and public posturing, it is clear from the history of Christian socialism that religion played an important role for those within the Christian community who chose a Socialist option. Moreover, religious language and symbols were part and parcel of many Socialist and radical analyses of the dehumanizing impact of capitalism on human life and shaped descriptions of alternative visions of human society in which human community, solidarity, and love could be kindled, fostered, and sustained. One of the best representatives of this other aspect of religion and socialism is Eugene V. Debs.

Nick Salvatore has noted how throughout his life Debs made constant use of religious imagery. This was but one indication of the extent to which the dominant Protestant culture had infused Americans' conception of themselves and their history. While Debs shunned religious labels and institutional affiliation, there was a Christocentric dimension to his self-understanding. Debs was disturbed, as were most working-class people, by the use of Christianity to legitimate the dominant social order. It seemed to him that those members of the clergy who most harangued Socialists about their supposed immorality were the very ones who lined their pockets with the profits obtained by human exploitation. They had their salaries paid by capitalists as they preached a "religion in the service of mammon." Debs dubbed these "preachers of capitalism" the real betrayers of the people and Christ's teachings, "the slimy, oily-tongued deceivers of their ignorant, trusting followers, who traffic in the slavery and misery of their fellow-beings that they may tread the paths of ease and bask in the favors of their masters." Denouncing such ministers as hypocrites, Debs contrasted this perversion of Christianity to the "religion of Jesus, the homeless wanderer who sympathized and associated with the poor and lowly, and whose ministrations were among the despised sinners and outcasts." Particularly during his imprisonment in the Atlanta Federal Penitentiary for violation of the Espionage Act, Debs drew strength from Christ's life of service and love. He spoke of Jesus as the "martyred Christ of the working class," whose life was given for the liberation of people from bondage and served as a model for others.[70]

Most Socialists, Christian or not, shared Debs's revolutionary understanding of Jesus. It was most powerfully expressed in the poem "Comrade Jesus" by Sarah N. Cleghorn, published in the radical journal *The Masses* in April, 1914. Cleghorn, a recent convert to socialism, was seeking to work out her newfound feelings about the meaning of socialism and her Christian faith.

> Thanks to Saint Matthew, who had been
> At mass meetings in Palestine,
> We know whose side was spoken for
> When Comrade Jesus had the floor.
>
> "Where sore they toil and hard they lie,
> Among the great unwashed, dwell I.
> The tramp, the convict, I am he;
> Cold-shoulder him, cold-shoulder me."
>
> By Dives' door, with thoughtful eye,
> He did to-morrow prophesy:—
> "The Kingdom's gate is low and small;
> The rich can scarce wedge through at all."
>
> "A dangerous man," said Caiaphas;
> "An ignorant demagogue, alas,
> Friend of low women, it is he
> Slanders the upright Pharisee."
>
> For law and order, it was plain,
> For holy Church, he must be slain.

The troops were there to awe the crowd,
And "violence" was not allowed.

Their clumsy force with force to foil,
His strong, clean hands he would not soil.
He saw their childishness quite plain
Between the lightnings of his pain.

Between the twilights of his end
He made his fellow-felon friend;
With swollen tongue and blinding eyes,
Invited him to Paradise.

Ah, let no Local him refuse;
Comrade Jesus hath paid his dues.
Whatever other be debarred,
Comrade Jesus hath his red card.[71]

"Comrade Jesus" represents an appropriation of religious imagery and language as a vehicle for conveying a Socialist vision, and it evinces the extent to which Socialists, like most American workers before them, readily distinguished between Jesus and institutionalized Christianity. For Debs and Christian Socialists alike, it was clear that Jesus had sided with the poor and oppressed, but his church had betrayed him. Christian Socialists posed an interesting question about what happens when the church ceases to be a visible sign of God's concern for the poor. Perhaps, in such instances, an option for socialism is a means of keeping alive the gospel as "good news" for all those who have been deemed expendable by those who wield power over them.

African-American Christianity and Socialism

The history of the struggle for socialism in America has most often been written as if it can be told in terms of the aspirations of only white workers and radicals, reinforcing a perception of socialism for whites only. Likewise, Christian socialism has been perceived as a white phenomenon, unrelated to the black community and the development of African-American Christianity. It is not surprising, as James Cone has observed, that most black preachers and theologians have assumed that "racism can be solved in the United States without a socialist transformation in the political economy." These thinkers have accepted as a given that racism has shaped the life and practices of the dominant institutions, but they have also believed that "American society is essentially just and consequently has the best of all possible political systems." Cone's observations, with some important exceptions, can be illustrated historically through a series of debates over socialism and the labor movement that took place in the late nineteenth century in the pages of the *A.M.E. Church Review*, an organ of the African Methodist Episcopal church, one of the oldest black denominations in the United States.[72]

Writing in the aftermath of the Paris Commune and the Haymarket tragedy of May, 1886, Alexander Clark, a "stalwart Republican" active in Republican political circles in Iowa, lawyer, and former slave, condemned socialism as "an aggregate of seditious and incendiary attacks upon law and order." At the same time, Clark was sympathetic to the goals of the Knights of Labor and critical of the excesses of industrial capitalism, which threatened to usurp the "function of popular government" and increase the already vast gap between the rich and the poor. But Clark believed that the existing system was fundamentally sound and amenable to change and that African Americans "want nothing of socialism or the Commune, the strike or the boycott, the mob or the riot. For us be it sufficient that we emulate the spirit and faith of Lincoln, Grant, Sumner . . . [who were] devoted to liberty and justice, but equally the friends and champions of law and order as the benign agencies of man's highest good." John R. Lynch, like Clark a former slave and a lawyer who served as speaker of the House of Representatives of Mississippi and as a Republican member of Congress, agreed with Clark in linking socialism with violence and anarchy. Less critical than Clark of the shortcomings of industrial capitalism, Lynch thought workers should look upon the owners of property as their friends, not their enemies. Black workers should not join any labor organization that had as its purpose the creation of "a feeling of antipathy and hostility between capital and labor, employer and employee."[73]

By contrast T. McCants Stewart, born of free black parents, lawyer, and AME preacher, maintained that America was increasingly ruled by a "moneyed oligarchy" that profited from a society in which "the rich get richer, and the poor get poorer. The production rather than the distribution of wealth seems to be the rule under which we are working at the labor problem of to-day. The laboring masses cry for bread, while their masters revel in luxury." Stewart differed with Lynch in seeing the future for black workers as tied less to the benefits capitalists might bestow on a docile work force than to what they could create for themselves as part of the labor movement. He drew hope from the history of working-class struggle against oppression and tyranny. African Americans, like other workers before them, should "by strong combination . . . strike back at oppression, wrong, or injustice." And yet, the situation facing black workers was not the same as that facing whites. For centuries they had been unable to enjoy the fruits of their own labor, had been valued as less than human and bound by the limits of a slave society. Although such a past lived on in the present, African Americans could look forward to a different future if they took pride in themselves and held fast to their dreams.[74]

Stewart was not alone in his judgment about the fundamental inequity of industrial capitalism. James Theodore Holly wrote: "There is no Gospel morality in our organized modern industry, and therefore offerings from such ill-gotten riches are made as if God could be bribed by the mammon of iniquity." Holly, like Stewart, was born of free black parents, and he was not only active in the abolitionist movement but an early advocate of pan-Africanism, an ordained Episcopal priest. He believed African Americans would never be truly at home in the United States, with its racism and "bastard democracy." Instead, he worked for emigration of black Americans to Haiti, where he believed there would be "far more security for the personal liberty and general welfare of the governed." Unlike Clark, Holly was not fearful of the Socialist movement, for he considered the aims and goals of socialism more in keeping with the dictates of the Bible than the "heathenism" of capitalism. It seemed to Holly that those who most condemned socialism did not hesitate to bless European domination of people of color, the conquest of Africa, and the filling of "the bottomless coffers of avaricious millionaires"—all in the name of Christian civilization. Socialism, for Holly, was a way by which a God of justice was calling an "apostate Christendom" to repent its allegiance to an order that brought death and destruction to millions of human beings.[75]

Only with the turn of the twentieth century and the formation of the Socialist Party of America did there emerge black preachers who took seriously the challenges socialism posed for the African-American community. The most important of these black Socialist preachers were George Washington Woodbey and George W. Slater, Jr., whose contributions have been recovered largely thanks to the work of Philip S. Foner, most notably in his study *American Socialism and Black Americans* and his collection of Woodbey's and Slater's writings, *Black Socialist Preacher*. Woodbey and Slater raised the issue of the importance of race within the context of the political economy of capitalism. It was Reverdy Ransom, however, who questioned any formulation of socialism unrelated to the struggle of African-American people for self-determination. Ransom questioned Socialists, white or black, who too quickly tried to reduce the problem of racism to class relations. Like W.E.B. Du Bois and Hubert Harrison, he explored the implications of African-American historical experience, particularly the liberative dimension of black Christianity and the importance of the black church as a community of resistance to the dominant culture.[76]

George Washington Woodbey

Biographical material on Woodbey is sketchy, but it is clear that he had a commanding presence as an orator, lecturer, and preacher and that he led a life dedicated to the service of others. Born a slave on a plantation in Johnson County, Tennessee, on October 5, 1854, Woodbey was largely self-educated, having attended only two terms of common school. As a young man, he worked as a miner, factory hand, or at whatever job could provide him with the necessities of life. After migrating to the Midwest, he was ordained a Baptist preacher in Emporia, Kansas, in 1874. He served a number of pastorates in Missouri and Kansas before settling in Nebraska in the early 1880s. There he immersed himself in struggles for social reform, including women's suffrage.[77]

Woodbey established a reputation as a gifted public speaker and ran as a candidate on the Prohibition Party ticket for lieutenant governor in 1890 and for Congress in 1894. In 1896 he joined a faction that bolted the Prohibition Party when it refused fusion with the Populist People's Party and endorsement of its presidential candidate, William Jennings Bryan. Even as Woodbey became a "Bryanite," he was beginning to have doubts about fusion politics. He was deeply disturbed by his reading of Edward Bellamy's *Looking Backward* and a copy of the Socialist *Appeal to Reason*. The Christian Socialist Eliot White observed that a good majority of those who joined the Socialist Party came to it "through the printed word," and Woodbey was no exception. Gradually it became clear to him that socialism had more to offer than did the tepid reformism of William Jennings Bryan.[78]

By 1901 Woodbey was a member of Debs's Socialist Party and thenceforth devoted himself to the cause of socialism. An early admirer of Woodbey, A. W. Ricker, chief editorial writer for the *Appeal to Reason*, described his role in the development of the Socialist movement in Omaha, Nebraska: "We remember him in the stirring days of the inception of the Socialist movement in Omaha. Night after night he spoke on the streets and in the parts of that city. Omaha has never had a speaker who could draw and hold the crowds that attended Woodbey's meetings. We have given it as our opinion that Comrade Woodbey is the greatest living negro in America. His style is simple and his logic invincible." Ricker, a former Populist organizer and onetime aspirant for the ministry, shared Woodbey's radical interpretation of the Christian tradition. One of Ricker's most noted writings was "The Political Economy of Jesus," wherein he summarized his views: "The first missionary work of Jesus and his followers was among the working class who heard him gladly. Jesus was crucified by the ruling class because He was a labor agitator, arousing discontent among the poor. The early Christians practiced communism and condemned private property until the wily Constantine corrupted the church. The dark ages began soon after Christianity became respectable and deserted the cause of the oppressed working class."[79]

In 1902 Woodbey moved to San Diego, California, to join his mother, whom he had not seen in years. He became active in California Socialist politics as he assumed a new pastorate, Mount Zion Baptist Church. He was a delegate from California to the Socialist national conventions in 1904, 1908, and 1912, elected to the state executive board of the Socialist Party, and a candidate for state treasurer in 1914. His gifted oratory made him a sought-after Socialist speaker throughout the state. One Socialist publication stressed, "He has done more good for the cause than any of our most eloquent speakers who have preceded him."[80]

Woodbey's approach was to persuade Christians that there was no inherent incompatibility between their Christian faith and the espousal of socialism; in fact, that the biblical tradition and the goals of socialism were the same, so that one had to "accept Socialism in order to stand consistent by the teachings of his own religion." Woodbey argued that the Bible's central focus was on the world of the poor, on issues, questions, and problems facing oppressed people. It seemed equally obvious to him that the God of the Bible sided with the poor and that Jesus' gospel was good news for poor people. His rendering of the biblical witness reminded Christians of the radicality of their own tradition, something socialism had made more evident than all the preachers of capitalism combined.[81]

In helping people to understand the Bible, Woodbey first stressed that the biblical story was "a history of the class struggle going on between the rich and the poor." The biblical authors, like modern Socialists, stood with the poor in opposition to private property, usury, and all that divided people against each other and diminished the possibilities of human solidarity, community, and co-operation. If one really listened to the biblical message, from Moses to Jesus, there emerged a consistent theme: the defense of the poor against their oppressors and the creation of a society in which human beings could share in the products of their own labor. By contrast, in the United States "extortionists" such as John D. Rockefeller were honored while more and more impoverished people struggled to survive. It is the Socialists, said Woodbey, "who stand up to plead the cause of the poor as against the rich . . . [who] stand with Christ." Like the biblical writers, Socialists understood that so long as a small minority controlled the goods of this earth, a class-divided society would perpetuate human misery and want.[82]

As long as the churches sought to legitimate the existing capitalist social order, a system predicated on the exploitation of the poor, "their prayer meetings and solemn assemblies" were a "mockery." Christians needed to realize that it was "the curse of private ownership of the means of production and distribution that stands in the way of the progress of the church, and socialism will enable her to return to her ancient moorings." Hence Woodbey, like many of his Christian Socialist contemporaries, believed that socialism offered Christians the possibility of rediscovering their own tradition of God's love for the poor and recovering their calling as prophetic witnesses against societal forces destructive of human worth and dignity.[83]

There was something refreshing about Woodbey's clarity of insight. Woodbey reminded people that Marx was part of a long Jewish tradition that included the prophets, Christ, and the earliest apostles. If Marx had been accused of stressing material aspects of human life, Christians must remember that so did the Bible. Both Marx and the biblical tradition underscored the degree to which human beings could create conditions in which they could shape their own lives, lives marked more by hope and the possibilities of human creativity than by laments over human failings and shortcomings. Woodbey readily agreed that

Marx was obviously not a Christian, but he insisted that the more important question was whether Marx and Socialists proposed ways to enrich human life, to permit oppressed people to have life in all its fullness.[84]

Woodbey's analysis foreshadows in a remarkable way the work of the Mexican scholar José Miranda. Woodbey argued that communism meant the sharing of one's resources and possessions so that human needs could be met, something practiced by Jesus, the apostles, and the early church. It seemed to Woodbey that the communism of the early church was one of the reasons for the persecution of the Christian community by "rich rulers" of the Roman Empire. When the church ceased "distributing wealth," it "opened the door for the entry of the rich, with all their robbery of the poor." What seemed tragic to Woodbey was that Christians had forgotten that the affirmation in the Apostles' Creed "I believe in the communion of saints" referred to the practice of the early church in which all "sold their possessions, put them into a common stock and every one was served as he had need, and no one said that aught that he had was his own." Those who objected to the very notion of communism ought first to come to terms with the communism of early Christians, who, like modern Socialists, required that the goods of this world be shared with the poor. Woodbey would agree with Miranda in asking, "What if in the history of the West, it is Christianity that *started* communism?"[85]

In addressing the black community, Woodbey maintained that socialism was a means by which "the race problem will be settled forever." There was, in Woodbey's mind, a historical link between racial and class domination; racial oppression was rooted in the development of capitalism. "The Negro was not enslaved because he was a Negro, but because it was supposed that more profit could be made out of his labor." The grueling poverty the majority of working-class African Americans faced daily could not be solved by capitalism, even black capitalism. Blacks needed to see themselves as workers, as workers who had more in common with white workers than with the capitalists who exploited both of them. Woodbey stressed that for too long "we poor whites and blacks have fought each other . . . and while we have fought, the capitalists have taken everything from both of us."[86]

Socialists understood not only the exploitative nature of a capitalist economy but the empty rhetoric of the political system. Socialism was opposed to both political and economic inequality: a government ruled by the rich and powerful was "only the shadow of a government representing the people." The Republican Party, to which African Americans had traditionally given their loyalty, had "abandoned the Negro." It was time for black people to realize that only socialism offered them a future in which they would "have an equal ownership in all that the public owns, and this will entitle him to an equal part of the good things produced by the nation."[87]

To his fellow Socialists Woodbey was a constant reminder to live up to their professed principles of the international solidarity of all working-class people.

In the debates that raged over immigration restriction, Woodbey said, "I am in favor of throwing the entire world open to the inhabitants of the world." He agreed with Thomas Paine that "the world is my country." If so, said Woodbey, if socialism is "based . . . upon the Brotherhood of Man," any stance the Socialists took that lessened the reality of their solidarity with all people, regardless of race or national background, diminished the meaning of socialism.[88]

George Washington Slater, Jr.

While it is difficult to measure the impact of Woodbey's Socialist preaching on the African-American community, it is clear that he made one important convert, George Washington Slater, Jr. Slater was born in Richmond, Missouri, on September 22, 1872. He was fortunate enough to obtain a high school education, graduating in 1890 in Aurora, Nebraska. In addition, he attended a number of colleges, Wesleyan University, Penn College, and the AME seminary, Payne Theological Seminary, in Wilberforce, Ohio. Licensed to preach in 1894, he was pastor of churches in Illinois and Ohio, among them Trinity Church in Wilberforce, Ohio, where he was also pastor of Wilberforce University and visiting lecturer at the university in psychology, moral philosophy, and political economy. By 1911 Slater had settled in Clinton, Iowa, where he became pastor of Bethel African Church.

Slater's first encounter with Woodbey came in 1908, when he was pastor of Zion Tabernacle in Chicago. Captivated by Woodbey's discussion of socialism, Slater began to read more on the subject. He soon discovered, says Philip Foner, that "the tenets of Socialism were the solution of our problem; the ethic of Jesus in economic action; the solution of the poverty question with its attendant evils; the making of a practical brotherhood; the solution of the more serious phases of the so-called race problem." Even though Chicago had grown in importance as a major industrial center, most African Americans still worked in "domestic and service trades, almost untouched by labor organizations and industrial strife." Slater had learned from bitter experience the limits of a socioeconomic system fundamentally insensitive to the needs of poor people. During the winter of 1907–1908, when most of the members of his congregation "had little work and little money, and the prices of food were exorbitant," he tried to establish a cooperative to provide affordable food. He soon learned that those who controlled the food industry were not interested in aiding anyone who might undermine the profit system. Slater came away from the experience indignant but clear in his own mind that an alternative was needed: this he found in socialism. He became an active member of the Socialist Party and established a reputation as an articulate and persuasive advocate. He later joined the Christian Socialist Fellowship and, in 1912, was appointed secretary of the CSF for the "Colored Race." [89]

Slater agreed with Woodbey that there was no contradiction in being both a Socialist and a Christian. In fact, he particularly took to task those who reduced Christian faith to the social gospel form of "social service," which dealt with the effects rather than the causes of injustice and oppression. He disagreed with R. R. Wright, editor of the AME *Christian Recorder* and Chicago social reformer, who stated that "the motive of Social Service in relation to the church differs from that of socialism. Socialism's motive is economic betterment. That of Social Service is spiritual and moral betterment." For Slater, "spiritual and moral betterment" was not truly possible without fundamental change. The "social message of Jesus" demanded a "kingdom of justice— justice in economics, food, shelter, clothing." This kind of justice could be realized only through the creation of a Socialist society, in which the practice of "brotherhood" would be possible, in which the differences that so marked the contemporary world—between men and women, Jew and gentile, whites and people of color—might be overcome. His vision was based on his belief that Socialists were dedicated to the struggle against all forms of oppression and domination: "Comrades, amidst the snows of the north, the vines of the west, the factory-coped plateaus of the east . . . [and the] cotton-fields, chain-gangs and peonage system in the south, comrades in these regions, tell my people that the day dawns, the sun is rising, the mist is dispelling, darkness is receding, the shout of universal brotherhood begins to rend the earth." [90]

Believing that the main obstacle in the appeal of socialism to African Americans was a compound of misinformation and misunderstanding, Slater worked to change the attitudes, beliefs, and political orientation of the black community. As a lecturer, writer, and organizer on behalf of the Socialist Party and the CSF, Slater argued that neither the Republicans nor the Democrats were concerned about the plight of the poor. The very same people who exercised political power in the country also managed the economy, making democracy a sham and justice an illusion. For Slater, one of the most graphic examples of what a society dominated by the rich could do to the human community was war. Rather than a means to defend a country's honor or principles, war was an opportunity for commercial expansion and a deadly game in which the poor were usually the ones who died. Furthermore, black Americans had exchanged the chains of chattel slavery for the chains of a "capitalist competitive system" in which "poor men fight and destroy each other for the crumbs under the rich man's table." The racial tensions between black and white workers were grounded in an industrial order that pitted workers against each other so as to rob them of the fruits of their labor. The only remedy Slater could envision was the destruction of competitive capitalism and its replacement by a cooperative Socialist society "wherein the government guarantees every man equal justice and opportunity." It was nonsense to argue that black Americans in time might share the benefits of capitalism. "A few leading Negroes may get a few political appointments and a little money," but the situation would not change for the mass of black people.[91]

Reverdy Cassius Ransom

Woodbey and Slater were not alone in testifying on behalf of socialism and in recognizing the challenge socialism presented to the black Christian community. Reverdy Ransom, described by David Willis as one of the "most important black churchmen of the first half of this century," was an AME bishop and a prophetic witness for social justice. "Socialism," he wrote, "like the inspired Carpenter of Nazareth, places more value upon man than it does upon riches. It believes that rights of man are more sacred than the rights of property, believes indeed, that the only sacred thing on earth is a human being. Socialism would bring all the people to participate in the rivalry of life upon a footing of equality, allowing each individual the widest possible range for development of his powers and personality, with freedom to follow wherever his abilities may lead him." [92]

Reverdy Cassius Ransom was born in Flushing, Ohio, on January 4, 1861, just before the outbreak of the Civil War; he died on April 22, 1959, at the age of ninety-eight. Raised in southeastern Ohio, Ransom's most enduring childhood memories were the hardships his mother endured, working as a domestic servant to support her family, and the prejudice and animosity of the white community. His mother hoped that her son would obtain more than the limited education offered by the local segregated schools. Ransom worked at varying jobs, was tutored in various subjects, and eventually enrolled in Wilberforce University in 1881. [93]

At Wilberforce, an AME institution and the oldest "black-controlled" college in the country, Ransom encountered a community he described as "a verification of the Negro's humanity and manhood. It proves that darkest centuries . . . have not been able to rob the Negro of his humanity or destroy within him the image of God." Ransom would always feel himself indebted to Wilberforce, but he felt compelled to expand his educational horizons. With a scholarship and the promise of part-time work, he transferred to Oberlin College. There, instead of educational opportunities and the liberalism for which the school was noted, he encountered discrimination. When segregated eating facilities for black women were introduced, Ransom organized a protest meeting, and the faculty voted to withdraw his scholarship. Returning to Wilberforce, he decided on a program in theological studies and graduated in 1886 with a Bachelor of Divinity. He was ordained as an AME pastor and served a number of churches in western Pennsylvania and Ohio for the next ten years. [94]

Ransom became active in the antilynching campaign, protested the increasing disenfranchisement of African Americans in the South, and urged the church to take a more active role in these struggles. From 1896 until 1905 Ransom was a pastor in Chicago, first at Bethel Church, where he was confronted with the poverty, wretched living conditions, and unemployment facing most African Americans, and he developed a new understanding of the ministry of the church. With the support of such well-known social settlement workers as Jane Addams, Graham Taylor, and Mary McDowell, Ransom looked for a way to move beyond sermons, prayer, and song to "the betterment of humanity and the . . . uplifting of . . . [the] race." In 1900 Ransom, with the financial assistance of the AME church, established the Institutional Church and Settlement House. It created programs for men, women, and children that extended from literary societies to training institutes and an employment bureau. Du Bois commented that it made "the church exist for the people rather than the people for the church." Through the Institutional Church, Ransom became involved in Chicago politics, and he fought those structures, institutions, and persons who exploited the poor. Ransom was particularly disturbed when those who controlled the numbers racket on the South Side tried to extend their influence to black schoolchildren. In response to Ransom's campaign against the racket, the Institutional Church was dynamited and his life was threatened.[95]

Chicago during this period was also the scene of violence against black workers who had been brought from the South by the meat-packing industry as strikebreakers. During a 1902 strike in the Chicago stockyards, Ransom mediated between black and white workers, arguing with union officials that black men "would be quite willing to join the union if permitted, but colored men were laborers, had families to support and wanted jobs, [and they] had no desire to take their jobs or deprive others from bread and butter [for] there were enough jobs for all if black and white workers would agree upon some plan of friendly cooperation." Although Ransom was instrumental in settling the strike, the conflict between black and white workers was not easily resolved.[96]

Ransom traced the tension between blacks and whites to the inability of white workers to recognize that African Americans were workers too, oppressed by the same capitalist system. Furthermore, since socialism was based on the solidarity of the working class, it was not a white phenomenon but a rallying point for all the oppressed. Workers and Socialists alike needed to understand that "while one class of toilers is outraged and oppressed, no man is free. When millions of toilers are degraded, labor is degraded, man is degraded." Black people would embrace socialism only when it could be truly said that socialism recognizes "the unity of the race and the brotherhood of man . . . [and] will accord to each individual the full reward which the exercise of his powers has won, and the right to stand upon an equal plane and share all of the blessings of our common heritage." It seemed to Ransom that, however liberative the socialist message, the reality was that black workers faced a world in which their skills, abilities, and knowledge were good only for work deemed "distasteful to white men." Barred from factories and mills by organized labor, the majority of black workers were still confined to agriculture and domestic service. The only exception, Ransom noted, was the railroad porter, as if the trains traveling across the country were "thought to be his place and plane." Ransom thus concluded that socialism would become a concrete option for African-American people only when Socialists understood the need for solidarity between black and white workers based on a realization of their common goals and enemies, a realization that their destiny as workers was bound together.[97]

In the years that followed, Ransom assumed a number of pastorates, serving the Charles Street AME Church in Boston from 1904 to 1907 and then Bethel AME Church in New York City from 1907 to 1912. In addition, Ransom established a mission church in Manhattan's "Black Tenderloin" district, the Church of Simon of Cyrene, to serve the needs of the poor. He became editor of the *A.M.E. Church Review*, a position he held from 1912 to 1924, the year in which he was elected bishop. Throughout this period of his life, Ransom became increasingly militant on behalf of rights too long denied black Americans. He spoke of the absolute necessity for resistance, not submission, to the politics and religion of the dominant culture, for defiance, not acceptance.[98]

On August 17, 1906, Reverdy Ransom addressed the second annual meeting of the Niagara movement, at Harper's Ferry, West Virginia. The Niagara movement, founded in 1905 at the initiative of W.E.B. Du Bois, consisted of those within the African-American community opposed to what they believed to be the accommodationist policies of Booker T. Washington and his associates. Advocating the principles of the "dignity of labor," "freedom of speech and criticism," "manhood suffrage," "recognition of the principles of human brotherhood as a practical present creed," and eradication of distinctions based on race and color, those who founded the movement intended to "claim for ourselves every single right that belongs to a freeborn American, political, civil, and social; and until we get these rights we will never cease to protest and assail the ears of America." Ransom was active from the beginning; Gayraud Wilmore has dubbed him "the unofficial chaplain of the Niagara movement."[99]

In Ransom's address at Harper's Ferry, titled "The Spirit of John Brown," it was clear that he shared Du Bois's admiration for Brown, a man who had understood the incompatibility of slavery with the word of God. Even though slavery had since been overthrown, Ransom argued, racism continued to reign, unhampered by law, government, or custom. In many senses, black Americans stood alone. One could not expect Republicans or Democrats to take any real interest in the plight of black Americans. Even the Republican Party, which the African-American community had supported for so long, abandoned them whenever it seemed politically expedient. The black community had two options. "The one counsels patient submission to our present humiliations and degradations; it deprecates political activity, ignores or condones the usurpation and denial of our political and constitutional rights, and preaches the doctrine of industrial development and the acquisition of property, while it has no word of protest or condemnation for those who visit upon us all manner of fiendish and inhuman indignities." The other option demands that black people "not submit to being humiliated, degraded and remanded to an inferior place . . .

[and] not believe that those who toil and accumulate will be free to enjoy the fruits of their industry and frugality, if they permit themselves to be shorn of political power." Du Bois recalled that Ransom's speech, more than any other, aroused those who had gathered at Harper's Ferry. He believed, in fact, that it was the eloquence and inspiration of Ransom's address that led to the founding of the National Association for the Advancement of Colored People.[100]

Ransom as pastor, editor of the *A.M.E. Church Review*, and witness for racial justice and equality again and again confronted the limits of the existing political system. In a moving address to the founding members of the NAACP, "Democracy, Disfranchisement, and the Negro," Ransom stressed that democracy as an aspiration for freedom belonged to no one people but embodied the historic struggle of human beings against all forms of tyranny. Those Americans who proclaimed the word *democracy* had to face the contradiction between the affirmation of certain inalienable rights in the Declaration of Independence and the exclusion of African Americans from the development of democracy in America. It was only with the abolition of slavery and the passage of the Fourteenth and Fifteenth Amendments to the U.S. Constitution that black Americans began to hope that democracy would be realized, but the experience of the black community after the Civil War eroded that promise. In the South especially, African Americans were reduced to a "condition of semi-slavery and serfdom." On other occasions Ransom remarked that African Americans faced not only disenfranchisement but the racism of organized labor and the indifference of a nation in which the "lynching of Negroes, or their burning at the stake no longer fills the country with horror." [101]

Racism and the history of the African-American community confronted the apologists for American democracy with the gap between word and deed; the same was true for American Christians. Ransom insisted that the "practical application of Christianity meets a real test every time it is confronted by our American Negro. The Negro here is a standing challenge to the earnestness of its faith, the strength of its courage, and the depth and sincerity of its love." It seemed that the ability of Christian faith to transform human life and modify the behavior of white Christians stopped at the "color line" and if "Jesus wept over Jerusalem, he should have for America an ocean of tears." Christianity, Ransom maintained, should be based on the teachings and practice of Jesus Christ, and there could be no racial component to the articulation of Christian faith. Even though Jesus lived in a world bound by antagonisms rooted in racial and class differences, what distinguished the early Christian community was its ability to overcome such distinctions. Any nation-state that professed itself to be Christian should have "no race problem." But, in point of fact, the self-described Christian nations were the very ones that dealt with racial issues by "rack, torch . . . political disability, social exclusion and by all other means passion and prejudice could devise." From the beginning the United States, which claimed to be "born with the Bible in its hands," compromised its professed ideals over the question of slavery and the status of people of color. Even more profoundly ironic was the very notion of American Christianity, which made a mockery of "the brotherhood of man" with its "hypocritical lips" that spoke of love of Christ and the church as the beloved community of the faithful.[102]

Ransom concluded that one of the tasks of the black church was to confront its white counterpart with its infidelity, its failure to live out the teachings of Christianity. To his own congregation, in particular, he spoke of a church that believed in the "absolute equality" of all persons, irrespective of race or color, and declared that this belief could not under any circumstances be compromised. The church must be a prophetic community that stands for justice and freedom, held together by a shared vision of the United States as "a land where all are free to preserve untarnished the crown of their manhood and womanhood, where neither class, nor blood, nor race shall separate man from his brotherman," in which "our strength is in God, and our unconquerable weapon is faith in the triumph of righteousness and justice among men." In addressing black pastors, Ransom recognized the difficulties of ministry in a society marked by racial hatred and nominal Christianity. At the same time, he saw in the mission of the black church an opportunity to demonstrate the fundamentally liberative nature of the Christian gospel, a gospel not identified with imperialism, racism, and the exploitation of the world in service to a small minority. Rather, as Ransom saw it, the gospel proclaimed "human life and conduct, that find the exaltation of humanity not in triumphant democracy, or the supremacy of race, but in triumphant brotherhood and the supremacy of love." [103]

Religion and Socialism, Race and Class

Marx and Engels in their *Communist Manifesto* rendered a telling judgment: "Christian Socialism is but the Holy Water with which the priest consecrates the heart-burnings of the aristocrat." This indictment by the founders of modern socialism was not shared by all Socialists. Christian Socialists of the Debsian period saw no incompatibility between their Christian beliefs and the espousal of socialism; they accepted the reality of class struggle and believed, as did most Socialists, in the working class as the agency for the establishment of a new social order. They saw their own specific task as converting their fellow Christians to the Socialist cause. The teachings of Christ demanded that Christians battle capitalism and work to create a society in which the ideals of Christianity might be realized. Furthermore, it was apparent to them that Christ stood in opposition to a culturally bound Christianity, especially one that aligned itself with the oppressive forces that must be overthrown. J. E. Franklin summarized their critique: "If the indictment drawn by socialism against our present industrial organization is measurably true; if our competitive system is the fruitful source of poverty, misery, and sin; if the cooperative commonwealth is an ideal that can be approximately attained and brings with it a state of society in which men can actually live the true Christian life; then the Christian church by all its ideals and traditions, should be squarely committed to this movement." [104]

The use of religious language was not limited to Christian Socialists alone. Debs and other Socialists appropriated religious imagery, underscoring the extent to which Socialists, like earlier generations of working-class radicals, pitted a revolutionary Christ against representatives of power and privilege. In answer to those who too quickly reduce the past to theoretical constructs that compartmentalize human experience, who assume that religion belongs to the private realm of human affairs, there were Socialists who rejected the privatization of religion. They declared that religion is more, is as much a manifestation of human wrestlings with the public dimension of life as is politics. Christian Socialists, in particular, viewed an option for socialism as a way of living out politically one's fidelity to the gospel, so that it could truly become good news for the poor and oppressed.

Black Christian Socialists agreed that the establishment of socialism would be a means to bring about the Kingdom of God and to permit a form of the human community no longer based on racial distinctions to flourish. Woodbey and Slater reminded those who would tarnish socialism and the gospel with racism that socialism is international; working-class solidarity transcends race and color, just as Christianity's affirmation of human equality includes all as children of God. To the black community they tried to make it apparent that capitalism robbed people of the fruits of their own labor, set black and white workers against each other, and made a mockery of the democratic republican tradition. Their message was also an implicit condemnation of white Socialists who excluded the black experience and the reality of race as a significant factors in the shaping of American history.

Reverdy Ransom joined Slater and Woodbey in their desire to affirm the unity of oppression based on race and class, but he maintained that class analysis alone could not explain the ongoing history of racism and the racial attitudes and practices of white Americans. If socialism was ever to be a concrete option for black Americans it had to be more than economic and political justice, as important as that might be. It had to be a new social order that understood the meaning of words such as *democracy, brotherhood,* and *equality.* Socialism would have to be part of a visible manifestation of what people could create together once they were no longer limited by class or race. To the black community Ransom preached the importance of drawing strength from the history of the black church and from African-American understandings of the Christian faith, which offered black people a means of confronting the principalities and powers of this life, so eager to deny the world black people had made.

Cornel West writes that the Socialist Party analysis of race and racism subsumed African-American oppression "under the general rubric of working-class exploitation. This viewpoint is logocentric in that it elides and eludes the specificity of Afro-American oppression outside of the workplace; it is reductionistic in that it explains away rather than explains this specificity." Christian Socialists were no exception; white Christian Socialists accommodated themselves to the racist social and political structures of American society, in spite of all their rhetoric to the contrary. James Cone in his study of the Methodist tradition makes an observation that is relevant to a critique of Christian Socialists: one of the central differences between black and white Methodism was the extent to which black people refused to make the experience of conversion coequal with an acceptance of racism and social injustice.[105]

Still, there is an almost natural reaction to engaging in judgment by hindsight. In the historical context, especially evident in the often simplistic analysis of racism offered by Socialists of this period, perhaps it would be too much to expect the Socialist Party to transcend the common racial rhetoric. But it must be remembered that there were Socialists and others sympathetic to the cause of socialism who saw the world differently, from the leaders of the Oklahoma Socialist Party to Harrison, Du Bois, Ransom, Woodbey, and Slater, though Woodbey and Slater shared many of the assumptions of their Socialist comrades about the "race problem." Socialist language, in the final analysis, is insular, limited to the rhetoric of class oppression while it ignores one of the most exploited sectors of the working class, African Americans. Clearly, class as a category of analysis cannot fully explain the realities of oppression and domination in American society. Yet, for all their limitations, Socialists did understand that there was a relationship between racial inequality and how an economy was structured. That is why at this juncture in our history we can learn from black radicals such as Woodbey, Slater, and Ransom, who grounded their analysis of race and class in the experience of black people. Whatever their shortcomings, they far exceeded their contemporaries within the religious community in understanding how the exploitation, misery, and suffering endured by people of color is rooted in the structure of economic life and that Christian faith has something very fundamental to do with values, institutions, programs, and policies that mean life rather than death for people of color.

In the mid-1940s W.E.B. Du Bois wrote a letter to his granddaughter about race relations, trying to help her come to terms with white children. He asked her to remember that as a group "person for person they have had in their lives better food, better homes, better clothes, better training than your little colored friends in Baltimore," but "they are not necessarily better people; they have had better opportunities."[106] These opportunities, which had to do with being white and privileged, were inseparable from the realities of race and class. It was also clear that racism as an ideology was rooted in an exploitative relationship that served the interest of the dominant people and classes by making property rights more important than human rights, that the very language and myths of American democracy were embedded in the protection and exercise of the rights of private property. Ransom, Du Bois, and Harrison again and again denounced a political system that could summarily disenfranchise millions of its citizens while it celebrated the glories of democracy, and inexorably exposed the history of dehumanization and oppression that lurked behind such words as *freedom* and *liberty*. Beyond the impact of racism on varying aspects of civil society was the issue of what happened to the human spirit. Reverdy Ransom equated segregation with degradation, for it diminished not only the quality of life but the realization of human aspirations.[107]

What Marable Manning has so aptly called the "blackwater" dimension of Christian faith was an acknowledgment of pride in being African American, of the mission of the black church as a prophetic witness to the truths of the gospel, and a vision of socialism organically related to the struggle of all people for liberation. It reflected the understanding that human dignity, worth, and community, grounded in Christian faith and practice, can give concrete hope to oppressed people in spite of the forces of the dominant culture, which deny a more egalitarian and participatory vision of society. Socialism became a sustained critique of capitalism on the grounds of its inherent incompatibility with the teachings of Jesus, became a community based on human dignity and worth shared by Christian Socialists black and white. Blackwater was a visible expression of faith that embodied the demands of the Kingdom for justice, freedom, and human liberation.

4

Radical Politics and

Southern Prophets

The Struggle for Racial Equality

On July 5, 1852, Frederick Douglass, abolitionist and former slave, delivered an address, "The Meaning of July Fourth for the Negro," in Rochester, New York. Douglass spoke of the glaring contradictions between America's professed ideals, its "shouts of liberty and equality," and the "gross injustice and cruelty" of which the slave was "the constant victim." He charged that slavery, with all its inhumanity, was given legitimacy by the religion of the Republic, which "favors the rich against the poor; which exalts the proud above the humble; which divides mankind into two classes, tyrants and slaves; which says to the man in chains, *stay there;* and to the oppressor, *oppress on;* it is a religion which may be professed and enjoyed by all the robbers and enslavers of mankind; it makes God a respecter of persons, denies his fatherhood of the race, and tramples in the dust the great truth of the brotherhood of man." [1]

Time has not moderated Douglass's harsh judgment of the hypocrisy of American political and religious life. Racism has shaped the character of national life and thought, and religion has often been enlisted to sanction injustice. Charles Long persuasively argues that dominant people use a cultural language—be it theological, political, or socioeconomic—of "conquest and suppression." The very terms Americans use to describe themselves render oppressed people "invisible" and prevent those who are more free from "seeing themselves as they really are." Christian ethics too often share in this process by accepting definitions of reality that obscure rather than expose the nation's longest and deepest injustice. Racism remains both an American and a Christian dilemma. To envision the world differently, to see ourselves as we really are, and to rethink the role the Christian faith can and must play in the struggle for racial justice are the central concerns of this chapter. Others have made this effort; Douglass was one. Here we will look at the courageous work of some remarkable people who spoke a different, more truthful, and more liberative language in the decades before the civil rights movement. [2]

Dr. Martin Luther King, Jr.'s famous "Letter from Birmingham City Jail," written in 1963, asked the white church and its clergy where Christians had been when black people were being lynched, brutalized, and forced to endure the chains of poverty and discrimination. Joel Williamson, in his study of black-white relations following the Civil War, observes that few southern whites have had the "sensitivity and imagination necessary to put themselves in the place of black people and to understand something of the burden that color carried with it in the South." But there were some.[3]

Howard Kester and Claude Williams were two southern Protestant pastors who attempted to understand the burden of color and to combat a system of domination in which poverty and racism seemed inseparable. They are part of an often untold story of faith in the midst of the violence and bloodshed of the South of the 1930s and 1940s. Interwoven with the life stories of Kester and Williams is the history of the Southern Tenant Farmers' Union and the People's Institute of Applied Religion, interracial organizations dedicated to empowering poor people and bringing about needed sociopolitical change. In addition, they provide a missing chapter in the often bleak history of Christian toleration of racial injustice. While many have pointed out that most adherents of social gospel Christianity ignored racism, few have noted that there were in fact white and black Christians telling the church that such a problem existed. Historians and ethicists, who often write off the history of the South, especially from the rise of white supremacy to the emergence of the civil rights movement, might learn something from poor people and the Christians who stood with them about a different South, a different history, and a different interpretation of Christian faith.

By temperament, background, and experience, Kester and Williams were very different personalities; their lives overlapped, at crucial points as friends, at other times as political opponents. Each in his own way sought to be faithful to Jesus as the bearer of good news to the poor and oppressed. In the process each confronted the contradictions Douglass had denounced nearly a century before, and each forged an alternative language to expose domination and oppression while reaffirming a Christian and American commitment to freedom, justice, and equality.[4]

Howard Kester

Howard Anderson Kester was born on July 21, 1904, in Martinsville, Virginia. He grew up at a time when whites regarded segregation as the only satisfactory means of establishing "proper" relations between blacks and whites, as taken for granted as the disenfranchisement of blacks in Virginia two years before Kester's birth. Between 1889 and 1946, approximately four thousand black men, women, and children were killed by lynch mobs in the United States. As a small boy Kester heard his father and neighbors speak in "hushed tones of lynchings that had taken place in the neighborhood." Kester's Pennsylvania-born father, a fairly successful farmer, was from a Quaker background and became a respected elder in the local Presbyterian church. His life exemplifies Charles Long's analysis of the culture of domination: he never questioned racial segregation, and for a time, he was even a member of the Ku Klux Klan. Yet that same culture contained the seed of another kind of consciousness. From his mother, the daughter of a plantation overseer, who was born just before the outbreak of the Civil War, Kester learned about lost causes. What Kester recalled as a relatively comfortable and tranquil life ended when he was eleven, and his father, after suffering financial setbacks, moved the family to the coal-mining fields of Beckley, West Virginia.[5]

At his baptism, Kester's parents had decided their son should devote his life to the ministry; he grew up convinced he would become a Presbyterian minister. In 1921, with a scholarship from the Presbyterian church, Kester returned to Virginia to attend Lynchburg College. There he became active in the YMCA and made the study of the Bible an important part of his life. For young Kester, Jesus' Sermon on the Mount was a "must system of morality." During the summer of 1923 he joined a YMCA-sponsored student "Pilgrimage of Friendship" to Europe to study the impact of the First World War. Kester came away shaken by the "brutal scars" left by war, moved by the popular desire for peace, and disturbed by European anti-Semitism, which he found similar to American racism. Returning to college, Kester served as director of European Student Relief in the South. In 1924 he organized a student interracial forum and began to discover what "it is to be a Negro in days like this." His dawning awareness of racism was soon coupled with his first exposure to economic contradictions during a summer student pastorate in Thurman, West Virginia. When miners and railroad workers went on strike, he found their complaints justified and took their side. His work on their behalf brought criticism from his home church in Beckley, which had supported his student ministry. With a developing pacifism, questions about established white "solutions" to black-white relations, doubts about the capitalism system, and problems with the institutional church, Kester entered Princeton Seminary in the fall of 1925.[6]

The Presbyterian church of the midtwenties was torn by the controversy raging between modernists and fundamentalists. Princeton Seminary was the home of A. A. Hodge, Benjamin B. Warfield, and J. Gresham Machen, defenders of a "Princeton Theology" based on scriptural literalism, rationalistic epistemology, and a deep pessimism about the possibilities of sociopolitical change. The most articulate spokesperson for fundamentalism at Princeton was Machen, a New Testament scholar who argued that the liberal interpretation of the Christian tradition relinquished everything distinctive about Christianity. To Kester, by now something of a rebel, Princeton seemed a sterile place, out of touch with people and a lived understanding of the Christian faith. The seminary's intolerance of divergent points of view and hostility to any questioning of faith motivated Kester to read "everything I could lay my hands on," seeking answers quite different from those of his teachers. By the end of the year, Kester decided Princeton was not the place where his questions could be answered; those answers would more likely be found in "the lives of common men and women" than in "scholarly treatises." [7]

Kester remained active in the YMCA, pressing it to desegregate its all-white leadership training programs held annually at Blue Ridge, North Carolina. Failing to break the "color line," Kester invited Mary McLeod Bethune, founder of Bethune Cookman College, and George Washington Carver, celebrated scientist of Tuskegee Institute, to speak to the Blue Ridge assembly. Kester's contact with Carver led to an invitation to spend part of the summer of 1926 at Tuskegee, and in the years that followed they became close friends. During that same summer Kester became the first white southerner invited as a "fraternal delegate" to the black YMCA conference held at Kings Mountain, North Carolina. At Blue Ridge Kester not only met Carver but also Alice Harris, a progressive student leader of the Young Women's Christian Association who, like Kester, was in the process of distancing herself from the conservative attitudes of her family. Three weeks after they met they were engaged; eight months later they married. Kester said of Harris that she was a "true friend, a comrade and co-worker." From Tuskegee, Alabama, Kester wrote to his fiancée about some of the changes overcoming him that summer of 1926:

> I look out and see men, rich men, honorable men, capable men leaning over tables planning wreck and ruin to countless thousands yet unborn; I look out and see boys and girls walking leisurely down the road that leads to disaster and ruin; I see old men and women broken in the wheels of industry, crying and in great bitterness; I look out and see Negroes pushed aside, Hindoos driven away, Chinese maltreated because their skin is not white. I see the misery and poverty in countless cities and hear the cry of little children for bread, and I grow weary and downcast. What is to be done? How am I to use my life, are questions I have asked myself thousands of times.[8]

In the fall he enrolled in Vanderbilt University's School of Religion, supporting himself as assistant secretary for the university's YMCA. Vanderbilt proved a far more supportive environment than Princeton, but again there were very definite limits for those who questioned the status quo. When Kester organized an interracial group to protest Western intervention in China, the university fired him from his job with the YMCA. Meanwhile, as an expression of belief in the power of nonviolence, he had joined the Fellowship of Reconciliation. Paul Jones, secretary of the FOR, offered Kester a job as secretary for its youth section; he wrote to Alice Harris that the job was "a real challenge to you and me to really lay our lives down in real service." [9]

Kester dropped out of seminary and after their marriage Alice and Howard moved to the New York area. For two years Kester crisscrossed the country, speaking and organizing, but all the while, he had the haunting feeling that he belonged back in the South. He convinced the FOR that it needed a secretary in the South, and he was appointed to a part-time position. In the fall of 1929 he reenrolled at Vanderbilt's School of Religion, where he came under the influence of Alva Taylor, a latter-day social gospel advocate and secretary of the Disciples of Christ's influential Board of Temperance and Social Welfare, who "brought Jesus to life and fitted Him into the picture of today." Here, Kester first encountered Claude Williams and other southern radicals who were to play an important role in his rethinking of the Christian faith. Kester's responsibilities for the FOR were directed toward building interracial student groups. He traveled throughout the South holding interracial conferences in Birmingham, Atlanta, Jackson, and elsewhere, often facing hostile whites and indifferent Christian ministers. Kester desperately wanted to reach such people; he believed that he had a particular responsibility to help whites understand the problems facing black people and how racism was embedded in the economic and political structures that governed everyday life. His sociopolitical awareness grew with his reading of the anarchism of Kropotkin, the nonviolence of Tolstoy and Gandhi, and the economic analysis of Marx, Engels, and Lenin. But most of all, Kester was drawn to the message of the biblical prophets, especially Amos, and to the life of Jesus and the witness of the early Christian community.[10]

By this time, Kester was not alone. In addition to friends such as Carver, Taylor, and Williams, through the FOR he met Norman Thomas and Reinhold Niebuhr, leaders of a generation of increasingly radicalized Christians. Thomas, raised in a comfortable, well-established Presbyterian parish, was an unlikely future presidential candidate for the Socialist Party. His father, like generations before him, was a Presbyterian minister, staunchly Republican, yet relatively open-minded. After graduating from Princeton and Union Theological Seminary, Thomas was ordained a Presbyterian minister and assigned to an immigrant parish in East Harlem, New York. His parish experience forced him to confront social, economic, and political realities for which his background had ill prepared him. The outbreak of the First World War, especially the U.S. entry into the war in April of 1917, tested Thomas's pacifist belief that war was a fundamental denial of the Christian tradition, and he responded by joining a tiny band of antiwar clergy. Thomas's work defending the religious and political rights of conscientious objectors drew him to the Socialist Party, which in April, 1917, declared "its unalterable opposition to the war just declared by the government of the United States." Thomas joined the party in 1918; ten years later he became its presidential candidate.[11]

Thomas's leadership of the Socialist Party indicated a gradual shift in its place in American life. Unlike his predecessor, Eugene V. Debs, Thomas had come to socialism not through involvement with the rank and file of the labor movement but out of moral and religious convictions. While Debs addressed himself to the working class and spoke in ways working-class people could

Mother Jones
and Terence Powderly.
*Courtesy of the Department of
Archives and Manuscripts,
Catholic University of America,
Washington, D.C.*

Top: Reverdy C. Ransom.
Courtesy of the Archives and
Special Collections, Wilberforce
University, Wilberforce,
Ohio.

Left: Frances E. Willard.
Courtesy of the Frances E.
Willard Memorial Library,
Evanston, Illinois.

Top: Howard Kester
(foreground), c. 1932.
*Courtesy of the Southern
Historical Collection,
Manuscripts Department,
University of North Carolina,
Chapel Hill.*

Right: Claude Williams,
c. 1975. *Courtesy of the
Archives of Labor and Urban
Affairs, Wayne State University,
Detroit, Michigan.*

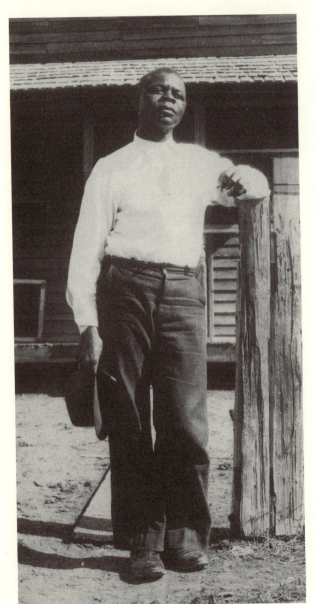

E. B. McKinney.
*Courtesy of the Southern
Historical Collection,
Manuscripts Department,
University of North Carolina,
Chapel Hill.*

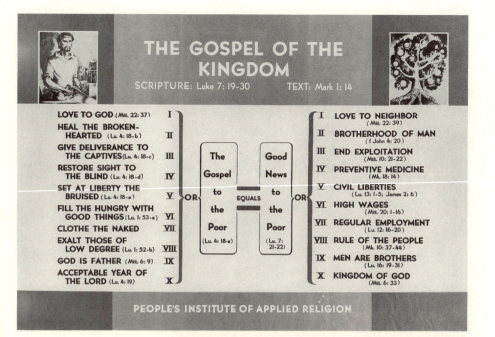

Top: "The Gospel of the Kingdom," a People's Institute of Applied Religion poster. *Courtesy of the Archives of Labor and Urban Affairs, Wayne State University, Detroit, Michigan.*

Right: Dorothy Day and A. J. Muste in Union Square, New York, at antiwar demonstration, November 6, 1965. *Courtesy of Tom Cornel and the Department of Archives, Memorial Library, Marquette University, Milwaukee, Wisconsin. Photo by Ben Fernandez.*

Harry F. Ward, c. 1941.
*Courtesy of Special
Collections, Union Theo-
logical Seminary, New York,
New York.*

understand, Thomas attracted middle-class reformers and intellectuals and gave socialism a religious sanction. When the Great Depression moved certain segments of the Protestant community to the left, many were attracted to the Socialist Party.

The most visible manifestation of the leftward shift among Protestants was the Fellowship of Socialist Christians, founded in 1931 under the leadership of Reinhold Niebuhr. Stressing the gulf between Christianity and capitalistic individualism, as well as the inability of liberal Christianity to deal with the social upheaval of the Depression, the FSC maintained that "a Christian ethic is most adequately expressed and effectively applied in our society in socialist terms." Unlike the earlier social gospel, the FSC saw the limitations of moral suasion and of Christian categories that ignored class conflict and the problems of power. Some found in Marxism an instrument of societal analysis and a way of understanding how middle-class Christianity often provided ideological and institutional justification of a capitalist society. They believed, along with many other Americans, that the nation's economic system was bankrupt and that socialism provided the only viable democratic alternative. Accordingly, the FSC worked with Thomas for a revitalized Socialist Party. In a 1934 *World Tomorrow* questionnaire, 28 percent of the over twenty thousand clerical respondents advocated socialism as the solution to the problems confronting the nation. Over one-half the clergy who replied favored a drastic reform of capitalism. Niebuhr commented, with some exaggeration, that "probably the church of no other country in the world would produce so large a number taking a completely revolutionary position." Regardless of the American church's complicity with the existing system, the questionnaire demonstrated, to Niebuhr's satisfaction, that the church "harbored a very healthy Left minority." [12]

Kester, one of those Protestants who found in Thomas and Niebuhr a bridge to socialism, joined the party in October, 1931, and with five other Socialists set up a party local in Nashville, Tennessee, with himself as secretary. From the beginning, the Nashville local was interracial. Its members believed that the only possible Socialist policy, in the South or anywhere else, was working-class solidarity, receiving "Negroes as genuine comrades." Socialism, for Kester, was a "philosophy of equality" that admitted no taint of discrimination. In addition to his role as secretary of the Nashville local, Kester served as chairperson of the state executive committee, drafted the Socialist Party of Tennessee's state constitution, and ran an unsuccessful congressional campaign in 1932 on the Socialist ticket. His activity on behalf of working people earned him threats against his life, which only solidified his belief in the necessity of radical overhaul of the capitalism system. He maintained that "within the framework of capitalistic society any attempt to build a decent world is a dream and an illusion and therefore until capitalistic society is uprooted, any efforts to achieve anything that even remotely resembles the Good Life are doomed to failure. . . . To attempt to emancipate the mass of white and Negro workers in the South, employed in mill, mine, farm and factory only through the methods of goodwill, moral suasion, and education is to invite the continued exploitation, misery, and suffering of generations yet unborn." [13]

Kester reached this conclusion through reading, reflection, and experience—especially eighteen months working on behalf of striking workers in Wilder, Tennessee, in the Cumberland region in 1932–1933. From his boyhood in West Virginia Kester knew well the conditions miners faced, but Wilder was the "worst I ever saw." It was a company town controlled by the Fentress Coal and Coke Company. Three hundred miners and their families were served by five water pumps, and the company store charged food prices two to three times higher than independently owned stores, making indebtedness to the company a fact of life. In the decade preceding the strike, miners were required to sign "yellow-dog" contracts vowing never to join a union or engage in strikes against the company. Nevertheless in June, 1931, the miners successfully organized a United Mine Workers local and won a contract. During the spring of 1932, however, the company fired the miners who had organized the union and began cutting wages. By May, there had been three wage cuts, amounting to almost half the 1931 wages. After a fourth wage cut, this one 20 percent, the miners went out on strike. All attempts to meet with mine operators were turned down, and the company refused to submit the strike to arbitration. In November, the company persuaded the governor to call in the state militia, and, wrote Kester, "the strikers were intimidated, beaten and brutalized by the guards in an effort to get them to return to the mines." The guards functioned as employees, setting up machine guns to protect the private property of Fentress Coal and Coke Company. In addition to the use of the state troops, the company resorted to injunctions against union leaders, violence, and scabs. [14]

Into this setting came Alice and Howard Kester, as directors of the Wilder Emergency Relief Committee, to distribute food and clothing collected by the Socialist Party and church groups. Before the committee was established, the only so-called relief program was run by the Red Cross under the control of the wife of the superintendent of the mines, who gave out flour and cloth only to those who supported the coal company. The Kesters set about trying to meet the needs of the striking workers and their families, coordinating their work with the union. Meanwhile, the strike dragged on. At every turn the company was guilty of bad faith, finally resorting to murdering strike leaders. In April, 1933, Barney Graham, president of the UMW local, was killed by company "thugs." "Ten bullets had entered his body from three types of guns," Kester wrote. "His head had been beaten in with the butt of a gun." Coal company guards stood over his body with a machine gun to keep the people away. At Graham's funeral Kester said, "I loved him as a brother, not alone for his own worth, but for his place in the leadership of America's toiling millions." Kester was deeply moved by the words of a mountain preacher, Brother Johnson, who officiated with him at the funeral. As Johnson saw it Graham was killed because he wanted to change things, and those who killed him were "the same kind of people—coal operators, thieves and robbers of women and little children, company thugs, and hired gunman—that murdered Jesus Christ. They crucified Christ because he was a friend to the poor man and because he stood up against the rich and powerful men of his day. Jesus wanted to change things in his day and they killed him. They killed Barney Graham because he wanted to change things in Wilder Hollow." Understandably, this experience brought the Kesters "bitterness and despair," but they continued to work with the miners and their families after the strike was broken, helping workers evicted from company shacks to relocate in Cumberland Homesteads, a program of the Resettlement Administration of Franklin Roosevelt's New Deal.[15]

The Wilder experience and Kester's own reading of the "signs of the times" persuaded him that the FOR should join forces with those seeking revolutionary change. Such a commitment was nothing less than acceptance of "the historic position of Jesus who definitely recognized the class struggle and set his face steadfastly against the oppressors of the poor, the weak and the disinherited." This shift in priorities led Kester to reconsider his commitment to nonviolence. For Kester and other Socialist members of the FOR, the tension between socialism and pacifism climaxed with the resignation of J. B. Matthews, executive secretary of the FOR. Matthews, more than any religious figure of the 1930s, represented the extremes of what Murray Kempton has called "multiple revelations." From a small town in Kentucky he traveled a path that led from missionary evangelist to pacifist, radical Socialist, and avowed revolutionary. Matthews came to question FOR policy; he challenged the religious character of the FOR and argued that violence was inevitable in the emerging confrontation between labor and capital. Finally, he resigned in 1933. In the wake of his resignation, the FOR canvassed its membership on the role of violence in the creation of a just social order; the results reaffirmed the organization's rejection of the use of violence, even in the pursuit of economic justice. It would "agitate, educate, and organize" to support workers' struggle for change, but always in a "non-warlike" manner.[16]

But Kester, Niebuhr, and some other members of the FOR had concluded that the injustices of capitalism could be not abolished by moral suasion. Niebuhr, in particular, argued that a Christian and Marxist reading of human and political realities called pacifism into question. The English Marxist John Strachey proclaimed that "the capitalist system is dying and cannot be revived." The latter half of 1933 witnessed the "largest number of work stoppages since 1921." Roosevelt's New Deal had not altered the bread lines, unemployment, or the widening differences between rich and poor. Given the depth of the crisis, Christian radicals read Fascist portents for the future unless some real reversals took place in American society. What was happening to the international Socialist movement intensified this sense of urgency. Hitler was firmly in power and the largest Socialist Party in Europe had been crushed without resistance. Then in 1934 Austrian fascism came to fruition with an abortive insurrection by Austrian workers and the eventual outlawing of the Austrian Social Democratic Party.[17]

In this context the FOR split, and Kester, with other Socialists, left the organization, feeling he could not continue as the southern secretary. Many of those who had supported his work did not want it to end, however. They organized the Committee on Economic and Racial Justice with Niebuhr as chairperson and Kester as executive secretary, a position he would hold from 1934 to 1941. Also in 1934 Kester received requests from Ward Rodgers, an old Vanderbilt friend, and Harry L. Mitchell to join them in building the Southern Tenant Farmers' Union. When he and Kester met, Mitchell remembered Kester was "wearing a pellet of cyanide on a chain around his neck." He had just completed an NAACP investigation of the savage lynching of a young black man, Claude Neal, in Marianna, Florida. He would eventually investigate twenty-five other lynchings for the NAACP, the American Civil Liberties Union, and the Workers Defense League. On this particular occasion he had stayed overnight with his old friend George Washington Carver on his way to Arkansas. Carver had made the cyanide pellet chain, advising Kester to use it if he found himself in a situation where he was to be tortured.[18]

Claude Williams

Claude Clossie Williams was born on June 16, 1895, near Union City, Tennessee, not far from the borders of Missouri and Kentucky. He and his family were sharecroppers and his earliest memories were of poverty, "kivver-to-kivver" biblical fundamentalism, and racism, for his father had taught him to believe black people were not really human beings. Until his teens he thought that "Damrepublican," like "Damyankee," was but one word. His family was a member of the Cumberland Presbyterian church, which was a product of the revivals that had swept through Kentucky and Tennessee in the early nineteenth century. Cumberland Presbyterians disagreed with the "fatalistic" tenor of the Westminster Confession of Faith and the need for an educated clergy, depending instead on the Bible and the outpouring of the spirit.[19]

When Williams was eleven years of age the majority of the Cumberland Presbyterian churches voted to merge with the Presbyterian Church, U.S.A. Only a conservative minority elected to maintain their separate identity; the Williams family's church stayed with this minority. Growing up, Williams felt that the fires of hell were as real as the glory of heaven. With no more than an eighth-grade education, Williams's life was bounded by work in the fields and jobs on the railroad and the Mississippi River boats. In 1916 he enlisted in the army; three years later, unable to decide whether or not to become a minister, he reenlisted. In 1921, his mind made up, he entered Bethel College with the help of a scholarship from the Cumberland Presbyterian church. While

Howard Kester was wrestling at Princeton with the limitations of the established church, Williams was taking for granted biblical literalism, orthodox theology, and a conservative approach to sociopolitical change. Yet Williams was impressed with the early church fathers' condemnations of wealth and privilege and moved by the personal vitality of the prophets.

At Bethel he met Joyce King, a descendant of the founders of the Cumberland Presbyterian church, who was preparing to become a missionary. She too came from rural Missouri and had a fundamentalist approach to Christianity. With little money and no support from the "old men who ruled" Bethel College, Joyce and Claude were married. By the time Claude Williams completed his studies in 1924, both he and Joyce had moved beyond the strictures of their families' church. Williams applied for a pastorate with the Presbyterian Church, U.S.A., and was appointed to serve six churches in Auburntown, Lebanon, and Watertown, Tennessee, not far from Nashville.[20]

Williams was a successful preacher. He preached "to save their never-dying, ever-precious souls from the devil's hell eternal," dutifully catered to his better-off parishioners, and gained a reputation as a scholar and orator who "started where Bill Sunday left off." Yet Williams was more than a simple country preacher. He possessed an almost photographic memory, an inquisitive mind, and a restless spirit—all eventually bound to raise doubts about a world circumscribed by a fundamentalist understanding of Scripture and life. Haunted by the demands Jesus placed on those who sought to follow him and an almost innate sympathy for the poor and dispossessed, he wanted to learn more.[21]

His life was never the same after he purchased a copy of *The Modern Use of the Bible*, by Harry Emerson Fosdick. That evening he and Joyce stayed up half the night working through what Fosdick had to say about the Bible, biblical criticism, and Jesus of Nazareth. Fosdick had thought that his approach to Scripture would be "distasteful to those bound by a theory of literal inerrancy in their approach to the Bible," but Williams experienced instead a feeling of liberation, a discovery of a God of life concerned more about hunger and oppression than the streets of heaven. Williams asked his church board for a leave of absence and in the summer of 1927 started taking summer courses at Vanderbilt University's School of Religion. Like Kester, he came under the influence of Alva Taylor and began to wrestle with liberal theology, the social dimensions of the gospel, and the centrality of Jesus' proclamation of the Kingdom of God. Taylor "had a way of removing the theological debris from the Son of Man under which he's been buried for all these centuries and making him appear human," Williams recalled later.[22]

At Vanderbilt, Williams also met Howard Kester, Ward Rodgers, and Don West, who were all active in union organizing and socialist politics. Through his contact with Kester, Williams attended his first interracial conference, held in Waveland, Mississippi, in 1928. Forced to deal with people not as stereotypes or racist abstractions but as concrete human beings, Williams felt a conversion that forever changed his understanding of black-white relations. His experience at Waveland, his changing attitudes toward fundamentalism, and his growing conviction of the importance of building the Kingdom by feeding the hungry and clothing the naked brought him into conflict with church leaders. Through a friend he learned of a parish in Paris, Arkansas, a small mining community in the west-central part of the state. In July, 1930, he was appointed pastor of the First Presbyterian Church, where he would remain for the next four years. Those were decisive years as Williams became an articulate, prophetic voice on behalf of poor and marginalized people, labeled "the South's most hated preacher" because of his commitment to social justice and racial equality.[23]

Williams assumed his pastorate hoping to develop a new type of ministry, one sensitive to the social and economic demands of the gospel. What he discovered was a "dead" church with a dwindling congregation, in the hands of people unresponsive to the needs of the community. The onset of the Depression had increased the problems facing the poor. The town had no organized program to deal with hunger, unemployment was especially high among the miners, and black and white tenant farmers lived a borderline existence on surrounding plantations. The town had no parks or library, and the only place young people could meet was the local pool hall. To create programs for the young, Williams transformed an unused wing of the church into a recreation center, with its own pool table, reading room, and social activities. An empty lot next to the church became a playground for basketball, baseball, and volleyball. Discussion groups were formed in which young people felt free to explore everything from sexual equality to war and peace. Gradually the church became a place where not only young but those traditionally excluded, miners and poor people, felt at home. One miner observed:

> When I came to Paris ten years ago the church was so dead that scarcely anyone realized it was present. Some way I started to come to the door to listen after Preacher Williams. I stood outside because I doubted preachers and the churches. Finally, I became so interested that I got closer. After a sermon on Sunday, we talked about it all week at the mine. . . . No matter what time of day or night, if someone came for help or information, he would respond. He would take stuff out of his own typewriter, and do work for others first. Men would be talking in the streets, and run up against something they wanted to know. Someone would say, "Well, let's go to the preacher to find out." Negroes have stopped me and told me how fine Williams was. He teaches young people to think for themselves.[24]

As he gained the miners' confidence, Williams was asked to help them reestablish a union. In the late 1920s there had been a local of the United Mine Workers, but it was crushed during a strike in 1927, which left in its wake dead miners and wages cut from $8 to $3.50 a day. By the early 1930s a family of five was living on less than $10 a week. In May, 1932, the local union was reorganized, and UMW District 21, which extended from western Arkansas to eastern Oklahoma, called a strike for union recognition. Claude and Joyce Williams devoted all their time and energy to supporting the striking miners and their families. Williams traveled thousands of miles throughout Arkansas and Oklahoma speaking on behalf of strikers. By now thoroughly committed to a Christian vision of justice and liberation, he told the miners: "You will not find true Christianity in most churches, but you will find it in a miners' union hall. I have seen it and tested it in my contact with the rank and file of the United Mine Workers throughout the field. The union is the only thing potentially stronger than the satanic system of capitalism. It is the living expression of the brotherhood of man, of the humble poor people who are the elect of God." [25]

Williams established contact not only with miners but with tenant farmers and sharecroppers. Near the end of the strike he helped organize one of the largest mass demonstrations by workers ever seen in the Southwest. The miners and their supporters, with donated trucks and cars, created a procession of working people that took over an hour to pass in front of the Herald-Tribune Building in Fort Smith, Arkansas. In the end, the strikers won union recognition, but many felt that their grievances about working conditions; lack of insurance against sickness, injury, and death; and continued low wages were not being addressed by John L. Lewis and the leadership of the UMW. Since the union contract agreed upon by the president of District 21 had been signed without consulting rank-and-file miners, Williams fought on their behalf for a reorganized local with autonomy within the UMW. Although workers filed for autonomy under section 7A of the National Industrial Recovery Act and overwhelmingly voted for autonomy, mine operators, the National Recovery Administration, and the UMW worked together to refuse them recognition. UMW leaders threatened Williams with physical violence if he continued to support the miners' cause. [26]

While Williams became an honorary member of the local miners' union, business and professional leaders made sure that he no longer received any financial support for the church. As traditional backing dried up, the young people and workers became more active in the church's ministry to the poor and oppressed. The community needed a center where union meetings could take place, farmers and workers could establish solidarity, programs could be launched to deal with black-white relations, and the social evils of industry could be debated. Just as important, the community needed a gymnasium and a house of worship sensitive to the needs of working people. Late in the summer of 1932 construction began on "the Proletarian Church and Labor Temple" on a half acre of land next to the church. People of the community donated labor, and the Williamses used all their savings, sold their car, and borrowed money against a government certificate. The purposes of the Proletarian Church and Labor Temple, according to Williams, were to "demonstrate the solidarity of labor, the independence of workers; that Labor can create its own institutions under the most adverse conditions," and to demonstrate that Christian faith, not marred by distinctions of race and class, affirmed the dignity of labor. By "seeking the Kingdom of God, we are to seek to change the conditions which give rise to want, suffering, insecurity and crime." The Labor Temple was a challenge to the church and organized labor to work for the redistribution of wealth and a more democratic society. It also challenged workers and farmers to create forms of political action that would deprive the "unscrupulous industrialists who live as parasites upon society" of power over the political life of the country.[27]

By now Williams had forged out of his experience an understanding of Christian responsibility, a political theology quite different from the social gospel popular among concerned Christians removed from such realities. One morning Williams preached a sermon called "The Dark Lines in God's Face." He told coal miners and sharecroppers that he saw "dark lines on God's face because I saw them in the faces of His children. I saw them in the wrinkled brows of sharecropper-mothers and in the glassy eyes and scrawny bodies of their babies. I saw them in the old bodies of young coal miners and in the broken bodies—and faces—of older ones. I knew that injustice had put dark lines in God's face. I knew that they were the same acts of injustice that put them in the faces of His children." [28]

Williams's commitment to such people brought problems with the union as well as with the establishment. Eleven UMW locals voted for a checkoff of a dollar per miner to help finance the Labor Temple; fifty-two hundred workers backed the action, with only one dissenting vote. Officials of the UMW, however, decided the checkoff was unconstitutional and denounced Williams as a meddling preacher. Local pastors, too, were alarmed by his preaching, personal life-style, and attractiveness to the young people of the community. The pillars of the church were even more disturbed by their loss of leadership, Williams's support of workers, and especially by his preaching against racism. Williams courageously incorporated into the service a prayer that asked God's forgiveness of a guilty nation that tolerated lynching, "the practice of vile mob murder of men." [29]

The straw that broke the proverbial camel's back was Williams's plan for a "New Era Forum" in which outside speakers would address topics of labor, race, and war. In the spring of 1934 a minority of eleven persons petitioned the Presbytery of Fort Smith to dissolve the relationship between Williams and the church, charging the pastor with dereliction of his duties, espousal of communism, and preaching religious views that deviated from established church teachings. Aided by the National Religion and Labor Foundation, headed by Willard Uphaus, Williams gained national publicity in his effort to maintain his parish. Support came from over twenty-eight organizations, most of them local unions. Miners in the Denning coalfields stated that they had known Williams for three years and found him to be "a man of courage, faith, devotion, ability, influence, and integrity, a man of power; a man that men can and do love and respect; a tireless worker; a Christian after Christ; a leader and a gentleman. . . . It is apparent that he is being removed from the church of his choice, because of his sympathies for the man with the hoe, and the shovel, and the plow." A farmer added that those who opposed Williams were "the old-time politicians, the Chamber of Commerce, Kiwanis, hangers on." It was all in vain.[30]

The processing of the case against Williams was riddled with irregularities; the presbytery never addressed the merit of the charges against him. Williams had given four years of his life and sacrificed, as he said, "money, time, labor, reputation, economic security of my family, health—everything," but he was dismissed. A fellow Presbyterian pastor, a southerner himself, son of a Confederate soldier, wrote to the head of the Presbyterian Board of Missions that all Williams was guilty of was preaching the "social gospel of Jesus." Williams had been removed, this minister felt, because he challenged the "best people"—those who wanted a minister to have "no political, or social opinions, at least which conflict with the 'large contributors' of the congregation. He is expected to deal in platitudes. His pastoral duties are to be merely perfunctory duties [and] when he is otherwise, he is dangerous and the local Pharisees seek to destroy him." [31]

After his dismissal, Williams reflected on what it meant to take "Jesus seriously." He concluded that following Jesus entailed taking stands at variance with what was considered Christian practice, and he developed six criteria of loyalty to Jesus:

(1) "If I believe in Jesus of Nazareth, I cannot believe in imperialist war." He noted that he had resigned his reserve officer's commission and felt that patriotism and the flag were really code words for imperialism and profits. Historically, it seemed, the church had violated its own principles, legitimating everything from Constantine to "the militarized Boy Scouts." In sanctioning war the church ceased to be a disciple of the "murdered Nazarene" and became instead "the murderers of the Nazarene."

(2) "If I believe in Jesus of Nazareth, I cannot believe in capital punishment."

(3) "If I believe in Jesus of Nazareth, I cannot believe in our present capitalist practice." Capitalism was an order founded on "acquisitiveness, the profit motive, competition, selfish ambition, all from the basic sin, human greed." The Sermon on the Mount turned the capitalist world upside down, affirming the solidarity of all races, human brotherhood, love, and cooperation. It seemed difficult to reconcile the breadlines and starving people with the luxury of Park Avenue and debutantes. Christians who had adapted the gospel to exploitation had created a "tommy-rot" gospel. It was "not good news to the poor, it does not release the prisoners of war, it does not send away free those whom tyranny has crushed." The Morgans, Phelpses,

Vanderbilts, Rockefellers, Dukes had "robbed the consumer, exploited the worker, wasted the natural resources and drained the wealth of the nation into their powerful coffers. They have conducted Homestead, Ludlow, Harlen and Franklin massacres; led us into war to save the world from democracy; loaned our marines to supervise their Nicaragua elections; enslaved the Cubans, the Haitians, the Filipinos, the Puerto Ricans and to a lesser degree, the Mexicans and the Chinese." Why, then, he asked, was he forced to preach about such inconsequential things as the length of women's dresses, or smoking and playing cards, when capitalists sent millions into "premature graves because of economic servitude."

(4) "If I believe in Jesus of Nazareth, I cannot believe in race prejudice and race discrimination."

(5) "If I believe in Jesus of Nazareth, I cannot believe in class barriers."

(6) "If I believe in Jesus of Nazareth, I cannot believe in the mores of society, the traditions of the elders or southern provincialism." For Williams it was impossible to identify Jesus with either racial superiority or "bourgeois respectability"; he must instead acknowledge a Jesus who "identified himself with the masses, and gave his life in an attempt to establish a righteous religion upon the earth." [32]

When the decision was made to remove him, Williams was told to vacate the manse. He had no resources to support his family; the church still owed him more than two thousand dollars in back salary. After leaving Paris, Claude and Joyce Williams lived with uncertainty, not sure where the next dollar would come from. Sometimes it came from friends, such as Willard Uphaus and the National Religion and Labor Foundation, or from money raised on speaking tours in places like New York, or even from those whose lives were more marginalized than their own: tenant farmers, miners, the unemployed. They finally settled in Fort Smith, Arkansas, where Williams hoped to establish a school for workers with classes in the history of trade unions, economics, politics, and prophetic Christianity. Just as important would be practical courses in the tactics of union organizing and the empowerment of people for action.

Before the school opened, Williams became involved in the organizing efforts of the Workers Alliance. A friend of his, Horace Bryan, a union organizer who had assisted his attempt to establish miners' autonomy within the UMW, was leading a strike of unemployed workers. At the time the unemployed were earning thirty cents an hour on government relief projects. Arkansas state authorities, who administered the federal funds, decided to cut these wages to twenty cents an hour to coincide with a reduction in wages of miners, whose union contract was up for renewal. When the unemployed responded with a strike, Bryan was arrested and Williams was asked to take his place. He led demonstrations and hunger marches throughout the Fort Smith area; during a protest meeting, as a fellow preacher led the strikers in prayer, Williams was arrested and thrown in jail. He was found guilty of the charges and fined a hundred dollars, and he spent a month in jail before he was able to make bail.

Jail became for Williams a "postgraduate course in the pain of the despised and rejected." Like Dr. King a quarter of a century later, he wondered about the readiness of the institutional church and its clergy to compromise the gospel for the sake of comfort and privilege. Williams asked why it was that those who were called Communists were more apt to side with the poor than were Christians, whose faith was founded on the life and teachings of an assassinated prophet. Upon his release from jail, Williams and his family moved to Little Rock, Arkansas, to escape vigilantes. There, Williams finally established a center for workers' education, the New Era School of Social Action and Prophetic Religion. Supported by Socialists and Communists as well as the leadership of the Southern Tenant Farmers' Union and the Workers Alliance, the school became a training center for black and white labor organizers throughout the state of Arkansas. Pitting himself against the established jim crow of Little Rock, Williams became active in the organizing efforts of both the Workers Alliance and the STFU. By the mid-1930s, he had joined the Socialist Party, was a member of the Arkansas State Executive Committee, and ran for the Senate on the Socialist Party ticket in the 1936 election. Always primarily committed to the poor as people, he was wary of a "middle-of-the-road" brand of southern socialism that substituted compromised policies and elitist posturing for revolutionary commitment. As he put it, "Southern Socialism and a Quaker Prayer meeting must no longer be synonymous terms." [33]

Southern Tenant Farmers' Union

The South of the 1930s represented the changing face of American agriculture. Prior to the Civil War, two-thirds of the labor force was engaged in agriculture. By 1880 that figure was reduced to one-half, and 37 percent of those people were tenant farmers. Behind the shrinking number of farmers who did own land were the bank, with its control of mortgages, and the merchants, sources of credit for the farmers but often themselves indebted to the banks. In the South the percentage of the landless increased with each passing decade; by 1920 tenancy reached 49.6 percent, a decade later 55.5 percent. The major crop was still "King Cotton" and over 60 percent of those involved in cotton production were tenants. In some states the percentage of tenant farmers was very high; it was 72 percent in Mississippi, for example. About 60 percent of southern tenant farmers were white, and 40 percent black. Two kinds of tenancy were common: share tenants had their own farm tools and animals and paid a set amount of the money they earned for the use of the land; sharecroppers farmed on "halves," half of the proceeds going to the landlord, who furnished everything from housing to seed. The system bred dependency and poverty. Inadequate housing, poor health, and a meager diet were the lot for most sharecroppers, the majority of whom were black, and their marginal existence, subject to the whim of the landlord, was worsened by Roosevelt's New Deal for agriculture. The Agricultural Adjustment Act of 1933 aided southern planters by providing "benefit payments" for crop acreage reduction. According to Jerold S. Auerbach, by directing payments for reduced acreage to the landlords, the AAA policy "tended to drive sharecroppers and tenant farmers from the land, to lower their status still further, or to reinforce their subservience." Their situation was most vividly captured by Erskine Caldwell: "In parts of the South human existence has reached its lowest depths. Children are seen deformed by nature and malnutrition; women in rags beg for pennies; and men are so hungry that many of them eat snakes, cow dung, and clay. These are the unknown people of today, the tenant farmer of the South. These are the people who hide their nakedness behind trees when a stranger wanders off the road. There is hunger in their eyes as well as in their bellies." [34]

Into this explosive situation came the Southern Tenant Farmers' Union, formed in July, 1934, in Tyronza, Arkansas, through the organizing efforts of two Socialists, Harry L. Mitchell and Clay East. Mitchell, the son of a Tennessee tenant farmer, became a Socialist through his reading of socialist tracts and the work of Upton Sinclair. In the late twenties, he moved to Tyronza and opened a small dry-cleaning business. Here he met Clay East, who ran a gasoline station and whose family had been among the early settlers of eastern Arkansas. Mitchell introduced East to Sinclair's writings and to Oscar Ameringer's *American Guardian*, an Oklahoma socialist newspaper. After hearing a speech by Norman Thomas in Memphis, Tennessee, during his 1932 presidential campaign, the two men formed a local of the Socialist Party in Tyronza. They met with Thomas on a number of occasions, showing him firsthand the conditions facing sharecroppers and tenant farmers. Thomas encouraged them to organize. Tyronza was part of the cotton-growing delta counties of eastern Arkansas, where the norm was large plantations, often owned by absentee owners who left the running of the plantation to hired managers and "riding bosses." The first local of the STFU was formed at a meeting in a dilapidated one-room schoolhouse in Sunnyside, Arkansas, near Fairview Plantation. Hiram Norcross, a St. Louis lawyer, had recently purchased the plantation and evicted a number of sharecropper families that had received more credit from his company store than he deemed warranted.

Mitchell and Clay met with eleven white and seven black sharecroppers, most of whom either worked on the Norcross plantation or had recently been evicted. At that meeting, an older black man recalled other attempts of black people to form their own unions; each time they had been broken by planters and the law. He particularly reminded those present of the Massacre of 1919 in Elaine, Arkansas, in Phillips County, a cotton-growing region in east-central Arkansas, not far from the Mississippi border. Black sharecroppers had organized their own union, the Progressive Farmers and Household Union of America. They were particularly frustrated over the low prices they received for the cotton they produced for plantation owners, even though cotton prices were soaring, and the high charges they had to pay for the supplies they purchased from local merchants. One of the union's circulars declared: "The time is at hand that all men, all nations and tongues must receive a just reward. This union wants to know why it is that the laborers cannot control their just earnings." The union decided to hire a lawyer to obtain an exact statement of their accounts and contemplated work stoppages and charging the landlords with peonage. White reaction to the organized resistance of black people bordered on hysteria. An exchange of gunfire took place after whites attempted to break up a union meeting at a local church. This precipitated attacks on black people throughout the county as plantation owners called for reprisals and armed whites from surrounding states poured in to help put down the supposed "insurrection." Federal troops were summoned, and a thousand black men and women were rounded up and placed in a stockade. When it was over, five whites and an unknown number of black people (estimates varied from twenty-five to several hundred) had been killed. Retelling the story fifteen years later, the old man stressed how important it was for all sharecroppers, black and white, to work together:

> We colored people can't organize without you . . . and you white folks can't organize without us. Aren't we all brothers and ain't God the Father of us all? We live under the same sun, eat the same food, raise the same crop for the same landlord who oppresses and cheats us both. For a long time now white folks and colored folks have been fighting each other and both of us has been getting whipped all the time. We don't have nothing against one another but we got plenty against the landlord. The same chain that holds my people holds your people too. If we're chained together on the outside we ought to stay chained together in the union. . . . The landlord is always betwixt us, beatin' us and starvin' us and makin' us fight each other. There ain't but one way for us to get him where he can't help himself and that's for us to get together and stay together.[35]

The STFU shared this vision and fought for the right of sharecroppers and tenant farmers to establish an organization that could give them bargaining power with planters. In theory the AAA provided for "parity" payments to sharecroppers and tenant farmers for cotton land that was plowed under and guaranteed them certain protection as part of the AAA crop reduction program. But in practice federal money went straight into the hands of planters, who evicted almost a million sharecropper families from the land. After Norcross evicted STFU members from his plantation, the union attempted to force the U.S. Department of Agriculture to live up to the provisions of the AAA, only to discover that the government would not act against the planters and would do nothing to prevent evictions.

The STFU received little help from Washington, but it kindled a response among tenant farmers and sharecroppers. From fifteen locals with a few hundred members in late 1934, the STFU grew in a year to an organization of over fifteen thousand members and seventy-five locals. In September, 1935, the STFU launched a strike against cotton planters who planned to reduce the price paid for picking a hundred pounds of cotton from sixty to forty cents; the union demanded a dollar. As circulars stating union demands mysteriously appeared throughout northeastern Arkansas, planters responded with violence, intimidation, and the jailing of STFU organizers. In spite of planter terrorism, the strike spread and the price paid in some places rose to seventy-five cents. On the heels of what the union felt to be a significant gain, more than thirty new locals were organized in forty-five days. The following May, the STFU waged a general strike of cotton choppers, tenant farmers, sharecroppers, and day laborers for union contracts and a wage of $1.50 a day for ten hours' work. Although the strike was not successful, it led to nationwide publicity for the union. The governor of Arkansas called in the National Guard to break the strike, and strikers were featured in a documentary film titled *Land of Cotton*, which was shown nationally. By June of 1937, STFU membership stood at over thirty-four thousand, with 410 locals in Arkansas, Mississippi, Missouri, Oklahoma, Tennessee, and Texas.[36]

One explanation for the rapid expansion was that the STFU was more than a trade union seeking to organize the unorganized. In point of fact, the STFU functioned as a community organization for the sharecroppers, who had always felt so powerless, an organization that, in Howard Kester's words, gave them "a new voice, created . . . [a] collective will, discovered a forgotten hope, brought to life new meaning to ancient concepts, struggled heroically against tyranny and oppression, risked their all that all might share and have abundantly, fashioned a new faith, built a mighty union." To forge such a sense of community among blacks and whites, some of whom were former Klan members, was possible in large measure because of the religious character of the union, evident not only in its language and music but in its leadership, organizing tactics, and orientation toward life.[37]

Three visible symbols of religious presence were prayer, churches, and preachers. Every gathering of the STFU, from local union meetings to the annual convention, to a general strike, opened with a prayer. Prayer became a means of establishing solidarity between black and white sharecroppers rather than a vehicle for rationalizing the need to submit to hardship and suffering. In prayer, the Bible was evoked to afflict the comfortable more than to comfort the afflicted. E. B. McKinney, a "gray-haired preacher and veteran organizer," for example, prayed that men and women who knew that imprisonment and bloodshed might lie ahead would remember that God was with them in their struggle, giving them the courage to know that poverty, want, and injustice were not in keeping with God's Kingdom. An Oklahoma preacher reminded sharecroppers: "God is God and Man is Man: be a Man. God has done his work, now you do yours. You want freedom, you want bread, you want a better world in which to live. You can have it but you've got to work for it. You've got to organize like the bees and the ants, you've got to have power, you've got to build a union strong and mighty, you've got to be the army of the disinherited marching toward the promised land, but you've got to be men." [38]

Because churches, particularly black churches, were most often the central meeting places for STFU members, they became the targets of planter violence, routinely attacked and often burned to the ground. Nor was violence limited to property. Organizing sharecroppers was in some cases tantamount to signing one's own death warrant. The *Sharecroppers' Voice*, an STFU mimeographed publication edited by Howard Kester, described how

> in northeastern Arkansas a reign of terror has been inaugurated by an illegal minority of Ku Kluxers and Vigilantes. Democracy—if there ever was any—has utterly disappeared. Innocent men, women, and children have been assaulted, mobbed and beaten with pistols, clubs, and flashlights. Officers, members, and friends of the Southern Tenant Farmers Union have been illegally arrested and jailed. Homes and churches have been riddled with bullets. Whole families have been driven from their homes. Men and women have been shot. Every act on the calendar of terrorism has been practiced against the members of the union. Starvation, eviction, attempted lynchings, death threats, attempted murders. [39]

Lay preachers, black and white, did the day-to-day organizing of the union. John Steinbeck, moved by their courage, portrayed one such preacher in *The Grapes of Wrath*. He was killed by the landowners' hired thugs as he fought for better wages and conditions for the poor people. Tom Joad, the central figure of the novel, following in the preacher's footsteps, vowed that "wherever they's a fight so hungry people can eat, I'll be there. Wherever they's a cop beatin' up a guy, I'll be there . . . an' when our folks eat the stuff they raise an' live in the houses they build, why, I'll be there." One of the first victims of planters' violence was C. H. Smith a black preacher and sharecropper from Tyronza, who, along with Ward Rodgers, was sent to organize in Crittenden County, Arkansas. During an organizational meeting in a black church, a group of plantation riding bosses broke in. Rodgers made it to the safety of the county line, but Smith two days later was hauled out of his car by riding bosses and sheriff's deputies, badly horsewhipped, and thrown in the Marion jail. The union hired C. T. Carpenter, a Mark Tree, Arkansas, attorney, and forty to fifty sharecroppers demonstrated their solidarity with Smith by their presence in the courtroom. Smith, released without a trial, remarked that "the union is the only thing that will help my people—and all of you people, whether white or black, are my people." [40]

Smith was but one of many black preachers who joined Claude Williams and Howard Kester in the work of the STFU. Eventually six of the fourteen members of the National Executive Committee of the STFU were preachers. A. B. Brookins was a seventy-year-old Holiness preacher who became chaplain of the STFU and one of its many song writers. Like Smith, Brookins was subjected to intimidation and jailed for his organizing efforts. Edward Britt McKinney, known as Britt or E.B., was a powerful, charismatic Baptist preacher who at one point in his career was responsible for overseeing thirty-six black congregations in eastern Arkansas. Influenced by the nationalism of Marcus Garvey, he worked to instill among black sharecroppers a sense of pride and dignity in being black. He constantly struggled with those white STFU members who wanted the union's banner of interracial justice to remain rhetorical. McKinney worked to prevent both the pitting of poor blacks and whites against each other and the sacrifice of lives of black people to call public attention to the plight of white sharecroppers. For McKinney it was not a question of mistrust of white people, for there were some white members of the STFU in whom black sharecroppers had more confidence than "they do [in] any people of their own race." McKinney simply wanted an organization in which accountability and trust between black and white sharecroppers was based on an acknowledgment of the overwhelming predominance of black sharecroppers and the necessity to combat racism in all its forms. He became the first vice-president of the STFU. Claude Williams noted that black sharecroppers all over Arkansas referred to themselves as "an 'E.B.' man; right or wrong I am an 'E.B.' man!"[41]

Another black Baptist who joined the ranks of the STFU was Owen H. Whitfield, sharecropper and preacher. Born in 1892 in Jonestown, Mississippi, of sharecropper parents, he spent much of his youth traveling throughout the South, earning his living by working on farms, stoking a train, and even tap dancing in a traveling minstrel show. At nineteen he married Zella Glass, only thirteen and herself the daughter of sharecroppers; together they would raise fifteen children. In the early 1920s he and his family settled down to sharecropping on a plantation near Charleston, Missouri, not far from the Mississippi River. At the same time he became a Missionary Baptist preacher. The Whitfields' lives were shaped by poverty and uncertainty about the future, but they had a deep sense of God's presence among the poor who were striving to be more than an extension of a plow, working only to harvest planters' cotton, earning profits they would never share. Early on, Whitfield realized that preaching was more than "just gettin' the people ready to die" by focusing on the vivid contrast between the toil and hardship of this life and the supposed heavenly realm after death. He concluded that there was a difference between preaching the gospel and delivering sermons: "A sermon sends you home happy [and] the Gospel sends you home mad." The gospel had to do with the nature of this life and why people were exploited and forced to live in poverty, bound by sickness, hunger, and an early grave. He told his people, "Take your eyes out of the sky because someone is stealing your bread." Convinced that "the brotherhood of man" was "applied religion," he joined the STFU after attending a church

156

meeting at which the main speaker was Claude Williams. Williams described Whitfield as "the most effective union organizer, the most effective speaker that I've seen or heard." [42]

Although Whitfield was elected vice-president of the STFU in 1937, he never shared the preoccupation of Mitchell and other leaders of the STFU with the traditional trade-union strategy of strikes on behalf of better wages. His greatest contribution to the cause was his organization of the Missouri sharecroppers' highway demonstration of 1939. On January 10, 1939, in the bootheel region of southeastern Missouri, some seventeen hundred sharecropper families were handed eviction notices for their protest of planters' plans to reduce them to day laborers. Whitfield responded by organizing a massive public demonstration. Seeing their situation as analogous to that of the children of Israel under the pharaoh, Whitfield led an "exodus" of sharecroppers out of the plantations to the highways of routes 60 and 61, where thousands of black and white sharecroppers set up roadside camps that stretched for hundreds of miles. Soon newspaper reporters gathered to describe men, women, and children "singing hymns lustily to banjos and violins between piles of junk that were their worldly possessions—corn shuck mattresses, battered pots and pans, wire coops of chickens, and relics of iron cookstoves; pouring coffee for each other around the camp fires and calling each other 'Sister Almeada' and 'Brother Otis.' " Amid the snow and ice of winter, the sharecroppers' demonstration drew the attention of the American public. Planters responded with police and vigilante committees who hauled the "embarrassing" sharecropper families off the highways and dumped them in abandoned buildings, or on top of levees; in one case a hundred families were taken to the New Madrid County Spillway and placed under armed guard, with no access to either food or water. In spite of the reaction of the planters, Whitfield gained national sympathy for the plight of sharecroppers, won some temporary concessions from state authorities, and eventually obtained federal housing for displaced sharecroppers. More important, Whitfield demonstrated to the STFU the importance of protest demonstrations as a means of social change. [43]

Howard Kester was an important link among the STFU, the Socialist Party, and left-leaning Protestant groups such as the Fellowship of Socialist Christians and the Fellowship of Southern Churchmen. The Fellowship of Southern Churchmen was founded in 1934 as the Conference of Younger Churchmen and changed its organizational name in 1936. Historian David Burgess says that the ministers who built the fellowship were individuals whose "dreams of a better Southland were haunted by the specter of hunger amidst plenty, by bitter racial antagonisms which again and again boiled over into brutal lynchings and riots, by mile and mile of desperate men hunting a lonely job, by bread lines and soup kitchens, by intimidation and violence upon those who dared organize the unemployed . . . and lethargy and remoteness from the struggles of the people on the part of the ecclesiastics." Given the difficulty of collecting union dues from members who had so little money (at best only 10 percent of STFU members could manage to pay their dues), the STFU was dependent on outside funding. The Socialist Party and church groups, with their extended financial networks, were sources of tangible support.[44]

Kester also served as an organizer, leader, theoretician, and one of the STFU's more visible public spokespersons. As such, he consistently defined its work in religious terms. In an address before an annual meeting of the NAACP, he described the role of the STFU in the fight against peonage and argued that his hope for the South was a new day, a "society in which there shall be economic, political, and social equality for every man, woman and child who wants it; a society in which a man can call another brother and mean it." Racist America, he went on, was something he did not wish to die for, and the sooner it was buried the better would be the cause of freedom. The STFU was not only a movement for creating new relations between black and white Americans but a means by which Christians might realize that "they can serve God best by abolishing the power that holds their people in poverty, ignorance, and hopelessness." Jesus came alive when Christians participated with oppressed people in building a new society, for "true Christianity" was expressed when people "are clothing the naked, feeding the hungry, ministering to the sick, speaking and living a gospel of neighborliness and love." Kester believed that as poor people learned that building the Kingdom meant seizing the future with their own hands, their hopes for a juster social order might become less of a dream and more of a lived reality. Hence as the STFU did all it could to "sweep into hell the system" that held black and white sharecroppers in bondage, its members were living out their faith in the Kingdom of the Good Life.[45]

Religion, for Kester and his STFU colleagues, was concerned with the totality of life, not only its brokenness. It provided a means by which life might be made whole, dreams might be realized, hopes made concrete. Kester believed that religion had to do with material needs, most visibly symbolized by bread, which sustained life, but also with beauty, for he contended that "bread alone is insufficient. Men must have beauty in their lives if their lives are to be fruitful of the better things in our world." The great tragedy facing southern tenant farmers, sharecroppers, and day laborers was that they had access to neither bread nor beauty. That was why fundamental structural change was so necessary if the South was not to be a wasteland populated with wasted people. Kester's understanding of the role Christian faith should play in the lives of poor people was embodied in a ritual titled "Ceremony of the Land," which he wrote with Evelyn Smith, who served for many years as a secretary and later educational director of the STFU. Much of the ceremony, first performed at the Third Annual Convention of the SFTU in January of 1937, was composed of a reader-response exchange between biblical texts and quotations from Kester's *Revolt among the Sharecroppers*. The demands of the biblical prophets for justice for the poor were seen as alive in the STFU's struggle against racism, hope for a new social order, and celebration of the worth and dignity of oppressed people. Voicing together the claim that "the land is the common heritage of the people" and "to the disinherited belongs the future," those present closed with a prayer composed by Walter Rauschenbusch: "Speed now the day when the plains and the hills and all the wealth thereof shall be the people's own and free men shall not live as tenants on the earth which thou hast given all." [46]

For Kester, as for most members of the STFU, the union was part of the quest for a new South where neither people nor resources would be exploited, a place where the "Lord of Life" would be present in the very structure of daily life. The STFU was "a movement for social emancipation," for a total reordering of southern society:

> The land must be restored and the people must be restored to the land. There can be no health for this nation so long as these millions of men, women, and children, are homeless and landless. I want decent homes, decent schools, for old and young alike, health clinics, and kindly country doctors, freedom from the tyranny of oppressors on the land or in the courts of justice; freedom from drudgery and monotonous toil, from loneliness, emptiness, and despair. I want to see men possessed of the knowledge that they are loved and wanted; that they have talents which are needed in building the world of tomorrow. I want to see them breathe the air of freedom, and have a share in the ongoings of a great democracy. I want to see men liberated from the tyranny of ignorance and poverty, to see them bless the earth with intelligent labor, and love, and honest sweat and to enjoy the rewards of their toil in peace and security. I want to see mothers and fathers rejoice over the birth of children without the fear of having to later apologize to their children for the mess they have made of their lives. I want to see man call his brother "friend" and mean it.[47]

Claude Williams shared Kester's vision of a new South, and of the prophetic role of Christians in making such a society possible. Williams devoted himself to STFU organizing with the same energy and commitment that marked his earlier ministry. As a member of the National Executive Committee, Williams was a constant opponent of racial discrimination; he supported E. B. McKinney's struggles on behalf of black sharecroppers, sharing McKinney's mistrust of white STFU members who were not willing to acknowledge solidarity between blacks and whites. J. R. Butler, president of the STFU, said of Williams that "he can organize more sharecroppers in ten days than I can in three months." Williams would travel along country dirt roads, often at night to avoid plantation riding bosses or enraged vigilantes, and meet with sharecroppers in churches or fields. In black churches he joined the congregations in singing "Steal Away to Jesus" and "Swing Low, Sweet Chariot" and preached about how God, through his servant Moses, had organized Israelite bricklayers to oppose the tyranny of the pharaoh just as the STFU was organizing to resist the oppression of the cotton planters.[48]

A good example of his work was Williams's response to the appeal of a black sharecropper who worked on the Red River Plantation in Fulton, Arkansas, a small town in the southwestern part of the state. The sharecropper wrote: "We are in a suffering condition, men, with children seven to eight in family, without food or clothes. We are tired of wearing cotton sack, flour sack. . . . we are working men, and till the soil, and all we want is justice, but these people are far worse than Pharaoh was in his day. . . . So if we can get your cooperation to . . . guide and lead us to the land of promise. May God bless the union." Arriving in Fulton, Williams learned how local sharecroppers had been reduced to day laborers and forced to live on forty to fifty cents a day, how people were trying to exist on what they could glean from the wilds. Meeting only at night, Williams spoke of God's justice and how union solidarity would prevail over all the violence the landowners might muster.[49]

Williams's own encounter with plantation violence came in the summer of 1936 when H. L. Mitchell asked him to conduct a funeral service for a black STFU organizer, Frank Weems. Weems had been part of a picket march in Crittendon County, Arkansas, when he was attacked and killed by riding bosses with baseball bats. En route to the funeral, Williams, accompanied by Willie Sue Blagden, who was a Socialist from a well-established Memphis family, was accosted by a group of angry planters, taken into the backwoods, and beaten so badly that his back looked like jelly and he could hardly walk. Blagden was beaten less severely and put on a Memphis-bound bus. The attackers drove around with Williams until midnight, debating whether to kill him. Finally he was released with a warning never to set foot in Crittendon County again. This incident made immediate headlines; when such things happened to black people, as they all too often did, they were not given so much attention.[50]

Williams's organizing abilities were also utilized in the educational work of his New Era School of Social Action and Prophetic Religion. The New Era School became a training center for organizers, a place where black and white workers could meet in safety, far from the terrorism of the plantations. Williams focused his school program on teaching workers how to develop their own ability to deal with the hard, day-to-day realities of southern life. In his view the central need was "to point out general trends; to tell them why [they] must organize; and to teach them how to organize." He worked out of his own home with a volunteer staff, often bringing the school to the workers.[51]

In the summer of 1937 Williams became director of Commonwealth College, a labor college in Mena, Arkansas, founded in 1923. The college founders had understood that the established educational system did not serve the needs of working-class people but was, rather, an instrument for the perpetuation of bourgeois values, interests, and goals. Since the early 1930s students and faculty had been involved in strikes and organizing efforts throughout the South and Midwest. The college community, made up of people of varying political stripes, from old-time Wobblies to Socialists and Communists, was constantly hounded by state authorities, especially witch-hunting state legislative committees. During the 1930s Commonwealth's most important link to organized labor was the STFU. Mitchell and Kester were not particularly enthusiastic about Commonwealth's affiliation with the STFU because of the Communists among both the faculty and students, but Williams viewed the situation differently. On becoming director, he sought to relate the college more organically to the needs of the labor movement. He believed that the STFU had played an important role in creating a "sharecropper consciousness" among the American public, in "forcing the recognition of plantation conditions and practice by the state and federal authorities; in setting up tenancy commissions; in proposed legislation; in securing convictions for peonage." Now the most pressing need was to provide STFU members with organizing skills and knowledge. He also hoped Commonwealth might devote some of its resources to educating black sharecroppers and for that purpose a black staff member was hired.[52]

As Williams saw it, black and white preachers were crucial to the future success of the STFU for they were "key persons in the struggle to organize agricultural workers and generally improve their lot." Accordingly, he set about establishing institutes for rural pastors, one for white preachers and ministerial students at Commonwealth and another for black preachers, church workers and rural schoolteachers at his New Era School in Little Rock. In the summer of 1938 Williams held his first institute for "Cotton Preachers" at New Era School, sponsored by Commonwealth College. Some of the topics were "the role of the country church in organizing rural workers, various methods of organizing sharecroppers and tenant farmers; religion and reaction; the history and economic significance of the STFU." In addition, Williams tried to educate self-styled radicals about the importance of religion in the life of working-class people. Against those who viewed religion as simply an opiate of the people that substituted a future world of happiness for the pains of this life, he argued that religion was in reality a dynamic force for social change. In a lecture to Commonwealth students and faculty Williams reminded them that

> Moses was the first labor agitator. He organized a walkout of bricklayers and led them out of Egypt to the land of Canaan, their own land, where each man could have forty acres and a mule. All through the Old Testament you find the prophets crying out against the rich and selfish who have forgotten the Hebraic laws against monopolizing the fruits of the earth. And in the New Testament you discover Jesus driving the money-changers from the temple, championing the common people, Paul declaring that those people who do not work have no business eating. James denouncing the landlords who cheat their tenant farmers. The Bible has as many texts for organizational speeches as it has for sermons on other-worldliness.

Williams remained director of Commonwealth until the summer of 1939, when he resigned to devote all his energies to the work of the People's Institute of

Applied Religion. The college lasted for another year and folded in September of 1940.[53]

Williams, Kester, and other preachers helped to forge solidarity among traditionally powerless sharecroppers. They gave voice to those the system tried to silence, making the gospel truly good news for the poor. Yet, it was difficult to replace fear with hope when every aspect of people's lives was permeated by violence. John Henry, a black poet and STFU organizer, composed a poem for the STFU, including this verse: "We have never broke up your meetings or your churches burned; nor beaten with an axhandle, shot in the back or put in jail; labor has never shot in your homes or thrown dynamite; landlord what in the Heaven is the matter with you?" The STFU concluded that what was wrong was to believe that violence could solve anything. Sharecroppers could begin to replace fear with hope only when they learned to trust one another by acknowledging that nothing could divide them, that love was stronger than hatred and the thirst for justice more enduring than planter terrorism. Kester still wanted a revolution, but he now believed that whatever success the STFU had was due in large measure to the unwillingness of the union to engage in violence "even though we worked in the midst of one of the most volcanic and violent areas in America." To use the weapons of the system to bring about a more equitable order of peace and justice would contradict the stated purpose of the STFU.[54]

If nonviolence was the union's fundamental mechanism of social change, then music was the means by which the union maintained solidarity, built community, and kept hope alive. Given the centrality of Christian faith, and the importance of the church as a meeting place for the STFU, it was natural that much of the music was created by adapting well-known hymns and spirituals. "Jesus Is My Captain" became "We Shall Not Be Moved," of which a black member of the STFU commented, "That song I Do believe sprung from our Lips with the voice of God, it re[mem]bered my mind Back to the time when Moses was Leading the children of Israel. I believe that Was Handed Down for this Day for some of us are getting shot and some getting beaten." "The Old Ship of Zion" became "Union Train" when a woman STFU member gave it new words declaring that the union "will carry us to freedom." One of the more prolific song writers was John Hancock, black sharecropper, STFU organizer, lay preacher, and former Commonwealth student. Hancock composed "Hungry, Hungry Are We," which spoke about how sharecroppers "don't get nothin' for our labor," and transformed "Roll the Chariot On" into "Roll the Union On," in which the union would not be stopped by bosses, scabs, or hired goons. Mrs. M. H. Barnes of the STFU local in Blytheville, Arkansas, adapted "Swanee River," a well-known popular song that celebrated the traditional southern way of life, to affirm "long have we suffered in the struggle, dark clouds are rolling now behind us, the day of redemption's arrived, come join us in friendly union." [55]

As new words to old music gave strength to poor people, they wondered how planters and their hired clergy could so easily overlook their sufferings. One noted apologist for the planters was an Arkansas Methodist pastor, J. Abner Sage, of Mark Tree, Arkansas. He characterized sharecroppers as a "lazy lot of poor whites and Negroes." It seemed to sharecroppers that he was more preoccupied with speaking to fancy Rotary Club dinners than discovering the conditions under which sharecroppers were forced to live. Sage was perceived as only another example of those who "spoke more for his masters, rather than for The Master." It seemed to sharecroppers that Sage's distortion of the Christian message to salve the conscience of the powerful no longer had any power over them, for they knew they could no longer be manipulated and used as those in power saw fit. The STFU was a visible sign that other ways of being human were possible and that poor people could be the instruments of their own liberation.[56]

People's Institute of Applied Religion

By the late 1930s, Williams and Kester had gone their separate ways. Socialist members of the STFU, particularly Kester and Mitchell, regarded Williams with suspicion as he aligned himself with Communists and adamantly opposed any form of "red-baiting." Ward Rodgers, a longtime friend of both Williams and Kester, felt Kester and Mitchell were "making asses" of themselves by getting the STFU embroiled in the Socialist Party's conflicts with Communists. Much of this animosity came to a head in September, 1937, when delegates to the annual STFU convention voted to affiliate with the United Cannery, Agricultural, Packinghouse and Allied Workers of America, a newly organized CIO international. Kester and Mitchell worried about the status of the STFU as part of the UCAPAWA, and they distrusted Communist leaders within the CIO and the UCAPAWA. Williams, by contrast, enthusiastically urged STFU members to join the new union: "The Lord spake unto the children of Moses: Go Forward! He that putteth his hands to the plow and looketh backward is not fit for the Kingdom of God. Go forward, FORWARD INTO THE CIO!" The head of the UCAPAWA was Donald Henderson, a former economics instructor dismissed by Columbia University for his radical politics, who later worked with farm and cannery unions in California and New Jersey and was an active member of the Communist Party. Mitchell and others felt that Henderson was not sensitive to the differences between organizing wage workers and organizing cotton pickers, especially what it meant to organize rural southern agricultural workers. This mistrust, coupled with ideological conflicts, was exacerbated by misunderstandings and personality feuds within the STFU.[57]

Williams wanted to expand STFU organizing among tenant farmers, believing that this was part of the task of creating a strong and vibrant CIO; meanwhile people such as Norman Thomas worried about "scheming" Communists. In this atmosphere, in the late summer of 1938, J. R. Butler discovered a piece of paper Williams had left in his coat pocket after staying with him on his way to the Memphis area to do field work for the STFU. The unsigned document was a draft of an appeal to the Communist Party for support for Commonwealth College, which exaggerated Communist strength at the college and within the STFU. Although Williams had nothing directly to do with the drafting of the document and felt its characterization of the facts was untrue, Butler interpreted it as proof of Communist subversion of the STFU. He immediately called a press conference and asked for Williams's resignation. Later he retracted this request, but Williams's old friend Howard Kester pressed for his expulsion. In September the Executive Council of the STFU expelled Williams and, in the early months of 1939, the STFU withdrew from the UCAPAWA. The months between Williams's expulsion and the STFU's secession from the CIO were a period of confusion and turmoil as the STFU and UCAPAWA fought for the loyalty of the members in a battle that eventually led to the demise of the STFU. Claude Williams and some of the most brilliant of the STFU's black leaders, E. B. McKinney and Owen Whitfield among them, continued their affiliation with the CIO.[58]

With the collapse of the STFU and the later disbanding of his Committee on Economic and Racial Justice, Kester devoted more of his time to the Fellowship of Southern Churchmen. Eventually even his interest in the progressive agenda of the fellowship would wane, and his earlier radicalism would be replaced by a liberal anticommunism shared by many former Christian radicals of the 1930s, the most visible being his great mentor Reinhold Niebuhr. Claude Williams, on the other hand, built upon his experience of the thirties by forming the People's Institute of Applied Religion in 1940. He was still convinced that Christianity had a prophetic role to play and that grass-roots religious leaders were the key to any hope for social change in the South. The PIAR was based on Williams's belief that "to preach the Good News of freedom, peace, security and personal dignity, to preach these things to the poor, an army of new preachers to the poor were needed, and to apply the teachings of the Gospel of the Kingdom to the problems of here and now, a truly non-sectarian, wholly independent religious movement was necessary. The People's Institute of Applied Religion was therefore developed to enlist, train, select and inspire leaders from the people to preach and practice the Gospel of the Kingdom of God on earth." Initially, the PIAR worked with sharecroppers in Arkansas and Missouri, setting up short-term leadership training institutes. Later it became involved in the CIO's efforts to organize workers throughout the South.[59]

Williams's old STFU allies Owen Whitfield, W. L. Blackstone, and Leon Turner aided in the development of the PIAR. Joining Williams from Commonwealth College was Winifred Chappell, who had known Joyce and Claude Williams from their days in Paris, Arkansas, and was an important staff member of Harry F. Ward's Methodist Federation for Social Service. She and Whitfield became associate directors of PIAR. Don West, Williams's friend since they had studied together with Alva Taylor at Vanderbilt's School of Religion, directed the work of the PIAR in Georgia. Three other leaders were Harry and Grace Koger and A. L. Campbell. Harry had once been a YMCA secretary but became disillusioned with what he perceived to be the YMCA's lack of commitment to the pressing issues of social justice. At the time the PIAR was founded he was the regional organizer for UCAPAWA in Memphis. Campbell was a white, Free-Will Baptist sharecropper preacher from eastern Arkansas. He had once been an active member of the Ku Klux Klan and in the spring of 1941 was recruited by local planters as a spy on an upcoming PIAR institute for cotton-patch preachers in St. Louis, Missouri. Campbell left Williams's institute as a PIAR convert.[60]

In the beginning, the PIAR's program centered around three- to ten-day institutes that brought together about fifty men and women, evenly divided between black and white participants. Gathered together were not only lay preachers but church deacons and evangelists, Sunday school teachers and Sunday school superintendents—all those who were "the natural and accepted leaders of the peoples of the rural South." Centrally important to Williams was the interracial character of the institutes, which brought blacks and whites together, often for the first time, to talk about their common problems. Williams related how many of them "had never sat down to a meal together, and most of them thought they never would—especially the whites. The blacks never thought they'd have the opportunity. A black man got up and wept . . . [when] Winifred Chappell called him 'brother.' He never thought he'd ever live to see the day when a white woman said 'brother' to him." Problem sharing was accompanied by prayer, Scripture reading, and song. Williams also believed that a reliance upon written material was not the best approach for dealing with sharecroppers and community leaders, so he developed a series of visual aids and outlines of central biblical themes. Before leaving Commonwealth College, Williams had developed some basic charts he felt were particularly adapted to people "in preaching timely social messages to their folk." The charts had titles such as "The Galilean and the Common People," "Religion and Progress," "Anti-Semitism, Racism, and Democracy," and "King Cotton, His Lord and Slaves." In later years he added others, including "Religion and Labor," "World Brotherhood," and "The Gospel of the Kingdom." [61]

Williams's approach was based on a series of assumptions about Scripture and popular religion. For one thing, he thought that those who had worked with the "masses," be they sharecroppers, farmers, or workers, had done so in a condescending way. This was evident especially in their attitudes toward popular religion, which they often regarded as simply superstition or, worse yet, an "opiate of the people." Rather than speak to oppressed people in language they could understand, they employed "bookish jargon" or fell into the use of mechanistic leftist rhetoric that substituted quotations from Marx and

Lenin for analysis of fundamental human needs. It seemed ironic to Williams that the "rocking-chair reds" who so easily "dismiss[ed] religion," which is a fundamental part of the lives of oppressed people, were the same ones likely to celebrate the common people and talk about the masses' contribution to music, art, and literature.

Beyond an appreciation of the role of religion in the lives of the poor, it was necessary more fully to "understand the forces which have exploited them, victimized them, and divided them." Williams knew that the rural poor of the South, unable to understand the "forces which crushed them," used religion as a means of consolation rather than a path of liberation. Hence it was crucial to develop religious programs that dealt with people in "terms of meat, bread, shelter, health, freedom," and "security." These could be fostered by working with "work-a-day" preachers of the South, who were, Williams believed, "basically honest, sincere, and zealous." And the way to work with lay preachers was to acknowledge that the "Bible is the vernacular of mass America." Given the importance of the Bible for common people, a "people's interpretation of the Bible" was needed, that is, an understanding of the class basis of Scripture. The Bible was an ongoing story of the struggles of oppressed people against their oppressors and the "enemies of justice." [62]

Williams contended that the norm for a people's appropriation of Scripture was the "Galilean Carpenter" who sided with the poor and proclaimed the Kingdom of God as a project to be realized in history. Jesus needed to be freed from "the tomb of capitalist theology" in which he had been imprisoned by biblical interpreters and theological systems. Reclaimed by common people, Jesus once again became the "Nazarene Carpenter" who was "lynched because he stirred up the people, the common people; and in such numbers that the agents of Rome said, Behold, the whole world is gone after him (Luke 23:5; Mark 12:37; John 12:19). The Nazarene was a class-conscious leader of the people, the common people (Matt. 26:5)." A closer reading of the biblical text, Williams argued, shows that Jesus began his ministry by preaching the good news to the poor. Central to Jesus' preaching was that the poor should join together to obtain what was rightfully theirs, the goods of this life. Jesus was a person who "declared His oneness with the afflicted and announced that His purpose on earth was to carry out God's program for the poor, HERE and NOW!" [63]

Williams contrasted the words of Jesus to the religion about Jesus, which spoke only about the next life and overlooked the fact that Jesus, as well as the whole of the biblical story, "condemns the oppressors and demands that people be FREED from BONDAGE and have LAND and HOUSES and FOOD and CLOTHES and HEALTH and FREEDOM!" That was why Williams contended that Jesus was murdered not because he preached "theological abstractions" and "personal salvation" but because he dealt with the concrete problems of daily life. A religion of pious-sounding platitudes would have been no threat to Rome. Only a religion that wrestled with economic and political justice and sought, in the words of Mary, "to put down the mighty from their seats, to exalt them of low degree, to fill the hungry with good things, and to send the rich empty away (Luke 1:52,53)" was a threat to the existing social order. It seemed obvious to Williams that a reading of the biblical text from Genesis to Revelation showed a preoccupation with economic, political, and social problems as they affected oppressed people. Therefore, the Bible as the "People's Book" was a living book that spoke to common people about a God of life who demanded freedom, security, and brother/sisterhood. Religion became, in Williams's mind, a "vital force" in this life against all that sought to divide oppressed people, from racism to anticommunism. Hence it was not religion that was the "opium" but the uses to which religion was put. True religion was manifest in deeds and action, whereas false or bad religion was known by its "noble profession of words." Biblically based religion was that which fed the hungry, clothed the naked, healed the sick, and liberated the oppressed. Similarly, false religion was a torrent of words used to mask a legitimation of "oppression, deceit, and bigotry." [64]

Armed with Williams's charts and accompanying interpretative outlines, staff members of the PIAR spread out across the South, setting up scores of conferences and institutes. Vernon G. Olson, district representative of East Texas for UCAPAWA, who had long experience working with sharecroppers, tenant farmers, and agricultural workers, remarked that the PIAR represented one of the most effective means of transforming religion from the reactionary instrument of those who waged a "campaign of terror, racism, and subjection" into a way of arming "poor people of the South with a weapon of truth with which to win a kingdom of brotherly love and freedom on earth where true Christianity shall prevail." [65]

In the summer of 1941, Don Henderson of UCAPAWA invited the PIAR to work with the CIO in Memphis in its struggle against the political machine of Ed Crump, who maintained a jim crow city with low wages and antiunion policies. Union organizers were found floating in the Mississippi River, or they simply disappeared. Setting up offices in a CIO union hall in Memphis, Williams was joined by Harry and Grace Koger and Owen Whitfield. They began by holding classes using Williams's charts in an effort to bring black and white workers together by preaching the importance of racial unity based on a common faith, the Bible, and hope for the future. Not long after a successful meeting that drew five hundred men and women from Memphis and outlying plantations, Harry Koger was jailed, and Williams was arrested and held for two days, without being charged. The PIAR later established similar classes in Evansville, Indiana, and became involved in organizing tobacco workers in Winston-Salem, North Carolina. Then in 1942 a number of inner-city Presbyterian pastors in Detroit, impressed by Williams's work with southern workers and the overall approach of the PIAR, were instrumental in having Williams appointed as a "minister for labor" to the Detroit Presbytery.[66]

Detroit had undergone a number of significant changes since the turn of the century. During the initial expansion of the auto industry, the most important group of workers was immigrants from southern and eastern Europe. The outbreak of the First World War ended the immigrant labor supply, and auto manufacturers, in search of labor, recruited southern black workers. At the end of the war, the black population of Detroit had increased 400 percent over the preceding five years, and black workers constituted 8 percent of the work force, although they were largely confined to unskilled jobs. Still facing critical labor shortages, the companies then recruited southern whites, particularly during the late 1920s. With the beginning of World War II, the auto industry again faced a labor shortage; between 1940 and 1943, over half a million rural southern workers, the vast majority white, migrated to Detroit.

Newly arrived southern workers were confronted with well-established racist, even fascist organizations. The Ku Klux Klan, at its height, had more members in the state of Michigan than anywhere else in the country. In addition to the KKK, Detroit was home to the Liberty League, the pro-Nazi National Workers League, Silver Shirts, and the Black Legion, some of which received the backing of leading Detroit industrialists. In addition to organizations devoted to anticommunism, anti-Semitism, and racism, certain ministers, including Father Charles E. Coughlin, J. Frank Norris, and Gerald L. K. Smith, gave a religious coating to the climate of hatred and intolerance.[67]

Williams's appointment as labor minister established Detroit as the national headquarters for the PIAR. After analyzing the problems facing working people in Detroit, Williams set out to organize southern workers in the war plants and tried to defuse the racist and anti-Semitic atmosphere that gripped the city. Many rural southern whites had brought with them racist, anti-Jewish, anti-union, and anti-Yankee attitudes and were being recruited by the KKK and other reactionary organizations. Williams understood that southern whites had been denied adequate education, decent housing, and medical services and forced to work long hours for pay that could barely sustain a family at a minimal subsistence level, and he believed such "economic conditions and lack of understanding have made them intolerant." Their religious beliefs offered reassurance and consolation but reinforced religious bigotry and racial prejudice, and perpetuated their inability to understand the day-to-day realities of economic and political life.[68]

Working with the United Auto Workers, Williams first reached out to black and white southern lay preachers working in Detroit-area war plants. He estimated that there were over three thousand such preachers; over one thousand "shop preachers" were members of Ford Local 600 alone. These individuals preached to thousands of relocated southern black and white workers. In early

1943, with the support of the UAW's educational director, the PIAR began organizing in the auto plants. Setting up classes based on Williams's approach to scripture and utilizing his visual-aid charts, the PIAR taught hundreds of shop preachers how to come to terms with the "forces which exploited them, victimized them, and divided them." One of the PIAR's most impressive organizers was a black shop preacher named Virgil Vanderburg. Beginning with a group of twelve preachers in the Packard plant, in a matter of months he had expanded to forty black and white preachers who spread the PIAR's message to Murray Corporation, General Electric, Ford, and Briggs plants. Under Vanderburg's leadership, the Gospel Preacher's Council of Applied Religion was established at Packard; it was instrumental in supplying shop preachers for religious services throughout various Detroit war plants. At the same time the PIAR created interracial "Brotherhood Squadrons" drawn from Protestants and Catholics, and used musical groups as well as lay speakers to join in "fighting race prejudice." [69]

Williams also established a working relationship with two noted black church leaders, Charles Hill and John Miles. Both preachers had been using the PIAR's charts and methods in their ministries. Hill was pastor of Hartford Baptist Church and an honorary member of Ford Local 600. His church was a meeting place for the union because the local union hall had been infiltrated by spies from Ford Motor Company, and the members felt "it would be difficult for them to prove that we were just discussing union matters" if they met in church.[70]

In addition, the PIAR worked closely with various civil rights organizations, liberal groups, and church agencies and councils to confront Detroit's growing racial tension. Williams believed that if the church was to preach brother/sisterhood between blacks and whites and speak out against racial discrimination, it must itself give visible witness. Interracial services were established at a local Detroit Presbyterian church, which used the name Congregation of His People. There Williams insisted that

> we cannot preach the Fatherhood of God unless we believe in the Brotherhood of Man. We cannot believe in the brotherhood of man unless we accept the implications of such a brotherhood. We cannot believe in democracy unless we accept the implications of democracy. We cannot fight for a just and durable peace while we "ration" the four freedoms to "native-born Gentile whites." There is no such thing in the world today—nor can there be—as an "individual" Christian, an "isolated," "segregated," "jim-crowed," "Nordic" or "cautious" Christian; nor a class, caste, or "native born, Gentile, white" democrat. These are contradictions in terms, anti-religious and representative of the truly godless movements.

Williams reminded the congregation of the nature of Pentecost, when all were united together as one people, divided by neither race, gender, nor class. Again and again Williams hammered on the theme of the unity of all people. But unity could be established only when all God's people came to terms with the issues facing people of color. Hence, justice for African Americans was the litmus test of whether the ideals of democracy and Christian faith had become more than beautiful-sounding verbal pronouncements.

> The peoples of the world are predominantly colored. Therefore since all problems are world problems, the index of progress in this country is with the Negro people, i.e., if we are right on the issues pertaining to the interest of the Negro people we are right on most issues. If we are wrong on these issues, we are wrong on most issues. The Negro people constitute not only the largest and most conspicuous minority in the United States but also the minority most vitally connected—both economically (Mtt. 5:3) and racially (Mtt 25:40) with the world dynamic for democracy and freedom. Therefore reaction crystallizes against them more swiftly and easily than against any other group. . . . If the Church is to have any part in the establishment of a people's world, it must get in the gutter with the multitudes and again demonstrate its blood heritage. There is blood on Calvary, blood on the stones of the prophets, blood in the lion's dens of history. It is just as red as any red of history, and was shed in the same struggle for economic, social, and political and racial justice for all people. The church must reclaim this heritage.[71]

While Williams focused his energies on combatting reactionary forces opposed to democracy and freedom in Detroit, the PIAR continued its work throughout the South, setting up institutes, running conferences, and bringing new hope to downtrodden people. A. L. Campbell led "Anti-Semitism, Racism and Democracy" institutes in Arkansas and Missouri. He reported from Pocahontas, Arkansas; "Just came home from one of the biggest and best institutes which I believe we ever had. Some nights we had around three hundred people present." In St. Louis, Owen and Zella Whitfield led a PIAR institute of black and white sharecroppers to whom Owen Whitfield preached: "I say to you not blessed are the poor in spirit but rather: Blessed are the spirited poor. The poor won't inherit the earth until they get sassy enough to take it." When the war ended Claude and Joyce Williams returned to the South and set up the PIAR headquarters in Birmingham, Alabama. From there the Williamses and their supporters carried on their efforts for racial justice and the creation of unity among a poor and divided people. It was a difficult struggle. The PIAR was officially disbanded in March of 1949 because Williams felt that "the developing hysteria of the cold-war made it impossible to find a place where Negro and white working-preachers might meet together and speak truthfully about the problems of racial brotherhood, political equality, economic justice and permanent peace." Despite setbacks, Williams continued until his death in 1979 to battle against white supremacy and intolerance and for civil rights, racial justice, and equality. At a memorial service held in his honor, a tape recording of the words of old friend, biographer, and colleague Cedric Belfrage was played. Belfrage had sent his remarks from his place of exile in Mexico. He noted that Williams "recognized long before 99 percent of white Americans the truth of W. E. B. Du Bois's saying, 'The problem of the twentieth century is the problem of the color line.' " [72]

The Struggle for Racial Justice, an Enduring Commitment

Living as we do in the twilight of the twentieth century, it might be asked what Howard Kester, Claude Williams, the Southern Tenant Farmers' Union, and the People's Institute of Applied Religion contributed toward resolving what Gunnar Myrdal labeled "the American dilemma," racism. [73] First of all, Kester and Williams stressed that racism was more than a set of values and attitudes; it shaped structures of oppression that divided poor people, black and white, and maintained a privileged white elite in power, and it was rooted in an economic system, capitalism. Williams, in particular, sought to help poor whites understand that racism blinded them to the fact that the powerlessness they felt in their lives, the inability to provide for their families and realize their hopes and dreams, had more to do with class than race. Racism was not, he believed, some sort of ontological given, for if it was, then it was unalterable. Rather, racism had a history, and was part of a sociopolitical matrix intricately related to how an economy functioned, who benefited and who did not. Through the organizing efforts of the STFU and the institutes and conferences sponsored by the PIAR, poor whites learned that they had more in common with their black brothers and sisters than with the white planters and their hirelings who oppressed both of them. For Williams, racial unity was the same thing as class unity; it would permit oppressed people to join together to overthrow the forces of domination and claim their place in a democratic society.

Second, both Kester and Williams learned early on that the struggle against racism had its costs, costs that had so far been borne largely by black people. Williams had a way of bluntly stating the obvious, and he once said: "There is no way out of paying the price of brotherhood in blood; and the white man will have to pay his share. What we need is not the courage to stand for our convictions, but the courage to have convictions." It was one thing to proclaim human rights in seminaries, church conventions, and prosperous congregations, quite another to do so in Detroit defense plants and southern towns. To stand for racial unity, in such places, to proclaim in the midst of real conflict that poor people had as much right to share in the goods of this life as the privileged and powerful, was to feel the violence, hatred, and wrath of those who benefited from the status quo. [74]

Third, both Kester and Williams understood that the issue of race was as inseparable from religion as from class. They realized that religion was both part of the problem and part of the solution. It was one thing for sharecroppers to know that the white church had accommodated itself to the demands of King

Cotton and had served to legitimate the plantation system, but it was another thing to unravel how racism was intertwined with a disembodied fundamentalism and its ahistorical Jesus. Williams's approach to the Bible as the "People's Book" was one means of helping poor people to discover the prophetic and liberative nature of their own Christian faith. Williams began with what he perceived to be the very material basis of the biblical tradition. Jesus' preaching had to do with meeting material needs, from bread for the hungry to clothing for the naked and freedom for the imprisoned. Long before liberation theology, Williams argued that class struggle, oppression and liberation, rich and poor, poverty and wealth are salient themes of the biblical text. Likewise, Kester's experience with the STFU reinforced his conviction that religion could enable, indeed had enabled, poor people to sustain themselves against what seemed impossible odds. For both men, religion had to do with the basic wholeness of life; it not only gave meaning to social and political praxis, to human experience, but made the human spirit soar and allowed human eyes to behold the possibility of beauty. Kester wrote in 1940 that "Christianity is concerned with the welfare of the human body and the eternal flowering of the human spirit; it must, if it is true to its mission, be content with nothing less than the ordering of the total life of man." An important part of the reordering of life was the relationship between human beings, no longer separated by color but drawn together in freedom and equality. Williams would add that the mark of brother/sisterhood was the degree to which the "burden of color" was lifted and the worth and dignity of people of color were acknowledged.[75]

The interrelated experiences that marked the lives of Claude Williams and Howard Kester were more than their individual biographies, for these men were part of interracial organizations dedicated to making the good news of the gospel a reality for poor people. Given the institutionalized violence of the 1930s, the ability of the Southern Tenant Farmers' Union to forge a sense of community among black and white sharecroppers, however short-lived, was a remarkable accomplishment. Just as remarkable was the role cotton-patch preachers played in the organizational life of the union. Through word and deed they made possible a new vision of what the South might be when purged of racism, poverty, and hopelessness, a vision that would flower again in another generation. To a forgotten people, the STFU became a movement for social change, the basis for new life.

Likewise, Claude Williams's People's Institute of Applied Religion instilled in people not only a new sense of self but tools with which to understand how the system operated, that being poor did not mean one had to live poor for the rest of one's life. Poor people also learned that the Bible was their book, a book written about poor people, which celebrated not the mighty acts and deeds of the powerful and privileged but stories of the downtrodden, visions of prophets, and God's love for the poor and God's presence in their struggles to create a new social order. The experience of thousands of poor people who attended PIAR institutes throughout the South was best summed up by D. C. Williams, a sharecropper from East Prairie, Missouri, former member of the KKK and PIAR organizer. After attending a PIAR institute held in St. Louis, he underwent a conversion and became, along with A. L. Campbell, one of the PIAR's most effective leaders. After the St. Louis conference he wrote a poem he called "Startled":

> One thing I learned that startled me
> That if "ye know the truth it will make you free."
> I learned a lesson and learned it well
> This lesson to the people I wanted to tell.

> I received a chart from this college,
> Which revealed much Godly knowledge
> To us these charts were brought
> To reveal the system that Jesus taught.

> The truth I was teaching and doing no harm
> When some one sounded the danger alarm.
> "He's a 'Communist' and a dangerous foe"
> He's just returned from meeting the CIO.

> . . .

> It was not a union which I was seeking
> I was content with religious teaching
> But if those toppers want not a union to encircle their throng,
> They'd better leave old D. Williams alone.[76]

Christian ethicists could take some lessons from preachers such as D. C. Williams and other poor men and women who gave their lives so that justice, equality, and freedom might be more than hollow-sounding rhetoric. Ethical discourse takes on new meaning and gains credibility when spoken by those personally committed to social change and willing to suffer the risks such commitment might entail. It is one thing to speak about equality and justice to a polite middle-class audience, from the pulpit, in the classroom, or at a political conference where the most one can expect is a possible hostile word or gesture. It is quite another thing to speak of such ideals when violence or even one's own death is a real possibility. Williams's life in many ways is paradigmatic. During some of the most violent decades of this century, Williams was a consistent voice for the voiceless, but more important he empowered the oppressed to discover their own voice, words, and future. It is not enough to help people who are dependent upon the power of others, be they the government, the church, or even unions. People must take charge of their own lives, and the Christian faith can play an important role in enabling poor people to pursue freedom and equality. In the end, to take democracy seriously is to understand that those who have historically been used, manipulated, and controlled by others must have a central role in defining the nature of the political community.

173

5

The Great Evasion

Religion, Marxism, and the Politics of

Nonviolence

American historian William Appleman Williams contends that in reducing life to the dictates of the marketplace, we practice a "great evasion," for we avoid having to come to terms not only with our domination of nature and the meaning of human existence but with the necessary ingredients for the "building of a true community." As we stand on the brink of a new century, what we perhaps need to recapture more than anything else is a vision of community, a realization, writes Warren R. Copeland, of "what persons have in common rather than what we have apart." Human interdependence, it can be argued, rather than human antagonism, forms the basis for a community that can sustain a viable economic and sociopolitical order. We seem to have lost confidence in the redemptive power of Christian faith, ourselves, and the democratic processes that speak of the person-in-community and the common good.[1]

One avenue for restructuring a debate about the nature of community can be found through Williams's insistence on listening to what Marx has to say to us, especially when that discussion is conjoined with an analysis of nonviolence as the politics of empowerment. It is also important at the outset to note that a discussion of Marx and nonviolence is not a contradiction in terms. Marx believed in the necessity for workers to be engaged in the political process, emphasizing that violence was not always the best means for the establishment of workers' control of society. It seemed apparent to Marx that each country had its own "institutions, mores, and traditions," and in some contexts, such as the United States, England, and Holland, "the workers can attain their goal by peaceful means."[2]

However, to engage in a discussion about the essence of human community entails a word of caution. Community can become equated with forms of particularism that separate people from one another and reinforce modes of domination and control, such that the rhetoric of community becomes equal with feelings of belonging and security that are defensive and static, only perpetuating racism, exploitation, and inequality. On the other hand, note Sara Evans and Harry Boyle, community can mean participation and equality, as people who have been rendered powerless discover new modes of living together that "outgrow parochialisms of class, race, and sex, and form a broader conception of the common good." What is crucial, as Norman Birnbaum has said, is the ability to make links between community and polity that bind together "particular and universal social concepts." The struggle for community, then, is not distinct from the attempt to limit forms of nationalistic chauvinism, be they aspirations of empire building or preoccupations with national security to the exclusion of global realities and responsibilities. Furthermore, the attempt to translate concerns about community into programs, policies, and social visions has something to do with fundamental assumptions about human beings, their needs, wants, and hopes, and with questions of ends and means. In sum, how we deal with ourselves as a people, a community, and a nation is not unrelated to how we deal with the world and the categories, concepts, or values that make for peace and justice at home and abroad.[3]

Writing in 1941, the Scottish philosopher John Macmurray stressed that "freedom and equality are the keynotes of democracy. Democracy opposes privilege and social distinction, because these mean that some people or some classes of people are cornering freedom and responsibility for themselves at the expense of others. It bases rights upon common humanity and not any limited ground such as citizenship, or nationality, sex or race." By extension, democracy can flourish only to the degree to which "the spirit of community" based on the "service of the common life and its common needs" is recognized. Christianity, like democracy, Macmurray continues, is equally concerned about the nature of community, but its vision of community is revolutionary because it stands "for the oppressed against the rich, the common people against the rulers, both temporal and spiritual." The Christian social order "puts down the mighty from their seats and exalts the humble and meek." Christianity is future oriented because it strives for a new community in which people are bound not by distinctions based on class, race, or gender but by human relationships grounded in the "mutual service of equals." Democracy and Christianity share a refusal to legitimate hierarchy, authority, and privilege, placing their faith in a "common humanity."[4] Macmurray's language and analysis assume that freedom and equality have meaning, that human commonality is a shared experience. Part of what follows is a recovery of the givenness of a language that liberates and seeks to build community. To a degree each of the previous chapters has been about the search for community, and about meaning and value, especially in light of the destructive and exploitative nature of a developing capitalist system. This chapter is a more explicit attempt to deal with the issue of community by focusing on the life and thought of four individuals: Reinhold Niebuhr, Harry F. Ward, A. J. Muste, and Dorothy Day.

Niebuhr is particularly important because of his status as one of the most important theological figures in American history. Arthur Schlesinger, Jr., has called him the most influential "preacher" of his generation, in both the religious and the political realms. Niebuhr's stature as a theologian, ethicist, and political analyst has given his views on Marx, communism, the Soviet Union, and violence and nonviolence more weight than those of his religious contemporaries. In addition, as Beverly Harrison has noted, "Niebuhr's influence has conditioned both the practice and the ideological sensibility of religious ethicists." It has, it can be maintained, because Niebuhr embodied the essence of a "realistic" approach to religion and politics, which made distinctions, perceived nuances, and was critical of any political or religious belief, system, or ideal that claimed one's absolute loyalty. And he couched his views in irony, ambiguity, and paradox. By contrast, Ward, Muste, and Day have in common the extent to which they differed with Reinhold Niebuhr and his judgments about the constitution of Williams's "true community." [5]

The differences among Niebuhr, Ward, Muste, and Day are best understood in the context of Franz Hinkelammert's observation that our perceptions of economic, social, and political reality, as well as our theological or philosophical assumptions, are "strongly determined by the theoretical categories of the framework we use for interpreting that reality. Social reality is not reality pure and simple, but rather a reality perceived from a given standpoint. We can perceive only the reality that becomes apparent to us with the theoretical categories we use. It is within this framework that phenomena come to have some meaning." Thus, it can be argued that the theoretical categories, language, and analysis employed by Niebuhr, Ward, Muste, and Day can be understood as shaped by two approaches to social reality, which Gérard Fourez calls realism and utopia. Each interpretative stance represents a certain attitude, temperament, and strategy for dealing with the world and what is historically possible. Niebuhr in this case is the realist, and Ward, Muste, and Day are the utopians.[6]

Whereas Fourez's understanding of the realistic and utopian do not necessarily "fit" with every aspect of the life and work of Niebuhr, Ward, Muste, and Day, his remarks have a ring of truth that will become more apparent. The realist is, for Fourez, one who recognizes that we live amid conflict and that violence is rooted in the aggressive tendencies of human beings and human self-interest. There is an inherent distrust of idealistic ideologies that "aim too high," for if the limits of human possibility are overlooked, dreams can all too easily turn into nightmares. Politics is the art of the possible, a balance between contending forces and movements. Realism thus deals with what is, not with what should be. Utopians recognize human aggressiveness but nevertheless believe that people can change and that there is "reasonable hope for a better world." Likewise, they recognize the pervasiveness of violence, both personal and structural, but also realize that it is not as important to condemn violence as to search for alternatives to it. Politics is the art of imagination, of learning how to conceive the world differently and to create new human possibilities. Utopians see a fundamental contrast "between what human beings have been and what they could be," trusting that the history of humankind has yet to be told and acknowledging "a mystical dimension of hope for historical freedom that the realist's attitude lacks." [7]

Reinhold Niebuhr and Harry F. Ward

J. King Gordon, a leading Canadian Christian Socialist of the 1930s, was a graduate student at Union Theological Seminary in New York City during the early days of the Depression. He was appointed as a graduate assistant in Christian ethics to both Reinhold Niebuhr and Harry F. Ward. What struck him about Niebuhr was his consuming emphasis on the tensions between the dictates of an absolute ethic of love and the commitment to action in a world of injustice and power politics. Ward, by contrast, seemed to Gordon to have no tensions or constraints derived from a transcendental theology, only a social gospel that led directly to a revolutionary social ethic. Gordon's reflections on the 1930s are a reminder that Niebuhr was not the only ethicist who stalked the halls of Union Theological Seminary. In fact, Ward had been at Union since 1918 and had a well-established reputation as a noted Christian radical. In the thirties he was often paired with Niebuhr as a prophetic disturber of Christian complacency. His contribution to Christian ethics has been eclipsed by the cold war, during which he was dismissed as an "apologist" for the Soviet Union. To understand his contributions it is important to move beyond the labels or caricatures our historical experience has given us, especially those that have been painted with the brush of anticommunism or the ideological debates of another era. [8]

Reinhold Niebuhr and the Art of the Possible

The journey of Reinhold Niebuhr from radical critic of American society to celebrated figure in American life has been told and retold in varying ways, but the most perceptive and balanced treatment of the complexities of Niebuhr's life to date is that of Richard Fox. Here, there is no need to duplicate the work of Niebuhr's biographer, but it is crucial to try to understand the changes that took place in Niebuhr's formulation of an adequate social ethic, particularly how Niebuhr dealt with structural questions in terms of power politics rather than the political economy of capitalism. Such questions are not unrelated to Niebuhr's developing attitudes about the possibility for social change and what makes for a viable community. Before turning to the radical Niebuhr of the thirties, we can learn much about Niebuhr from his pastoral experience in the city of Detroit between 1915 and 1928. [9]

In 1915 at the age of twenty-three Niebuhr became pastor of Bethel Evangelical Church, a small congregation in Detroit, Michigan, made up largely of middle-class German Americans. Reflecting on his Detroit experience later in life, Niebuhr took particular care to emphasize that he was not the pastor of a "workers' church." He was confronted on a daily basis not with the problems facing working-class people but with "the social and moral irrelevance of a complacent middle class church." This did not mean that he was unaware of the issues facing workers in the auto industry, or that he did not have doubts about the policies and practices of Henry Ford's supposed humanitarianism, which, Niebuhr believed, could not mask the "groans of his workers . . . [which] may be heard above the din of his machines." But Niebuhr was less preoccupied with the realities of class and a class-divided society than with what he perceived as the tragic dimensions of human life. What contact he had with the labor movement led him to believe that the leaders of the American Federation of Labor had about as much "imagination as a group of village bankers" and that a new type of leadership was necessary. Niebuhr tended to assume that workers were a passive lot, easily swayed by conservatives and radicals alike. Furthermore, the country seemed to him to lack a democratic tradition of "radical idealism"; according to Niebuhr, "There is no real radicalism in America." He viewed Marxism as antithetical to people's aspirations for a democratic social order and perceived it as a rigid form of instrumentalism that had no "confidence in people," believing more in the power of impersonal economic and political forces than what people could create for themselves.[10]

Far more troublesome for Niebuhr was the liberal sentimentalism of fellow clergy who, because of their romantic notions of human nature, seemed unable to comprehend the degree to which the human person was "imperialistic and even parasitic in his nature." To think that people were otherwise, in their private and collective lives, was to fail to deal with "the brutalities of life." Nothing else could explain the realities of power and greed. And yet, for all Niebuhr's despair about human beings, he made a distinction between the individual and society that was to be the hallmark of his later work. It seemed to Niebuhr that "men are clearly not very lovely in the mass. One can maintain confidence in them only by viewing them at close range."[11]

Many interpreters have noted that Niebuhr, later the cold warrior, was in the 1930s a Socialist who used a Marxist analysis in his critique of religion and society and that his position as an architect of Cold War policy had evolved over time. Yet Niebuhr's socialism and anticommunism were not distinct phases in his life. There was no "epistemological break" between the young and old Niebuhr. The vehemence with which Niebuhr was to condemn communism and Marxism as he grew disillusioned with socialism and the working class was rooted in his reading of Marx, Marxism, and working-class realities in the 1930s.[12]

The onset of the Great Depression raised questions for Niebuhr about capitalism, politics, and the future of American society. Unemployment, which stood at 3.1 percent in 1929, rose by 1933 to 25.2 percent, so that by March of 1933 over fifteen million people were out of work. U.S. industrial output fell by 47 percent from 1929 to 1934, and over half of the total decline in the world's industrial production took place in the United States. More dramatic examples of the human costs than any statistics can convey were the growing number of "Hoovervilles," nothing more than shantytowns, which sprang up across the country as jobless, homeless, and penniless people tried to ride out the worst depression in American history. And the problems were more severe than they might have been because "no major country in the world was so ill-prepared as the United States to cope with it." People were unable to come to grips with the Depression partly because they believed the myth of American uniqueness, that somehow the United States was exempt from the societal ills of the Old World. Thus, the effects were as much psychological as economic: confidence in the established order and the values upon which it was based was badly shaken. Thomas Wolfe's posthumously published *You Can't Go Home Again* vividly records how one writer measured the effects of the Great Depression.

> What happened in Libya Hill and elsewhere has been described in the learned tomes of the overnight economists as a breakdown of "the system, the capitalist system." Yes, it was that. But it was also much more than that. In Libya Hill it was the total disintegration of what, in so many different ways, the lives of all these people had come to be. It went much deeper than the mere obliteration of bank accounts, the extinction of paper profits, and the loss of property. It was the ruin of men who found out, as soon as these symbols of their outward success had been destroyed, that they had nothing left—no inner equivalent from which they might now draw new strength. It was the ruin of men who, discovering not only that their values were false but that they had never had any substance whatsoever, now saw at last the emptiness and hollowness of their lives. Therefore they killed themselves; and those who did not die by their own hands died by the knowledge that they were already dead.[13]

The Depression had a radicalizing effect on the left wing of mainline Protestant Christianity. The *World Tomorrow*, whose editors were Reinhold Niebuhr, Devere Allen, and Kirby Page, was by early 1931 supporting the Socialist Party, regarding both the Republican and Democratic parties as incapable of making the drastic economic and political changes necessary to deal with the Depression. The editorial policy of the *World Tomorrow* was that the only concrete alternative to American capitalism was socialism. Protestants, in particular, were attracted to the Socialist Party because the leadership of Norman Thomas drew to it a largely educated and middle-class constituency. With Thomas at the helm, the Socialist Party gained a religious legitimacy that could have been conferred by few others. Kirby Page believed that "the mantle of Debs has fallen upon Thomas and he has become the acknowledged spokesman of American Socialists."[14]

The Depression also gave birth to the Fellowship of Socialist Christians, founded in 1931 as the outgrowth of discussions among members of the New York–based Conference of Younger Churchmen. This association of clergy, academics, and radicalized church people, led by Reinhold Niebuhr, maintained that neither a bankrupt liberal Christianity, with its moral illusions about human beings and the nature of violence, nor capitalistic individualism could deal with the social upheaval of the Depression; the only answer was socialism. Only active Socialists were admitted to membership, and therefore most FSC members joined Thomas's Socialist Party. Although it was a small organization, the FSC was influential among the generation of men and women who came of age in the midst of the Depression and moved along a course from radical opposition to the status quo and into the mainstream of American life. It was Reinhold Niebuhr who gave a definite stamp to the form of socialism espoused by the fellowship.[15]

It was not surprising that the editors of the *World Tomorrow* supported Norman Thomas and the Socialist Party's bid in the presidential election of 1932, stressing that capitalism was dying and it was only a matter of time before its autopsy would be written. The triumph of socialism seemed, particularly to Reinhold Niebuhr and Kirby Page, inevitable. Niebuhr and other editors of the *World Tomorrow* harshly criticized those who abandoned the Socialist Party because it did not easily obtain power. They noted that if one "does not have a religious zeal for its cause and the attendant confidence in its ultimate victory, it will not be able to persist through the years of hardship until its final goal is reached." But Niebuhr's belief in Socialist inevitability was to be short-lived. By the 1936 election, Niebuhr questioned whether Thomas's Socialist Party was a viable political option, given its dwindling public and political support. Niebuhr concluded prior to that election that divisive and destructive factional debates within the Socialist Party meant that "American socialism as a whole is not ready to be an emancipating factor in our political situation." His reservations can be found in what he considered to be his most Marxist works, *Moral Man and Immoral Society* and *Reflections on the End of an Era*.[16]

John C. Bennett has commented that Niebuhr "hammered into our minds" the difference between individual action and collective behavior. Whereas the human individual might develop religious ideals, aspirations, and ethical models, these could not be extended to the collective or societal interaction of people without recourse to means that would greatly qualify the aims of such ideals on an individual scale. Self-interest manifested itself in all collective activity and affected the operation of disinterested moral or religious ideals that were possible between individuals. Religious idealism must thus be tempered by a recognition of human beings' collective proclivity toward selfishness. While love might be the ideal, justice was what was possible in the societal arena.[17]

In Marx and the Marxist tradition, Niebuhr discovered a concept he believed was central to an understanding of human history: the nature of power and the will-to-power, especially economic and political power, were "the distinctive feature of the Marxian dream . . . [and] the destruction of power is regarded as the prerequisite of its attainment." Marxism seemed to offer a form of social analysis that could address the contradictions of American society under capitalism. Thus Marxism served not only as an instrument of societal critique but also as a condemnation of what was felt to be bourgeois Christianity's ideological and institutional sanctification of the capitalist system. Niebuhr assigned the role of establishing a just social order to the proletariat. A self-conscious Marxian proletariat, aware of the various configurations that economic and political power have taken, was "potentially the strongest force of redemption in society." Yet for all his faith in the proletariat, Niebuhr had little faith in what people could accomplish, given the "stupidity of the average man." [18]

Niebuhr believed Marxism also contributed to a form of social realism that acknowledged the inevitability of social conflict in human history and underscored the necessity of being cognizant of the pitfalls of utopianism, be it religious, political, or socialist. He contended that unchecked utopianism, in its various idealistic guises, could foster both absolutism and fanaticism, which in its political form "shuts the gates of mercy on mankind." In his assessment of the prospects for socialism Niebuhr was absorbed by the debates in which European Socialists were engaging, particularly in England and Germany, and paid little direct attention to either the history or the experience of American Socialists and workers.[19]

By the time Niebuhr wrote *Reflections on the End of an Era* the stress he had placed on collective egoism and the demonic nature of utopianism in *Moral Man and Immoral Society* was sharpened and heightened to such a degree, as J. King Gordon has pointed out, that it was no longer a question of an immoral society but "a terribly immoral society." Marxism seemed to bolster belief in the destruction that awaits capitalism but also the fate of all human constructs that forget that the impulses of history are governed not by reason but by the order of nature, that they lead not to life but to death. While Marxism seemed to account for the crisis of a capitalist society, only the traditional Christian realization of human finitude and sinfulness could ultimately account for "the fact that every co-operative achievement in human history actually had the possibilities of providing collective egoism with wider and more destructive forms of expression." Niebuhr concluded that the will-to-power was inevitable, corrupting the Marxist belief in the possibility of a better order of things. In the American working class he saw little hope for the future. In this country, he said, "no authentic proletariat" existed, other than those unemployed who sporadically expressed a "spirit of rebellion," and there was no class consciousness among American workers. In place of his earlier hope for the revolutionary potential of the proletariat as the forerunners of a new social order, he now saw only signs of the perils of a form of barbarism "actuated by the spirit of vengeance as much as by the spirit of justice." [20]

As James Gilbert has noted, Niebuhr did not share with Marx the conviction that the "predominant characteristics of a period [are] reflected in its property forms and not in power relationships." In his preoccupation with power and the balancing of power relationships, Niebuhr overlooked the Marxist view that human exploitation of human beings is historical and not ontological. He failed to note that for Marx the class struggle leads not to a power equilibrium but to the older French Socialist idea of "from each according to his abilities, to each according to his needs." Furthermore, as Beverly Harrison points out, Marx was more concerned about "a critical description of what exists, not positive or predictive knowledge of what will be." Marx was interested not only in the destructive nature of a capitalist political economy but in wider social and cultural relations. In lamenting the nature of the American working class as a form of "exceptionalism," Niebuhr failed to examine its long history of resistance or to understand American workers' perceptions of class relations, which were indeed class conscious. At the same time Niebuhr neglected the extent to which the hegemonic power of capitalism is based on the exercise of varying forms of domination that range from the mechanism of state control to ideology.[21]

One of the most intriguing aspects of his radicalism is Niebuhr's understanding of the relation between Christianity and socialism. George Hammar contends that in the final analysis, there was no connection between the socialist elements of Niebuhr's social ethics and his religioethical thinking. Niebuhr's Marxism had no intrinsic relation to his Christian orthodoxy except where it coincided with his reading of political realities. It did not call his theological assumptions into question, because the tragedy of human existence was as much a given as the despairing realism of Niebuhr's theology. Only Christianity, with its understanding of human finitude and the depths of the collective human proclivity toward evil could offer a "realistic" appraisal of the human condition and the limits of human possibility. If Niebuhr had read Marx with greater care, he might have come to question his own reading of the Christian tradition. For all Niebuhr's supposed radicalism, the conservativeness of his interpretation of Jesus is striking. The teachings of Jesus were reduced to an individualistic ethic of love, from which one could derive neither a social ethic nor social implications, for Jesus' "chief interest was in the quality of the life of an individual." Jesus did not question the established political or social order; his life offered only the ideal of perfect love, which was impossible to realize within history. Given the nature of human self-interest, the most that could be hoped for was relative justice, that is, "the achievement of justice through equilibria of power." [22]

By the mid-1930s Niebuhr's ahistorical treatment of Marx would be set over and against the realism of Christianity. Marxism, for all its irreligious claims, functioned as a religion. It duplicated the errors of religious absolutism, and its secularized message contained not only romantic illusions about human nature but an oversimplified analysis of the human situation. Niebuhr came to believe that because of the human propensity for collective evil, a qualitatively better order of things was not possible and that all human projections and possibilities were tainted "with the force of human ego's will-to-live and will-to-power."

The problem rested once again with power, be it in the hands of the bourgeoisie or the proletariat. Niebuhr coined what he believed to be an apt axiom: "Trust no man." [23]

Niebuhr's final disillusionment with Marxism came with a series of events that marked the end of the 1930s. This was a period in which Niebuhr characterized the world as mad, for "step by step the nations rush toward disaster." The West was still recoiling from the Moscow trials and subsequent purges; Republican Spain was fighting for its existence against Franco and his fascist allies; China was open to Japanese aggression; and the so-called democratic powers stood by, hoping the Munich accord in 1938 would bring peace, as Europe was being dismembered by the Nazis. As the world seemed to totter on the break of disaster, Marxism, for Niebuhr, suffered a series of reversals. Events in the Soviet Union "seriously . . . [challenged] the Marxian interpretation of the state as an instrument of class domination which will wither away in a classless society" and threw doubt "upon the Marxian analysis of human nature." In contrast to the pronouncements of Leon Trotsky and the Communist Left, Niebuhr attributed the Stalinist repressions not to Stalin's machinations but to human nature. Like many of his contemporaries, he so identified Marxism with the fate of the Soviet Union that he judged the adequacy of Marxism as a form of social analysis to a significant degree on its application in the Soviet Union. The signing of the German-Soviet nonaggression pact on August 23, 1939, brought Niebuhr to the conclusion that the "tragedy of our era is not merely the decay of a capitalist bourgeois social order, but the corruption of its alternative socialist order almost as soon as it had established itself." [24]

Thus, Niebuhr concluded that both Marx and communism had an unrealistic view of human nature and human possibilities. Communism was not as bad as fascism, but its utopian assumptions about a new social order and working-class aspirations for justice were self-deceptions that turned out to be not dreams for human betterment but living nightmares. What Niebuhr found so objectionable about Marxism was its basic faith in the capacity of human beings to create something new in history. The world around him seemed to confirm only a pessimistic interpretation of human events, shoring up both his antiutopianism and his basic distrust of human nature. J. King Gordon believes that his realism and pessimism put Niebuhr at odds with those who had more "confidence in the redemptive power of Christianity" in the establishment of an infinitely better social order. [25]

With the conclusion of World War II, whatever qualifications Niebuhr had about the Soviet Union, Marx, and communism came to an end. The war and his own development led to what he called Christian realism. Many hailed Niebuhr as a hard-boiled realist who portrayed the Soviet Union as it really was and decried the destructive illusions of communism. Despite reservations about strategies that were "primarily military," Niebuhr never doubted that "communism must be contained." He chastised idealists who could not comprehend the fanaticism of Communists and the "reality of evil" that communism represented.[26]

One problem was that Niebuhr's ahistorical and abstract treatment of the Soviet Union as the embodiment of evil was set over and against another set of abstractions, the United States as the defender of freedom and justice. The opening lines of *The Irony of American History* (1952) maintained: "Everybody understands the meaning of the world struggle in which we are engaged. We are defending freedom against tyranny and are trying to preserve justice against a system which has, demonically, distilled injustice and cruelty out of its original promise of a higher justice." Drawing on themes he had developed in the 1930s, Niebuhr contended that the evil of communism was its "utopian illusions," which made it "more dangerous than Nazism." Its greatest danger was in its secularized version of Christian hopes for humankind, the belief that one could overcome "the ambiguities of history" and establish the Kingdom of God on earth. What most frightened Niebuhr were the religious and moral characteristics he attributed to Marxism and communism. Niebuhr, so fond of irony, failed to see the great irony of his critique of Marxists for exalting the poor, for believing that the poor should inherit the earth, as if solidarity with the poor and oppressed were not in keeping with the gospel as good news for the poor. One of Niebuhr's most acclaimed anti-Communist pieces, according to Richard Fox, was an article he wrote for the *New Leader* titled "The Evil of the Communist Idea," which was included in Niebuhr's collection *Christian Realism and Political Problems* (1953). Bertram Wolfe of the State Department's Ideological Advisory Staff used it for a radio broadcast. In the article, which appeared ten days before the execution of Julius and Ethel Rosenberg, Niebuhr described communism as "an organized evil which spreads terror and cruelty throughout the world and confronts us everywhere with faceless men who are immune to every form of moral and political suasion." The essay sounded like a movie script and it reduced whatever sense Niebuhr had of the ambiguities of life to something close to one-dimensional cold-war propaganda.[27]

Equally one-dimensional was Niebuhr's depiction of the United States as a society that had achieved justice through an equilibrium of power. Niebuhr, once critical of the shortcomings of American capitalism and an advocate of socialism, now argued that the Marxist analysis of capitalism was in error. American business had accepted the power of labor, had even acknowledged the rights of collective bargaining as part of the "American way of life." Thus Niebuhr ignored the possibility that the struggle against communism served the desire of the dominant elites to break the back of labor and destroy the Left in the labor movement. With the passage of the Taft-Hartley Act, especially its anti-Communist affidavits, "mass picketing, secondary boycotts, and sympathy strikes" were banned. Nor did Niebuhr mention how anticommunism led to the expulsion of progressive unions, such as the United Electrical

Workers Union from the CIO or how the Communist Party had organized black and Puerto Rican workers against racism. Christopher Lasch concludes that Niebuhr was not comparing differing social structures or systems but simply playing "one myth off against the other." Talking about "the Soviet Union as a monolith, obedient to some mysterious and inflexible law of totalitarianism, made very little sense at a time when the structure of Soviet society was undergoing important and far-reaching changes; to characterize American society as 'tolerant and modest' made very little sense at any time in American history." [28]

Niebuhr's anticommunism blinded him to the repercussions of domestic anticommunism in other ways. For example, he was critical of the tactics of Joseph McCarthy not because they violated people's civil liberties or established an atmosphere of suspicion and fear but because they were ineffectual in combatting communism. Similarly, when J. B. Matthews, who had become a "professional" authority on communism for the Committee on Un-American Activities, claimed that thousands of Protestant ministers were fellow travelers and Communist sympathizers, Niebuhr criticized him for the way in which he handled numbers and not for naming names. He had little sympathy for the Rosenbergs and felt the death penalty was not too severe for those he considered traitors. Niebuhr argued that "traitors are never ordinary criminals and the Rosenbergs are quite obviously loyal Communists. While the death penalty may be unprecedented, it is also obvious that the cold war in which we stand is an unprecedented form of peace and stealing atomic secrets is an unprecedented crime." [29]

In the international arena Niebuhr became an apologist for imperialism, criticizing those who saw it as an unambiguous evil. He believed that they had forgotten the great benefits of education and technical skills that came with the domination of most of the world by the West. Niebuhr neglected to come to terms with the resulting lack of control people had over their own economies, the collusion between domestic and foreign elites, and the role of U.S. business interests. For Niebuhr the real sin of imperialism was spiritual ("arrogance of power") rather than economic exploitation. Though he acknowledged that the United States was an imperial power, he maintained that the nation exercised its power in morally responsible ways that led to peace. The United States, he felt, used its political hegemony with firmness and soberness in its struggle with the Soviet Union. Niebuhr warned that "dangerous as they are, [military dictatorships] are at least reversible and Communist dictatorships, supported by religio-political dogma, are irreversible." It is no wonder that this liberal world view came to demand U.S. intervention in other countries and U.S. support of dictatorial regimes—all in the name of fighting communism—when such rhetoric painted the United States as the defender of justice, liberty, and freedom. Charles West observed decades ago that "it is hard for all believers in Niebuhr's type of Christian action of a pragmatic sort to understand that their 'realism' transported out of an Anglo-Saxon environment sounds to others like ideology . . . [that] it justifies so much of the Anglo-Saxon way of life that it builds up the authority of the white man. In relation to Communism it tends to presuppose a community of 'free' nations against a tyranny, whereas the perspective of another country sees the danger of the two great power colossi, one hard and direct, the other softer and much more diffuse to be sure, but neither welcome as dominating power." [30]

Harry F. Ward and the Struggle for a New Social Order

Harry Frederick Ward was born in the Brentford section of London, England, on October 15, 1873, and died almost a century later on December 9, 1966. His life contradicted the truism that people become more conservative as they age. Ward was raised in a pious middle-class Methodist family. His father, a successful lay preacher, was also a butcher with an entrepreneurial bent who had little sympathy for the labor movement or concern about the working conditions of those in his employ. The Methodism of Ward's youth had an evangelical cast with its stress on the importance of personal religious experience and a rejection of what was perceived as the rigidity of Wesleyan formalism in both worship and theology. There was a suspicion, which Ward always shared, about theological formulations that were detached from life. Ward later wrote that "a theology that is purely or predominantly metaphysical is foredoomed to lose in the struggle with sin, because it diverts man's energies elsewhere." His Methodist background also provided him with a belief in human potential and human possibilities, a conviction that with God's grace many things can be accomplished, for history is infused with a "not yet" quality that has as much to do with the human person as with human society.[31]

At the age of seventeen Ward emigrated to the United States largely because of his desire for a college education, which the English class system of the period made impossible. He did his undergraduate studies at the University of Southern California and Northwestern University and earned a master's degree at Harvard. Those who most influenced Ward at Northwestern were John H. Gray, an economist who taught Ward about the tensions between Christianity and a profit-driven economic order, and George Albert Coe, a philosopher and religious educator who stressed the social nature of the self. At Harvard, Ward studied with William James, Josiah Royce, and Francis Peabody, then Professor of Christian Morals, and he did much of the research for Peabody's book *Jesus and the Social Question*, which was published in 1900. Ward had very little formal theological training, just enough to pass the examinations for the Methodist ministry. After completing his work at Harvard, he returned to Northwestern and spent two years as head resident of the Northwestern University Settlement, augmenting his second year with an appointment as a lay preacher in a parish on Wabash Avenue, Chicago. Ordained in 1902, Ward would spend the next twelve years in the parish ministry, eight in the Stock-yard area of Chicago. Ward once remarked that he was part of a generation of "uplifters and converts," some of whom became settlement house workers, muck-raking journalists, and Socialists, while he entered the church.[32]

The social, living, and working conditions of the Stockyard area of Chicago came to the attention of most Americans with the publication of Upton Sinclair's novel *The Jungle*. One of Sinclair's contemporaries, Charles Bushnell, contrasted Hyde Park, just to the east, with its "green lawns, beautiful homes . . . and thousands of special places of aesthetic recreation and inspiration" with the Stockyards, where people "struggle to manifest themselves amid squalid and unlovely surroundings." The back of the yards, as it was known, was originally a marsh and later the city dump, but since 1865 it had housed the meat-packing industry. The Stockyards were famous for their unsanitary living conditions, crowded tenements, and dilapidated houses. According to Edith Abbott, people worked in "unclean, dark, ill-ventilated rooms in which the slaughtering was done, vaults in which the air was rarely changed; windows clouded by dirt, walls and ceilings so dark and dingy that natural light penetrated only 20 or 30 feet," and lacking sanitary arrangements so that "odors and fumes" filled the air. It was here that Harry F. Ward came face to face with the realities of class and a growing labor movement.[33]

While working with the Northwestern University Settlement, Ward became friends with Jane Addams of Hull House, and he met Mary McDowell, Graham Taylor and George Herbert Mead. He became involved in various progressive social movements. He worked with the Chicago Civic Committee in its struggle against political corruption, was chairperson of both the Committee on Labor Conditions of the City Club of Chicago and the Commission on Church and Labor, and helped organize the Industrial Committee of the Churches of Chicago. Like many progressives of the period, Ward wrestled with the inadequacies of traditional responses to societal ills, but it was his day-to-day contact with the problems facing unskilled immigrant stockyard workers and their families that radicalized him.[34]

He organized community programs but found that only women and children responded to his "social ministry." His church, like many others in Chicago, received financial support from Gustavus F. Swift, founder of Swift and Company, one of the "Big Seven" Chicago meat packers. Swift and Company had grown from a single plant with sixteen hundred workers in 1886 to seven plants employing over twenty-three thousand in 1903; however, according to David Brody, "the struggle for empire left little room for the problems of workmen." Ward soon learned that workers were well aware of the support Swift gave local churches, money that came from speedups, unpaid overtime, and the institutionalized exploitation of working people. Workers came to call the extra work without extra pay "working for the church," knowing well that Swift's generosity to the religious community was dependent on the money he extracted from their labor. Ward elected to join forces with the unionizing efforts of stockyard workers, and he soon learned that his choice labeled him a Socialist in the eyes of G. F. Swift.[35]

It seemed obvious to Ward that working-class people could almost intuitively comprehend the radicality of Christian faith. Like many workers before and since, they distinguished between Jesus and the church. Jesus they perceived as a rightful member of the working class, "a carpenter," as one put it, despised by the upper classes. Jesus understood the suffering of workers "and told them openly that the day of deliverance was at hand and that he had come to set them free." It was a disquieting message for those in power. Christianity and the working class had a common vision of the world vividly embodied in the ideal of solidarity advocated by the IWW, a feeling, spirit, and hunger for a community not bound by "color or sex or creed or race." If it was obvious that the Christian view was also the workers' view, it was equally clear that it differed markedly from Christianity as practiced.[36]

So often Christianity, especially in its liberal middle-class version, was separated from life, as if God were removed from the history of people's search for liberation. Standing with oppressed people one could more easily understand the radicality of Scripture, of a God of justice experienced by those who struggled against oppression and domination. In fact, Ward believed that the Bible was unique, for it was the "only literature written by common people." Issues of life and death were not theological mysteries but concrete realities that had to do with God's concern for how an economy was organized, how political power was distributed, and how people lived out their lives. An experience of God was more than feeling. It was the biblical understanding of how God's presence was manifest in people's actions and their interrelationships. If one's knowledge of God did not lead to "more passion for justice," then it was questionable if one really understood a God of life. The God of the Bible was not confined to a book. God was active in the ongoing social struggles of people.[37]

Working-class people also raised important questions about the role of the church in society. Ward concluded it was incumbent upon the churches to deal with both the causes and the symptoms of social injustice. To that end, he joined a coalition of social gospel advocates within the Methodist Episcopal church who formed the Methodist Federation for Social Service in 1907. In addition to Ward, the four other individuals most responsible for the creation of the federation were Frank Mason North, corresponding secretary for the New York Evangelization Union; Herbert Welch (later bishop), president of Ohio Wesleyan University; Worth Tippy, pastor of an inner-city parish in Cleveland, Ohio; and Robb Zarring, assistant editor of the *Western Christian Advocate*. The federation was the semiofficial social action agency of the Methodist Episcopal church until it was ousted from the church during the height of the anti-Communist hysteria of the 1950s. For more than forty years under the leadership of Harry Ward, as executive secretary, and Bishop Francis McConnell, as president, the federation advanced a radical social gospel within the Methodist Episcopal church against racism, American imperialism, class exploitation, and the profit motive. The distinctive aspect of the federation's social gospel radicalism was its sustained criticism of capitalism as formulated by Ward. Throughout its history the federation sought to be a conscience for the church, raising issues and confronting problems the church might otherwise wish to ignore.[38]

Although Ward has often been viewed as a radical champion of the social gospel, he was always uncomfortable with the notion of a social gospel. He criticized the moralistic idealism of the social gospel advocates who were so easily disillusioned by the First World War and the resistance of an acquisitive society to social transformation. Nor did he like their tendency to believe that public pronouncement of abstract principles, no matter how revolutionary they sounded, could substitute for concrete action. The ideals of the social gospel movement, Niebuhr and other critics claimed, permitted little understanding of the tragic dimensions of life or recognition of sin and evil in the world. Ward agreed that "our goodness is not adequate to remove the evil that is in the world" but at the same time wanted to stress that sin had to do with "particular attitudes and deeds of man" that could be altered. The acknowledgement of sin should lead not to passivity or hopelessness but to a commitment to the struggle against whatever debased, demeaned, and delimited human hope and possibilities. Faith, he said, is that which establishes a "new heaven and a new earth. It proclaims the illimitable possibilities. At its best it offers man a future to be made, not merely waited for, a future to be lived in its promise, its hope, and its continual coming." It was also clear to Ward that proponents of the social gospel were reacting to the privatization of religion and its excessive preoccupation with the individual to the exclusion of the social dimensions of faith. But they failed, he believed, to "recognize that the Gospel, like man whose redemption it seeks, is neither social nor individual but inseparably both."[39]

Evident in Ward's analysis of the social gospel was the influence of his former teacher and longtime friend and colleague George Albert Coe. Coe maintained that the individual, qua individual, is part and parcel of society and that human selfhood is a social product. One's knowledge of self comes through interaction with other persons. Like George Herbert Mead, who contended that "the individual self is individual only because of its relation to others," Coe asserted that the self had to be understood in interpersonal terms. Ward's approach to structural questions was predicated upon this belief in a social concept of the human person. Instead of assuming that the only way to change society was to convert individuals one by one, it was important to realize the reciprocal relationship between individuals and society. Thus, as one transforms society, one cannot help but change the individual and his/her perception of self.[40]

More important, Ward refused, like Marx, to believe that a capitalist portrait of the human being was essentially the "nature" of the human person, that other human beings are but means to our self-realization. In Marx's critique of the *Declaration of the Rights of Man* of the French Revolution he asserted that the rights proclaimed are only the "rights of egoistic man, of man separated from other men and the community" and that "liberty as a right of man is not founded upon the relations between man and man, but rather upon the separation of man from man. It is the right of self-interest. . . . It leads every man to see in other men, not the realization, but the limitation of his own liberty." [41]

In 1913 Ward accepted an appointment as professor of social service at Boston University's School of Theology on the condition that he would be able to continue his work as executive secretary for the Methodist Federation for Social Service. Five years later he became professor of Christian ethics at Union Theological Seminary, where he would remain for the next twenty-three years. In those years he would serve for two decades as chairperson of the American Civil Liberties Union and of the American League against War and Fascism (the most important United Front organization of the 1930s). During those decades Ward was a controversial figure—defender of the rights of working people, critic of the wealth and power of the comfortable, and voice of those seeking radical social change. He was known for his breadth of social vision, commitment to social justice, and knowledge of grass-roots movements, always ready "with an unquenchable arsenal of facts, faith, and fidelity—the facts as he saw them through sharp, intelligent eyes—the faith that God was revealing himself in Jesus the Christ—the unashamed fidelity to that revelation." Ward was rarely self-reflective, but the following words seem to capture the meaning of his life: "Only as one's job is part of the lessening of misery and ignorance, of the search for freedom, justice, and fellowship, does he find that spring of such happiness as is possible in this disordered world." His contribution to social ethics and his insights into the necessary ingredients for building community can best be seen in Ward's analysis of the tensions between Christianity and democracy, the political economy of capitalism, and in his treatment of Marx, the Soviet Union, and communism. [42]

The essence of democracy, Ward believed, is "faith in the capacities of the people." Democracy is both an end and a means by which the power of the people is maintained, for Ward agreed with Lincoln that democracy is "government of the people, by the people and for the people." To Ward these words from Lincoln's Gettysburg Address were not pious-sounding political rhetoric but an affirmation of democracy in which people have control "over their own lives and destinies—their government, their livelihood, their culture." But democracy would remain only an ideal unless people continually worked to extend social equality to all members of society. In a truly democratic society, Ward believed, "every child that was born would have an equal opportunity with every other child for the development and expression of all the capacities that were inherent with that child." Thus, for Ward, "the willingness to give equal rights to others is the final test of a democracy." Equality, moreover, is not simply equal opportunity "for people to climb the ladder of success"; it is the structuring of society so that people, irrespective of class, race, or gender, could have equal participation, voice, and role in its development.[43]

Democracy requires more, however, than free and equal individuals, for too often what was called freedom was simply "individual selfishness." What binds people together in a democracy is the recognition that "equal rights involve equal obligations," that, for example, the economy functions "for the good of the community rather than for personal gain." Ward conceived of obligations in terms of mutual service, meeting social needs, and the recognition of the worth of persons in human interrelationships. He was adamant in stressing that a democracy was viable only to the extent to which it encouraged people to help one another, insisting that "the meaning and end of individual life and of social living is reciprocal and inter-dependent . . . [and] the more the individual values the community, the more he contributes to it, and thereby enlarges his own life; the higher the community regards its constituent members, the more it provides for their development, the stronger and richer is its own life." Ward was trying to facilitate a needed societal conversation about our obligations to one another as members of a democratic society. Neither those who call themselves conservatives nor those who call themselves leftists, claims Alan Wolfe, have managed to find "a way of balancing obligations both to self and to others." Hence Ward's insistence upon human interdependency was a way of understanding that "obligations to family members and intimate others are equally as pressing as . . . obligations to strangers and future generations." Consequently an awareness of the moral obligations each person owes to others might be the beginning of the revitalization of a truly democratic society.[44]

For Ward, democratic capitalism was a contradiction in terms because capitalism was "essentially autocratic in principle, being organized on the right of the strong to rule . . . [and] it rejects completely the social equality for which democracy strives . . . [insisting] that inequality is necessary." American life seemed to be schizophrenic with a political system that was supposed to diffuse power and an economic order that promoted the "concentration of power." Ward believed, as do Joshua Cohen and Joel Rogers, that capitalism limited the functioning of political democracy because in a class-divided society justice was only "class justice" and the state really represented only the interests of an economic elite. The end result is that in a democratic society based on a capitalist economy political rights are formal or procedural rather than substantive because inequalities in the distribution of resources limit both the exercise and the power of political expression. In addition, capitalism limits "the effective expression of the formal rights" guaranteed by a democratic political system by making the "exercise" of those political rights in the interest, both domestic and foreign, "of the preservation of capitalism and the taking of profits."[45]

Capitalism is antithetical not only to democracy but to Christianity, in Ward's view. Christianity, seeks "human development directly through the limitation of self-interest by mutual adjustment and mutual aid," whereas capitalism aims at "economic efficiency and mutual advantage through the exaltation of self-interest." To Ward the entire biblical tradition seemed to speak on behalf of the poor and oppressed and to affirm that "the common welfare was to be found organizing society to meet the needs and develop the lives of the people at the bottom." It was a struggle against exploitation, profit takers, and possessors of privilege and power in favor of the "producer and server." It was just as obvious to Ward that biblical teachings so stressed the life of the community that they set human rights above property rights: property was to be "the servant and not the master of life" because property was for the betterment of the human community and not its subjugation.[46]

What most disturbed Ward were the anthropological assumptions that underlay capitalism. Its doctrine of the human person "believes man is essentially and irredeemably selfish; that his chief function is the creation and satisfaction of economic needs. So it holds that he can be moved to significant endeavors only by an appeal to acquisitiveness, by enlarging his tendency to exalt himself above his fellows and at their expense." Capitalism is thus a celebration of inhumanity, injustice, competition, and above all else, self-interest. By contrast, Ward asked, what if what makes us human is our capacity to share, to cooperate, and to work with one another for the enhancement not of the individual but of the common good. Christianity maintains a belief in the capacities of people to change and affirms that love, which seeks justice, is more powerful than self-interest. Jesus was "permanently revolutionary," for he believed "in the possibilities of all men, the worst and the lowest. His faith was in the infinite worth of the down-most man."[47]

In the end, Ward believed, capitalism was far more destructive than communism because it reduced the human person to a consumer of things and substituted modern forms of "bread and circuses" for human aspirations for justice, freedom, and equality. Ward asserted that capitalism was simply a modern-day form of idolatry, with its gods of prosperity that demanded human sacrifices for the sake of mammon. In the name of prosperity, he noted, "we sacrifice each year in this country more human lives in industrial accidents and diseases than we lost in a year of the World War." Furthermore, he questioned a system that "devitalized children" and "overworked mothers of mill and mine towns"—all to increase the accumulation of profit. Here was a "false faith" that in the "exaction of human sacrifice" destroyed lives with impunity. Ward concluded that the two great commandments of capitalism were "Thou shalt love the making of money with all thy heart and mind and soul and strength; and thou shalt love thy neighbor—enough to make a profit off him."[48]

Following in the footsteps of R. H. Tawney and others, Ward wrestled with the impact the rise of capitalism had on Christianity and the development of economics in an amoral vacuum with neither "heart nor conscience." Churches had failed to conform their own economic behavior to the demands of the gospel and the biblical tradition, substituting for a Christian ethic an ethic of expediency that insulated them from taking any responsibility for the functioning of the economy. Churches had decided that business was best left to businesspeople, and that the concerns of the church had little to do with economic ethics. But Christians must not leave economics to economists; they must develop an adequate Christian economic ethic. Surely, Ward believed, that ethic could not be capitalism, which rationalized greed, luxury, and power and valued the "enlargement of self-interest instead of [the] realization of the self through the enlargement of the common good." Christianity, Ward felt, was facing a choice, the option of being either an institutional or a prophetic religion:

> Institutional religion represents the vested interests of an organization in property, income, social prestige, political power, modes of thought. Prophetic religion represents the attempt to change human life in the direction of certain ideals worked out in the social struggle by joining the needs of the people with the insight and vision of the prophet . . . [by] raising their protest against injustice and oppression, crying their challenge to a new order. . . . [Such a religion] will bring them hope and courage, sharing the dangers and persecutions that are the lot of those who break new paths in the social order. In that experience it will find a new life for itself.[49]

In both personal conversations and decades of correspondence Ward and his lifelong friend George Albert Coe debated varying interpretations of Marx, Marxism, and communism. Not long after Coe's death Ward approvingly quoted Coe's observation that "we are not done with Marxism when we weigh the merits and demerits of the Soviet government, nor when we choose between communist and the anti-communist ideology: Marx raised the fundamental ethical question whether it is humane or just that a man's sustenance should depend upon his contributing by his labor to the private profit of another. This ethical core of Marxism is being ignored by both the political and ecclesiastical thought that is most characteristic of the United States today."[50]

Marxist fundamentalism was abhorrent to Ward, and he criticized those who were tempted to reduce the corpus of Marx's writings to dogmatic texts perceived as an infallible bible that required official interpreters. It was Marx's method of analysis for dealing with present-day realities that attracted Ward. He questioned those, like Niebuhr, who tried to turn Marx into a philosopher of history, preoccupied with some remote future. Just as problematic for Ward were readings of Marx that spoke of the inevitability of history as if it were predetermined, forgetting that for Marx "history is the activity of man in the pursuit of his ends."[51]

Ward believed that one of the challenges of Marx for America was that he forced people to confront certain myths about their history and the nature of their society. One cherished myth was that America was without class divisions, class conflict, or class consciousness. But how else, Ward argued, could one explain the "common line" that ran throughout our history of "debtors and creditors, tenants and landlords, workers and employers, small business and big business," which revealed "the creditors, the employers, the landlords, the monopolists" as the "common enemy" that exercised dominion based on ownership of property. The formation of a class society extended from the *Mayflower* to the present as the resources of the country, both productive and natural, had increasingly become concentrated in the hands of a small economic and political elite. The class-divided society affected everyone, not just workers but farmers, middle-class people, and all those who felt that their lives were marked by insecurity, lack of opportunities, and lack of hope for the future. Ward believed that in a democratic society there was a need for people to realize that "the extension of democracy to the whole of the common life" was impossible so long as a capitalist class had control over the forces of life and death.[52]

The insights of Marx were not limited to examining how domination stemmed from unequal property relations in a capitalist society but also encompassed capitalism as a system and "a way of life" that shapes our perception of ourselves, our culture, and our future. Ward focused on the cultural apparatus of domination, with its myths of individualism, capitalist efficiency, and social mobility—all of which required a new democratic culture. Samuel Bowles and Herbert Gintis have defined a democratic culture as "a broad diffusion of politically relevant information, skills, and attitudes of political effectiveness, as well as the availability of forms of discourse conducive to the effective functioning of democratic institutions." Such a vision of democracy, Ward believed, was possible only to the extent that people had control over both their political and their economic life.[53]

To raise the specter of the Soviet Union as an alternative to capitalism is to embroil oneself in debates ranging from the nature of Stalinism to the possible threats the Soviet Union has posed to American national security and American values. Stephen Cohen has pointed out the extent to which a model of totalitarianism has governed American interpretations and perceptions of the Soviet Union. At its worst, this model has substituted "labels, images, metaphors, and teleology" for explanation, with the end result that "orthodox Sovietology" has distorted the complex social and political realities that have shaped Soviet history since the Bolshevik Revolution.[54]

Similarly, simply to label Ward "pro-Soviet" and therefore to dismiss him is to forfeit all shades of meaning and nuance and to fall victim to a mode of interpretation that does little justice to Ward and his reasons for admiring the Soviet Union. Ward shared with Paul Robeson a basic trust, warmth, and affection for the Soviet people and especially Robeson's conviction that "a socialist society represents an advance to a higher stage of life—that it is a form of society which is economically, socially, culturally, and ethically superior to a system based upon production for profit." Whether that admiration necessarily translates into a support for Stalinism and all it represents is another question.[55]

For those who view Stalinism as a fundamental distortion of Marxism there is a great deal of truth in the observation of Cornel West that "Stalinism is to Marxism what the Ku Klux Klan is to Christianity: a manipulation of the chief symbols yet diametrically opposed to the central values." At the same time, as Alexander Cockburn stresses, those who focus only on the crimes of Stalin have missed not only the dynamics of Soviet history but the paradox of Stalin. In the midst of the worldwide depression of the 1930s, Stalin was pushing for education of the masses and making concrete achievements. One could also argue that labels such as "Stalinist" and "pro-Soviet" are "catchall [terms] of abuse for anyone who has an ideal of a classless society animated by socialist principles and who does not think that what are chastely called 'market forces' are the exclusive signposts to that goal."[56]

Ward's attitudes toward the Soviet Union evolved over time. For many, the Bolshevik Revolution raised the possibility of a new social order. The American Left was generally supportive of the Bolshevik Revolution, and John Reed captured the excitement of the period in *Ten Days That Shook the World*. "No matter what one thinks of Bolshevism," Reed declared, "it is undeniable that the Russian revolution is one of the great events of human history, and the rise of the Bolsheviki a phenomenon of world-wide importance." Eugene Debs spoke for many of his Socialist comrades when he proclaimed, "From the crown of my head to the soles of my feet I am Bolshevik, and proud of it." Yet however much sympathy for the revolution existed among Socialists, they did not necessarily view the events taking place in Russia as a model that could be applied to the United States. Meanwhile, the reaction of the U.S. government ranged from simple antagonism toward the Soviet Union to rampant paranoia.[57]

Writing in 1919, Ward initially assessed what was taking place in Russia as positive, particularly as it related to the attempt to organize a society around the principle of labor rather than property. While Ward condemned the excesses of the Bolshevik regime, he also emphasized that they had to be understood against the background of what he believed to be historical Russian brutality and the atmosphere created by the civil war. He stressed his opposition to the establishment of the dictatorship of the proletariat by force but insisted that when peaceful change was no longer possible people would inevitably turn to other means. Ward questioned the antireligious attitudes and policies of the Soviet government but at the same time was enamored of a vision he believed was not distinctively different from the goals sought by Christian social ethics: a vision of a society in which every individual would be accorded the means of development and all would be expected to contribute to the common welfare of the nation. In the creation of a new social order, the value and authority of the church could not be assumed as it had been in the past, but Ward felt that the acts of cruelty that had accompanied the disenfranchisement of the church were unjustified.[58]

Ward alienated certain segments of the American religious community with his statement that "the aim of the Bolsheviki is clearly the creation of a state composed entirely of producers and controlled by producers. This is manifestly a Scriptural aim." Various individuals attacked him as a dangerous Socialist agitator. The publishers of the Graded Lesson Syndicated, for whom he had prepared Sunday school material in the form of a column called "The Bible and Social Living" for ten years, went so far as to discontinue his column, destroying both the materials and the plates of Ward's writings they had on hand.[59]

In the summer and fall of 1924 Ward had the opportunity to visit the Soviet Union during a year's sabbatical from Union Theological Seminary. His friend Sherwood Eddy arranged for Ward and his wife to stay in the apartment of Julius Hecker, who at the time occupied a chair in sociology and social ethics at the reopened Moscow Theological Academy. Ward interviewed people from all walks of life, toured factories, and visited governmental and educational institutions. Upon leaving Russia, he wrote that "there was at work a tremendously powerful human machine, the likes of what has seldom been assembled in human history. Roughly speaking it is the sense of concentrated power which is my chief impression now." It seemed to Ward that Russia was in an intermediate stage between capitalism and whatever form of socialism would emerge in the future. His reflections on the Soviet Union did not glow with the enthusiasm evident in his portrayal of the revolution, but he had faith in Russian youth, whom he saw as the vital sector in the shaping of Soviet history. He was not impressed with what he conceived to be a regimented society in the making and was critical of the policies of the General Political Administration and the apparent lack of civil liberties. What particularly disturbed him was the attitude of the Communist Party toward religion. He traced the roots of this antireligious policy to the apathy the Orthodox church had historically shown toward the suffering of workers and peasants and to its organic link to the repressive rule of the czars. But whatever stance the new government took toward the church and institutional religion, he felt that the religious sensibilities of the Russian people would never perish.[60]

The market crash of 1929 and the events that followed created a new climate of opinion with respect to the Soviet Union. In the early 1930s, Russia seemed a sign of hope to people caught up in what was perceived as a failing economic order. Under the First Five-Year Plan, the Soviet Union was undergoing rapid industrialization, especially in iron and steel, coupled with massive collectivization of agriculture. Louis Fischer, Moscow correspondent for *The Nation*, observed that in spite of the hardship which the Russian people were experiencing, there was "a bright and encouraging side: the birth of new 'Socialist' cities, the erection of grain factories and farms, the thrill of a whole continent tapping new sources of creative energy and marching toward economic independence and a better standard of living." It was within this context of raised hopes and expectations that Ward returned to the Soviet Union from fall 1931 till spring 1932. The purpose of this second trip was "to satisfy myself whether the building of socialism was developing incentives which promised more for the continuing of human society than those which are manifestly failing in the capitalist world." At stake, Ward understood, was an economy based on use rather than profit, one that substituted "the will to serve for the will to gain." [61]

Once again, with the aid of Julius Hecker, Ward interviewed people and worked through the documents and records made available to him on every aspect of Soviet life and thought. He traveled extensively throughout the Soviet Union, collecting data on various facets of agricultural and industrial life. The result was his massive and detailed study *In Place of Profit*, his effort to document a unique historical event in which a social philosophy was being established that exalted the creative desires over the possessive appetites by abolishing the possibility of acquisition, limiting ownership to purely personal property, and opening up for masses of people new possibilities whose social ends were more important than personal reward. It was evident to Ward that cooperation was replacing competition, service to others was being substituted for self-interest, human solidarity was supplanting relationships based on unequal patterns of property ownership, and sacrifice was being exalted over egoistic gain. Cooperation was manifest in the conscious expression of the primacy of collective efforts over personal exploits. Just as clearly, the economic means of life was being democratized by social ownership of the means of production through workers' control of industry. Individuals seemed to work together for the common good by striving for human solidarity rather than for human individuality. Finally, there was the sacrifice of the present for the future; present enjoyment of certain goods was being sacrificed in order that capital might be used for building the industrial foundation for the future. Ward realized that the Soviet state rested upon an iron will that suppressed all dissent, but he felt that the repressive aspects of the dictatorship were only instrumental and that its main objective was constructive. Ward would continue in subsequent years to contend that Soviet society took seriously the priority of organizing the economy in service of human need. Irrespective of its failures, and there were many, socioeconomic planning would permit the use of both human and natural resources for the common good, not just for the enlargement of the private good. He also maintained that what was happening in the Soviet Union could not necessarily be applied to the United States, for "the job of developing democracy as the people's power and government by common consent has to be done differently from theirs." [62]

Whatever reservations Ward had about the Soviet Union were far less important to him than the weakness of a capitalist system that "is now bringing such misery to the lives of human beings as it has long brought such corruption to their hearts and souls." In answer to those who decried the inadequacies of the Soviet experiment, Ward pointed to the rise of fascism as an attempt to save a bankrupt capitalist order. It was clear to him that fascism posed a far greater threat to the survival of humankind than did the Soviet Union. At this same time, some within the Soviet Union viewed Soviet society very differently from Ward. Nikolai Ivanovich Bukharin, later condemned to death by Stalin during the purge trials of 1938, favored a different road to socialism, one that was less brutal, more conciliatory and gradualist, based on what Stephen Cohen calls "socialist humanism." It seemed to Bukharin, Cohen writes, that Stalin's First Five-Year Plan was less an advance toward socialism than a step toward a future in which people "perish from hunger and lay down . . . [their] bones to die." In response to those who celebrated the glories of forced collectivization Boris Pasternak wrote in the early 1930s that he too had wanted to see the "new life of the village" but instead found "such inhuman, unimaginable misery, such a terrible disaster, that it began to seem almost abstract, it would not fit within the bounds of consciousness." [63]

By the end of World War II it seemed to Ward that all too quickly our Soviet allies became the new enemy at the same time as the cold war turned the United States into "a political and ideological system for organizing and ordering world power." Ward criticized certain elements of Soviet ideology and policy but refrained from open condemnation of the Soviet Union, lest his words and analysis give comfort to those eager to dismiss all the Soviet Union had been able to accomplish as a beginning step in the creation of an alternative economic order. If Niebuhr can rightly be accused of growing increasingly uncritical of America under capitalism, the same may also be said of Ward and the Soviet Union. For all his political and intellectual acumen, Ward so desired to see profit replaced by a more humane and juster social order that he could not see that in Soviet society, too, there was a conflict between rhetoric and reality.[64]

Whatever the shortcomings of Ward's analysis of the Soviet Union it is important not to lose sight of the significance he placed on refusing to be "drawn into the whirlwind of anticommunism," which obliterated distinctions, serving the interests of those who sought to make a mockery of democratic process. At the same time, Ward intended no "abdication of the right of criticism of communism and opposition to it," as was particularly evident in his analysis of the tensions between Christianity and communism. Ward was critical of Communists' understanding of religion, for it was not truly dialectical. Because they reduced religion to a one-dimensional phenomenon through a static interpretation based on "insufficient data and limited experience," Communists were unable to understand how religion could be a means of human liberation. That did not mean that there were no similarities between Christianity and communism, for did not Christians and Communists both have concern for those who had been most exploited, and did they not both promulgate a society based on values that might expand human possibilities and concrete hopes for the future? In addition, it seemed obvious to Ward that those who so easily criticized communism as "a menace to mankind" needed first to search through historical records and ask themselves how Christianity had been "related to the economic imperialism long practiced by the European powers and now being developed in the name of democracy by our own nation." As to the atheistic dimension of communism, with its critique of God and the transcendental view of life as a "hindrance to man's development," was there not a tendency to deify "economic law and science," portraying them as beyond human control just as if they were gods of the cosmos? Ward believed that communism was a challenge to Christians, but he doubted whether the churches could "match" the Communists in their commitment to the "emancipation and education of the people at the bottom." [65]

A. J. Muste and Dorothy Day

The lives of A. J. Muste and Dorothy Day challenge our imagination and the limits of current political wisdom as to what constitutes a viable political system. Richard Falk has argued that the eclipse of vision that bars images of human community based on the liberative capacity of human beings and the enduring quality of the human spirit can lead to a political system that is closed to the idea of transformation. The political system of the United States is closed because it is in fact a "war system" geared to the defense and protection of what are perceived to be national security interests. The structures of militarism, not unlike any feature of the status quo, are legitimated by specific language employed by the dominant culture: words such as *practical, realistic,* and *feasible* mask the root causes of war and violence and the alternatives of peace and nonviolence. Perhaps that is why Gordon Zahn has so stressed that "pacifism is visionary," for it is "more realistic and certainly [more] practical than the fatalism which would see 'no alternative' but ride with the course of events, never questioning how they came to be what they are or the consequences they are certain to bring. The chain must be broken at some point and, the pacifist insists, this can only be done through the total renunciation of war and ways of violence. Having reached this conclusion, he finds it equally obvious that it is up to the self-proclaimed followers of Christ to show the way." Those who chose to follow in Christ's footsteps not only learn about the revolutionary nature of nonviolence but experience anew the radicality of the Christian faith in their solidarity with God's poor, learning that peace based on justice demands foremost an ability to perceive the gospel as good news for the poor.[66]

Abraham Johannes Muste: Journey on the Left

At the height of a developing protest movement against the intervention of the United States in Vietnam, A. J. Muste made two trips to Vietnam, one in April,

1966, to Saigon and the other the following January to Hanoi. Shortly after his return from Hanoi, Muste died, at the age of eighty-two. In the words of his close friend David Dillinger, he had "put an intolerable strain on his system by working overtime." As a tireless activist on behalf of a peaceable kingdom, Muste had been deeply involved in organizing broad-based opposition to the Vietnam War through his work with groups ranging from the Committee on Nonviolent Action to the National Mobilization Committee to End the War. When Muste was in Saigon, he and a group of American pacifists held a nonviolent protest in response to Nguyen Cao Ky's recent mandate of the death penalty for anyone who publicly advocated peace. Muste, Barbara Deming recalled, "was assaulted at a press conference by some of Ky's agents" and later arrested and deported. The other demonstrators were also arrested. All spent hours on a broiling hot day in a paddywagon and later in a detention area in the airport awaiting deportation. Through it all, said Deming, Muste had smiled and said, "It's a good life!" [67]

Muste was born on January 8, 1885, in the small port city of Zierikzee, in the province of Zeeland in the Netherlands. His parents named him Abraham Johannes which Muste thought a "sonorous name" for a young child, though he later reflected that the Abraham tied him to the biblical past and reminded him that God was at work in moving history forward. Six years after his birth, in 1891, he and his family emigrated to the United States hoping to escape the constraints placed on them by his father's job as a coachman to a local noble family. After crossing the Atlantic in steerage during the middle of winter, the Muste family joined relatives in Grand Rapids, Michigan, where Dutch immigrants had settled since before the Civil War, drawn by the need for skilled and unskilled workers in lumbering and furniture manufacturing. By 1890, the Dutch community numbered about ten thousand people. The Muste family became members of the Reformed church, rather than the Christian Reformed church to which their American relatives belonged. The Christian Reformed church had been founded in 1857 over dissatisfaction with the Reformed church in the United States and the Netherlands on grounds of both doctrine and church polity. The Reformed church was to a great degree more Americanized, but it was still part of a community that valued sobriety and industriousness and was as critical of labor unions as it was of the Democratic Party. Its members were solid Republicans who regarded voting Democratic as an unpardonable sin, equal only to physical abuse, stealing, or extramarital sex.[68]

Little of Abraham Muste's future radicalness seems traceable to the conservative Calvinist Reformed church. Muste himself later recalled the writings of Ralph Waldo Emerson, the mythic stature of Abraham Lincoln, and a close familiarity with the Scriptures as formative influences that "molded my mind and spirit." He was educated at institutions founded by the Dutch Reformed settlers of western Michigan, first the Preparatory School of Hope College and later Hope College, from which he graduated in 1905 with a classical education. He taught in Iowa for a year before entering the Reformed church's New Brunswick Theological Seminary in New Jersey. The seminary was at a low point in its history, and he found more intellectual stimulation in philosophy courses at New York University and Columbia University, especially the lectures of John Dewey and William James. Graduating from seminary in 1909, he was ordained and became a minister at the oldest Reformed church in New York City, Fort Washington Collegiate Church in Washington Heights. What pleased Muste most about his new appointment was the opportunity to take courses at Union Theological Seminary.[69]

At Union, Muste was particularly intrigued by Arthur Cushman McGiffert's courses in church history, which seemed to open new avenues, both intellectual and religious. He soon discovered that he could no longer accept a literalist approach to Scripture, and he was increasingly uncomfortable with the Calvinist tradition in which he had been raised. At Union Muste wrestled with questions of structural injustice and was forced to come to terms with a set of experiences he had had as a student at New Brunswick Theological Seminary. During his second and third year of seminary he was a supply pastor on New York's East Side, where he discovered the realities of poverty, so very different from what he had known in the Midwest. When making calls on sick and aged parishioners, he had sometimes "been barely able to endure the fetid smells and unceasing raucous noises." He began to understand the reasons for the conflict between labor and capital when he saw the horrific conditions in the sweatshops where garment workers were employed. These came to public attention through the tragedy known as the Triangle Fire. On March 25, 1911, a fire erupted at the Triangle Shirtwaist Company in New York, which was located on the eighth floor of a ten-story building. The doors to the eighth floor had been locked to discourage both union organizers and the easy exit of employees. Thus, when the fire broke out, the workers' only means of escape was to jump from the windows. Over one hundred and forty-three women lost their lives. By the 1912 presidential election, it was apparent to Muste that Eugene V. Debs was the only viable candidate, and from this time forth, he wrote, he never "voted for any Democrat or Republican for any major state or national office." [70]

No longer able to accept what he perceived to be a dogmatic interpretation of Christianity, Muste resigned from the Fort Washington Collegiate Church at the end of 1914 and changed his denominational affiliation. The following year Muste became pastor of the Central Congregational Church in Newtonville, Massachusetts, a church composed mainly of professional people who were supportive of his ministry. Contacts with other clergy and theologians made Newtonville seem almost "idyllic" until Muste began openly criticizing those who sought to involve the United States in the Great War. For Muste, the First World War was a crisis of conscience. He came to believe that biblical teachings on nonviolence could not be modified for public consumption. The irony was that throughout his biblical training, at both New Brunswick, which Muste characterized as the "citadel of orthodoxy," and Union "the hotbed of heresy," no one had ever raised the possibility of "a pacifist interpretation of the Gospel." It was his own religious upbringing, with all its rigidity, that had shaped his belief that the ethical demands of the gospel were always in conflict with the sirens of war. As he wrestled with his conscience and Christian responsibility, he found the works of the noted Quaker scholar Rufus M. Jones and the long history of Quaker "peace testimony" particularly helpful. He concluded: "My reading of the New Testament and of the witness of the Inner Light makes me a conscientious objector to all war. I am convinced that it is a tragic mistake for people to think God wants them to kill each other wholesale in order to keep the world from falling to pieces . . . [and] that war is foolish and ineffective as well as wrong." A year after assuming his new pastorate he became an active member of a newly formed chapter of the Fellowship of Reconciliation, established at Cambridge University in England in December, 1914.[71]

The congregation of Central Congregational at first accepted Muste's advocacy of Christian pacifism, but as time wore on and Muste's antiwar activism increased, some members of the congregation, especially the wealthier ones, became uneasy with Muste's commitment to a pacifist interpretation of Christianity. Even though most of his congregation continued to support him, he resigned in December, 1917, because he found that he could not in all conscience fully comfort parents whose sons had died in war. For Muste the real tragedy of war was revealed most clearly by actions of those who sent their own children to die, only compounded by the failure of the religious community "to stop the war and render all wars unthinkable." Instead of being "driven out of a pulpit which for my predecessors had proved a stepping stone to highly distinguished careers in the ministry," Muste remarked, he had been "marked as a pacifist and a possibly dangerous character." After his resignation he worked with what was later to be known as the American Civil Liberties Union to help conscientious objectors, who were subject to federal prosecution because of their violation of conscription laws and, if convicted, were often brutalized by prison authorities.[72]

Gradually, Muste became involved with labor issues. Toward the end of 1918 he and two other pacifist ministers, Harold Rotzel and Cedric Long, and their families, plus Ann Davis and Ethel Paine, formed a group called the Comradeship. They rented a house in the Back Bay section of Boston and tried to organize their lives, Muste wrote, "so that they would truly express the teachings and spirit of Jesus . . . [and] faith in the way of truth, nonviolence and love." It was not enough, they believed, to deal with the nature of war; they must also enter the struggle for economic and racial justice. Moreover, abstract discussion of peace and justice was insufficient; it must be translated into reality.[73]

In 1919 in nearby Lawrence, Massachusetts, thirty thousand textile workers, largely unskilled immigrants, struck for a shorter work week with no reduction in pay. The United Textile Workers, which represented only the interests of skilled workers, refused to sanction the strike, and the Lawrence workers formed their own provisional strike committee. Muste and other members of the Comradeship who traveled to Lawrence with the intention of offering their support very quickly found themselves not only speaking out on behalf of striking workers but appointed as members of the strike committee, of which Muste was made executive secretary. As head of the strike committee, Muste organized strike relief and nonviolent confrontations with police from Lawrence and Boston, and he had to deal with labor spies and threats of the use of machine guns against workers. After over four months of resistance, when it seemed that the strike was on the verge of collapse, the mill owners agreed to workers' demands. Muste was elected general secretary of a newly formed industrial union, the Amalgamated Textile Workers of America, modeled after the Amalgamated Clothing Workers of America. The new union was short-lived. Although it had some forty thousand members in 1920, the depression of the early 1920s took its toll and by 1925 the union was defunct.[74]

In the summer of 1921 Muste resigned as general secretary of the Amalgamated Textile Workers to become education director of Brookwood Labor College in Katonah, New York. Brookwood was supported by those segments of the labor movement critical of the American Federation of Labor, and on its board were trade unionists such as John Fitzpatrick, president of the Chicago Federation of Labor, James H. Mauer, Socialist and president of the Pennsylvania Federation of Labor, Rose Schneiderman of the New York Women's Trade Union League, and John Brophy, president of the District No. 2 of the United Mine Workers. Students came from coal mines, factories, and a variety of occupations. They were native-born and recent immigrants, black and white, and about a third were women. At the college workers were to receive an education that would help them serve the labor movement. They would "go back to the shop or mine," writes Arthur Gleason, "to be active in local unions, perhaps, in time, to be elected to higher union offices but to 'remain in the struggle'—not to acquire an itch to get on the payroll—to retain a fighting edge and a dynamic idealism." Students were trained not only in basic skills but also in the social and natural sciences. Courses ranged from labor journalism to law. Everyone in the college community, both faculty and students, performed common tasks from maintenance of the school to food preparation, all infused with laughter, caring, and debate. Sinclair Lewis called Brookwood "the only self-respecting, keen, alive, educational institution I have ever known."[75]

In 1928 controversy emerged over the aims and goals of Brookwood. The executive committee of the AFL condemned the school as a dangerous institution that was "disloyal to the labor movement," antireligious, and Communist, but the AFL never made the charges public, and there was no opportunity for a hearing to respond to the allegations. In reality, wrote Muste, the charges were nothing more than an attempt to smear "the progressive trade union leaders of the time." Despite the attack, Brookwood retained the support of certain sectors of the labor movement.[76]

Over the next few years Muste divided his time between the work with Brookwood and an evolving labor organization known as the Conference for Progressive Labor Action, which was launched in 1929 and held its first official convention in 1932. Membership of the CPLA was made up of Socialists, trade unionists, and labor educators, such as Muste—all critical of the conservative leadership of the AFL and the approach of the Communist Party to labor organizing. The CPLA briefly became an independent Marxist party known as the American Workers Party, but by December, 1934, had merged with the Trotskyite Communist League of America to become the Workers Party. In 1936 Muste experienced a reconversion to Christianity and broke with the Workers Party.[77]

The years preceding Muste's reconversion were marked by numerous crises, both personal and political. Even though it was one of the most unsettling periods of his life, he believed that it was a challenging time in which to be alive. Muste's involvement with the labor movement and the political Left increased his disenchantment with the church. It seemed ironic to him that throughout the twenties and thirties, when war was not being waged, most mainline Protestant denominations had become pacifist in orientation. When the economic system crumbled about them, the churches "identified with the *status quo,* middle-class in composition and coloration," and were as unconcerned with the problems facing working-class people as they had been about peace when the nation was at war. It was evident to Muste that "it was the radicals, the Left-wingers, the people who adopted some form of Marxian philosophy, who were *doing something* about the situation. . . . it was on the Left—and here again the Communists cannot be excluded—that one found people who were truly 'religious' in the sense that they were virtually completely committed, they were betting their lives on the cause they embraced. Often they gave up ordinary comforts, security, life itself, with a burning devotion which few Christians display toward the Christ whom they profess as Lord and incarnation of God." As Muste moved from pacifist to Trotskyist to pacifist he learned that he had to "*experience* ideas, rather than *think* them." Being responsible meant being involved in "the struggle against injustice and tyranny" and striving for a new social order.[78]

Muste resigned from Brookwood Labor College in 1933. He continued to devote his energies to labor education through the work of the CPLA in meeting the needs of the unemployed and organizing the unorganized into industrial unions, especially in textiles and mining. The CPLA developed unemployed leagues, which attempted to organize people around self-help projects while instructing them in the nature of unemployment as a structural contradiction of a capitalist economy and inspiring them to political struggle. Socialists and

Communists were also organizing the unemployed, but the CPLA was more flexible organizationally and ideologically. The CPLA had adopted some of the tactics used by the Unemployed Citizens' League of Seattle Labor College in which the unemployed could barter labor for food and fuel. This was not enough. The CPLA's leagues also fought evictions, agitated for increased relief for the unemployed, and worked for better living conditions. According to a league organizer in Pittsburgh, Ernest McKinney, "We had a very practical program in the unemployed league. We actually got them placed on relief, we actually kept them on relief. . . . We got food orders for them, we supplied them with concrete things, with food, clothing, and shelter, the basic demand of the masses of the people." [79]

Unemployed leagues established workers' schools, organized social events, and promoted a rank-and-file movement for social change. Ohio and Pennsylvania had the greatest number of leagues, and state organizations also existed in Virginia, North Carolina, and New Jersey. Most were concentrated in rural communities and small industrial and mining towns. Roy Rosenzweig concluded that the leagues had helped "to improve concretely the living conditions of the jobless—relief was increased, the relief structure was made more humane and just, work relief jobs were created, and evictions were halted. They also helped to preserve the self-respect and morale of their idle members. Through membership in the ULs, the jobless realized that they were not alone and were not to blame for their condition." [80]

In some cases the leagues served as a basis for union organizing. In early 1934 in Toledo, Ohio, a newly chartered AFL auto union struck the Electric Auto-Lite Company, which was a major auto parts company, and three small auto parts firms. The union demanded a 10 percent wage increase, a seniority system, and union recognition. Auto-Lite refused to negotiate under any conditions and the strike escalated. The CPLA, now the American Workers Party with Muste as executive secretary, came to the aid of the union through its Lucas County Unemployed League. It became clear that mass picketing had to be used in order to deal with strikebreakers and to provide support for the striking workers. Auto-Lite hired armed guards and special deputies to protect strikebreakers and won an injunction against all picketing, but picketing continued and league members were arrested wholesale. It was a remarkable strike, a reporter for the Scripps-Howard newspapers declared, for the unemployed "appeared on the picket lines to help striking employees win a strike, tho you would expect their interest would lie the other way—that is, in going in and getting the job the other men had laid down." [81]

On May 23, 1934, a battle erupted. The police had arrested a number of picketers and, while a crowd of about ten thousand strikers and their sympathizers watched, had brutally beaten an old man. The outraged crowd surrounded the company building, where approximately fifteen hundred strikebreakers were working. Auto-Lite barred its doors, and from the roof and windows special deputies threw tear gas bombs at the people below. They also used "bolts and iron bars, water hoses, and occasional gunfire." The strike supporters responded with stones and bricks and on three occasions were able to break into the factory where hand-to-hand fighting took place before they were driven out. The following morning nine hundred soldiers of the Ohio National Guard arrived on the scene. When fighting broke out between the National Guard and the crowd, the troops fired, killing two persons and wounding fifteen. A threat of a general strike by the Toledo Central Labor Union in support of the striking Auto-Lite workers eventually led to a settlement. The American Workers Unemployed League had been central to the success of the strike.[82]

The American Workers Party was formed as a revolutionary political party, an alternative to both the Socialist Party and the Communist Party. Muste contended that Communists had never taken American workers seriously, relying too heavily on Russian and European experience. By contrast, the American Workers Party was to be "rooted in American soil, its eyes fixed primarily upon American conditions and problems, attracting American workers who are concerned about their own situation." It was open to all working people, industrial workers and farmers, men and women, and committed to "complete equality for the Negro people." While the American Workers Party stressed the importance of the electoral process, it had more faith in the effectiveness of mass action, arguing that people were living in a revolutionary era and that a democratically organized party could make a difference for the future.[83]

In this same period those most influenced by Leon Trotsky had formed the Communist League of America. They approached the American Workers Party with the idea of a merger of the two parties, which led in December, 1934, to the creation of the Workers Party. From 1934 until he broke with the Workers Party in 1936, Muste was embroiled in interparty politics that centered around the "French Turn," that is, whether the new party should follow the French Trotskyites' example and join the Socialist Party of Norman Thomas, with the supposed goal of creating a more militant political party. Muste vigorously opposed the move. The political debates of the period increased his disillusionment with Trotsky, and while he admired him for both his critique of Stalin and "his intellectual versatility and brilliance," he found his instrumentalist approach to violence very questionable and thought that his followers were as "autocratically" controlled as those of Stalin.[84]

The Workers Party merged with the Socialist Party in 1936, and not long after, Muste was active in a strike in Akron, Ohio, at the Goodyear Rubber Company. It was the first use by American workers of the sit-in technique, already successful in France. Muste's close friends could see that he was emotionally and physically drained after years of work in labor struggles. They encouraged him and his wife to take a vacation to Europe and offered financial support. Muste accepted an invitation to meet with Trotsky in Norway, attended a secret conference with leaders of the Fourth International near Paris, and then finally had a vacation in Switzerland and France.[85]

While touring Paris, Muste happened upon the massive old church of Saint Sulpice. He sat and looked up at the cross on the front of the church. Suddenly came the realization, " 'This is where you belong' and 'belong' again, in spirit, to the Church of Christ I did from that moment on. I felt as if the hand of God had drawn me up out of those 'titanic glooms of chased fears' of which Francis Thompson sings and had catapaulted me back into the Church." Later he reflected that the experience could be explained psychologically, but he believed it to be a religious reconversion. It took place at a time when he acutely felt the reality of impending war. Neither the labor movement nor left-wing political parties would be prepared to deal with this war, for neither was willing to acknowledge the folly of war and violence as solutions for a world on the brink of catastrophe.[86]

In the years that followed, Muste once again would become active in the Fellowship of Reconciliation, first as industrial secretary and later as executive secretary from 1940 to 1953. For a brief period, 1937–1940, he was director of the Presbytery of New York's Labor Temple, located on the East Side. It had been founded in 1910 by the social gospeler Charles Stelzle. Muste continued the educational and social service work of the Labor Temple as it reached out to the immigrant community, radicals, and disaffected intellectuals. He questioned those on the Left who too easily substituted authority, particularly that of the "Party," for the exercise of critical intelligence and human freedom and who succumbed to the violence of a system they so opposed.[87]

At the age of sixty-eight Muste retired from the Fellowship of Reconciliation. He became active in the civil rights and disarmament movements and protested both nuclear testing and civil defense exercises. He was at the center of the burgeoning antiwar movement of the 1960s and his radical pacifism was in many ways a bridge between the "Old Left" of the 1930s and what emerged decades later as the "New Left." The Old Left, he said, and here he might include the New Left, "had the vision, the dream, of a classless and warless world . . . [for] here was a fellowship drawn by the Judeo-Christian prophetic vision of a 'new earth in which righteousness dwelleth.' " Christians who "scorned" such a vision as naive or utopian overlooked the revolutionary character of Christianity, which "demanded revolutionary living and action." Muste understood the importance of such a vision—of a world not based on war, violence, and exploitation—and he contributed that understanding to the discussion of what constitutes the human community. His views are most evident in his critique of Christian realism and in his writings on violence and nonviolence and on the relationship of politics and ethics in the making and shaping of human relationships.[88]

Muste considered Reinhold Niebuhr a theologian of despair and defeatism.

Convinced of human depravity and "futility," Niebuhr held fatalistic assumptions about human history, attributing "inevitability" even to the Marxism he so despised. Muste granted that Niebuhr and advocates of a neo-orthodox interpretation of Christianity were right in criticizing those who underestimated the "depth of depravity in certain persons and systems" and in insisting that there were no easy solutions to international problems. Nevertheless, the neo-orthodox reading of Scripture seemed to be an extended commentary on one text: "The good that I would I do not; the evil that I would not, that I practice. . . . Wretched man that I am, who shall deliver me?" (Romans 7:19, 24). Any acknowledgment of the power of God's grace was qualified by expression of the human propensity toward sin, Muste argued, so that they seemed to be saying, "Where grace abounds sin much more abounds!" For Muste, God's grace was something revolutionary, a witness to the power of God to alter human life, and he approvingly quoted Daniel Day Williams's affirmation that "the Christian religion has always created hope in the human spirit. It has produced men who lived in the world of affairs with a unique expectancy." Muste, like Williams, understood grace in much the same way as the Latin-American theologians of liberation—namely, that through grace faith liberates us "for something definitive and indeed eschatological: the building up of the kingdom of God." [89]

Muste's belief that human beings, and human society, could be otherwise was based on faith in the transforming power of God's grace and a conviction that we are "beings of moral dignity and worth, capable of discerning good and evil and choosing good voluntarily." Conceivably, those who were so preoccupied with human failings and the impossibility of social change were "usually thinking of human beings as exemplified in themselves." Far more real for Muste were the words of Ignazio Silone's character Pietro Spina, a revolutionary masquerading as a priest in Silone's novel *Bread and Wine*, who asserts, "It is a matter of conversion. It is a matter of becoming a new man" who partakes of a "Christianity that neither abdicates in the face of Mammon, nor proposes concordats with Pontius Pilate, nor offers easy careers to the ambitious, but leads to prison, seeing that crucifixion is no longer practiced." Just as conversion created a new person, so the demands of the Kingdom moved human history forward. To hold that the Kingdom of God is "beyond history," that the struggle for a world of justice and peace is illusionary, Muste said, is a misreading of the biblical tradition and a distortion of the centrality of the coming of the Kingdom of God in history. The end result of placing "limits to the realization of the Kingdom of God on earth, to the banishment of social evils, to building economic and political life . . . on the standards set forth by Jesus and the prophets" was defeatism. If the Christian message was reduced to what was "practical and feasible," stripped of the revolutionary vision of the Kingdom of God, then the church was almost certain to succumb to the constant temptation to acquiesce in the status quo, for "where the church provides 'no vision, the people perish.' " [90]

The banishing of the demands of the Kingdom of God from history indicated to Muste a fundamental dualism underlying neo-orthodox Christianity. Niebuhr, in particular, had maintained that a Christian espousal of love, while the ideal and perhaps a norm for interpersonal relations, was not possible in "the real world." The best one could obtain in a world of power, domination, and conflict was relative justice. Muste's response was to draw no clear line between love and justice, for the demand for justice within the biblical tradition was based on dealing with persons as "ends in themselves." Love includes justice, and those who try to escape the complexities and obligations of an ethic of love by demanding only justice, "lapse into moral relativism" because they join justice with power rather than love. Basing justice on power produces a situation in which Christian ethics seem irrelevant for addressing political problems because possibility, practicality, and justice are framed within "the existing power structure, and what is 'responsible' behavior within that context." It was apparent to Muste that if "problems of politics are dealt with on a nonmoral basis, political life tends to become immoral. A power-entity with no element of morality and nobility in it degenerates into a tyranny or a fascist regime." By contrast, to speak about love is to affirm that domination is not the "final reality" and that liberation from bondage—be it economic, political, or racial—is possible. [91]

On the other hand, love is not reducible to sentimental "feelings"; it is other-directed behavior that demands justice for the poor and oppressed. Muste's understanding of the relationship between love and justice is best captured by Paul Ricoeur. Like Muste, he links love to Jesus' proclamation of the Kingdom of God, affirming that love is "co-existent with justice, its soul, its impulse, its deep motivation; it lends it its vision. . . . At the same time, justice is the efficacious, institutional realization of love." It is the task of Christian ethics, Muste believed, to speak about love and justice, of the struggle to relate the coming of the Kingdom of God to history. He himself had been preoccupied with this task since 1915, pursuing, in words he used to describe the work of Albert Camus, a consistent "determination to reintroduce the language of ethics into the language of politics." [92]

Muste regarded Niebuhr's attempt at a Christian justification of power politics as indistinguishable from the political machinations of John Foster Dulles and thought it ironic that "Reinhold Niebuhr, the radical, and John Foster Dulles, the Wall Street attorney and one of the chief architects of the bipartisan foreign policy of the United States, should be virtually a team." In advocating the use of political and military means to defend ourselves from the peril of communism both tended to blur all distinctions and divorce political behavior from ethical judgment. While Muste was as critical of communism and the

Soviet Union as Niebuhr, for him it was clear that Christian ethics had something to say about the political behavior of the United States in the international
arena and that the assessment of global conflict should not be left in the hands
of those who wanted only to extend U.S. hegemony in the world. Borrowing
from Martin Buber, Muste asked if it were not essential to attempt, in spite
of all the difficulties, " 'to drive the plowshare of the normative principle'—
i.e. love—'into the hard soil of political fact.' " Christians, like Jews, Muste
asserted, were the inheritors of a prophetic tradition that saw no separation of
the religious from the political, in which the prophets judged both individual
actions and national policy and which insisted that "the will of God . . . should
be done on earth, His Kingdom of righteousness and brotherhood made actual
in men, but also by and among them, on this earth naturalized for the human
spirit." [93]

Champions of "realpolitik" dismissed ethical questions because they exposed the degree to which power politics was directed toward the maintenance
of privilege and domination. In answer to the argument that political realism
required the defense of United States national security interests, Muste asked
whose interests were being served, those of the dominant elite or the majority
of the American people? Were American interests only a favorable balance of
trade and stable markets for investment so that the United States could "continue to control half the wealth of the world . . . and maintain the armed forces?"
Even the word *security* bothered Muste, for how secure were the American
people, or any people for that matter, in a world dominated by atomic weapons
and growing military power? Was it not the case, Muste asked, that the security
that came out of the barrel of a gun produced only "insecurity, fear, and greed
of both neighbor and myself"? Richard Barnet has likewise asked whether
the endless preoccupation with "military hardware," the equation of military
might and national power, has been purchased at the expense of the diminishing
quality of American life. Americans would be better served if national security
were related not just to matters of foreign policy but to domestic issues as well.
It is necessary to see that national security is in fact "a desired state of physical
safety, economic development, and social stability within which there is space
for individuals to participate in building an American community free of both
foreign coercion and manipulation by government." [94]

Those who resort to violence, Muste maintained, have concluded that people
can be treated as objects and things and thus be more easily killed. The objec-
tification of human beings is rooted in the loss of human solidarity that results
when a society so stresses greed and competition that it blots out the fact that
we are all "brothers and sisters." The wielders of violence dehumanize not only
others but themselves, for in employing violence they also become "things,"
and cease to be sensitive and responsive human beings who deal with others
as equals. Simon Weil poignantly described for Muste what happens when a

person becomes not a subject but "a thing in the most literal sense: it makes a corpse out of him." Is not violence, Muste reasoned, a sign of the lack of community, a situation in which "bitterness and hostility" govern human relations?[95]

Muste was particularly troubled by those who justified violence if it was used to defend others, especially when the cause was "just," for they employed a "double standard of morality." How can "we constantly condone or justify in ourselves and those who are on our side what we subject to the severest condemnation when practiced by others"? The classic example of "double morality" for Muste occurred during the First World War when Americans were outraged by what they perceived to be the atrocities committed by Germans, but were indifferent to the "Easter Massacre" and "the injustices to Negroes or laborers at home and . . . practically without exception they unequivocally condemn [a] resort to violence on the part of these victims and on behalf of the cause of social or economic emancipation." It was also clear to Muste that in any discussion of violence distinctions had to be made. Pacifists, in particular, had to understand that the violence that emerged in a people's struggle for liberation, where avenues to peaceful social change had been closed, was not the same as the violence used by "imperialist powers" such as the United States during the Vietnam War.[96]

Muste agreed with Reinhold Niebuhr that evil was real, just as real as the violence that leads to the suffering and death of innocent people. The advocacy of nonviolence does not easily diminish the overwhelming nature of violence in the world, but a refusal to participate in "hunting, hurting, killing another human being," whatever the circumstances, is a refusal to succumb to the violence that surrounds us. In the end it is up to the individual to decide whether to join with the "hunters" in the maximization of hurting and violence or to believe in the power of love that seeks the welfare of other human beings above all else. The price of a commitment to nonviolence is "the willingness and ability to die at the hands and on behalf of the evildoer." In waging peace, like war, there are costs and sacrifices, not self-seeking martyrdom but redemptive suffering in light of the cross that affirmed the ultimacy of love and a God of life.[97]

Nonviolence is both a way of life and a method of social change. As a method, nonviolence is revolutionary because it ceases to collaborate with a system based on exploitation, militarism, and domination. One cannot practice nonviolence and benefit from the profits of a capitalist economic order, for capitalism, directly and indirectly, is predicated on violence: the violence of profits, the violence of imperialism, and the violence of a class-divided society. People too quickly lose sight of the fact that the security and possessions that govern their lives are most often purchased through the oppression of others. Consequently violence and suffering come to seem acceptable because they bring about "social peace," the peace of the tomb. "In a world of violence," Muste concluded, "one must be a revolutionary before one can be a pacifist; in such a world a non-revolutionary pacifist is a contradiction in terms, a monstrosity." [98]

Muste's understanding of the tactics and goals of revolutionary nonviolence was influenced by the experience of Mohandas Gandhi in India. The West could learn much from Gandhi, Muste believed, especially that a mass-based nonviolent movement for liberation must be religiously rooted in "convictions about the very nature of life and the universe, convictions held not merely by the mind but by a moral commitment of the whole being to the practice of them." Muste considered the Gandhian symbol of the spinning wheel important because it represented the need to return to a premodern and precolonial mode of production that united farmers and workers. Within the context of the United States the spinning wheel embodied the truth of the inseparability of nonviolence from a reordered economic and social life, of the necessity of cooperative ways of living and a realization that a new economy is something we enact in the present, not to be postponed for some day in the far distant future. Socialists and Communists could take a lesson from Gandhi about the significance of living now what one envisions for the future. A new society would only come about only as people lived together in different ways, something early Christians, Franciscans, and Quakers understood. They discovered that people "who have entered into the spirit of community will inevitably be driven to seek to give expression . . . to their inner spirit in economic relationships." [99]

While it was clear to Muste that nonviolence and capitalism were incompatible, he was reluctant to identify an alternative, though a decentralized form of democratic socialism seemed most in keeping with his pacifist convictions. It would be a society in which there was a fundamental respect for civil liberties and some form of social ownership of production that did not lead to individual or class exploitation. He realized that the attempt to create economic alternatives within the framework of a capitalist order was difficult, and yet he had little sympathy for intentional communities that became "a shelter for the saints or a secular elite." Intentional communities took on meaning only to the degree that they were "a model of how society could, and eventually might, be organized," with a cooperative economy substituted for a competitive economy. [100]

Above all, Muste saw Gandhi's movement as a political expression of the aspirations of oppressed people for liberation. American advocates of nonviolence could learn much about themselves and their society from oppressed people, be they African Americans, sharecroppers, or industrial workers. [101]

For Muste, revolutionary nonviolence necessitated a direct confrontation with racism. Racial discrimination was an affront to God, for it did violence to the equality and dignity all people shared by being made in the image of God. It was a "denial of brotherhood by drawing lines that shut some in and others out." In 1943 it seemed to Muste that Hitler's treatment of Jews was analogous to the segregation of African Americans in the United States, which prevented them from participating fully in the life of their own country. Muste discerned that words could never be a substitute for action. He declared that if black churches took the lead in a nonviolent struggle against segregation, "it would constitute another great step toward the achievement of a revolution greater and more beneficent than all the revolutions of the past." [102]

Years later Martin Luther King, Jr., stated "unequivocally," writes Nat Hentoff, that "the current emphasis on nonviolent direct action in the race relations field is due more to A. J. than to anyone else in the country." King's observation was based on the civil rights work of the Fellowship of Reconciliation under Muste's leadership, and the role of those who had worked closely with Muste, especially James Farmer, Bayard Rustin, A. Philip Randolph, Glenn Smiley, George Houser, and James Lawson. Out of the FOR grew the Committee for Racial Equality, later called the Congress of Racial Equality. CORE was established in the spring of 1942 by James Farmer, a recent Howard University Divinity School graduate and race relations secretary for the FOR. Farmer had sent a memorandum to Muste about how to apply Gandhi's tactics of nonviolent resistance, from civil disobedience to noncooperation, in the "battle against segregation." Supported by the FOR, James Farmer formed the first chapter of CORE in Chicago, made up largely of students from the University of Chicago who were part of a FOR "peace team" at the university. Joining Farmer as a staff member of CORE was George Houser, a former student at Union Theological Seminary who had refused to register for the draft and was sentenced to a year in the Danbury Penitentiary. The first chapter of CORE comprised six persons, four white and two black, all pacifists, assisted by Bayard Rustin, FOR youth secretary and longtime peace activist. Two years later CORE had eight chapters, from New York to San Francisco. In the North and West, CORE used sit-ins and boycotts to attack discrimination in the public arena, especially in the areas of housing and jobs, and to combat segregation in all its manifestations, from public accommodations to movie theaters. In 1947 CORE moved south and in cooperation with the FOR launched the "Journey of Reconciliation" as a test of a recent Supreme Court decision about the unconstitutionality of segregated interstate bus seating. After intensive training in the techniques of nonviolence, sixteen people, eight white and eight black, traveled the Upper South for two weeks. They were arrested twelve times. Although the Journey of Reconciliation failed to overturn southern jim crow legislation it provided a precedent for the later Freedom Ride movement of the 1960s. In addition, throughout the 1940s and 1950s, CORE and the FOR worked together organizationally and "kept the tradition of nonviolent protest action alive within the circles of a few black American leaders." [103]

At the time of the 1955–1956 Montgomery Bus Boycott led by King and the Montgomery Improvement Association, FOR organizers Glenn Smiley (minister, southerner, and FOR secretary) and Bayard Rustin provided training in nonviolence as an instrument of social change. The bus boycott was the first use of the tactics of nonviolence on a mass scale, and as Aldon Morris notes, it "became an example to blacks throughout the South of what could be accomplished with organized protest." As nonviolent resistance to segregation spread throughout the South during the late 1950s, Smiley and Rustin were there to offer support, training, and their experience in the practice of nonviolence.[104]

A sit-in at a lunch counter at Woolworth's in Greensboro, North Carolina, by black students sparked similar protests across the South and captured "the imagination of an entire generation of young people." In Nashville, Tennessee, James Lawson, son of a black Methodist minister, was southern field secretary for the FOR. Influenced by A. J. Muste and Bayard Rustin and his experience in India he worked with black leaders to create a mass-based nonviolent movement. Lawson joined with students in their attempt to desegregate the city of Nashville. Julian Bond, at the time a student at Morehouse College in Atlanta, remembers attending a student conference in the spring of 1960 in Raleigh, North Carolina, and how moved he was by Lawson's commitment to nonviolence. Lawson had a vision of "a militant nonviolence, an aggressive nonviolence. You didn't have to wait for evil to come to you, you could go to the evil." [105]

Student sit-ins were followed in 1961 by Freedom Rides, inspired by the earlier Journey of Reconciliation. CORE and FOR activists organized an interracial group of thirteen freedom riders to test the Supreme Court decision against segregated seating on interstate buses and trains as well as segregated terminal. Freedom riders were subjected to the hostility of white mobs, beatings, fire bombing of their buses, and arrest. Nevertheless, what Manning Marable has labeled a "Second Reconstruction" had begun, bringing about "a series of massive confrontations concerning the status of Afro-Americans and other national minorities in the nation's economic, social and political institutions." The Second Reconstruction would permanently dismantle jim crow structures and testify to black people's enduring commitment to a vision of democracy, equality, and freedom.[106]

Muste believed that the civil rights struggle was not just a witness to the power of nonviolence but an organic part of "building the beloved community." But the beloved community could not be built as long as violence reigned both at home and abroad. A new community was an expression of a people's desire for liberation, but the desire could not be achieved if one sided "with any force that obstructs liberation." One of the major obstacles to the liberation of people throughout the world was the foreign and military policy of the United States. Muste concluded, as King would later, that civil rights leaders could not be silent about the war in Vietnam.[107]

The aspiration for liberation embodied an enduring lesson for Christians, Muste believed. Human relations, he thought, are rooted in what humanity shares as "that of God," a Quaker phrase that conveys that all—even the oppressors—are sisters and brothers. Those who exploit, dehumanize, and oppress others are also human beings. The phrase signified to Muste that what happened to black Americans could not be separated from what that meant for white Americans, for we are all part of a shared humanity. Muste found insight in Gandhi's observation that we constantly have to recognize the "humanity of the enemy," who is in fact our "other self." Being made in the image of God implies that we must "try and reach and touch the human in them," the oppressors. The overcoming of oppression and domination will not occur until we realize that a world organized around injustice is held together by fear, fear of freedom, fear of being human, and fear of community.[108]

Dorothy Day: Living Out an Option for the Poor

The story of Dorothy Day and the Catholic Worker movement has been told and retold in many different ways, each trying to capture or portray her importance for American life and the history of Catholicism in the United States. Storytelling, not unlike ways of doing theology and ethics, assumes that we participate in the story, particularly as it reveals insights into our own lives. Perhaps that is why biographies are so different from autobiographies. While telling the story of another person's life, the biographer is interpreting events from a particular point of view, one with which the subject under question might not always agree. This was the case with Dorothy Day. Her biographer William Miller states that one of the reasons Day so resisted the idea of a biography was that it "represented a placing of her life into someone else's hands—and that she could not abide." Keeping in mind Day's reservations about biographers, what follows has less to do with the exact details of her life than with what we can learn from Dorothy Day and the Catholic Worker movement, that is, something fundamental about what Virgil Elizondo calls the transmission of faith from the periphery, from those who have been rendered powerless by the status quo and exist on the margins of both the church and society.[109]

Dorothy Day believed that throughout her life there were various turning points when she envisioned the totality of her life differently: times of searching as well as times of loneliness and joy. She often liked to emphasize, in words she knew were downright flippant, that "the mass of bourgeois smug Christians who denied Christ in His poor made me turn to Communism, and that it was the Communists and working with them that made me turn to God." Over the years she came to feel that there was a world of difference between being part of a radical movement that sought justice for the oppressed and living in solidarity with them. Accepting "hardship and poverty as the way of life in which to walk," she remarked, "lays [one] . . . open to this susceptibility to the sufferings of others." [110]

Dorothy Day was born in Brooklyn, New York, not far from the Brooklyn Bridge on November 7, 1897. She was one of five children. Her father was a sports writer who moved often, finally settling in Chicago, where Day grew up on the North Side. Books, especially the works of Peter Kropotkin and

Upton Sinclair's novel *The Jungle*, exposed her to the plight of the poor. Sinclair wrote about a Chicago she never knew and opened up for Day the realities of immigrant life. She found herself exploring Chicago's West Side, fascinated by the sounds and smells of urban poverty, feeling that "from then on my life was to be linked to theirs, their interests were to be mine; I had received a call, a vocation, a direction to my life." At the age of sixteen she entered the University of Illinois. By the end of her first year she had joined the Socialist Party. The IWW and Debs seemed to embody hope for working-class people, and she questioned an industrial society that left in its wake disabled workers, hunger, sickness, and disease. Friendships with other student radicals went hand in hand with her growing radicalization. She had aspirations of being a writer and even at an early age was able to observe the world around her acutely and to find the words to express what she saw. She left the university in 1915 after two years and took her first job as a reporter for the *Call*, a New York Socialist paper.[111]

In her work for the *Call*, she covered strikes, investigated the slum conditions of New York, and followed the debates of a developing opposition movement to the First World War. She was particularly drawn to those such as Bill Haywood and Elizabeth Gurley Flynn of the Wobblies, who were working to transform American society. Day was surrounded by radical artists and writers in New York's Greenwich Village and after two years of working for the *Call* became a staff member of *The Masses*. Here she met and grew close to writers such as Floyd Dell and Max Eastman, political cartoonists such as Art Young, and a range of artists, poets, and critics on the Left whose purpose was best described by John Reed as "a social one: to everlastingly attack old systems, old morals, old prejudices—the whole weight of outworn thought that dead men have saddled upon us—and to set new ones in their places. . . . We intend to be arrogant, impertinent, in bad taste, but not vulgar. We will be bound by no one creed or theory or social reform, but will express them all, providing they are radical." [112]

When America entered the First World War it was governmental policy to suppress any form of dissent, and the U.S. Post Office banned radical and Socialist material, including *The Masses*, from the mails. Just after *The Masses* was shut down, Day joined a friend as part of a demonstration of suffragettes picketing the White House on behalf of political prisoners. She was arrested and spent the next month in prison. Day soon discovered that suffragettes were subject to brutal treatment from prison authorities and learned firsthand something about the bleak and "barbarous" nature of imprisonment. Upon her release from prison Day thought that she wanted to become a nurse and spent a year as a nurse probationer at King's County Hospital in Brooklyn. She soon realized that she still had "a longing to write" and moved back to Chicago, taking various jobs to support herself while she worked for the newly established successor to *The Masses*, the *Liberator*, coedited by Crystal and Max Eastman.[113]

Chicago was still an exciting place for Dorothy Day. She found solace in meetings of immigrant workers or their Sunday afternoon picnics in Lincoln Park, sharing their dreams of a new day and their belief that change was possible. Her solidarity with working-class people was enough to land her in jail. Attorney General A. Mitchell Palmer, riding on a tide of postwar hysteria over the Bolshevik Revolution, was given almost carte blanche to repress any movement, organization, or individual deemed subversive. Thousands of immigrants were deported with little public protest, and organizations such as the IWW were depicted "as an American appendage of the Bolsheviks." Day was associated with the Wobblies in Chicago, and one evening when she was staying at a Wobbly "flop house" she was arrested by police for being in a "disorderly house," a humiliating experience she never forgot.[114]

While living in Chicago, Day wrote an autobiographical novel, *The Eleventh Virgin*, which she later labeled "a very bad book." It was not a best seller, but it did produce enough interest to sell the motion picture rights, enabling her to move back to New York and purchase a small house on Staten Island, where she could write. She wrote for local papers and published articles for the *New Masses*, a publication closely associated with the Communist Party. She admired the Communists' dedication to the cause of working people, though Day never became a party member herself.[115]

The middle and late twenties were a period of "natural happiness" for Dorothy. She gave birth in spring, 1926, to a daughter, Tamar Teresa. By the time her daughter was baptized that summer, it was clear to Day how dissimilar she was from her common-law husband, Foster Batterham, though she loved him very much. As close as she was to Battterham, he remained an anarchist and an atheist with little sympathy for Dorothy's growing interest in Catholicism. She felt that she had come to a point in her life where she had to choose between God and "human love," and initially, she believed that her conversion was incompatible with her radicalism: "I was betraying the class to which I belonged, you my brother, the workers, the poor of the world, the class which Christ most loved and spent His life with." Only gradually did she come to understand that her commitment to the Catholic church was an affirmation of God's love for the poor and oppressed.[116]

In the years that followed her conversion, Dorothy supported herself and her daughter by writing articles for the Catholic press and lived in both New York and Mexico. Daily, she discovered new dimensions to her newfound faith and became attentive to what the poor had to teach her. The onset of the Depression increased her desire to be of service, but it was not clear the direction her life should take. In December, 1932, as a reporter for *The Commonweal*, she covered a hunger march in Washington, D.C., organized by Communist

Unemployment Councils. Feeling a natural kinship with the unemployed, she lamented: "I stood on the curb and watched them, joy and pride in the courage of this band of men and women mounting in my heart, and with it a bitterness too that since I was now a Catholic, with fundamental philosophical differences, I could not be out there with them. I could write, I could protest, to arouse the conscience, but where was the Catholic leadership in the gatherings of bands of men and women together, for the actual works of mercy that the comrades had always made part of their technique in reaching the workers?" It was at this point that Peter Maurin entered her life. On returning from Washington to New York she found Peter waiting for her, having been sent to her by George Shuster, editor of *The Commonweal*.[117]

Although Dorothy Day and Peter Maurin founded the Catholic Worker movement together, Dorothy contended that "the story of the *Catholic Worker* begins with Peter." Peter Maurin was born twenty years before Day, on May 9, 1877, in the small village of Oultet in southeastern France. He was the eldest of twenty-two children of devout Catholic parents of peasant background and was educated in Christian Brothers' schools. Drawn to the Christian Brothers order by both its simplicity and its dedication to teaching, Maurin became a teacher devoted to serving the poor and working class. He spent a number of years as a teacher but eventually left the order in 1902 because of his attraction to the Le Sillon movement founded by Marc Sangnier. Le Sillon was an expression of a form of Catholic activism attentive to the growing distance between the church and the working class and the need for Catholics to respond to the exploitation of working people, especially in light of Pope Leo XIII's encyclical *Rerum Novarum*. Sangnier had an inherent belief in democracy and the role popular organizations and institutions could play in the life of impoverished people, and Le Sillon supported the creation of political and economic institutions that would defend the rights and dignity of workers and advocated consumer and producer cooperatives. Difficulties with military service led to Peter Maurin's departure from France for Canada in 1909. This was the beginning of a long odyssey as an itinerant worker, from homesteading in western Canada to a journey across the United States, working in steel mills, coal mines, lumber camps, and on the railroads. Over the years he struggled to think through what it meant to be responsive to the poor and for Catholics to incorporate the social teachings of the church into their daily lives. At the time he first met Dorothy Day he was living in the Bowery, speaking on street corners and in public places and trying to get the Catholic press to publish his writings on the need for voluntary poverty and works of mercy. He was, Day wrote, a "troubadour of God" who sought to convey to his listeners the relevance of the teachings of the church in addressing the contradictions of the established social order.[118]

Maurin became Day's teacher, educating her about the history of the Catholic church, the radicality of the Bible, and the religious tradition of those who had sided with the poor and oppressed. It seemed to Day that Maurin was visionary who held fast to the ability of human beings to "build a new society within the shell of the old." She insisted that Maurin's capacity to dream was deeply rooted in his belief in the love of God and what God's love of creation made possible. This was manifest in the ability to see Christ in others, especially the poor.[119]

Maurin presented Day with a threefold program. The first part he called round-table discussions. These would bring together various segments of the community, be they workers, intellectuals, or members of middle class, to wrestle with the problems confronting society, each learning from the other. Maurin's "Easy Essays" conveyed what he envisioned:

> We need round-table discussions
>   to keep trained minds from being academic.
> We need round-table discussions
>   to keep untrained minds
>   from being superficial.
> We need round-table discussions
>   to learn from scholars
>   how things would be,
>   if they were as they should be.
> We need round-table discussions
>   to learn from scholars
>   how a path can be made
>   from things as they are
>   to things as they should be.

The round-table discussions were the efforts of a teacher to radicalize people, but Day's imagination was caught by his talk about the need for a labor paper as a means of "popularizing the teachings of the Church in regard to social matters, bringing to the man in the street a Christian solution of unemployment, a way of rebuilding the social order." [120]

The second part of the program was the establishment of houses of hospitality as an expression of the gospel command to feed the hungry, cloth the naked, and shelter and comfort the homeless. Houses of hospitality would present people with the opportunity of serving the poor and taking personal responsibility for their own lives. The third part was the creation of farming communes where people could live off the land and be freed from dependence on the wage system for their existence. The farming communes were a means of instilling in people the dignity of work and the understanding that they were cocreators with God in the creative process. They were also an immediate answer to unemployment and the crisis of a failing industrial order, and they would allow people to rediscover the values of cooperation and community.[121]

Peter Maurin's dreams took on reality with the publication in May, 1933, of the first issue of the *Catholic Worker*, which sold for a penny a copy to Com-

219

munists and trade unionists who had gathered at New York's Union Square to celebrate May Day. The first issue was produced in the kitchen of Day's apartment on the Lower East Side of New York. By the end of the year the circulation of the paper reached 100,000; by 1936 it rose to 150,000. Houses of hospitality were established in New York and other cities, and toward the end of the thirties there were twenty-three hospices and four farming communes. As Day has said, what subsequently happened "was history"—a history of all those "who have been part of the Catholic Worker family . . . a family spread across all the cities and states of this country." [122]

The Catholic Worker movement became a concrete embodiment of Saint Paul's description of Christian life as manifested in faith, hope, and charity and as witnessed in the struggle for social and racial justice. Christian life was made real "every time hand bills are passed out on the street, every time one walks a picket line, or sits down in factory or before a factory gate, or at the world's fair, or in front of the Waldorf, every time a voice is lifted to call attention to man's joblessness, his homelessness. . . . We cannot be silent." [123]

Dorothy Day was never silent. From the first publication of the *Catholic Worker* until she died on November 29, 1980, she lived as a Catholic Worker with the urban poor. As Peter Maurin had been her teacher, she became a teacher for all those who sought to live on the boundary between faith and politics, searching for the meaning of individual responsibility before God and human aspirations for community. Her legacy to us is most vividly conveyed through an examination of her understanding of faith as an option for the poor and her critique of the limits of our political imagination. [124]

Day took with absolute seriousness Jesus' declaration that what we do to the least of our brothers and sisters we do unto him. Christ was visibly present for her in the faces of the poor. The tragedy of contemporary Christianity, in her view, was how Christians, by both word and deed, turned their backs on the poor, who were "herded like brutes in municipal lodging houses, tramping the streets and roads hungry, working at starvation wages or under an inhuman speed-up, living in filthy degrading conditions." Just as surely as Christ was present in the faces of the poor, so was he present in every step toward justice. He stood with those who suffered in the struggle for a better social order, for "He was the I.W.W. who was tortured and lynched out in Centralia and Everett . . . [and] there was never a Negro fleeing from a maniacal mob whose fear and agony and suffering Christ did not feel." In response to the indifference of many Christians to the plight of the poor, the Catholic Worker movement called for solidarity with the poor and a rediscovery of a Christianity dedicated to the interests of the oppressed and the cause of justice for the poor. Christians must "always be thinking and writing about poverty, for if we are not among its victims its reality fades from us. We must talk about poverty, because people insulated by their own comfort lose sight of it." [125]

Day recognized two different forms of poverty: one she labeled "inflicted poverty" and the other "voluntary poverty." "Inflicted poverty" described the destitution, bleakness, and misery that poor people endured. It was the world of tenement houses and forced evictions, of homeless people, and children with little hope for the future. This form of poverty denied people the basic necessities of life, what Peter Townsend defines as "the lack of resources necessary to permit participation in the activities, customs, and diets commonly approved by society." By contrast, voluntary poverty was a way of life that one chose to adopt out of fidelity to the teachings of Jesus. Day's model was Saint Francis who joyfully and gladly embraced "Lady Poverty," becoming totally dependent upon what God provided. She approvingly quoted the words of Maurin that "voluntary poverty is the answer. We cannot see our brother in need without stripping ourselves. It is the only way we have of showing our love." Living a life of voluntary poverty was conceived as nonparticipation in a society that determines value and worth only in materialistic terms. Day considered *materialism* just another word for exploitation, the amassing of comforts and luxuries at the expense of others.[126]

Day took literally the injunction "While our brothers suffer from lack of necessities, we will refuse to enjoy comforts." Tom Sullivan, active in founding the first Catholic Worker house in Chicago in the midthirties, recalled that Day spoke about the saints "like they live in our midst." Saints who had dedicated their lives to service of the poor became role models for Sullivan. He quickly learned what following in their footsteps entailed as he and other young Catholics became "completely uprooted from our former attitudes and values. At the same time, most of us literally deserted our families and friends. A Catholic Worker way of life was sheer madness to all of them, so many of us felt as though we were outside of the mainstream of everyday life of jobs and business." Day stressed that people should hold jobs that were in some way a "category of the Works of Mercy"—"having to do with food, clothing and shelter, health and education, re-creation, and should be not only to earn a living . . . but to earn a living for others who suffer involuntary poverty and destitution." One would have to "exclude jobs in advertising, which only increases people's useless desires, and in insurance companies and banks, which are known to exploit the poor of this country and of others. Whatever has contributed to the misery and degradation of the poor may be considered a bad job, and not to be worked at." [127]

Day agreed with Saul Alinksy that it is difficult for people of privilege, because of their education, family background, and experience, to comprehend the nature of poverty. Only by self-discipline and a generosity made concrete in the sharing of one's material goods did Catholic Workers learn a new kind of poverty that did not contribute to the continuing cycle of the exploitation of the poor. In the late 1950s the New York Catholic Worker house was taken over by the city under the right of eminent domain in order to build an extension of the subway. The city treasurer sent a check for over three thousand dollars to the Catholic Worker for interest on money they were awarded in a property settlement. The check was promptly returned because, Day affirmed, "we do not believe in the profit system, and so we cannot take profit or interest on our money. People who take a materialist view of human service wish to make a profit but we are trying to do our duty by our service without wages to our brothers as Jesus commanded in the Gospel (Matt. 25)." Profit making was just another part of a system that defrauded the poor and robbed people of their dignity and worth.[128]

Day asserted that the poor were a challenge to the church and the entire Christian community because Christ "is incarnate today in the poor" and "it is through the poor that we achieve our salvation; Jesus Himself has said it in His . . . [description] of the Last Judgment. It is through the poor that we can exercise faith and learn to love Him." Yet, Day did not romanticize the poor. She saw them as human beings. She was amazed that the poor were never deprived of hope, that "they have hoped against hope," and she was inspired by the endurance of human nature. Working with the poor was above all a striving for community, a community of the dispossessed, who in some mysterious way gave evidence of the immanence of God through the love of people for one another.[129]

To side with the poor meant that Catholic Workers would find themselves working with all who sought justice for the poor, including Communists. It also meant a demand for an economy based on meeting human needs rather than accumulating profit. In spite of her belief in the possibility of a more humane and just society, Day still maintained that no matter what form of social transformation took place there would always be poor and marginalized people. God did not create poverty or the poor; thus a class-divided society was of human doing and capable of human alteration. Like Virgil Elizondo, Day understood what it was to live in a competitive society that worshiped the idols of winning and success, blaming all those who did not make it—the millions of people who were forced to feel rejection, shame, and guilt, as if failure was their own doing. For both Elizondo and Day, in such a society it becomes impossible to "meet the God of Jesus since we tend to worship more naturally Prometheus masked as the Christian God than the God of the weak and powerless who presents himself to us throughout the pages of scripture." It was the God of the poor that Day discovered throughout her long life as a Catholic Worker, the God revealed in a carpenter from Nazareth who preached good news to the poor and commanded all his followers by word and deed to identify with the poor and oppressed. As she proclaimed, we need "to grow in the love of God, by seeing Christ in each one who comes to us, especially in all these neglected ones on our skid rows." [130]

Dorothy Day considered politics to be a reappropriation of personal responsibility for the way in which the human community is structured. She was an astute observer of American society and was well aware of the extent to which so much of what went under the guise of politics was nothing more than the constant search for new and more effective means of exerting power over others. Various interpreters of Day and the Catholic Worker movement have pointed out the anarchist dimension to her thought and her opposition to working "through the state." To her mind, those who sought to reform society by means of the existing political process were interested only in palliatives, unwilling to acknowledge that it was the "whole system that was out of joint. And it was to reconstruct the social order, that we were throwing ourselves in with the workers, whether in factories or shipyards or on the sea." Catholic Workers thus shared with Communists a belief in the withering away of the state but only insofar as it involved an increase in people's control over their own lives. Communism appealed to Day because it implied a threat to money and property and was an attempt "at a more equitable distribution of this world's goods." Nevertheless, what intrigued Dorothy about communism was less the political connotations than its reminder to Christians of the communism of the early church and the success of medieval religious orders that shared all things in common.[131]

Day's anarchism was shaped by a number of factors that included her reading of Kropotkin, her experience with the IWW, her encounter with Peter Maurin, and her own wrestling with the contemporary relevance of the Catholic tradition. For her a Christian expression of anarchism stressed the importance of mutual aid, a decentralized economy, and the assumption by ordinary people of personal responsibility for each other. One of the distinctive features of Catholic Worker anarchism was its radical egalitarianism, an ontological belief in the absolute worth and dignity of all people, especially those whom society disregarded, neglected, and marginalized. Mary Segers concludes from her study of the Catholic Worker movement that "an egalitarian society will not be a reality unless an attitude of ontological equality which perceives human beings as basically equal conditions and influences all of one's relations with others, public and private." [132]

Robert Coles captures the essential character of Catholic Worker politics in the expression "localist politics," which implies that politics has to do with accountability and control of the political process on the local level and speaks of communities of people, of neighborhoods, and of "working from the bottom," never losing sight of one's accountability to the poor. Day believed that localism was concerned with what is real—clothing the naked, feeding the hungry, and sheltering the homeless—much more real than "living in the corridors of power, influence, money, making big decisions that affect big numbers of people." Whether localist politics are effective was not a key question for Day. The more appropriate question was the degree to which a locally based political vision could address the need for community by a reordering of values, perceptions, and world views that enhances the quality of the common good. The Catholic Worker position was "that success, as the world determines it, is not the criterion by which the movement should be judged . . . the important thing is that we adhere to values which transcend time and for which we will be asked a personal accounting." Daniel Berrigan observes that Dorothy Day hoped that by her commitment to the poor others might learn that a political system that sustains both war and poverty can be broken only by a "renewal of imagination" born out of living the gospel and turning things around so that a "well ordered heart can sustain, penetrate, interpret, resist, minister to, even at times heal, or at least mitigate the whirlwind. This she lived, so living, taught." [133]

Anarchism, localist politics, life among the poor, and the renewal of imagination were all rooted in Day's belief in what God could accomplish through people committed to living out the Sermon on the Mount. It was something so simple and yet so difficult, for it entailed the ability not to compromise, to say no when it was so easy to say yes, to realize the countercultural nature of Christianity. The problem with so much of Christian thinking about politics is that it assumes that the correct political agenda for Christians is to find a place, a voice, or a role for themselves within the political system. In so doing, Christianity succumbs to the questionable task of justifying the status quo.

Mel Piehl has noted the difference between the Catholic Worker movement and progressive Protestant movements, such as the social gospel, in their respective relationships to American culture. Protestantism has historically identified itself with the dominant values and institutions of American society to such a degree that critical distance has been difficult for Protestants to achieve. Thus, those who sought to Christianize the industrial order, to make it more responsive to the demands of the gospel, were confronted with members of their own community who assumed a natural compatibility between Christianity and the capitalist values of individualism, competition, self-sufficiency, and material success. Some Catholics also strove to Americanize the church and to adapt Catholicism to the ethos of a capitalist society. Others, however, such as Day, drew on a tradition of Catholic piety, social teachings, and radical spirituality that remained at odds with the demands of an acquisitive society. Rather than seek to transform society as a whole, Catholic Workers tried to lead lives as a dedicated minority of committed Christians. Whereas Protestants argued over where to draw the line between religion and politics, David O'Brien notes, Catholic Workers "did not see themselves as acting as members of a polity." Catholic Workers made a distinction between politics and radical Christian commitment. They were more concerned about empowering others than engaging in a politics of power. [134]

In her autobiography, Day wrote that community "was the social answer to the long loneliness." She believed that people long for fellowship, a sense of belonging and human interconnectedness. In words reminiscent of the hopes of religious radicals throughout human history, Day spoke of the desire for "land, bread, work, children, and joys of community in play and work and worship." Such a community would come into being only as people substituted the materialistic priorities of getting and having for being and becoming, out of love for their neighbor. As idealistic as such language sounds, it reflected her experience of working and living with the poor, which is quite different from the experience of lecturing about poverty and the poor. Given how much society has harmed, wounded, and abused most poor people, it is a considerable feat that the cry for community has stayed alive among them as long as it has.[135]

Dorothy Day felt a great deal of kinship with Martin Buber, who shared her distrust of centralist political organizations, of bureaucracy and top-down decision making that exalted the state, crushed the dreams of individuals, and diminished people's sense of personal responsibility. Both found mutuality, reciprocity, and dialogue more appropriate, words that underscored the desires human beings hold in common and structured human relationships that made possible "rootedness and community." Buber maintained that community must have a center, that which affirms the social dimension of our humanity. Community is an "inner disposition or constitution of a life in common, which knows and embraces in itself hard 'calculation,' adverse 'chance,' and the sudden access of 'anxiety.' It is community of tribulation and only because of that community of spirit; community of toil and only because of that community of salvation." [136]

For both Day and Buber, communities were not an escape from life but an immersion in the real world, with all its pain, hardship, tears, and joy. The search for community was embodied in the struggle to relate religion and socialism. They agreed that religion was an expression of their commitment to God, which could find its realization only in the service of others. That is why Day was so intrigued with Buber's conception of socialism as "possible only thru the formation of small voluntary groups . . . who not merely share the means of production, or the forces of labor, but who, as human beings, enter into a direct relationship with one another and live a life of genuine fraternity. Such a socialism would have to resist any mechanization of living. The association of such groups would have to resist the dictates of an organized center, accumulation of power, and a political superstructure." Thus, for Buber, "religion without socialism is disembodied spirit, and hence not authentic spirit; socialism without religion is body emptied of spirit, hence also not genuine body." Consequently, religion and socialism were not abstractions for Buber and Day, but manifestations of two aspects of human history, the struggle with God to achieve meaning for our lives and a means of embodying that meaning in our quest for authentic human communities.[137]

If the poverty of our political imagination has to do with lack of vision, lack of sensitivity to the poor, and lack of political will to transform our own lives, then Dorothy Day and the Catholic Worker movement are as realistic as those who advocate a politics of power that measures success only by the stick of what is possible. David O'Brien has noted that Day's "personalist radicalism" is a recognition that "the beginnings of real social change . . . lie in the human heart and revolution begins with conversion." It is important to take personal responsibility for one's actions and life in light of the demands of God's concern for the poor and oppressed, but doing so still leaves untouched the structural dimensions of oppression that no personal decision alone can alter. Thus community and solidarity with others is necessary in the creation of a new social order. We are indebted to Dorothy Day and the Catholic Worker movement for making us realize how prophetic are the words of Marie Augusta Neal that "the world's poor are reaching out to take what is rightfully theirs. How to respond to that fact is a major challenge facing Christians in the late twentieth century." [138]

Struggle for an Equitable Community.

Reinhold Niebuhr, Harry F. Ward, A. J. Muste, and Dorothy Day represent differing streams of twentieth-century Christian thought and practice. One of the assumptions of this chapter is that Niebuhr overlooked the contribution William Appleman Williams attributes to Karl Marx, namely, that he brings "our capitalist ego into a confrontation with our capitalist reality." [139]

Marx can be viewed as constantly raising the possibilities of what human beings can create from their own will, imagination, and organization. Niebuhr believed that Marx was mistaken in his assessment of human possibilities. He refused to allow either Marx or Marxism to call his own theological assumptions into question. The tragedy of human existence seemed to him as much a given as the despairing realism of his own theology. Scripture and the Christian tradition, according to Niebuhr, confirmed that human freedom and the exercise thereof are fraught with danger and error when they overstep the bounds of the political arena. The Kingdom of God might be a depository of hope, but living without illusions as to the nature of evil and the corruptibility of power, he believed that a qualitatively different order of human existence was not possible. The best possibility is relative justice and a balance of power in a world of conflict. Politics as the art of the possible has left a chastened legacy for Christian ethicists, who too often forget the words of Max Weber: "Man would not have obtained the possible unless time and time again he had reached out for the impossible." [140]

Christian ethics does the community of faith a disservice when it seeks to appease the powerful, striving for relevancy at the expense of prophetic insight. Christian ethics, as Archbishop Oscar Romero points out, has more to do with giving voice to the voiceless than with legitimating the power of the powerful.[141] The life of Dorothy Day demonstrates that Christian ethicists can learn a great deal about themselves and their faith by living and working with those at the bottom of society, by incorporating the cry of the poor into their reflections and analysis of both church and society.

The perspectives Ward, Muste, and Day offer about nonviolence, democracy, community, and a viable economy can be summed up in a series of images Wendell Berry evokes to describe how we treat the land and the natural world. Berry is a poet, writer, and farmer who over the years has voiced his concern about the environment and the impoverishment of our ability as human beings to communicate about issues of meaning. These issues vary from how we deal with our economy to the indifference of the dominant culture to the distortion of language that expresses our desires for community and wholeness. Berry describes how Europeans who came to the United States never considered it a "homeland." It was a place, a territory, a frontier to be exploited and used. The violence that has been done to nature has also been done to human beings: violence of wasted resources, violence of people, and violence of power over both people and nature. A utilitarian approach to life has reduced the world to a marketplace that exalts the supposed benefits of competition, which lead not to community but to winners and losers. The losers, like industrial waste, become "human dumps." Berry believes organized Christianity "makes peace with a destructive economy and divorces itself from economic issues because it is economically compelled to do so." The church's existence is dependent on not asking certain questions about the "link between economy and ecosystem" or how an industrial economy destroys community.[142]

Wendell Berry's experience of rural America makes him suspicious of those who speak in terms of the nation and the national economy, often interchangeable with the corporation and business. Rural people, he says, "see all around them, every day, the marks and scars of an exploitative national economy. They have much reason, by now, to know how little real help is to be expected from somewhere else. They still have, moreover, the remnants of local memory and local community." This is not to romanticize rural America but to recall that this country is composed of a set of communities, be they rural or urban, that know and understand the sources of their problems better than those at a distance who measure the world in terms of profitability and the dictates of the market, unconcerned about what is done to the human landscape.[143]

From his study of Appalachian society John Gaventa concludes that democracy divorced from a capitalist-based economy should be synonymous with people's aspiration for human community, supportive of the common good rather the good of a few individuals of wealth and power. Harry F. Ward insisted on the contradiction between democracy as the diffusion of power and capitalism as the concentration of power. But for all Ward's critique of capitalism and the profit motive, it was Muste and Day who realized that a sustainable future depends on allowing people control over their own lives and on making the institutional apparatus of a democracy accountable to people.[144]

The notion of a decentralized economy and political system was for Day and Muste not a flight from the complexities of the modern world so much as a renewal of democracy as a political possibility. In the same manner Sara Evans and Harry Boyte have stressed that the "eclipse of community" is the loss not only of belonging and identity but of active and participatory citizenship. For neoconservatives, notions of community are wedded to the maintenance of a marketplace mentality, with little sense of the collective reality of human experience. By contrast, Evans and Boyte speak about community as something that "sustains and reproduces a group's shared bonds of historical memory and culture," that is related to ways in which oppressed people come to self-consciousness in both the private and public dimensions of their lives. Community is thus an integral part of the recovery of democratic values in which powerless people act to transform the world about them. It is crucial that people connect what is happening in their personal lives to the structures of the dominant society, as both Muste and Day realized.[145]

The beginning section of this chapter drew on Gerald Fourez's analysis of the difference between realistic and utopian approaches to human history. A fitting response to the realists was Harry Ward's statement that "a new world can never come without the insights of prophets, the visions of seers, and the dreams of poets." Two persons who embodied for Ward such dreams, visions, and insights were Jesus and Marx, who understood the realities of poverty and spoke out against "the sufferings of the poor and the oppressed." Thus they were "dangerous to the lords and rulers of the earth, a menace to the comforts, privileges and powers of all who live, in whole or in part, on the labor of others without due return, they inherited the persecutions that were the labor of their forerunners." Whereas Marx pointed to the role a self-conscious working class could play in overthrowing structures of domination, Jesus proclaimed how a restructured life in service of the poor and marginalized could alter the "relation between the individual and society, the self and others, and from taking to sharing." Ward emphasized that for Jesus people are ends and not means and that human rights are far more important than the rights of property. Marx and Jesus agree that the road ahead for humankind is dependent upon the "exercise of mind and spirit." Dogma, be it political or religious, is antithetical to human development. Whatever truth we are to discover can be verified only by action. Ward concluded that Christianity as a religion "started out to change the world, [but] became controlled by the world," and perhaps the same could be said of Marxism. Both need to rediscover the revolutionary sources of their own beginnings and their ultimate accountability to the poor and oppressed of this world.[146]

Conclusion

The life histories of individuals, movements, and organizations have taken us on a journey that has encompassed more than a century of American history. It is a collection of stories that tell us something about ourselves as a people, a nation, and a religious community. If the past is to inform our understanding of the present, it will be, as Vincent Harding says, because we have come to know "the lives of women and men who provide intimations of our human grandeur, who open doors beyond darkness and invite us all toward the magnificent light of our own best possibilities, as mature, compassionate, evolving human beings." [1] As we have examined the lives of people who have envisioned a different structure for our society, a new way of living, we have encountered central questions about how we understand the relationship between the past and the present, the nature of Christian ethics, and religion and radical politics.

History

As we rediscover our historical memory, we need to recall that the past is never remembered in the same way. So often the history of Christianity in America has focused primarily on institutional development, disembodied theological debates, and the experience of transplanted European immigrants. It is not surprising that our religious self-understanding has been frequently indistinguishable from the dominant social values of American society. Hence to reread the past from the bottom up is literally to turn history upside down. Gustavo Gutiérrez has deemed this reversal "subversive history," that which makes history "flow backward—makes it flow not from above but from below." Such an approach is subversive not because it makes room for the history of oppressed people or allows traditionally excluded groups to be heard but because it alters our overall understanding of what constitutes our past as members of a believing community. It assumes that memories are a constituent part of our struggle in the present, for in reconstructing our conceptions of the past we are also redefining present and future possibilities. In turn, history becomes a memory of hope, creativity, and liberation on the part of marginalized people. This method implies that we take seriously a view of history that is political, political to the degree that one acknowledges how concepts of the past affect contemporary memories and ideologies. This kind of sociohistorical analysis is part of what Bill Schwartz describes as an "active construction of conceptions of the past as a continual and defining moment in political practice" as well as in struggles within the cultural arena.[2]

In examining the past with new eyes we have discovered an expression of Christian faith that has been inseparable from a fundamental commitment to the poor and the oppressed, an empowering of those rendered voiceless, and a constant awareness of the disquieting power of dreams and the exercise of social imagination. What is perhaps most unsettling for those who wield power over others, be they within the church or the society at large, is that ordinary people, who have been excluded on the basis of race, class, and gender, have clearly understood that the gospel is good news for the poor. It has been evident to them that the face of God was to be found in the struggle for justice, that God was present where people sought to substitute human solidarity for racial hatred, sexual equality for patriarchical domination, and democratic participation in the economic and political life of one's society for tunnel-vision politics and the dictates of corporate profit making.

To assert that God is actually present where barriers that separate people from one another are torn down and despair is replaced by hope is to raise questions about the theological reflection and ethical analysis that have traditionally informed our interpretation of American Christianity. If God is to be found at the margins of our society, where people are hurting and struggling for social transformation, then we need to question how we speak about God, understand the role of the Christian community, and proclaim our faith. Perhaps that is why Claude Williams could maintain that "the Lord of Hosts is the people's God. He has through the ages been with the people in their fight for righteousness. He is today with the people over the earth in their struggle for justice, political [autonomy], religious freedom; for homes, for land—and the question is not how far they are consciously going with God but how far are we conscious He is going with them. The people have in times past been His instruments to forge moral, ethical, and spiritual values. They are today His witnesses for peace, democracy, and security."[3]

To claim that God takes sides, that God is more responsive to the needs of the poor and oppressed than those of the complacent and comfortable, is to insist that our history is not inseparable from what God has done throughout human history. It follows that a critical dimension of a reunderstanding of our past is how it bears on our appropriation of Scripture and the Christian tradition. If we begin by viewing the Christian tradition and Scripture in terms of fidelity to the gospel as good news to the poor, we are presented with a challenge to reexamine the meaning of Christian faith and the legitimacy of

Christian practice. Pablo Richard has maintained that the poor and oppressed offer the key to biblical understanding, because only in solidarity with them in the struggle for liberation can we really understand the militant character of biblical faith. In a similar fashion the poor throughout the history of the United States read Scripture, preached the gospel, and lived out the Christian faith in tension with "official" church teachings, practices, and compromises. Reverdy Ransom believed that it was only because of God's ever-present spirit dwelling in the hearts of human beings that there have been "the visions of prophets, the dreams of poets, and the hopes and longings of the poor and oppressed" in the face of oppression and domination.[4]

By telling the story of this country differently we not only listen to different voices, explore different options that were historically possible, but hold up to ourselves a mirror in which we see ourselves differently. At the same time, as John Howard Yoder has stressed, an alternative historical narrative not only sheds light on how we discern the past, but "sustains a different understanding of how we want to help history move." It is told as "a subject for repentance and not merely remembering, for making amends as well as for giving thanks."[5]

Christian Ethics

James Gustafson emphasizes that students of ethics are inclined to neglect the importance of history. When ethicists do attempt to come to terms with history, the crucial question is often how to transcend ethical claims that seem trapped in either historical relativism or an absolutism that is unwilling to acknowledge historical change. While it is important to grapple with such problems as historical relativism or the "objective" grounding for moral reflection, too often history is treated as yet another abstraction. The relationship between ethics and history too easily becomes ideational when concrete historical situations are ignored or when history is treated only at a high level of generalization. Ideas and concepts become more important than human beings, and ethical discourse and analysis are detached from the lives of the women and men and the movements they created.[6]

Ethics, according to the traditional definition, deals with human conduct as it relates to choice, judgment, and the decision to act. Christian ethics is also concerned with choice, judgment, and decision, but within the context of moral reflection on the central symbols of Christian faith. By extension, Christian social ethics depends upon similar moral reflection, but as Gibson Winter has noted, social ethics emphasizes that the inquiry takes place within a community committed to the struggle for social justice. But there is a methodological shift if one situates ethical reflection and social analysis as organically connected with "the hopes and longings of the poor and oppressed." Ethics becomes a part of the material practice of people struggling to create historical alternatives. It is an acknowledgment that ethics must be historically grounded in the concrete struggles of oppressed people for liberation. Such a sociohistorical analysis, in the words of Beverly Harrison, "enables several forms of empowerment. It aids recovery of social memory and awareness of the struggle of our forebears. It aims to represent the past to us in specific ways—as the result of collective human agency."[7]

Christopher Lasch has observed the failure to link ethical reflection and analysis with the history of people's resistance to domination. One of the strengths of the Right, he argues, is that it has "identified itself with the aspirations of ordinary Americans and appropriated many of the symbols of popular democracy." For when one speaks about a new vision of society or of empowering people in the creation of a juster, more egalitarian, more human social order, the very historical symbols, myths, and experiences have often been "appropriated" by the Right in such a way that the liberative nature of a popular and democratic tradition have been privatized and distorted beyond historical recognition. Crucial struggles concerning the workplace, the incompatibility of democracy and capitalism, and the cry for responsive and participatory institutions and structures become trivialized, and a sophisticated blame-the-victim syndrome is substituted for concrete social analysis. It is at this juncture that constructive social ethics based upon historical knowledge and understanding can make an important contribution to ethical analysis. It connects a liberative tradition that has sought to be faithful to the demands of the gospel as good news for the poor with the aspirations of people for a democratic socialist future.[8]

An exploration of the relationship of ethics to the history of oppressed people also entails an acknowledgment, as Michael Harrington puts it, that "truths about our society can be discovered only if one takes sides." That is, "you must stand somewhere in order to see social reality, and where you stand will determine much of what you see and how you see it." That is why those who have historically chosen to stand with the marginalized, listen to their voices and identify with their struggles, have been able to provide us with insights into the nature of American society and the radicality of Christian faith.[9]

Seeing the world from the side of the marginalized has a very partisan ring, something not usually associated with Christian ethics, even Christian social ethics. To conceive of Christian ethics as part of the aspirations of oppressed people for liberation is to affirm that ethics can actively aid people to come to terms with the social, economic, and political forces that have shaped human life so that they can become subjects of their own history. Gustavo Gutiérrez asserts that "reasoning from a concrete situation is quite different from (but no less rigorous than) reasoning from a priori 'first principles'—unfamiliar though the ruling classes and their ideological dependents may have found it. Furthermore participation in a concrete historical process—such as the lives of the oppressed—enables one to perceive aspects of the Christian message that theorizing fails to reveal."[10]

Our attentiveness to issues related to class, race, and gender has brought forth insights into the role Christians have played in combatting racism, challenging the dominant socioeconomic order, and confronting patriarchal and sexist distortions of what it means to be created in the image of God. The lives of black and white sharecroppers, Socialist and union organizers, and women activists, among others, have given witness to how people can learn to empower themselves, to discover their own voices and name their own reality. Christian faith has been an important part of people's abilities to change the world around them. We have learned that by creating more responsive forms of social organization, people have been able to establish innovative models of human relationships while striving for economic democracy and a just and equitable social order.

If there is one common theme that links the past and the present, it is how the contradictions of a capitalist economy affect human beings. Economists, in particular, continue to overlook the fact that people matter in how we structure our economic life and that those who have raised the issue of class are talking not just about income and the distribution of wealth but about the degree to which people exercise control over the conditions that govern their lives. The lives of working-class people, Karen Bloomquist asserts, "are so enmeshed in a web of forces that dominate or exercise control over them that their religious yearning is for freedom, dignity, and a sense of worth. They want to be somebody amid the forces that treat them as nobody." [11] It also follows that racism and sexism are not unrelated to the structural arrangements and patterns that influence behavior, attitudes, and institutional practices.

Cornel West argues that the oppression of African Americans, the "basic form of powerlessness in America," has more to do with people's "class position, not their racial status." That is not to deny the ongoing reality of racist practices but to point out how racism is used "in buttressing the current mode of production, concealing the unequal distribution of wealth, and portraying the lethargy of the political system." Critical of narrowly defined black nationalism and black economic development for their political shortsightedness, West believes, as did Dr. Martin Luther King, Jr., that the future of "black America is inextricably bound with that of America." [12]

Therefore, to raise the issue of the interrelationship of race and class is to point to the experiences of poor and oppressed people across the country—how a capitalist economy has fostered a false consciousness about the source of our society's inability to handle problems of equity, about the responsiveness of social institutions, and about questions of individual ability and development. Every organ of established society seems to cloud the real issue of control by misdirecting anger and producing resignation, thereby assuring the perpetuation of the status quo. In this context racism creates mutual distrust among oppressed people, often pitting one racial group against the other. Those who might otherwise come together in a common struggle against the sources of their oppression fail to understand that effective power is beyond the range of those whose labor sustains a privileged minority.[13]

Sexism has to do with the fundamental oppression that is maintained by the structure of our economic life. Capitalism is not only an economic system but a way of organizing society that affects all dimensions of life, both public and private. Domination, exploitation, and dehumanization touch not just the world of work, for women are oppressed not only in terms of "their roles in production" but in terms of their roles in "reproduction, socialization, and sexuality." In exploring the relationship between class and gender one is forced to grapple with issues that extend from the sexual division of labor to the increasing feminization of poverty, particularly among women of color. Although women have entered the labor force in large numbers in the past decades, their pay and standard of living with respect to men has not significantly improved, and the Knights of Labor cry "for both sexes equal pay for equal work" is as valid now as it was over a century ago. We are living through a period in our history when more and more poor women are the heads of households and when women and people of color are funneled into a service-oriented economy in which pay is low and job insecurity is high.[14]

In addressing questions of race, class, and gender Christian ethicists have too often uncritically accepted the perimeters set by a market economy. We seem to lack the facility to conceive creative alternatives that address the ways in which capitalism has historically inhibited the development of responsive institutions and structures that might sustain an egalitarian and participatory vision of society grounded in an affirmation of human worth and dignity. It is no wonder that we lack the analytical tools to deal with the moral and human challenge of poverty and homelessness facing our society.

Fyodor Dostoyevsky once stated that if you want an insight into the soul of a people, look at their prisons. I maintain that if you want to discern what a people value, look at how they treat their children. The United States ranks eighteenth in the world in terms of infant mortality, lagging behind Singapore and Hong Kong. Twice as many black children die as white; a black child is more likely to live if she or he is born in Trinidad and Tobago, Chile, or the Soviet Union than in such cities as Indianapolis and Detroit. One out of every five children in this country lives in poverty, and the rate of children who suffer the hardships of homelessness, the emotional and physical pains of abuse, and day-to-day alienation is on the increase in communities across the country. As John C. Bennett has perceptively noted, "The issues we face are so grave, the simplest requirements of human concern for others are so clear, that a deep change in what people feel to be important to them and a real conversion of the mind and heart is called for." [15]

The conversion of the mind and the heart of the American people is predicated for Bennett on the development of ethics. Bennett probably would agree with Michael Harrington that an ethical examination of the pitfalls of our present economy needs to go beyond simply eliciting sympathy for the oppressed to an analysis of "macroeconomic structures" that would help us to understand why our economy functions the way it does so that we might begin to explore viable options. Irrespective of the changes taking place in the world around us, especially in Eastern Europe and the Soviet Union, the judgments made by Karl Marx about capitalism are still valid. The realities of class and how they have shaped social relations have not somehow suddenly vanished, any more than the adherents of the marvels of a market system have become more responsive to the basic needs of the poor or to the call for economic democracy.[16]

In pressing for economic ethics one is confronted by issues ranging from structural unemployment and deindustrialization, with its accompanying plant closings and capital flight, to the day-to-day problems facing women, racial minorities, and working-class people. Economic ethics, moreover, might force the church to come to terms with its own attitudes, social practices, and institutional priorities and programs. In so doing, the church could rediscover what Christians who have sided with the poor have known all along. "The values of capitalism," as James Cone has observed, "are so ingrained into American culture that church persons assume that they are the same as Christian values." It is therefore not difficult to understand how "the belief that capitalism is Christian and Marxism is godless is one of the major reasons why the church has been a consistent supporter of capital against labor, the rich against the poor." Self-examination might facilitate new directions and possibilities for the life and mission of the church.[17]

In raising the importance of the political economy for Christian ethics, one also needs to ask whether sexism or racism can be understood through an examination of the contradictions of capitalism alone. Or in wrestling with race and gender, are we bordering on something more central to the perception of self and society? Racism and sexism are related to the powerlessness that stems from people's lack of control over the political and economic arena, and to the distortions of human hopes, sensibilities, and aspirations. Robert Blauner notes that "racism excludes a category of people from participation in a society in a different way than class hegemony and exploitation. The thrust of racism is to dehumanize, to violate dignity, degrade personalities in much more pervasive and all-inclusive ways than class exploitation. . . . Racist oppression attacks selfhood more directly than does class oppression." Even so, it is clear that racism cannot be fully understood independent of capitalist social relations.[18]

If race relations are not wholly reducible to class relations, neither are the relationships between women and men. Sexism has to do with the treatment of women as the "other." It is the denial of the legitimacy of women's experiences and a prevailing ethos that consciously and unconsciously presents women as somehow "alien and less desirable than their male counterparts." By extension, a sexist society not only denies women equal access to the resources of life on the basis of gender but hinders the creative potential and strivings of women for liberation. The key word is *domination,* for sexism presupposes a disproportionate allocation of power, privilege, and knowledge. Throughout American history sexism, like racism, has contributed to our refusal to recognize our need for community, cooperation, and human interdependence.[19]

Confronting the relationship among race, gender, and class, in all their complexities, might lead to the development of a holistic approach to Christian ethics. This is especially true if Christian faith is grounded in a sociopolitical praxis that gives concrete hope to oppressed people in spite of the forces of the dominant culture, which deny a more egalitarian and participatory vision of American society.

Religion and Radical Politics

Various sectors of the secular Left in the United States have reevaluated their analysis of religion, particularly in response to the development of Latin American liberation theology and the vital role Christians have played in movements for liberation. Moreover, the Left in this country has included many Christians who have been involved in antiimperialist struggles, challenged institutionalized racism and sexism, and been witnesses for peace and justice. Concrete issues have been raised, from the limitations of orthodox Marxist interpretations of religion to the need for coalition building among progressive forces. There is a growing recognition on the Left of the bankruptcy of sociopolitical movements that are not attentive to the struggles of people in the cultural arena and everyday life, including religious belief and practice.[20]

This leftist reassessment of the liberative function of religion should extend to the past as well. The traditional Marxist tendency has been to understand religion only as an instrument of class domination. There needs to be a methodological unblocking of this static view of religion and an openness to the ways in which religion has been an integral part of people's struggle for social transformation. This is not to reduce religion to a mere instrumentalism but to see the seeds of revolutionary hope and practice as coming from "within the religious consciousness itself."[21]

If segments of the American Left are reassessing their understanding of religion, the same should hold true of Christians' perception of the Left. Those on the Left who have historically been faithful to the gospel as good news for the poor have worked more consistently to create a just and equitable social order and have given their lives so that people might taste the fruits of freedom. Theologically, the church must acknowledge that God is to be found where we least expect, present among those "disfigured by oppression, despoliation, and alienation." Probably that is why Dorothee Sölle says, "Sometimes I feel that Christ today is more homeless in our churches than ever before because he finds worshipers there but no friends; admirers, but not followers."[22]

236

In the final analysis what is needed is not a reevaluation of the Left so much as an integration into our historical consciousness of the realization that the options Christians on the Left have made were integral to the search for a concrete and visible political mediation of Christian faith and practice. We must realize that there is a relationship between affirming that the gospel is good news for the poor and Christian political involvement. But according to Robert McAfee Brown the question for Christians is no longer whether to mix religion and politics but what "kind of politics" to mix religion with. Too often right-wing politics has been accepted as appropriate for Christians, and left-wing politics has been condemned. There is a need to establish a greater "degree of congruence . . . between the nature of the God we worship and the nature of the human actions we undertake in God's name." To take Brown seriously would be to acknowledge with Vicky Randall that politics "at a minimum . . . is about how people influence the distribution of resources," whether economic, social, or cultural. Thus, Christians need to learn how to take responsibility for the lives of others and for the course of human history. One of the lessons learned from Christian involvement on the Left in the United States, like Christians in Latin America, notes José Míguez Bonino, has been that "the primary and decisive factor is and must remain the struggle of the oppressed themselves." At the same time we must recognize that "those who [are] caught up in the structures of oppression need to hear the call to conversion; they need to hear the good news that the option for the poor is open to them." [23]

The cry for the exercise of political imagination has never been more pressing than it is now, when "too much of our political discourse is 'trivial,' 'obscurantist,' and defined by the search for image, code, or picture that will grab" the attention of the American public. Congressional Representative David Obey rightly asks, "Is American politics so brain-dead that we are reduced to having political shysters manipulate symbols?" Obey's question about the bankruptcy of our contemporary political discourse is not unrelated to limits a profit-driven capitalist economy has imposed on our understanding of what constitutes a democratic society. American workers, Socialists, and radicals of varying persuasions have understood that there is a fundamental difference between democracy as popular participation and popular control and the liberal notion of democracy, with its fetish preoccupation with elections and free speech as the form and substance of the meaning of democracy.[24]

Our aspirations for a participatory expression of democracy and a moral vision that has come to grips with the varying forms of our public and private lives have yet to be realized. But if we acknowledge, with Vincent Harding, "how much of our life and hope arises out of our encounters with the personal and the concrete," then we can see the past as offering promise for the future.[25]

The challenge that lies ahead has been posed most eloquently by Dr. Martin Luther King, Jr. King understood better than most Americans the need for fundamental changes in the basic structures of American society. One year to the day before his assassination, on April 4, 1967, at Riverside Church in New York, King delivered an address titled "A Time to Break Silence." He expressed his opposition to the war in Vietnam and condemned racism, poverty, and militarism. "Our hope today," King affirmed, "lies in our ability to recapture the revolutionary spirit [to make democracy real] and go out into a sometimes hostile world declaring eternal hostility to poverty, racism, and militarism. With this powerful commitment we shall boldly challenge the status quo and unjust mores and thereby speed the day when 'every valley shall be exalted, and every mountain and hill shall be made low, and the crooked shall be made straight and the rough places plain.' " It was also clear to King that a "genuine revolution of values" demanded a loyalty to humankind and a world order in which we are no longer defined by "tribe, class and nation," but governed by unconditional love for all humanity. Edward Said has most vividly captured King's revolution of values when he declares that we "need to reorient education so that central to common awareness is not a paranoid sense of who is top or best but a map of this now tiny planet, its resources and environment nearly worn out, its inhabitants' demands for better lives nearly out of control. The competitive, coercive guidelines that have prevailed are simply no good anymore. To argue and persuade rather than to boast, preach and destroy, *that* is the change to be made." [26]

At the same time King held out to all Americans a vision of what this country ought to be. According to Cornel West, King made a contribution to that which is distinctive about the Left in the United States, the "substance of its moral vision and the relevance of its economic programs for the common good of the nation." The life of Dr. Martin Luther King, Jr., and the black freedom movement in which he was engaged, also reminds us, Clayborne Carson notes, that "participants in social movements can develop their untapped leadership abilities and collectively improve their lives." [27]

It is appropriate to conclude with words from a sermon by Dr. King, "A Knock at Midnight," addressed to the church and the Christian community at the midnight hour of a world in moral and social crisis.

> The church must be reminded that it is not the master or the servant of the state, but rather the conscience of the state. It must be the guide and critic of the state, and never its tool. If the church does not recapture its prophetic zeal, it will become an irrelevant social club without moral or spiritual authority. If the church does not participate in the struggle for peace and for economic and racial justice, it will forfeit the loyalty of millions and cause men everywhere to say that it has atrophied its will. But if the church will free itself from the shackles of a deadening status quo, and, recovering its great historic mission, will speak and act fearlessly and insistently in terms of justice and peace, it will enkindle the imagination of mankind and fire the souls of men, imbuing them with a glowing and ardent love for truth, justice, and peace.[28]

Notes

Introduction

1. Paul Deats, Jr., "The Quest for a Social Ethic," in *Toward a Discipline of Social Ethics: Essays in Honor of Walter George Muelder*, ed. Deats (Boston: Boston University Press, 1972), pp. 24–34; Mel Piehl, *Breaking Bread: The Catholic Worker and the Origin of Catholic Radicalism in America* (Philadelphia: Temple University Press, 1982), pp. 25–55; David J. O'Brien, "Social Teaching, Social Action, Social Gospel," *U.S. Catholic Historian* 5/2 (1986): 195–224.

2. Karl Marx, *The Eighteenth Brumaire of Louis Bonaparte* (1852; New York: International, 1963), p. 15.

3. Eduardo Hoornaert, *The Memory of the Christian People* (Maryknoll: Orbis Books, 1988), pp. 3–5; Christopher Hill, *Change and Continuity in Seventeenth Century England* (London: Weidenfield and Nicolson, 1974), p. 284.

4. Wendell Berry, *The Hidden Wound* (San Francisco: North Point Press, 1989), p. 135; Wendell Berry, *Home Economics* (San Francisco: North Point Press, 1987), p. 179.

5. Clodovis Boff and George V. Pixley, *The Bible, the Church, and the Poor* (Maryknoll: Orbis Books, 1989), pp. 159–201; Penny Lernoux, *People of God* (New York: Penguin Books, 1989), pp. 6–9; E. P. Thompson, *The Making of the English Working Class* (New York: Vintage Books, 1963), p. 9.

6. Lernoux, *People of God*, p. 79.

7. José Míguez Bonino, *Doing Theology in a Revolutionary Situation* (Philadelphia: Fortress Press, 1975), pp. 89–93; Gustavo Gutiérrez, *The Truth Shall Make You Free* (Maryknoll: Orbis Books, 1990), pp. 94–95; Mary Potter Engel and Susan Brooks Thistlethwaite, eds., *Lift Every Voice: Constructing Christian Theologies from the Underside* (San Francisco: Harper and Row, 1990), p. 8.

8. Martin Duberman, *Black Mountain: An Exploration in Community* (Garden City: Anchor Books, 1973), p. xiii.

Chapter One

1. David Hollenbach, "Liberalism, Communitarianism, and the Bishop's Pastoral Letter on the Economy," in *The Annual of the Society of Christian Ethics*, ed. D. M.

Yeager (Washington, D.C.: Georgetown University Press, 1987), pp. 33–35; Center for Popular Economics, *Economic Report of the People* (Boston: South End Press, 1986), pp. 21–158; Samuel P. Hays, "Theoretical Implications of Recent Work in the History of American Society and Politics," *History and Theory* 26/1 (1987): 16–18.

2. Otto Maduro, "Marxist Analysis and the Sociology of Religion: An Introduction," *Social Compass* 22 (1975): 313; Karl Marx and Frederick Engels, *German Ideology*, ed. C. J. Arthur (New York: International, 1976), p. 64.

3. Gwynn Williams, "Gramsci's Concept of Egemonia," *Journal of the History of Ideas* 21 (October–December, 1960), quoted in John Cammett, *Antonio Gramsci and the Rise of Italian Communism* (Stanford: Stanford University Press, 1969), p. 204. See also Otto Maduro, *Religion and Social Conflicts* (Maryknoll: Orbis Books, 1982), pp. 136–137.

4. James R. Green, "Rewriting Southern History: An Interview with C. Vann Woodward," *Southern Exposure* 12/6 (November–December, 1984): 90. Herbert Gutman's essay has appeared in various publications. Perhaps the most accessible is the collection of his writings *Work, Culture, and Society in Industrializing America: Essays in America's Working Class and Social History* (New York: Alfred A. Knopf, 1976), pp. 87–117.

5. Michael Reich, "The Evolution of the United States Labor Force," in *The Capitalist System*, ed. Richard C. Edwards, Michael Reich, and Thomas E. Weisskopf (Englewood Cliffs: Prentice-Hall, 1972), p. 175; Susan E. Hirsch, *Roots of the American Working Class* (Philadelphia: University of Pennsylvania Press, 1978), pp. xvii–xx; Alan Dawley, *Class and Community* (Cambridge: Harvard University Press, 1976), pp. 91–96; Douglas F. Dowd, *The Twisted Dream: Capitalist Development in the United States since 1776* (Cambridge, Mass.: Winthrop, 1977), p. 131; John McDermott, *The Crisis in the Working Class: Some Arguments for a New Labor Movement* (Boston: South End Press, 1980), p. 57.

6. Jackson Lears, *No Place of Grace* (New York: Pantheon Books, 1981), p. 7; Samuel Hays, *The Response to Industrialism, 1885–1914* (Chicago: University of Chicago Press, 1957), p. 22; Knut Hamsun, *The Cultural Life of Modern America* (Cambridge: Harvard University Press, 1889, 1969), pp. 19, 124; Andrew Carnegie, "Triumphant Democracy," in *The Transformation of American Society, 1870–1890*, ed. John A. Garraty (New York: Harper and Row, 1968), p. 23.

7. Katherine Stone, "The Origins of Job Structures in the Steel Industry," *Review of Radical Political Economy* 6 (1974): 115–70. Robert Bennett's statement is part of a symposium "Views of Working-men" as found in *The Labor Problem*, ed. William E. Barns (New York: Harper and Brothers, 1886), pp. 115–116.

8. Melvyn Dubofsky, *Industrialism and the American Worker, 1865–1920* (Arlington Heights, Va.: AHM, 1975), pp. 19–20; "Illinois Bureau of Labor Statistics Report" (1884), as found in *Transformation of American Society*, p. 129; David Montgomery, "Labor in the Industrial Era," in *The U.S. Department of Labor History of the American Worker*, ed. Richard B. Morris (Washington, D.C.: U.S. Government Printing Office, 1976), pp. 117–118.

9. Jeremy Brecher, *Strike!* (Boston: South End Press, 1972), pp. 1–96; John Swinton, quoted in Richard O. Boyer and Herbert M. Morais, *Labor's Untold Story* (New York: United Electrical, Radio, and Machine Workers of America, 1955), p. 68;

Gerald G. Eggert, *Railroad Labor Disputes* (Ann Arbor: University of Michigan Press, 1967), p. 232.

10. Dowd, *Twisted Dream*, pp. 48, 57–58; Gardiner Means, "Business Concentration in the American Economy," in *The Capitalist System*, p. 147; James Weinstein, *The Corporate Ideal in the Liberal State, 1900–1918* (Boston: Beacon Press, 1968), pp. ix–xv.

11. Joseph R. Buchanan, *The Story of a Labor Agitator* (New York: Outlook, 1903), p. 133; Massachusetts Bureau of Statistics of Labor, *Report of the Bureau of Statistics of Labor, 1870* (Boston: Potter, 1870), pp. 304–307; H. Francis Power, "The Workingman's Alienation from the Church," *American Journal of Sociology* 4 (March, 1899): 626.

12. Yehoshua Arieli, *Individualism and Nationalism in American Ideology* (Baltimore: Penguin Books, 1966), p. 247; Martin E. Marty, *The Righteous Empire: The Protestant Experience in America* (New York: Dial Press, 1970), pp. 151–153; Henry Ward Beecher, "The Tendencies of American Progress," in *God's New Israel*, ed. Conrad Cherry (Englewood Cliffs, N.J.: Prentice-Hall, 1971), pp. 229–243; Henry F. May, *Protestant Churches and Industrial America* (New York: Harper and Row, 1967), pp. 188–90, 199; Russell H. Conwell, "Acres of Diamonds," in *Issues in American Protestantism*, ed. Robert L. Ferm (Garden City: Anchor Books, 1969), pp. 237–238; Iring Fetscher, "The 'Bourgeoisie' (Buergertum, Middle Class): on the Historical and Political Semantics of the Term," *Christianity and the Bourgeois*, ed. Johann Baptist Metz, Concilium Series (New York: Seabury Press, 1979), pp. 9–10; Lears, *No Place of Grace*, pp. 17–25.

13. Marty, *Righteous Empire*, p. 179; May, *Protestant Churches and Industrial America*, p. 235; David Noble, *The Paradox of Progressive Thought* (Minneapolis: University of Minnesota Press, 1954), pp. 229–31, 250; William R. Hutchison, *The Modernist Impulse in American Protestantism* (Cambridge: Harvard University Press, 1976), pp. 164–174; Charles Sheldon, *In His Steps* (New York: Hurst and Company, 1899), pp. 17–18; Robert C. White and C. Howard Hopkins, *The Social Gospel: Religion in Changing America* (Philadelphia: Temple University Press, 1976), pp. 143–146, 254–272; Daniel D. Williams, *The Andover Liberals: A Study in American Theology* (New York: King's Crown Press, 1940), pp. 154–70; Graham Taylor to Frank Mason North, September 7, 1908, Graham Taylor Papers, Newberry Library, Chicago.

14. Noble, *Paradox of Progressive Thought*, p. 250; Shailer Matthews, *The Social Gospel* (Boston: Griffith and Rowland Press, 1910), p. 76.

15. Washington Gladden, *Working People and Their Employers* (Boston: Lockwood, Brooks, 1876), p. 43; Josiah Strong, "What Must Society Do to Be Saved?" *Gospel of the Kingdom* 1 (May, 1909): 58; John A. Hutchison, *We Are Not Divided: A Critical and Historical Study of the Federal Council of Churches of Christ in America* (New York: Round Table Press, 1941), p. 117; Walter Rauschenbusch, *The Righteousness of the Kingdom*, ed. Max Stackhouse (Nashville: Abingdon Press, 1968), p. 285; Walter Rauschenbusch, *Christianizing the Social Order* (New York: Macmillan, 1912), pp. 468–469; Walter Rauschenbusch, "Organization of Industrial Workers," Syracuse *Herald*, February 11, 1911, as cited in John R. Aiken and James R. McDonnell, "Walter Rauschenbusch and Labor Reform: A Social Gospeller's Approach," *Labor History* 2 (Spring, 1970): 149; May, *Protestant Churches and Industrial America*, p. 235.

16. Timothy L. Smith, "Religion and Ethnicity in America," *American Historical Review* 83 (December, 1978): 1155–1185; Jay P. Dolan, *The American Catholic Experience* (Garden City: Doubleday, 1985), pp. 294–335; Robert T. Handy, *A Christian America* (New York: Oxford University Press, 1971), pp. 73–75; Daniel Dorchester, "The City as a Peril," in *National Perils and Opportunities*, ed. Evangelical Alliance (New York: Baker and Taylor, 1887), p. 32; Philip S. Foner, *History of the Labor Movement in the United States* (New York: International, 1947), p. 72; Henry J. Browne, *The Catholic Church and the Knights of Labor* (Washington, D.C.: Catholic University of America Press, 1949), pp. 8–14; James Cardinal Gibbons, *A Retrospect of Fifty Years*, vol. 1 (Baltimore: John Murphy, 1916), pp. 186–209; Joseph M. McShane, *"Sufficiently Radical": Catholicism, Progressivism, and the Bishop's Program of 1919* (Washington, D.C.: Catholic University of America Press, 1986), pp. 1–6; Marc Karson, *American Labor Unions and Politics, 1900–1918* (Boston: Beacon Press, 1958), pp. 212–284; David O'Brien, "The American Priest and Social Action," in *The Catholic Priest in the United States: Historical Investigations*, ed. John Tracy Ellis (Collegeville, Minn.: Saint John's University Press, 1971), pp. 426–427.

17. McShane, *"Sufficiently Radical,"* p. 3; Aaron I. Abell, "The Catholic Factor in Urban Welfare: The Early Period, 1850–1880," *Review of Politics* 14 (July, 1952): 289–324; Browne, *Catholic Church and the Knights of Labor*, pp. 17–33; James Cardinal Gibbons, *Our Christian Heritage* (Baltimore: John Murphy, 1889), pp. 450–455; John Ireland, *The Church and Modern Society*, 2nd ed. (Chicago: D. H. McBride, 1897), pp. 106–110, 191–192. For a critique of the Protestant understanding of wealth see the work of Bishop John Lancaster Spalding, *Essays and Reviews* (New York: Catholic Publication Society, 1877), pp. 88–117.

18. Richard T. Ely, "Socialism," *Inter-denominational Proceedings* (Cincinnati: n.p., 1885), pp. 12–14 as cited in Mel Piehl, *Breaking Bread: The Catholic Worker and the Origin of Catholic Radicalism in America* (Philadelphia: Temple University Press, 1982), pp. 35–36; Victor Greene, *The Slavic Community on Strike* (Notre Dame: University of Notre Dame Press, 1968), pp. 46–47, 87, 106, 141, 147; Leon Fink, *Workingmen's Democracy: the Knights of Labor and American Politics* (Urbana: University of Illinois Press, 1983), p. 77; William B. Faherty, "Father Cornelious O'Leary and the Knights of Labor," *Labor History* 11 (Spring, 1970): 175–189.

19. Stephan Thernstrom, *Poverty and Progress* (Cambridge: Harvard University Press, 1964), pp. 171–180; Brian Greenberg, *Worker and Community* (Albany: State University of New York Press, 1985), pp. 128–134; John T. Cumbler, *Working-Class Community in Industrial America: Work, Leisure, and Struggle in Two Industrial Cities* (Westport: Greenwood Press, 1979), pp. 48–49.

20. James Paul Rodechkno, *Patrick Ford and His Search for America* (New York: Arno Press, 1976), pp. 60–67, 156–157; Francis G. McManamin, "John Boyle O'Reilly, Social Reform Editor," *Mid-America* 43 (January, 1961): 36–54.

21. Aaron I. Abell, *American Catholicism and Social Action: A Search for Social Justice, 1865–1950* (Garden City: Hanover House, 1960), pp. 55–59; Editorial, "Workingman's Friends," *Quincy Monitor* 3 (July, 1886): 4.

22. Richard Orsi, "The Laity and the Americanization of the Catholic Church: The Career of Humphrey J. Desmond, 1880–1915," in *An American Church*, ed. David J. Alvarez (Moraga: Saint Mary's College of California, 1979), pp. 76–82.

23. James Dombrowski, *The Early Days of Christian Socialism in America* (New York: Columbia University Press, 1936), p. 77; Edward H. Rogers, "Relation of the Church to the Capital and Labor Question," in *National Perils and Opportunities*, pp. 235–236; "The Auto-biography of Edward H. Rogers, of Chelsea, Mass., Reformer in Religion, Education and Labor," unpublished manuscript (1902), chap. 21, p. 1, Edward H. Rogers Papers, State Historical Society of Wisconsin, Madison; George McNeill, "Progress of the Movement from 1861 to 1886," in *The Labor Movement: The Problem of To-day*, ed. McNeill (Boston: A. M. Bridgman, 1887), p. 146; Massachusetts Bureau of Statistics of Labor, *Report of the Bureau of Statistics of Labor, 1879* (Boston: Rand, Abery, 1879), p. 138; "The Platform of the Boston Eight-Hour League," *Equity* 2 (June, 1875): 18–19; "Platform of the Socialist Labor Party," *The Labor-Balance* 1 (April, 1878): 14–15; editorial, "Platform of the Christian Labor Union," *Equity* 2 (June, 1875): 17–18; "The Christian Labor Union, of Boston," circular (n.p., n.d.), Rogers Papers.

24. May, *Protestant Churches and Industrial America*, pp. 73–79; C. Howard Hopkins, *The Rise of the Social Gospel in American Protestantism, 1865–1915* (New Haven: Yale University Press, 1967), p. 42.

25. Halah H. Loud, "Biographical Sketch of the Reverend Jesse Henry Jones," in Jesse H. Jones, *Joshua Davidson Christian*, ed. Loud (New York: Grafton Press, 1907), pp. vii–xiv; Williams, *The Andover Liberals*, pp. 1–7, 158–160; Jones, *Know the Truth* (New York: Hurd and Houghton, 1865), pp. 159–199; Jones, *The Kingdom of Heaven* (Riverside: H. O. Houghton, 1871), pp. 1–36, 201–214; David Montgomery, *Beyond Equality—Labor and the Radical Republicans, 1862–1872* (New York: Vintage Books, 1967), pp. vii–x, 117–119; James R. Green and Hugh Carter Donahue, *Boston's Workers: A Labor History* (Boston: Trustees of the Public Library of the City of Boston, 1979), pp. 29–32; Jesse H. Jones, editorial, "Wage Slavery," *Equity* 1 (July, 1874): 26–27.

26. Loud, "Biographical Sketch of Jones," pp. vii–xiv; Jesse H. Jones, *Shall We Have a New Labor Reform Paper?* broadside (n.p., n.d.), reprinted in *Labor Standard*, August 16, 1879; "Editorial Notes," *Equity* 2 (December, 1875): 28.

27. May, *Protestant Churches and Industrial America*, p. 79; Jesse H. Jones, "Our Ideal," *Equity* 1 (April, 1874): 1.

28. Rogers, "Auto-biography," chap. 1, p. 3, chap. 8, pp. 1–3, chap. 10, pp. 8–11, chap. 21, pp. 1–8; Montgomery, *Beyond Equality*, pp. 122, 200; Edward H. Rogers, "Reminiscences," unpublished manuscript, pp. 29, 37–38; clipping from the *Boston Sunday Globe*, February 5, 1905, Rogers Scrapbook, both in Rogers Papers; Rogers, "The Building Trades," in *The Labor Movement*, pp. 338–341; Edward Pessen, *Most Uncommon Jacksonians* (Albany: State University of New York Press, 1967), pp. 39–43.

29. Montgomery, *Beyond Equality*, pp. 122, 209; clipping from the *Boston Sunday Globe*, February 5, 1905, Rogers Scrapbook; Edward H. Rogers, *A Lecture: Eight Hours a Day's Work*, pamphlet (Boston: Weekly American Workman, 1872), pp. 3, 13, 18, copy in Rogers Papers (first printed and distributed by the Boston Eight-Hour League).

30. Robert C. Reinders, "T. Wharton Collens: Catholic and Christian Socialist," *Catholic Historical Review* 52 (July, 1966): 221; Edward H. Rogers, *"Like unto Me"*:

or, The Resemblance between Moses and Christ, pamphlet (Chelsea, Mass: the author, 1876), pp. 7, 11–15, copy in Rogers Papers.

31. Montgomery, *Beyond Equality*, p. 210; Rogers, "Auto-biography," chap. 20, pp. 6–15; Hopkins, *Rise of the Social Gospel*, pp. 177–180; Edward H. Rogers, "To the Professing Christians of Chelsea—Greetings," circular, Richard T. Ely Papers, Correspondence, box 34, folder 5, State Historical Society of Wisconsin, Madison.

32. Rogers, "Auto-biography," chap. 17, p. 1; T. Wharton Collens to Edward H. Rogers, January 7, March 30, 1874, Rogers Papers; Jesse H. Jones, "Died," *Labor Standard*, November 15, 1879, p. 4; Reinders, "T. Wharton Collens," pp. 213–214; James E. Winston, "Thomas Wharton Collens," *Dictionary of American Biography*, vol. 4 (New York: Charles Scribner's Sons, 1930), pp. 300–301; Pessen, *Most Uncommon Jacksonians*, pp. 173–174; T. Wharton Collens, "Labor-Time, or Cost," *The Labor-Balance*, November 18, 1877, p. 13.

33. Reinders, "T. Wharton Collens," pp. 217–18; Collens to Rogers, March 30, 1874, Rogers Papers; T. Wharton Collens, "Views of the Labor Movement," *Catholic World* 10 (March, 1870): 784–798; José Porfirio Miranda, *Communism in the Bible* (Maryknoll: Orbis Books, 1985), pp. 8–12.

34. Collens to Rogers, January 7, 1874, Rogers Papers; Collens, "Views of the Labor Movement," pp. 790–798; T. Wharton Collens, letter to the editor, *Equity* 1 (November, 1874): 62; Collens, "The Bible and the Rights of Labor," *The Labor-Balance* 1 (February, 1879): 3–4; Collens, "Proportionalism," *The Labor-Balance* 1 (January, 1878): 5–8; Collens to Rogers, December 24, 1876, Rogers Papers; Jones, "Died," p. 4. Collens's major work during this period was *Eden of Labor; or, The Christian Utopia* (Philadelphia: Henry Carey Baird, 1876).

35. Minister quoted in Massachusetts Bureau of Statistics of Labor, *Report of the Bureau of Statistics of Labor, 1871* (Boston: Wright and Wright, 1871), p. 474; William E. Barns, ed., *The Labor Problem*, p. 104; Montgomery, *Beyond Equality*, p. 231.

36. "Editorial Notes," *The Labor-Balance* 1 (January, 1878): 15; T. Wharton Collens, "The Measure of Hardship," *The Labor-Balance* 1 (October, 1877): 8. My approach to a theology of life has been greatly influenced by a very important collection of writings of some former colleagues in Latin America edited by Pablo Richard titled *The Idols of Death and the God of Life* (Maryknoll: Orbis Books, 1983).

37. Jesse H. Jones, editorial comment at the end of an article by Collens titled "The New People on the Labor Question," *The Labor-Balance* 1 (April, 1878): 14; editorial, "Platform of the Christian Labor Union," *Equity* 2 (June, 1875): 18; Ronald P. Formisano, *The Transformation of Political Culture* (New York: Oxford University Press, 1983), pp. 228–236; Green and Donahue, *Boston's Workers*, pp. 24–26; Thomas Dublin, *Women at Work* (New York: Columbia University Press, 1979), pp. 108–131; Norman Ware, *The Industrial Worker, 1840–1860* (Chicago: Quadrangle Books, 1964), pp. 154–162.

38. Karl Marx, *Capital*, vol. 1, ed. Frederick Engels (New York: International, 1967), p. 301; David Roediger, "Ira Steward and the Anti-slavery Origins of American Eight-Hour Theory," *Labor History* 27 (Summer, 1986): 421–426; Kenneth Fones-Wolf, "Boston Eight Hour Men, New York Marxists, and the Emergence of the International Labor Union: Prelude to the AFL," *Historical Journal of Massachusetts* 9 (June, 1981): 47–49; Ira Steward, "Labor Reform and Its Critics," *The Commonwealth*, June 29,

1872, p. 1, Ira Steward Papers, State Historical Society of Wisconsin, Madison; Steward, *The Meaning of the Eight Hour Movement*, pamphlet (Boston: the author, 1868), pp. 2–15; Steward, *A Reduction of Hours an Increase of Wages*, pamphlet (Boston: Boston Labor Reform Association, 1865), reprinted in *A Documentary History of American Industrial Society*, vol. 9, ed. John R. Commons et al. (Cleveland: Arthur H. Clark, 1910), pp. 284–301.

39. Fones-Wolf, "Boston Eight Hour Men," pp. 48–49; Arthur Mann, *Yankee Reformers in the Urban Age* (Cambridge, Mass.: Belknap Press, 1954), pp. 179–181; "George E. McNeill," *Biographical Dictionary of American Labor*, ed. Gary M. Fink (Westport: Greenwood Press, 1984), p. 384; McNeill, "Hours of Labor," in *The Labor Movement*, pp. 470–471.

40. Rogers, *A Lecture: Eight Hours a Day's Work*, pp. 5–16; Edward H. Rogers, "Hours of Labor," *The Labor-Balance* 1 (October, 1877): 9–12; Rogers, "Income versus Accumulation," *The Labor-Balance* 1 1(January, 1878): 8–12; Dublin, *Women at Work*, p. 156; Formisano, *Transformation of Political Culture*, pp. 283, 339–40.

41. "Editorial Notes," *Equity* 2 (June 1875): 20; Jesse H. Jones, "Eternal Life," *Equity* 1 (September, 1874): 41–42; Jones, "The Two Methods," *Equity* 1 (April, 1874): 2–3; Jones, "The Labor Movement," *Equity* 1 (April, 1874): 4–5; Jones, "Wage Slavery," pp. 26–27; Roediger, "Ira Steward and the Anti-slavery Origins," pp. 419–426.

42. Jones, "The Labor Movement," p. 5; Philip Foner, "Songs of the Eight-Hour Movement," *Labor History* 13 (Fall, 1972): 571, 580–81; "Eight Hours," *The Labor-Balance* 1 (April, 1878): 2–3.

43. "Remonstrance of the Christian Labor Union," *Equity* 2 (March, 1875): 7; Jesse H. Jones, "The Marriage of God and Mammon," *Equity* 2 (December, 1875): 25–26.

44. London *Standard*, quoted in Paul A. Carter, *The Spiritual Crisis of the Gilded Age* (Dekalb: Northern Illinois University Press, 1971), pp. 111, 122; Jesse H. Jones, "The Great Scandal," *Equity* 1 (October, 1874): 50; Jones, "Why Should This Paper Be Started?" *The Labor-Balance* 1 (October, 1877): 2–4.

45. Edward H. Rogers, "Gain or Godliness?" *Equity* 2 (December, 1875): 26–27; Rogers, "Labor Reform in the Church," *Equity* 1 (April, 1874): 5–6; Rogers, *"Like unto Me,"* pp. 11–14; T. Wharton Collens, "Philosophy and Communism," *The Labor-Balance* 1 (April, 1878): 3–12; Collens to Rogers, August 8, 1879, Rogers Papers.

46. Fink, *Workingmen's Democracy*, p. xii; Richard Jules Oestreicher, *Solidarity and Fragmentation: Working People and Class Consciousness in Detroit, 1875–1900* (Urbana: University of Illinois Press, 1986), p. 245; Jonathan Garlock, Foreword to *The Terence Vincent Powderly and John William Hayes Papers: A Guide to the Microfilm Edition*, ed. John A. Turchenesky, Jr. (Glen Rock: Microfilming Corporation of America, 1975), pp. 1–4; Oestreicher, "A Note on Knights of Labor Membership Statistics," *Labor History* 25 (Winter, 1984): 102–108; Montgomery, "Labor in the Industrial Era," p. 126; Leon Fink, "The Uses of Political Power: Toward a Theory of the Labor Movement in the Era of the Knights of Labor," in *Working-Class America*, ed. Michael H. Frisch and Daniel J. Walkowitz (Urbana: University of Illinois Press, 1983), p. 119; Steven J. Ross, *Workers on the Edge: Work, Leisure, and Politics in Industrializing Cincinnati, 1788–1890* (New York: Columbia University Press, 1985);

Faye Dudden, "Small Town Knights: The Knights of Labor in Homer, New York," *Labor History* 28 (Summer, 1987): 307–327; Jama Lazerow, " 'The Workingman's Hour': The 1886 Labor Uprising in Boston," *Labor History* 21 (Spring, 1980): 200–220; Michael J. Cassity, "Modernization and Social Crisis: The Knights of Labor and a Midwest Community, 1885–1886," *Journal of American History* 66 (June, 1979): pp. 41–61; Elizabeth and Kenneth Fones-Wolf, "Knights versus the Trade Unionists: The Case of the Washington, D.C., Carpenters, 1881–1896," *Labor History* 22 (Spring, 1981): 192–212; Susan Levine, *Labor's True Woman* (Philadelphia: Temple University Press, 1984); Melton Alonza McLauren, *The Knights of Labor in the South* (Westport, Conn.: Greenwood Press, 1978), p. 189; Gregory S. Kealey and Bryan D. Palmer, *Dreaming of What Might Be: The Knights of Labor in Ontario, 1880–1900* (Cambridge: Cambridge University Press, 1982), p. 278.

47. T. V. Powderly, *Thirty Years of Labor, 1859–1889* (Columbus, Ohio: Excelsior, 1889), pp. 131–222; George McNeill, "History of the Knights of Labor," in *The Labor Movement*, pp. 399–428; Garlock, Foreword, pp. 1–5; William C. Birdsall, "The Problem of Structure in the Knights of Labor," *Industrial and Labor Relations Review* 6 (July, 1953): 533–546; Fink, "Uses of Political Power," pp. 105–106; David Montgomery, *The Fall of the House of Labor* (Cambridge: Cambridge University Press, 1987), pp. 158–160.

48. Nicholas O. Thompson, "An Important Question," *Journal of United Labor*, June 15, 1881, p. 127; Oestreicher, "Notes on Knights of Labor Membership Statistics," pp. 102–106.

49. George McNeill, "The Problems of Labor To-day," in *The Labor Movement*, p. 459; Alfred F. Young, "Revolutionary Mechanics," in *Working for Democracy*, ed. Paul Buhle and Alan Dawley (Urbana: University of Illinois Press, 1985), pp. 6–9; Paul Gustaf Faler, "Workingmen, Mechanics, and Social Change: Lynn, Massachusetts, 1800–1860" (Ph.D. diss., University of Wisconsin, 1971), pp. 68–70; Howard B. Rock, *Artisans of the New Republic* (New York: New York University Press, 1979), pp. 141–143; Sean Wilentz, *Chants Democratic: New York City and the Rise of the American Working Class, 1788–1850* (New York: Oxford University Press, 1984), pp. 92–93.

50. Bruce Laurie, *Working People of Philadelphia, 1800–1850* (Philadelphia: Temple University Press, 1980), pp. 81–82; Oestreicher, *Solidarity and Fragmentation*, p. 42; Powderly, *Thirty Years of Labor*, p. 245; Lydia E. Drake, "Open Letter to the Knights of Labor," *Journal of United Labor* 3 (March, 1883): 423–424; "Shall Women Vote?" *Journal of United Labor*, July 25, 1885, p. 1041; Levine, *Labor's True Woman*, pp. 118–121, 132–134, 152–153.

51. "Assemblies of Colored Men," *Journal of United Labor*, August 15, 1880, p. 49; Sidney H. Kessler, "Organization of Negroes in the Knights of Labor," *Journal of Negro History* 37 (July, 1952): 275–276; Fink, *Workingmen's Democracy*, p. 169; Terence V. Powderly to Brother Wright, September 9, 1879, Terence Powderly Papers, reel 44, Department of Archives and Manuscripts, Catholic University of America, Washington, D.C.; John Devlin to A. W. Fletcher, January 7, 1892, Powderly Papers, reel 89. On the Knights' work among African Americans in the South, see Philip S. Foner, *American Socialism and Black Americans: From the Age of Jackson to World War II* (Westport: Greenwood Press, 1977), p. 63; McLauren, *Knights of Labor in the South*, pp. 147–148; Kenneth Kann, "The Knights of Labor and the Southern Black Worker," *Labor*

History 18 (Winter, 1977): 49–55. See also C. Vann Woodward, *Origins of the New South, 1877–1913* (Baton Rouge: Louisiana State University Press, 1951), pp. 350–353.

52. Powderly, *Thirty Years of Labor*, p. 243; "Labor as a Commodity," *Journal of United Labor* 4 (January, 1884): 624.

53. Joseph Labadie, "To the Editor of the Labor Enquirer," *Labor Enquirer*, March 17, 1883, p. 1; "Inquisitorial," *United Journal of Labor*, August 25, 1884, p. 774; McNeill, "History of the Knights of Labor," p. 402; S. M. Jelley, *The Voice of Labor* (1888; New York: Burt Franklin, 1970), pp. 201, 356; Fink, *Workingmen's Democracy*, pp. 9–10, 33–35.

54. Thomas Bender, *Community and Social Change in America* (New Brunswick: Rutgers University Press, 1978), pp. 110–115; Cassity, "Modernization and Social Crisis," pp. 41–61; Fink, *Workingmen's Democracy*, p. xii; Beaton quoted in Jelley, *The Voice of Labor*, p. 356.

55. Fink, *Workingmen's Democracy*, p. 169; Herbert Gutman, *Power and Culture*, ed. Ira Berlin (New York: Pantheon, 1987), p. 332; Joseph P. McDonnell, unpublished address (c. 1874), Joseph P. McDonnell Papers, State Historical Society of Wisconsin, Madison, pp. 1, 18, 38.

56. David Montgomery, "To Study the People: The American Working Class," *Labor History* 21 (Fall, 1980): 501; E. P. Thompson, *The Making of the English Working Class* (New York: Vintage Books, 1966), p. 9; Kealey and Palmer, *Dreaming of What Might Be*, pp. 278–279; Oestreicher, *Solidarity and Fragmentation*, p. 65. For a perceptive analysis of the issue of class formation, see Ira Katznelson, "Working-Class Formation: Constructing Cases and Comparisons," in *Working-Class Formation: Nineteenth-Century Patterns in Western Europe and the United States*, ed. Katznelson and Aristide R. Zolberg (Princeton: Princeton University Press, 1986), pp. 3–41; Milton Cantor, Introduction to *American Workingclass Culture*, ed. Milton Cantor (Westport: Greenwood Press, 1979), p. 3; Gregory S. Kealey, "Labour and Working-Class History in Canada: Prospects in the 1980s," *Labour/Le Travailleur* 7 (Spring, 1981): 80–91. On the influence of E. P. Thompson, see especially Gutman, *Work, Culture, and Society*.

57. McNeill, "The Problems of Labor To-day," p. 464; Kealey and Palmer, *Dreaming of What Might Be*, pp. 283–289; "Secret Work," an appendix to Browne, *Catholic Church and the Knights of Labor*, p. 360; Terence V. Powderly, *The Path I Trod*, ed. Harry J. Carman, Henry David, and Paul N. Guthrie (New York: Columbia University Press, 1940), pp. 50–51; "Evils Resulting from Long Hours and Exhaustive Toil," *Journal of United Labor*, October 15, 1881, p. 160; "Politics," *Journal of United Labor*, November 15, 1881, p. 68; Leonard M. Wheeler to J. P. McGaughey, May 24, 1886, John Samuel Papers, State Historical Society of Wisconsin, Madison, box 1.

58. Wilson Carey McWilliams, *The Idea of Fraternity in America* (Berkeley: University of California Press, 1973), pp. 393–394; Oestreicher, *Solidarity and Fragmentation*, pp. 61–65; Martin Shefter, "Trade Unions and Political Machines: The Organization of the American Working Class in the Late Nineteenth Century," in *Working-Class Formation*, pp. 204–224; "An Appeal for Aid, Noble Order of the Knights of Labor," circular, October 6, 1882, Samuel Papers.

59. George Doyle to the Co-operative Board, April 13, 1885, circular of the Burlington Assembly, no. 3135, Burlington, Iowa, May 20, 1885, both in Samuel Papers; Jonathan Garlock, "A Structural Analysis of the Knights of Labor: A Prolegomenon

to the History of the Producing Classes" (Ph.D. diss., University of Rochester, 1974), p. 7.

60. Thomas B. McGuire, "Our Fifteenth Anniversary," *Journal of United Labor*, December 10, 1884, pp. 856–857.

61. Terence V. Powderly to Archbishop Patrick Ryan, October 24, 1884, Powderly Papers; Norman J. Ware, *The Labor Movement in the United States, 1860–1890* (New York: Vintage Books, 1929, 1964), p. 75; Stephens quoted in McNeill, "History of the Knights of Labor," pp. 402–403, 407–409; "Our Past Grand Master Workman," *Journal of United Labor*, August 15, 1881, pp. 137–138; Powderly, *Thirty Years of Labor*, p. 168.

62. McNeill, "History of the Knights of Labor," pp. 402–409.

63. "The Political Parson," *Labor Enquirer*, March 1, 1884, p. 2; "Heartlessness," *Labor Enquirer*, November 5, 1883, p. 1; "Evils Resulting from Long Hours and Exhausive Toil," p. 160.

64. McNeill, "Problems of Labor To-day, pp. 468–469. Criticisms of Beecher appear in "Teachers and Toadies," *Journal of United Labor*, August 15, 1884, p. 774; and "Labor, Religion, and Capital," *Journal of United Labor*, October 10, 1884, p. 811.

65. Paul Avrich, *The Haymarket Tragedy* (Princeton: Princeton University Press, 1984), p. 316; Eugene V. Debs, "Jesus," in *The Cry for Justice: An Anthology of the Literature of Social Protest*, ed. Upton Sinclair (Philadelphia: John C. Winston, 1915), p. 345; Oestreicher, *Solidarity and Fragmentation*, p. 90; McNeill, "Problems of Labor To-day," pp. 468–469.

66. William B. Faherty, "Father O'Leary and the Knights of Labor," pp. 175–189; Browne, *Catholic Church and the Knights of Labor*, p. 158; Montgomery, *Fall of the House of Labor*, p. 49.

67. *Philadelphia Inquirer*, June 26, 1924, quoted in Henry J. Browne, "Terence V. Powderly: His Relations with the Catholic Church, 1878–1888" (M.A. thesis, Catholic University, 1924), pp. 121–122; Henry J. Browne, "Terence V. Powderly and the Church-Labor Difficulties of the Early 1880s," *Catholic Historical Review* 32 (April, 1946): 1–27; Ware, *The Labor Movement in the United States*, pp. 73–101; Gerald N. Grob, *Workers and Utopia* (Evanston, Ill.: Northwestern University Press, 1961), pp. 40–41; Richard Oestreicher, "Terence Powderly, the Knights of Labor, and Artisanal Republicanism," in *Labor Leaders in America*, ed. Melvyn Dubofsky and Warren Van Tine (Urbana: University of Illinois Press, 1987), p. 42; Samuel Walker, "Terence V. Powderly, Machinist, 1866–1877," *Labor History* 19 (Spring, 1978): 180; Edward T. James, "T. V. Powderly: A Political Profile," *Pennsylvania Magazine of History and Biography* 99 (October, 1975): 459.

68. Powderly, *The Path I Trod*, pp. 4–5, 8, 23–27, 39–45, 56–57; Oestreicher, "Powderly, the Knights of Labor, and Artisanal Republicanism," pp. 31–35, 41–44; Walker, "Terence Powderly, Machinist," pp. 165–184; John R. Commons et al., *History of Labour in the United States*, vol. 2 (New York: Macmillan, 1918–1935), pp. 56, 200; Montgomery, *Beyond Equality*, p. 162.

69. McNeill, "Progress of the Movement," p. 153; Terence V. Powderly, "The Army of the Discontented," *North American Review* 140 (April, 1885): 371; James, Powderly: A Political Profile," pp. 443–447.

70. Oestreicher, "Powderly, the Knights of Labor, and Artisanal Republicanism," pp. 32, 41; Powderly, *The Path I Trod*, p. 35; Harold W. Aurand, "The Workingmen's Benevolent Association," *Labor History* 7 (Winter, 1966): 19–27.

71. "Our Grand Master Workman," *Journal of United Labor*, May 15, 1880, p. 2; Mother Jones to Terence V. Powderly, May 9, 1906, in *The Correspondence of Mother Jones*, ed. Edward M. Steel (Pittsburgh: University of Pittsburgh Press, 1985), p. 59.

72. Terence V. Powderly to Archbishop Patrick Ryan, October 10, 1884, Powderly Papers; Powderly Diaries, 1869–1890, Powderly Papers; Powderly to Sister Rose Mary (niece), December 1, 1915, William Joseph Kerby Papers, Department of Archives and Manuscripts, Catholic University of America, Washington, D.C.

73. Browne, "Powderly: Relations with the Catholic Church," pp. 37, 56 (Powderly's statement on membership of the clergy); Powderly, *The Path I Trod*, pp. 263–264.

74. Powderly, *The Path I Trod*, pp. 38–39, 265, 342; Terence V. Powderly to Daniel O'Donoghue, March 23, 1886, Powderly Papers. For the assessment of Powderly's critique, see David J. O'Brien, "Social Teaching, Social Action, Social Gospel," *U.S. Catholic Historian* 5/2 (1986): 214–215.

75. Terence V. Powderly, "Poems and Speeches," Powderly Papers; Powderly, *The Path I Trod*, pp. 378–379.

76. Dawley, *Class and Community*, p. 192; James Weinstein, *Ambiguous Legacy: The Left in American Politics* (New York: New Viewpoints, 1975), pp. 4–7; Weinstein, "Socialism's Hidden Heritage," in *For a New America*, ed. Weinstein and David W. Eakins (New York: Vintage Books, 1970), pp. 229–231; Bender, *Community and Social Change in America*, p. 115.

77. John Swinton, *A Momentous Question* (1895; New York: Burt Franklin, 1971), pp. 276–277; Oestreicher, *Solidarity and Fragmentation*, p. 253; Kealey and Palmer, *Dreaming of What Might Be*, pp. 381–382; Sara M. Evans and Harry C. Boyte, *Free Spaces: The Sources of Democratic Change in America* (New York: Harper and Row, 1986), p. 23.

78. Jerome Davis, *Capitalism and Its Culture*, 2nd ed. (New York: Farrar and Rinehart, 1936), p. 372.

79. Ralph Milliband, *The State in Capitalist Society* (New York: Basic Books, 1969), p. 182; William Hayes Ward, "Church Attendance," *North American Review* 137 (July, 1883): 81; Merril E. Gates, "The Misuse of Wealth," in *National Perils and Opportunities*, pp. 81–93; "Testimony of R. Heber Newton before the Senate Committee upon the Relations between Labor and Capital, 1883," in *Labor and Capital in the Gilded Age*, ed. John A. Garraty (Boston: Little, Brown, 1968), p. 175.

80. Franz Hinkelammert, "The Economic Roots of Idolatry: Entrepreneurial Metaphysics," in *The Idols of Death and the God of Life*, p. 192.

Chapter Two

1. Linda Gordon, "What's New in Women's History," in *Feminist Studies/Critical Studies*, ed. Teresa de Lauretis (Bloomington: Indiana University Press, 1986), p. 23; Donald Matthews, "Women's History/Everyone's History," in *Women in New Worlds: Historical Perspectives on the Wesleyan Tradition*, ed. Hilah F. Thomas and Rosemary

Skinner Keller (Nashville: Abingdon, 1981), p. 37. The term "sex/gender system" is Gayle Rubin's, used in an analysis by Mary P. Ryan, *Womanhood in America*, 2nd ed. (New York: New Viewpoints, 1979), p. viii.

2. To stress the differences between women and other oppressed groups and to avoid the tendency to blur the degree to which the experiences and goals of women are different, Gerda Lerner distinguishes women's "emancipation" from the "liberation" of other groups. See Lerner, "Politics and Culture in Women's History," *Feminist Studies* 6 (Spring, 1980): 54.

3. Janet Wilson James, "Women in American Religious History: An Overview," in *Women in American Religion*, ed. James (Philadelphia: University of Pennsylvania Press, 1980), p. 1.

4. Beverly Wildung Harrison, *Making the Connections: Essays in Feminist Social Ethics*, ed. Carol S. Robb (Boston: Beacon Press, 1985), pp. 233–234.

5. Hannah Whitall Smith, Introduction to Frances E. Willard, *Glimpses of Fifty Years: The Autobiography of an American Woman* (Chicago: Woman's Temperance Publication Association, 1889), pp. v–vi; Ruth Bordin, *Frances Willard: A Biography* (Chapel Hill: University of North Carolina Press, 1986), pp. 5–7; Joseph R. Gusfield, *Symbolic Crusade* (Urbana: University of Illinois Press, 1963), pp. 98–100.

6. Willard, *Glimpses of Fifty Years*, pp. 1–72.

7. Mrs. A. J. Graves, *Woman in America* (New York: Harper and Brothers, 1841), reprinted in *Roots of Bitterness: Documents of the Social History of American Women*, ed. Nancy F. Cott (New York: E. P. Dutton, 1972), pp. 145–146. See also Cott, *The Bonds of Womanhood* (New Haven: Yale University Press, 1977); Nancy Woloch, *Women and the American Experience* (New York: Alfred A. Knopf, 1984), pp. 113–131; Barbara Leslie Epstein, *The Politics of Domesticity: Women, Evangelism, and Temperance in Nineteenth-Century America* (Middletown, Conn.: Wesleyan University Press, 1981), pp. 67–87. Harvey Green, a historian at the Margaret Woodburg Strong Museum in Rochester, New York, also provides an interesting insight into the Victorian period. See Green, *The Light of the Home: An Intimate View of the Lives of Women in Victorian America* (New York: Pantheon Books, 1983).

8. Willard, *Glimpses of Fifty Years*, pp. 25, 69–72.

9. Ibid., pp. 109–110; Woloch, *Women and the American Experience*, pp. 283–287.

10. Bordin, *Frances Willard*, pp. 52–64; Mary Earhart, *Frances Willard: From Prayers to Politics* (Chicago: University of Chicago Press, 1944), pp. 1–143; Mary A. Lathbury, "Frances E. Willard, of Illinois," in Frances E. Willard, *Women and Temperance* (Hartford: Park, 1883), pp. 24–28; Willard, *Glimpses of Fifty Years*, pp. 199–239, 342, 574–589.

11. Epstein, *Politics of Domesticity*, p. 90; Ruth Bordin, *Woman and Temperance: The Quest for Power and Liberty, 1873–1900* (Philadelphia: Temple University Press, 1981); Mari Jo Buhle, *Women and American Socialism, 1870–1920* (Urbana: University of Illinois Press, 1983), pp. 62–66; Wendy Mitchinson, "The WCTU: 'For God, Home, and Native Land': A Study in Nineteenth-Century Feminism," in *A Not Unreasonable Claim: Women and Reform in Canada, 1880s–1920s*, ed. Linda Kealey (Toronto: Women's Press, 1979), pp. 151–167; Mari Jo Buhle, "Politics and Culture in Women's History," and Ellen DuBois, "Politics and Culture in Women's History,"

both in *Feminist Studies* 6 (Spring 1980): 37–42, 28–36; *Feminist Studies* 6 (Spring, 1980): 28–36; DuBois, "The Radicalization of the Woman Suffrage Movement: Notes toward the Reconstruction of Nineteenth-Century Feminism," *Feminist Studies* 3 (Fall, 1975): 68–70; Carolyn DeSwarte Gifford, "For God and Home and Native Land: The W.C.T.U.'s Image of Woman in the Late Nineteenth Century," in *Women in New Worlds*, pp. 310–327.

12. Ruth Bordin, "A Baptism of Power and Liberty": The Women's Crusade of 1873–1874," in *Woman's Being, Woman's Place: Female Identity and Vocation in American History*, ed. Mary Kelley (Boston: G. K. Hall, 1979), pp. 283–295.

13. Willard, *Woman and Temperance*, pp. 50–79; Epstein, *Politics of Domesticity*, pp. 95–100; Frances E. Willard, Introduction to Annie Wittenmyer, *History of the Woman's Temperance Crusade* (Boston: James H. Earle, 1882), pp. 14–21; Leonard Woolsey Bacon, *A History of American Christianity* (New York: Christian Literature, 1897), pp. 366–367; Carrie Chapman Catt and Nettie Rogers Shuler, *Woman Suffrage and Politics*, Introduction by T. A. Larson (c. 1926; Seattle: University of Washington Press, 1969), p. 134.

14. Bordin, *Frances Willard*, pp. 97–111; Willard, *Glimpses of Fifty Years*, pp. 368–369.

15. Aileen S. Kraditor, *The Ideas of the Woman Suffrage Movement, 1890–1920* (New York: Columbia University Press, 1965), pp. 14–28; Edward D. Cope, "The Relation of the Sexes to Government," in *Men's Ideals/Women's Realities: Popular Science, 1870–1915*, ed. Louis Michele Newman (New York: Pergamon Press, 1985), pp. 210–216; "Remarks of Senator George G. Vest in Congress," in *Up from the Pedestal: Selected Writings in the History of American Feminism*, ed. Aileen S. Kraditor (Chicago: Quadrangle Books, 1968), p. 196.

16. Epstein, *Politics of Domesticity*, p. 118; Bordin, *Frances Willard*, pp. 100; Willard, *Women and Temperance*, pp. 452–459; Willard, *Glimpses of Fifty Years*, pp. 380, 419–421.

17. Willard, *Glimpses of Fifty Years*.

18. Bordin, *Frances Willard*, pp. 100–103; Bordin, *Woman and Temperance*, p. 120.

19. Steve M. Buechler, *The Transformation of the Woman Suffrage Movement: The Case of Illinois, 1850–1920* (New Brunswick: Rutgers University Press, 1986); Kraditor, *Ideas of the Woman Suffrage Movement*; William L. O'Neill, *Everyone Was Brave* (Chicago: Quadrangle Books, 1969); Alma Lutz, *Susan B. Anthony: Rebel, Crusader, Humanitarian* (Boston: Beacon Press, 1959). Frances E. Willard, "Power of Organization as Shown in the Work of the Woman's Christian Temperance Union," *Lend a Hand* 1 (March 1886): 168–172; Willard, *Glimpses of Fifty Years*, p. 592; "Annual Address of Frances E. Willard," in *Minutes of the National Woman's Temperance Union, 13th Annual Meeting, 1886* (Chicago: Woman's Christian Temperance Union Publication Association, 1886), pp. 70–72, copy in the Frances E. Willard Memorial Research Library, Evanston, Illinois.

20. Kenneth Cathen, *The Impact of American Religious Liberalism* (New York: Harper and Row, 1962), pp. 5–29; Emory Stevens Bucke, gen. ed., *The History of American Methodism*, vol. 2 (New York: Abingdon Press, 1964), pp. 592–618; Willard, *Glimpses of Fifty Years*, pp. 622–631; Donald W. Dayton, "Whither Evangelicalism?" in *Sanctification and Liberation*, ed. Theodore Runyon (Nashville: Abingdon Press,

1981), pp. 142–163; Timothy L. Smith, "Holiness and Radicalism in Nineteenth-Century America," in *Sanctification and Liberation*, pp. 116–142; Nancy Hardesty, Lucille Sider Dayton, and Donald W. Dayton, "Women in the Holiness Movement: Feminism in the Evangelical Tradition," in *Women of Spirit*, ed. Rosemary Ruether and Eleanor McLaughlin (New York: Simon and Schuster, 1979), pp. 142–163; Timothy Smith, *Revivalism and Social Reform* (New York: Harper and Row, 1957); Frances E. Willard, "Symposium on Religious Perils," in *Boston Monday Lectures*, supp. 1, ed. Joseph Cook (Boston: Rand Avery, 1887), p. 217.

21. "Annual Address of Frances E. Willard" (1886), pp. 41–42; Willard, "Woman as Preacher," *Our Day* 1 (April, 1888): 289.

22. James F. Findlay, Jr., *Dwight L. Moody: American Evangelist, 1837–1899* (Chicago: University of Chicago Press, 1969); William G. McLoughlin, Jr., *Modern Revivalism: Charles Grandison Finney to Billy Graham* (New York: Ronald Press, 1959), pp. 232–233; Willard, *Glimpses of Fifty Years*, pp. 356–360.

23. Willard, *Glimpses of Fifty Years*, pp. 615–621; Bordin, *Frances Willard*, pp. 160–168.

24. "President's Annual Address," *Minutes of the National Woman's Christian Temperance Union, 15th Annual Meeting, 1888* (Chicago: Woman's Temperance Publication Association, 1888), p. 42, copy in Willard Memorial Library; Frances E. Willard, "Woman as Preacher," *Our Day*, 1 (January, April, 1888), pp. 21–35, 286.

25. Willard, "Woman as Preacher," pp. 290, 293. Willard's "creed" on women as preachers is found in an article by Rosalita J. Leonard, librarian of the Willard Memorial Library. See Leonard, "The Secret History of Frances Willard's Library," *Union Signal* 102 (February, 1972): 10.

26. Frances E. Willard, "The Woman's Cause Is Man's," *The Arena* 5 (May, 1892): 712–725; Willard, *Glimpses of Fifty Years*, p. 613.

27. "President's Annual Address," *Minutes of the National Woman's Christian Temperance Union, 20th Annual Meeting, 1893* (Chicago: Woman's Temperance Publishing Association, 1893), pp. 104–112, copy in Willard Memorial Library.

28. Frances E. Willard, "Temperance and the Labor Question," *Signal Lights* (pamphlet), no. 18 (Chicago: Ruby I. Gilbert, n.d.), p. 2, copy in Willard Memorial Library; Willard, "Christian Socialism," *Union Signal*, May 29, 1890, p. 8; Terence V. Powderly, *Thirty Years of Labor, 1859–1889* (Columbus, Ohio: Excelsior, 1889), pp. 587–611; Samuel Walker, "Terence V. Powderly, the Knights of Labor, and the Temperance Issue," *Societas* 5/4 (1975): 279–293.

29. Willard, *Glimpses of Fifty Years*, pp. 423, 525; Frances E. Willard, "Three Weeks of Campaigning," *Union Signal*, February 17, 1887, p. 4; Willard to Richard T. Ely, April 30, December 12, 1887, Richard T. Ely Papers, box 1, folder 5, State Historical Society of Wisconsin, Madison; Willard to Henry Demarest Lloyd, January 2, 1894, Henry Demarest Lloyd Papers, State Historical Society of Wisconsin, Madison.

30. Willard, *Glimpses of Fifty Years*, pp. 413, 522–525.

31. Frances E. Willard, "Work," in *Mothers and Daughters*, vol. 2, ed. G. S. Reaney (London: A. W. Hall, 1893), p. 87; "President's Annual Address, 1893," p. 107; Willard, *Occupations for Women* (New York: Success, 1897), pp. 90–94; Willard, "The Coming Brotherhood," *The Arena* 6 (August, 1892): 320–321.

32. Earhart, *Frances Willard*, p. 247. Frances E. Willard to Richard T. Ely, Decem-

ber 30, 1887, Ely Papers, box 1, folder 6; "President's Annual Address, 1893," pp. 105–110; "President's Address," *21st Annual Meeting, 1894, Minutes of the National Woman's Christian Temperance Union* (Chicago: Woman's Christian Temperance Union Publishing Association, 1894), pp. 114–120, copy in Willard Memorial Library; "President's Address," *24th Annual Meeting, 1897, Report of the National Woman's Christian Union* (Chicago: Woman's Christian Temperance Union Publishing Association, 1897), pp. 113–120, copy in Willard Memorial Library.

33. Willard, "The Coming Brotherhood," p. 322.

34. Earhart, *Frances Willard*, pp. 257 (quoting Willard), 252–253; Frances E. Willard to Henry Demarest Lloyd, November 27, 1895, Lloyd Papers; "President's Address, 1893," p. 93; Henry Demarest Lloyd, *Men, the Workers* (New York: Doubleday, Page, 1909), p. 186; Nick Salvatore, "Eugene V. Debs: From Trade Unionist to Socialist," in *Labor Leaders in America*, ed. Melvyn Dubofsky and Warren Van Tine (Urbana: University of Illinois Press, 1987), pp. 89–94.

35. Willard, "Coming Brotherhood," pp. 321; Laurence Gronlund, *The Cooperative Commonwealth*, ed. Stow Persons (Cambridge, Mass.: Belknap Press, 1965), pp. 6–7, 90, 449–451; Gronlund, *Our Destiny: The Influence of Socialism on Morals and Religion* (London: S. Sonnenschein, 1890), pp. 128–136.

36. Willard, "The Coming Brotherhood," p. 321; Howard H. Quint, *The Forging of American Socialism* (Columbia: University of South Carolina Press, 1953), p. 79; Buhle, *Women and American Socialism*, p. 75; Arthur E. Morgan, *Edward Bellamy* (New York: Columbia University Press, 1944), p. 372; Edward Bellamy, *Looking Backward, 2000–1887* (Boston: Ticknor, 1888); Bellamy, *Talks on Nationalism* (Freeport: Books for Libraries Press, 1938, 1969), pp. 21–30; William Leach, "Looking forward Together: Feminists and Edward Bellamy," *Democracy* 2 (January, 1981): 120–134; Quint, *Forging of American Socialism*, p. 92.

37. "President's Annual Address," *16th Annual Meeting of the National Woman's Christian Temperance Union, 1889* (Chicago: Woman's Christian Temperance Union Publishing Association, 1889), pp. 114–117, copy in Willard Memorial Library.

38. *Woman's Journal*, October 5, 1888, cited in Leach, "Looking forward Together," p. 126, and see 123–124; Buhle, *Women and American Socialism*, pp. 75–79; *Address of Frances E. Willard, Woman's National Council of the United States*, pamphlet (Washington, D.C.: Woman's National Council of the United States, 1891), pp. 20–21, copy in Willard Memorial Library; Willard, "The Dawn of Woman's Day," *Our Day* 2 (November, 1988): 352–355. See also Dolores Hayden, *The Grand Domestic Revolution: A History of Feminist Designs for American Homes, Neighborhoods, and Cities* (Cambridge: MIT Press, 1982), pp. 135–136, 147–148.

39. Frances Willard, "Christian Socialism," *Union Signal*, July 25, 1889, pp. 8–9; Willard, "Christian Socialism" (1890), p. 8; Earhart, *Frances Willard*, pp. 289–290. "President's Annual Address, 1893," pp. 88–98.

40. "President's Address," *22nd Annual Meeting, Report of the National Woman's Christian Temperance Union, 1895* (Chicago: Woman's Christian Temperance Union Publishing Association, 1895), pp. 103–106, copy in Willard Memorial Library.

41. "President's Address," *24th Annual Meeting, Report of the National Woman's Christian Temperance Union, 1897* (Chicago: Woman's Christian Temperance Union Publishing Association, 1897), pp. 113–120, copy in Willard Memorial Library. See

also Paul F. Laubenstein, "A History of Christian Socialism in America" (S.T.M. thesis, (Union Theological Seminary, 1925), pp. 42–50; Quint, *Forging of American Socialism*, pp. 103–126; James Dombrowski, *The Early Days of Christian Socialism in America* (New York: Columbia University Press, 1936), pp. 96–109.

42. Earhart, *Frances Willard*, p. 291.

43. Debra Campbell, "Reformers and Activists," in *American Catholic Women: A Historical Exploration*, ed. Karen Kennelly (New York: Macmillan, 1989), p. 189; Dale Fetherling, *Mother Jones, the Miners' Angel* (Carbondale: Southern Illinois University Press, 1974), p. 10; *Washington Star*, December 11, 1930, clipping, Mother Jones Papers, Department of Archives and Manuscripts, Catholic University of America, Washington, D.C.; Joseph R. Buchanan, *The Story of a Labor Agitator* (New York: Outlook, 1903), p. 49. Karen Kennelly's collection should be supplemented by the work of Mary Jo Weaver, *New Catholic Women: A Contemporary Challenge to Traditional Authority* (San Francisco: Harper and Row, 1985); and James J. Kenneally, especially his article "Eve, Mary, and the Historians: American Catholicism and Women," in *Women in American Religion*, and *The History of American Catholic Women* (New York: Crossroad/Continuum, 1990).

44. Aileen S. Kraditor, *Means and Ends in American Abolitionism* (New York: Pantheon Books, 1969), pp. 18–32, 203; Saul D. Alinsky, *Reveille for Radicals* (New York: Vintage Books, 1969), pp. 209, 219. For an attempt to give an historical overview to the role of the agitator in American history, see Charles W. Lomas, *The Agitator in American Society* (Englewood Cliffs: Prentice-Hall, 1968).

45. Fred Mooney, *Struggle in the Coal Fields: The Autobiography of Fred Mooney*, ed. J. W. Hess (Morgantown: West Virginia University Library, 1967), p. 21.

46. Judith Nies, *Seven Women: Portraits from the American Radical Tradition* (New York: Viking Press, 1977), pp. 97–98; Priscilla Long, *Mother Jones, Woman Organizer*, pamphlet (Boston: South End Press, 1981), p. 2; Edward M. Steel, Introduction to *The Correspondence of Mother Jones*, ed. Steel (Pittsburgh: University of Pittsburgh Press, 1985), p. xiii; Steel, Afterword to *The Speeches and Writings of Mother Jones*, ed. Steel (Pittsburgh: University of Pittsburgh Press, 1988), pp. 259–260.

47. *The Autobiography of Mother Jones*, 3rd ed. rev. (Chicago: Charles H. Kerr, 1980), p. 11; Fetherling, *Mother Jones*, pp. 1–3; James S. Donnelly, Jr., *The Land and the People of Nineteenth-Century Cork* (London: Routledge and Kegan Paul, 1975), pp. 14–23; Samuel Clark and James S. Donnelly, Jr., eds., *Irish Peasants, Violence, and Political Unrest, 1780–1914* (Madison: University of Wisconsin Press, 1983), pp. 25–36, 98; Linda Atkinson, *Mother Jones: The Most Dangerous Woman in America* (New York: Crow, 1978), pp. 9–12; Mother Jones to William E. Borah, c. February 2, 1913, *Correspondence of Mother Jones*, p. 107; Helen C. Camp, "Mary Harris Jones ('Mother Jones')," in *American Reformers*, ed. Alden Whitman (New York: H. W. Wilson, 1985), p. 483.

48. *Autobiography of Mother Jones*, p. 11; Atkinson, *Mother Jones*, pp. 13–16; Bryan D. Palmer, *Working-Class Experience: The Rise and Reconstitution of Canadian Labour, 1800–1980* (Toronto: Butterworth, 1983), pp. 26–28; Gregory S. Kealey, *Toronto Workers Respond to Industrial Capitalism, 1867–1892* (Toronto: University of Toronto Press, 1980), p. 3.

49. Elizabeth Graham, "Schoolmarms and Early Teaching in Ontario," in *Women at Work in Ontario, 1850–1930*, ed. Janice Action, Penny Goldsmith, and Bonnie Shepard (Toronto: Women's Press Publication, 1974), pp. 165–187; Mother Jones to Mrs. Potter Palmer, January 12, 1907, *Correspondence of Mother Jones*, p. 61. See also Marta Danylewycz and Alison Prentice, "Teacher's Work: Changing Patterns and Perceptions in the Emerging School Systems of Nineteenth and Early Twentieth Century Central Canada," *Labour/Le Travail* 17 (Spring, 1986): 59–75; Atkinson, *Mother Jones*, pp. 19–23; Robert T. Handy, *A Christian America: Protestant Hopes and Historical Realities* (New York: Oxford University Press, 1971), pp. 101–105; Fetherling, *Mother Jones*, p. 3.

50. Atkinson, *Mother Jones*, pp. 24–32; Jonathan Grossman, *William Sylvis, Pioneer of American Labor* (New York: Columbia University Press, 1945), pp. 40–43, 150–151 (quoting Sylvis); David Montgomery, "William H. Sylvis and the Search for Working-Class Citizenship," in *Labor Leaders in America*, pp. 9–10.

51. Thomas Stritch, *The Catholic Church in Tennessee* (Nashville: Catholic Center, 1987), pp. 193–195; D. A. Quinn, *Heroes and Heroines of Memphis; or, Reminiscences of the Yellow Fever Epidemics That Afflicted the City of Memphis during the Autumn Months of 1873, 1878, and 1879* (Providence: E. L. Freeman and Sons, 1887); *Autobiography of Mother Jones*, p. 12.

52. Lawrence J. McCaffrey, "The Irish-American Dimension," in *The Irish in Chicago*, ed. McCaffrey et al. (Urbana: University of Illinois Press, 1987), pp. 7–8; Ellen Skerrett, "The Catholic Dimension," in *The Irish in Chicago*, pp. 25–29; Michael F. Funchion, "Irish Chicago: Church, Homeland, Politics, and Class—the Shaping of an Ethnic Group, 1870–1900," in *Ethnic Chicago*, rev. ed., ed. Melvin G. Holli and Peter d'A. Jones (Grand Rapids: William B. Eerdmans, 1984), pp. 31–33; Ray Ginger, *Altgeld's America* (New York: Funk and Wagnalls, 1958), pp. 15–34; *Autobiography of Mother Jones*, p. 13.

53. James W. Sheahan and George P. Upton, *The Great Conflagration: Chicago, Its Past, Present, and Future* (Chicago: Union, 1872), p. 282; *Autobiography of Mother Jones*, p. 13. See also Robert Cromie, *The Great Chicago Fire* (New York: McGraw-Hill, 1958); Adade Mitchell Wheeler and Marlene Stein Wortman, *The Roads They Made: Women in Illinois History* (Chicago: Charles H. Kerr, 1977), p. 57.

54. *Autobiography of Mother Jones*, pp. 14–16; Mother Jones, "Testimony before the Commission on Industrial Relations, Washington, D.C., August 23, 1912," in *Mother Jones Speaks: Collected Speeches and Writings*, ed. Philip S. Foner (New York: Monad Press, 1983), p. 404; Affidavit of Mother Jones, January 31, 1911, Cook County, Illinois; *Correspondence of Mother Jones*, p. 87; Philip S. Foner, *The Great Labor Uprising of 1877* (New York: Monad Press, 1977), p. 8; Samuel Yellen, *American Labor Struggles* (New York: S. A. Russell, 1956), pp. 3–9; Paul Avrich, *The Haymarket Tragedy* (Princeton: Princeton University Press, 1984), p. 97.

55. Yellen, *American Labor Struggles*, pp. 4–38; Jeremy Brecher, *Strike!* (Boston: South End Press, 1972), pp. 1–14.

56. Foner, *Great Labor Uprising*, pp. 55–67; Robert V. Bruce, *1877: Year of Violence* (Indianapolis: Bobbs-Merrill, 1959).

57. *Autobiography of Mother Jones*, pp. 14–16; Mother Jones, "Testimony before

the Commission on Industrial Relations," pp. 404–405; Susan Levine, "Labor's True Woman: Domesticity and Equal Rights in the Knights of Labor," *Journal of American History* 70 (September, 1983): 325.

58. Brecher, *Strike!* pp. 15–22; Foner, *Great Labor Uprising*, pp. 7, 44–45 (quoting manifesto).

59. *Autobiography of Mother Jones*, pp. 17–23, 28–29; Affidavit of Mother Jones, January 31, 1911; Howard H. Quint, *American Socialism: Origins of the Modern Movement* (Indianapolis: Bobbs-Merrill, 1964), pp. 293, 320; Elliott Shore, *Talkin' Socialism: J. A. Wayland and the Role of the Press in American Radicalism, 1890–1912* (Lawrence: University Press of Kansas, 1988), pp. 29, 75; Mother Jones to Walter Wayland, November 15, 1918, *Correspondence of Mother Jones*, p. 184.

60. "An Interview with Mother Jones," *Appeal to Reason*, September 14, 1901, p. 2; Kate Richards O'Hare, "How I Became a Socialist Agitator," *Socialist Woman* 2 (October, 1908): 4–5; Neil K. Basen, "Kate Richards O'Hare: The 'First Lady' of American Socialism, 1901–1971," *Labor History* 21 (Spring, 1980): 166, 172–173.

61. Mother Jones to William B. Wilson, February 2, 1902, *Correspondence of Mother Jones*, p. 21.

62. *Autobiography of Mother Jones*, pp. 24–27, 30–39; Steel, Introduction to *Correspondence of Mother Jones*, p. xxv; David J. McDonald and Edward A. Lynch, *Coal and Unionism: A History of the American Coal Miners' Unions* (Silver Springs, Md.: Cornelius Printing, 1939), pp. 22–28.

63. H. B. Humphrey, *Historical Summary of Coal-Mine Explosions in the United States, 1810–1958*, Bulletin 586, Bureau of Mines (Washington, D.C.: United States Printing Office, 1960), pp. 17, 19; A. T. Shurick, *The Coal Industry* (Boston: Little, Brown, 1924), p. 305. See also McAlister Coleman, *Men and Coal* (New York: Farrar and Rinehart, 1943), pp. 45–53; Priscilla Long, *Where the Sun Never Shines: A History of America's Bloody Coal Industry* (New York: Paragon House, 1989), pp. 140–155; William Graebner, *Coal-Mining Safety in the Progressive Period* (Lexington: University Press of Kentucky, 1976), p. 6; John B. Andrews, "Needless Hazards in the Coal Industry," in *The Price of Coal: Annual of the American Academy of Political and Social Science*, vol. 111 (Philadelphia: American Academy of Political and Social Science, 1924), pp. 24–25; Homer Lawrence Morris, *The Plight of the Bituminous Coal Miner* (Philadelphia: University of Pennsylvania Press, 1934), p. 176; Philip Foner, *Women and the American Labor Movement* (New York: Free Press, 1979), p. 281.

64. Donald L. Lewis, *Black Coal Miners in America: Race, Class, and Community Conflict, 1780–1980* (Lexington: University Press of Kentucky, 1987), pp. 121–123, 146; David Alan Corbin, *Life, Work, and Rebellion in the Coal Fields: The Southern West Virginia Miners, 1880–1922* (Urbana: University of Illinois Press, 1981), pp. 2–3, 8–11; Winthrop D. Lane, *Civil War in West Virginia: The Story of the Industrial Conflict in the Coal Mines* (1921; rpt. New York: Oriole Chapbooks, n.d.), pp. 21–23; Howard B. Lee, *Bloodletting in Appalachia* (Morgantown: West Virginia University Press, 1969), p. ix; Morris, *Plight of the Bituminous Coal Miner*, pp. 85–87.

65. *Autobiography of Mother Jones*, pp. 24–25; Mother Jones, "The Lives of Coal Miners," *Boston Herald*, September 11, 1904, in *Mother Jones Speaks*, p. 73; Corbin, *Life, Work, and Rebellion*, pp. 47–48; *Autobiography of Mother Jones*, pp. 45–48; Mother Jones to John Mitchell, March 14, May 5, 1902, *Correspondence of Mother*

Jones, pp. 25–26, 29–31; Mother Jones, "A Picture of American Freedom in West Virginia," *International Socialist Review* 2 (1901–1902), in *Speeches and Writings of Mother Jones*, pp. 270–271.

66. Edward M. Steel, "Mother Jones in the Fairmont Field, 1902," *Journal of American History* 57 (1970): 290–301; *Autobiography of Mother Jones*, pp. 40–45, 49–55; Jackson, quoted in Fetherling, *Mother Jones*, pp. 31–34.

67. Corbin, *Life, Work, and Rebellion*, pp. 87–90; Lee, *Bloodletting in Appalachia*, pp. 15, 20–24; Lawrence R. Lynch, "The West Virginia Coal Strike," *Political Science Quarterly* 29 (December, 1914): 632–633; Mooney, *Struggle in the Coal Fields*, pp. 16, 35; Jones, "Barbarous West Virginia," in *Mother Jones Speaks*, p. 159; Ralph Chaplin, *Wobbly: The Rough-and-Tumble Story of an American Radical* (Chicago: University of Chicago Press, 1948), pp. 119, 123.

68. Corbin, *Life, Work, and Rebellion*, p. 89; *Autobiography of Mother Jones*, p. 152; Mooney, *Struggle in the Coal Fields*, pp. 26–28. For Mother Jones's own account of the incident, see *Autobiography of Mother Jones*, pp. 156–159.

69. Chaplin, *Wobbly*, p. 120.

70. Jones, "Speech at a Public Meeting on the Steps of the Capitol, Charleston, West Virginia, August 15, 1912," and "Speech at a Public Meeting in the Courthouse Square, Charleston, West Virginia, September 6, 1912," both in *Speeches and Writings of Mother Jones*, pp. 89–91, 104, 106–108, 114; Jones, "Barbarous West Virginia," p. 157; Lee, *Bloodletting in Appalachia*, p. 33.

71. Corbin, *Life, Work, and Rebellion*, pp. 95–96; Mother Jones to Terence V. Powderly, March 3, 1913, Mother Jones to Caroline Lloyd ("sympathetic guards"), March 17, 1913, *Correspondence of Mother Jones*, pp. 108, 109; Lee, *Bloodletting in Appalachia*, pp. 33, 44; Fetherling, *Mother Jones*, pp. 96–99; Jones, "Barbarous West Virginia," pp. 160–162; Corbin, *Life, Work, and Rebellion*, pp. 97–100.

72. Jones, "Speech at the Convention of the United Mine Workers of America, Indianapolis, Indiana, January 29, 1909," "Speech at the Convention of the United Mine Workers of America, Indianapolis, Indiana, January 26, 1910," "Speech at a Meeting of the Pan-American Federation of Labor, Mexico City, January 13, 1921," in *Speeches and Writings of Mother Jones*, pp. 32–33, 112, 130–131, 233–237; Mother Jones to the *New York Call*, January, 1917, *Correspondence of Mother Jones*, p. 175; John O. P. Hall, ed., *A Miner's Life: John Brophy* (Madison: University of Wisconsin Press, 1964), p. 74.

73. Weaver, *New Catholic Women*, p. 24; Mother Jones to Terrence V. Powderly, March 22, 1914; Mother Jones to William B. Wilson, February 19, 1902, *Correspondence of Mother Jones*, pp. 122, 21; Lee, *Bloodletting in Appalachia*, pp. 18–21; Mooney, *Struggle in the Coal Fields*, p. 167; Mother Jones to Terence V. Powderly, September 20, 1913, *Correspondence of Mother Jones*, p. 119.

74. *Autobiography of Mother Jones*, pp. 178–183; Long, *Where the Sun Never Shines*, pp. 272–284; Mother Jones to Terence V. Powderly, March 22, 1914, *Correspondence of Mother Jones*, p. 122.

75. Jones, "Speech at a Public Meeting on the Levee, Charleston, West Virginia, August 1, 1912," "Speech at a Public Meeting at the Baseball Park, Montgomery, West Virginia," "Speech at a Public Meeting on the Steps of the Capitol, Charleston, West Virginia, March 15, 1912," "Speech at a Public Meeting in the Courthouse

Square, Charleston, West Virginia, September 6, 1912," "Speech at a Public Meeting in the Labor Temple, Pittsburg, Kansas, August 7, 1912," "Speech at a Public Meeting, Princeton, West Virginia, August 15, 1920," all in *Speeches and Writings of Mother Jones*, pp. 63, 67, 75, 81, 83, 93, 133, 161–163, 225; Long, *Where the Sun Never Shines*, pp. 291–294; George S. McGovern and Leonard F. Guttridge, *The Great Coalfield War* (Boston: Houghton Mifflin, 1972), pp. 215–231; Barron B. Beshoar, *Out of the Depths: The Story of John R. Lawson, a Labor Leader*, 3rd ed. (Denver: Golden Bell Press, 1957), pp. 166–179.

76. Jones, "Speech at the Baseball Park, Montgomery," "The Coal Miners of the Dominion," "Governor Comer's Alabama Cotton Mills," all in *Speeches and Writings of Mother Jones*, pp. 73–75, 85, 272–273, 283.

77. Jones, "Speech on the Steps of the Capitol, March 15, 1912," "Speech at the Pan-American Federation of Labor," January 13, 1921," both in *Speeches and Writings of Mother Jones*, pp. 90–91, 234.

78. Gregory Baum, "Sociology and Salvation: Do We Need a Catholic Sociology?" *Theological Studies* 50 (December, 1989): 735; Jones, "Speech at the Baseball Park, Montgomery," in *Speeches and Writings of Mother Jones*, p. 85; Mother Jones to Mrs. Potter Palmer, January 12, 1907, *Correspondence of Mother Jones*, pp. 60–61; *Autobiography of Mother Jones*, pp. 236–242. An interesting perspective on the sorts of conclusions about the nature of Christian faith to which Mother Jones came can be found in Matthew Lamb, *Solidarity with Victims: Toward a Theology of Social Transformation* (New York: Crossroad, 1982). For an insightful analysis of the meaning of workers' solidarity, see Rick Fantasia, *Cultures of Solidarity: Consciousness, Action, and Contemporary American Workers* (Berkeley: University of California Press, 1988).

79. Foner, "Mother Jones: Dynamic Champion of the Oppressed Multitudes," in *Mother Jones Speaks*, pp. 25–28. For a critique of Mother Jones, see Long, *Mother Jones, Woman Organizer*, pp. 28–35; and Susan Estabrook Kennedy, *If All We Did Was to Weep at Home: A History of White Working-Class Women in America* (Bloomington: Indiana University Press, 1979), pp. 115–116.

80. Hasia R. Diner, *Erin's Daughters in America: Irish Immigrant Women in the Nineteenth Century* (Baltimore: Johns Hopkins University Press, 1983), pp. 19–20, 99, 146–152.

81. Mother Jones to Mrs. Potter Palmer, January 12, 1907, *Correspondence of Mother Jones*, p. 61; Mother Jones, "Fashionable Society Scored," *Miners Magazine* (April 1, 1915), in *Mother Jones Speaks*, pp. 468–471; Jones, "Speech on the Levee, August 1, 1912," in *Speeches and Writings of Mother Jones*, p. 59.

82. Jones, "You Ought to Be Out Raising Hell," in *Mother Jones Speaks*, p. 290. On domestic violence, see Diner, *Erin's Daughters in America*, pp. 106–119.

83. Jones, "Speech at the Convention of the United Mine Workers of America, Indianapolis, Indiana, January 25, 1901," "Speech at the Convention of the United Mine Workers of America, Columbus, Ohio, January 21, 1911," both in *Speeches and Writings of Mother Jones*, pp. 4–6, 45; Jones, "This Is Not a Play, This Is a Fight!" and "You Ought to Be Out Raising Hell!" both in *Mother Jones Speaks*, pp. 137, 290.

84. *Autobiography of Mother Jones*, pp. 30–36, 145–147.

85. Jones, "Speech at a Special Convention of the United Mine Workers of America,

Cincinnati, Ohio, March 24, 1910," "Speech on the Levee, August 1, 1912," both in *Speeches and Writings of Mother Jones*, pp. 42, 65; *Autobiography of Mother Jones*, pp. 237–238.

86. Alan P. Grimes, *The Puritan Ethic and Woman Suffrage* (New York: Oxford University Press, 1967); Jones, "Speech in the Labor Temple, August 7, 1915," "Speech at a Public Meeting, Williamson, West Virginia, June 20, 1920," both in *Speeches and Writings of Mother Jones*, pp. 162, 219.

87. Archie Green, "The Death of Mother Jones," *Labor History* (Winter, 1960): 80.

88. Terence V. Powderly, "Mother Jones" (n.d.), Terence V. Powderly Papers, Department of Archives and Manuscripts, Catholic University of America, Washington, D.C.

89. Rosalynd Baxandal, *Words on Fire: The Life and Writings of Elizabeth Gurley Flynn* (New Brunswick: Rutgers University Press, 1987), p. 1; Elizabeth Gurley Flynn, *I Speak My Own Piece* (New York: Masses and Mainstream, 1955), p. 75.

Chapter Three

1. Mario Barrera, *Race and Class in the Southwest: A Theory of Racial Inequality* (Notre Dame: University of Notre Dame Press, 1979), pp. 206–209; Harry Chang, "Toward a Marxist Theory of Racism: Two Essays by Harry Chang," ed. Paul Liem and Eric Montague, *Review of Radical Political Economics* 17 (Fall, 1985): 41–45; Oliver Cromwell Cox, *Caste, Class, and Race* (New York: Monthly Review Press, 1948, 1970), pp. 330–345; Robert Staples, *The Urban Plantation: Racism and Colonialism in the Post–Civil War Era* (Oakland: Black Scholar Press, 1987); Michael Reich, *Racial Inequality: A Political-Economic Analysis* (Princeton: Princeton University Press, 1981); Manning Marable, *How Capitalism Underdeveloped Black America* (Boston: South End Press, 1983).

2. George P. Rawick, *From Sundown to Sunup: The Making of the Black Community* (Westport: Greenwood, 1972), pp. 150–151; Cedric J. Robinson, *Black Marxism: The Making of the Black Radical Tradition* (London: Zed Press, 1983), pp. 442–443.

3. Philip S. Foner, Introduction to *Black Socialist Preacher: The Teachings of Reverend George Washington Woodbey and His Disciple Reverend George W. Slater, Jr.*, ed. Foner (San Francisco: Synthesis, 1983), p. 1.

4. Reinhold Niebuhr, "Radical Religion," *Radical Religion* 1 (Autumn, 1935): 3; W.E.B. Du Bois, *The Souls of Black Folk*, 20th ed. (Chicago: A. C. McClurg, 1935), pp. 3–4.

5. Manning Marable, *Blackwater: Historical Studies in Race, Class Consciousness, and Revolution* (Dayton: Black Praxis Press, 1981), p. 40.

6. Cornel West, *Prophesy Deliverance!* (Philadelphia: Westminster Press, 1982), pp. 106–107.

7. Eugene V. Debs, "Outlook for Socialism in the United States," *International Socialist Review* 1 (September, 1900): 135; Robert H. Craig, "The Underside of History: American Methodism, Capitalism, and Popular Struggle," *Methodist History* 27 (January, 1989): 80–81; James Weinstein, *Ambiguous Legacy: The Left in American Politics* (New York: New Viewpoints, 1975), p. 7; James Weinstein, "Socialism's Hidden Heritage," in *For a New America*, ed. Weinstein and David W. Eakins (New York: Vintage

Books, 1970), pp. 229–231; Henry G. Stetler, *The Socialist Movement in Reading, Pennsylvania, 1896–1936* (1943; Philadelphia: Porcupine Press, 1974), pp. 90–92; James R. Green, *Grass-Roots Socialism: Radical Movements in the Southwest, 1895–1943* (Baton Rouge: Louisiana State University Press, 1978), pp. xi–xxi.

8. Mike Davis, *Prisoners of the American Dream* (London: Verso, 1986), pp. 45–51; Paul Buhle, *Marxism in the USA* (London: Verso, 1987), pp. 86–120; Robert Hyfler, *Prophets of the Left* (Westport: Greenwood Press, 1984), pp. 3–40; and Donald Stabile, *Prophets of Order* (Boston: South End Press, 1984), pp. 149–180. Some of the same kinds of questions have been raised by earlier studies of the Socialist Party, among them David A. Shannon, *The Socialist Party of America* (New York: Macmillan, 1955); Ira Kipnis, *The American Socialist Movement, 1897–1912* (New York: Columbia University Press, 1952); and the essays found in *Failure of a Dream? Essays in the History of American Socialism*, ed. John H. M. Laslett and Seymour Martin Lipset (Garden City: Doubleday, 1974).

9. James R. Green, "The 'Salesmen-Soldiers' of the 'Appeal Army': A Profile of Rank-and-File Socialist Agitators," in *Socialism and the Cities*, ed. Bruce M. Stave (Port Washington, N.Y.: Kennikat Press, 1975), pp. 23–37; J. L. Burke, "What Is Socialism?" *Appeal to Reason*, November 1, 1902, p. 3; Eugene V. Debs, "Industrial Unionism: A Letter to Tom Mann," *International Socialist Review* 11 (August, 1910): 90–91; Debs, "The Crime of Craft Unionism," *International Socialist Review* 11 (February, 1911): 465–468; *Bill Haywood's Book: The Autobiography of William D. Haywood* (New York: International, 1929), pp. 181–182; William D. Haywood, "Socialism, the Hope of the Working Class," *International Socialist Review* 12 (February 1912): 461–471.

10. Hal Draper, *The Two Souls of Socialism*, rev. ed., pamphlet (Detroit: Sherrico, 1966), pp. 3–6.

11. Haywood, "Socialism," p. 464; Gerald Friedberg, "Marxism in the United States: John Spargo and the Socialist Party of America" (Ph.D. diss., University of Chicago, 1964), pp. 48–49; Green, *Grass-Roots Socialism*, pp. 10–11.

12. Charles Edward Russell, *Bare Hands and Stone Walls* (New York: Charles Scribner's Sons, 1933), p. 196; Kate Richards O'Hare, quoted in Green, *Grass-Roots Socialism*, pp. 436–437.

13. Russell, *Bare Hands and Stone Walls*, p. 227; R. Laurence Moore, "Flawed Fraternity—American Socialists' Response to the Negro, 1901–1912," *The Historian* 26 (November, 1969): 1–14; Eugene V. Debs, "The Negro in the Class Struggle," *International Socialist Review* 4 (November, 1903): 257.

14. Ernest Untermann, excerpted in *The Socialism of To-day*, ed. William English Walling et al. (New York: Henry Holt, 1916), pp. 497–498. The 1907 meeting of the Socialist International was also important for adopting the anticolonial resolution that was to be the official Socialist position for the next two decades. Julius Braunthal, *History of the International*, vol. 1: *1864–1914* (New York: Frederick A. Praeger, 1967), p. 319.

15. Philip S. Foner, *American Socialism and Black Americans: From the Age of Jackson to World War II* (Westport: Greenwood Press, 1977), pp. 94–99. See the text of the resolution in *The Socialism of To-day*, pp. 504–505.

16. Charles Dobbs, "The Farmer and the Negro," *International Socialist Review*

4 (April, 1904): 613–614; Clarence Meily, "Socialism and the Negro Problem," *International Socialist Review* 4 (November, 1903): 266–267.

17. W.E.B. Du Bois, ed., *The Negro Artisan*, Atlanta University Publications, 7 (Atlanta: Atlanta University Press, 1902), pp. 156–158; Marc Karson and Ronald Radosh, "The American Federation of Labor and the Negro Worker, 1894–1949," in *The Negro and the American Labor Movement*, ed. Julius Jacobsen (Garden City: Anchor Books, 1968), p. 158; W.E.B. Du Bois and Augustus Granville Dill, eds., *The Negro American Artisan*, Atlanta University Publications, 17 (Atlanta: Atlanta University Press, 1912), pp. 82–114; Sterling D. Spero and Abram L. Harris, *The Black Worker: The Negro and the Labor Movement* (New York: Columbia University Press, 1931), pp. 87–105; Philip S. Foner, *Organized Labor and the Black Worker, 1619–1973* (New York: Praeger, 1974), pp. 65–73; Bernard Mandel, *Samuel Gompers* (Yellow Springs, Ohio: Antioch Press, 1963), pp. 234–236.

18. Herbert Gutman, "The Negro and the United Mine Workers of America," in *The Negro and the American Labor Movement*, pp. 110–127; Jim Green, "The Brotherhood," in *Working Lives: The Southern Exposure History of Labor in the South*, ed. Marc S. Miller (New York: Pantheon Books, 1980), pp. 22–39.

19. Robert Hunter and Untermann excerpted in *The Socialism of To-day*, pp. 495–504; Victor Berger and Barney Berlyn, quoted in Sally M. Miller, "The Socialist Party and the Negro, 1901–1920," *Journal of Negro History* 56 (July, 1971): 221–222. See also Kipnis, *American Socialist Movement*, p. 285; Charles Leinenweber, "The American Socialist Party and 'New' Immigrants," *Science and Society* 32 (Winter, 1968): 7, 23; Paul Buhle, "Debsian Socialism and the 'New Immigrant' Worker," in *Insights and Parallels: Problems and Issues of American Social History*, ed. William L. O'Neill (Minneapolis: Burgess, 1973), pp. 249–277; Sally M. Miller, *Victor Berger and the Promise of Constructive Socialism, 1910–1920* (Westport: Greenwood Press, 1973), pp. 38–39, 81–82.

20. Carole Marks, "Black Workers and the Great Migration North," *Phylon* 46 (June, 1985): 148; Ida M. Raymond, "A Southern Socialist on the Negro Question," *New Review* 10 (1913): 990; A. T. Cuzner, "The Negro or the Race Problem," *International Socialist Review* 4 (November, 1903): 261–264; Oscar Edgar, "A Study of Race Prejudice," *International Socialist Review* 4 (February, 1904): 462–465; E. F. Andrews, "Socialism and the Negro," *International Socialist Review* 5 (March, 1905): 524–526; Green, *Grass-Roots Socialism*, p. 95 (quoting Dennett).

21. Foner, *American Socialism and Black Americans*, pp. 131–137, 242; Eraste Vidrine, "Negro Locals," *International Socialist Review* 5 (January, 1905): 389–392.

22. Garin Burbank, *When Farmers Voted Red: The Gospel of Socialism in the Oklahoma Countryside, 1910–1924* (Westport: Greenwood Press, 1976), pp. 8, 57, 69–87; Green, *Grass-Roots Socialism*, pp. 94–109; Foner, *American Socialism and Black Americans*, pp. 223–237; Oscar Ameringer, *If You Don't Weaken* (New York: Henry Holt, 1940), p. 197.

23. Debs, "The Negro in the Class Struggle," pp. 257–260; Debs, "The Negro and His Nemesis," *International Socialist Review* 4 (January, 1904): 391–397; Meily, "Socialism and the Negro Problem," p. 265.

24. Nick Salvatore, *Eugene V. Debs: Citizen and Socialist* (Urbana: University of Illi-

nois Press, 1982), pp. 226–228; Ray Ginger, *Eugene V. Debs: A Biography* (New York: Collier Books, 1962), pp. 275–276; Cornel West, "Marxist Theory and the Specificity of Afro-American Oppression," in *Marxism and the Interpretation of Culture*, ed. Cary Nelson and Lawrence Grossberg (Urbana: University of Illinois Press, 1988), p. 19.

25. Martin Luther King, Jr., "Honoring Dr. Du Bois," in W. E. Burghardt Du Bois, *Dusk of Dawn* (New York: Schocken Books, 1940, 1968), p. xv; *The Autobiography of W.E.B. Du Bois* (New York: International, 1968), pp. 254; John Henrike Clarke et al., *Black Titan: W.E.B. Du Bois* (Boston: Beacon Press, 1970), pp. 304–306; Herbert Aptheker, ed., *The Correspondence of W.E.B. Du Bois*, vol. 1: *Selections, 1877–1934* (Amherst: University of Massachusetts Press, 1973), p. 82; Manning Marable, *W.E.B. Du Bois: Black Radical Democrat* (Boston: Twayne, 1986), pp. 89–90; Mary White Ovington, *The Walls Came Tumbling Down* (New York: Harcourt, Brace, 1947), pp. 101–107; Charles Flint Kellogg, *NAACP: A History of the National Association for the Advancement of Colored People*, vol. 1: *1900–1920* (Baltimore: Johns Hopkins University Press, 1967), pp. 9–12, 291. For an interesting assessment of Du Bois's contribution to the development of a black radical tradition, see Robinson, *Black Marxism*.

26. *Autobiography of W.E.B. Du Bois*, pp. 256–258; Du Bois to Mary White Ovington, April 9, 1914, *Correspondence of W.E.B. Du Bois*, pp. 188–191.

27. W.E. Burghardt Du Bois, "A Field for Socialists," *New Review*, January 11, 1913, pp. 54, 57; Du Bois, "Socialism and the Negro Problem," *New Review*, February 1, 1913, pp. 138–142.

28. W.E.B. Du Bois, *Darkwater* (New York: Schocken Books, 1920, 1969), pp. 138–142; Du Bois, "The Problem of Problems," *Intercollegiate Socialist* 6 (December, 1917–January, 1918): 8–9; *Autobiography of W.E.B. Du Bois*; Henry Lee Moon, *Emerging Thought of W.E.B. Du Bois* (New York: Simon and Schuster, 1972), pp. 267–269.

29. J. A. Rogers, *World's Great Men of Color*, vol. 2 (New York: J. A. Rogers, 1947), pp. 611–615; Wilfred D. Samuels, "Hubert H. Harrison and 'The New Negro Manhood Movement,' " *Afro-Americans in New York Life and History* 5 (January, 1981): 29–39; Ira Katznelson, *Black Men, White Cities* (London: Oxford University Press, 1973), pp. 75–76; Foner, *American Socialism and Black Americans*, pp. 207–216.

30. Cox, *Caste, Class, and Race*; Hubert H. Harrison, *The Negro and the Nation* (New York: Cosmo-Advocate, 1917), pp. 21–58.

31. Harrison, *The Negro and the Nation*, pp. 21–58.

32. Hubert H. Harrison, *When Africa Awakes* (New York City: Porro Press, 1920), pp. 5–7, 14–16, 22–24, 76–82, 96–98.

33. Allen D. Grimshaw, ed., *Racial Violence in the United States* (Chicago: Aldine, 1969), pp. 111–112; description of the riot quoted in Joseph Boskin, *Urban Racial Violence in the Twentieth Century* (Beverly Hills: Glencoe Press, 1969), pp. 24–25; Harrison, *When Africa Awakes*, pp. 20–22.

34. Harrison, *When Africa Awakes*, pp. 77–79, 84–86.

35. Ibid., pp. 91–95, 112–113. For an analysis of the developing black nationalist tradition, see Wilson Jeremiah Moses, *The Golden Age of Black Nationalism, 1850–1925* (Hamden: Archon Books, 1978); and V. P. Franklin, *Black Self-Determination: A Cultural History of the Faith of the Fathers* (Westport: Lawrence Hill, 1984).

36. Eric Hobsbawm, "Religion and the Rise of Socialism," *Marxist Perspectives* 1 (Spring, 1978): 14–33. For an analysis of the increasing secularization of the European working class, see Hugh McLeod, "The Dechristianisation of the Working Class in Western Europe (1850–1900)," *Social Compass* 27/2–3 (1980): 191–214; Rufus W. Weeks, "What the Christian Socialists Stand For," *Christian Socialist*, June 1, 1908, p. 1.

37. Martin E. Marty, *The Righteous Empire: The Protestant Experience in America* (New York: Dial Press, 1970), p. 179; Robert H. Craig, "Friend or Foe? Social Christianity's Response to Socialism prior to the Great Depression," *Radical Religion* 1 (Winter, 1973): 50–52; Paul F. Laubenstein, "A History of Christian Socialism in America" (S.T.M. thesis, Union Theological Seminary, 1925), p. 42; Morris Hillquit, *A History of Socialism in the United States* (New York: Funk and Wagnalls, 1906), p. 320; Joseph Dorfman, *The Economic Mind in American Civilization*, vol. 3 (New York: Viking Press, 1949), p. 157; Howard H. Quint, *The Forging of American Socialism* (Columbia: University of South Carolina, 1953), pp. 114, 121–124, 224, 256–263; Solomon Gemorah, "Laurence Gronlund—Utopian or Reformer?" *Science and Society* 33 (Fall–Winter, 1969): 446–458; Laurence Gronlund, *Our Destiny: The Influence of Socialism on Morals and Religion* (London: S. Sonnenschein, 1890), p. 136.

38. *American Fabian* 1 (February, 1895): 5, as cited in Quint, *Forging of American Socialism*, p. 121.

39. Craig, "Friend or Foe?" pp. 52–53; Howard H. Quint, Introduction to the Greenwood Press reprint of *The Socialist Spirit* (Westport: Greenwood Press, 1970), p. 2; George D. Herron, *Between Caesar and Jesus* (New York: Thomas Y. Crowell, 1899), pp. 94–95; Quint, *Forging of American Socialism*, p. 134. My interpretation of Herron is drawn from the work of Robert T. Handy, both his "George D. Herron and the Social Gospel in American Protestantism" (Ph.D. diss., University of Chicago, 1949), p. 110, and "George D. Herron and the Kingdom Movement," *Church History* 19 (1950): 110–113, and from a reading of Herron's works, especially *Between Caesar and Jesus* and his writings after he joined the Social Democratic Party.

40. George D. Herron, *Why I Am A Socialist*, pamphlet (Chicago: Charles H. Kerr, 1900), pp. 6–12; Herron, "Socialism and Religion," *International Socialist Review* 1 (January, February, 1901): 434, 501–504; Quint, *Forging of American Socialism*, pp. 134, 137–138.

41. George D. Herron, "A Plea for the Unity of American Socialists," *International Socialist Review* 1 (December, 1900); Kipnis, *American Socialist Movement*, p. 223; Laubenstein, "History of Christian Socialism," p. 93; Robert T. Handy, "Christianity and Socialism in America, 1900–1920," *Church History* 21 (March, 1952): 47–48.

42. Craig, "Friend or Foe?" pp. 55–56; "The Christian Socialist Fellowship," *Christian Socialist*, August 15, 1907, p. 5; Edward Ellis Carr, Editorials, *Christian Socialist*, May 1, June 1, 1906, pp. 4, 3; Rufus W. Weeks, Letter to the Editor, *Christian Socialist*, July 15, 1905, p. 3; Minutes of the CSF as published in *Christian Socialist*, July 1, 1906, p. 4. The other Christian Socialist organization of this period was the Church Socialist League, formed in 1911 on the model of the English Church Socialist League, which had been created in 1906. The league was mainly composed of Episcopal clergy and laity. By 1916 it began to take on more of an organizational structure, but its membership remained fewer than a hundred. Spencer Miller, Jr., and Joseph F. Fletcher, *The Church*

and Industry (New York: Longmans, Green, 1930), pp. 93–94. A rather laudatory assessment of the Christian Socialist League was written for the Socialist *American Labor Year Book, 1917–1918* by A. L. Byron-Curtiss, national secretary of the league. He believed that the league's "influence within the Episcopal church is not at all measured by its numerical strength. In spite of the conservativism of the Episcopal church . . . that church has officially adopted radical and even revolutionary resolutions, and the influence of the CSL is discernible as giving color to them. A considerable share of the clergy are tinctured with Socialism. With but 6,000 clergy, several hundred are avowed Socialists and nearly one hundred are members of the Socialist Party. The League is able to present the parallel demands of militant socialism to this communion as no other society can." A. L. Byron-Curtiss, "The Christian Socialists," in *The American Labor Year Book*, ed. Alexander Trachtenberg (New York: Rand School of Social Science, 1918), p. 300.

43. Handy, "Christianity and Socialism in America," p. 44; Eliot White, "The Christian Socialist Fellowship," *The Arena* 41 (January, 1909): 47, 49; James Weinstein, *The Decline of Socialism in America, 1912–1925* (New York: Vintage Books, 1969), p. 95; Edward Ellis Carr, "Economic Science or Sectarian Dogmatism," *Christian Socialist*, May 15, 1907, p. 1; J. Peter Brunner, "Prayer," *Christian Socialist*, September 1, 1908, p. 1.

44. J. O. Bentall, "Why I Am a Christian Socialist," *The Arena* 37 (June, 1907): 602; Weeks, "What Christian Socialists Stand For," pp. 1–2; George H. Strobell, *A Christian View of Socialism*, pamphlet (Girard, Kans.: Appeal to Reason, 1917). This was a reprint of an address Strobell first delivered before the Presbyterian Ministers' Association of New York City in 1905.

45. Purpose of the movement quoted in C. Howard Hopkins, *The Rise of the Social Gospel in American Protestantism, 1865–1915* (New Haven: Yale University Press, 1967), p. 296, and see 296–298; Walter Rauschenbusch, *Christianizing the Social Order* (New York: Macmillan, 1912), p. 20; "Who Are the 'Intellectual Asses?' " *Christian Socialist*, February 15, 1912, pp. 1–6. See also Elizabeth and Kenneth Fones-Wolf, "Trade-Union Evangelism: Religion and the AFL in the Labor Forward Movement, 1912–16," in *Working-Class America*, ed. Michael H. Frisch and Daniel J. Walkowitz (Urbana: University of Illinois Press, 1983), pp. 155–157.

46. Edward M. Duff, "The Men and Labor Forward Movement as a Capitalist Propaganda," *Christian Socialist*, February 22, 1912, pp. 1–3; Hugh D. Camitta, "Raymond Robins: A Study of a Progressive" (Honors in History paper, Williams College, 1965); Raymond Robins to Margaret Dreier Robins, February 3, May 17, 1910, Florence Kelley to Raymond Robins, June 20, 1917, Raymond Robins Papers, State Historical Society of Wisconsin, Madison.

47. J. O. Bentall, "Christian Socialist Fellowship Center," *Christian Socialist*, January 1, 1907, p. 3; "Christian Socialist Fellowship Center Organized in New York," *Christian Socialist*, November 15, 1907, p. 1; "Detroit Center Organized," *Christian Socialist* 12 (December, 1915): 6. "A Center Formed at Denver," *Christian Socialist*, February 15, 1908, p. 1; "The Christian Socialist Fellowship," *Christian Socialist*, September 15, 1910, p. 5; "The Christian Socialist Fellowship," *Christian Socialist* 12 (December, 1915): 6; J. O. Bentall, "Socialist Sunday Schools," *Christian Socialist*, August 15, 1907, p. 4; "A Socialist Prayer," *Christian Socialist*, May 9, 1912, p. 1.

48. "Our District Secretaries," *Christian Socialist*, April 15, 1909, p. 8; "The Revival at McKeesport," *Christian Socialist*, January 1, 1907, p. 7; "Notes and Comments," *Christian Socialist*, January 15, 1907, p. 7.

49. "Second Annual Summer Meeting of Graves County, Ky., Socialists," *Christian Socialist*, September 14, 1911, pp. 1, 3–4, 7.

50. *Christian Socialist*, November 1, 1907, September 1, December 1, 1908, March 15, 1909, February 23, 1911, August 1, 1912; "Women in the Fellowship," *Christian Socialist*, August 1, 1907, p. 6; "Woman's Day at the Chicago Christian Socialist Fellowship," *Christian Socialist*, April 15, 1910, pp. 1–3; Anna K. Hulburd, "Socialist Women and the Suffrage Association," *Christian Socialist*, April 15, 1910, p. 3; "Women and the Gospel," *Christian Socialist*, March 15, 1914, pp. 12–13.

51. Edward Ellis Carr, "A Personal Word," *Christian Socialist*, July 20, 1911, p. 7; White, "Christian Socialist Fellowship," p. 49; Weinstein, *Decline of Socialism in America*, p. 20.

52. Carr, "The Social Message of Jesus," *Christian Socialist*, June 1–15, 1909 (double issue), pp. 7–8; Carr, "Program of Christian Socialism for Churches," *Christian Socialist*, September 15, 1908, pp. 1–2; Carr, "The Church and Capitalism," *Christian Socialist*, March 1, 1908, p. 4.

53. J. O. Bentall, "Why I Am a Christian Socialist," *Christian Socialist*, November 1, 1907, p. 7.

54. Edward Ellis Carr, "A Strong Man Joins Us," *Christian Socialist*, January 1, 1907, p. 1; "Bentall's Letter of Resignation," *Christian Socialist*, January 1, 1907, p. 2; White, "Christian Socialist Fellowship," p. 48.

55. Russell, *Bare Hands and Stone Walls*, p. 207; Weeks, "What the Christian Socialists Stand For," p. 1; Rufus W. Weeks, Letter to the Editor, *Christian Socialist*, July 15, 1905, p. 3; Weeks, "Why I Am in the Socialist Movement," *Christian Socialist*, August 1, 1912, pp. 1–2.

56. *The American Catholic Who's Who*, vol. 14: *1960–1961* (Gross Point, Mich.: Walter Romeg 1960), p. 456; Irwin St. John Tucker, "How I Became a Socialist," *Christian Socialist*, February 1, 1914, pp. 7–8.

57. Irwin St. John Tucker, "The Religion of a Socialist," *Christian Socialist*, March 1, 1914, pp. 1–2; Leslie Marcy, "The Emergency National Convention," *International Socialist Review* 17 (May, 1917): 670; Robert Justin Goldstein, *Political Repression in Modern America* (Cambridge: Schenkman, 1978), pp. 119–127; Tucker, "Apologia Pro Vinculis Meis," *Social Preparation for the Kingdom of God* 6 (October, 1919): 20; Shannon, *Socialist Party of America*, p. 113; Tucker, *The Geography of the Gods* (Chicago: the author, 1919), p. 150.

58. Ray H. Abrams, *Preachers Present Arms*, rev. ed. (Scottdale, Pa.: Herald Press, 1969), p. 50; Edward Ellis Carr, "Remove All Profits from War," *Christian Socialist*, May 2, 1917, p. 4; Carr, "The Future of Socialist Parties and of Socialism in America," *Christian Socialist* 14 (November, 1917): 11–12; Kenneth E. Hendrickson, Jr., "The Pro-War Socialists: The Social Democratic League and the Ill-Fated Drive for Industrial Democracy," *Labor History* 11 (Summer, 1970): 304–322; Weinstein, *Decline of Socialism in America*, p. 303.

59. Weinstein, *Decline of Socialism in America*, p. 22; William English Walling, *Progressivism and After* (New York: Macmillan, 1914), pp. 377–389; Edward Ellis Carr,

"White Women and Negroes," *Christian Socialist* February 23, 1911, p. 5; fund-raising advertisement in *Christian Socialist*, February 1, 1912, p. 4.

60. Robert H. Craig, "Liberative History and Liberation Ethics: A Case Study of American Methodism and Popular Struggle," in *The Annual of the Society of Christian Ethics*, ed. D. M. Yeager (Washington, D.C.: Georgetown University Press, 1987), pp. 151–153; Green, *Grass-Roots Socialism*, pp. 126–175; Burbank, *When Farmers Voted Red*, pp. 6–9, and Spratt quoted p. 21.

61. Burbank, *When Farmers Voted Red*, pp. 19–26.

62. William A. Ward, "Great Fighter against Socialism in Texas Surrenders," *Christian Socialist*, September 21, 1911, p. 1.

63. J. L. Hicks, "A Visit to Hamilton," *Christian Socialist*, September 21, 1911, pp. 1–2; "Hamilton's New Confession of Faith Ringing Message of Social Redemption," *Christian Socialist*, September 21, 1989, pp. 2–3.

64. Craig, "Friend or Foe?" pp. 54–60; "Julian," "Paganism and Christianity," *International Socialist Review* 1 (June, 1901): 753; Robert Rives LaMonte, Letter to the Editor, *International Socialist Review* 2 (December, 1901): 435–437.

65. "Mrs. O'Hare to the Preachers," *Christian Socialist*, March 30, 1911, p. 12; Friedberg, "Marxism in the United States," pp. x–xi, 2–7, 94–95; John Spargo, "Christian Socialism in America," *American Journal of Sociology*, May 1, 1907, p. 2.

66. Ernest Untermann, "Inductive Dialectic or Metaphysical Speculation," *Christian Socialist*, May 1, 1907, p. 2.

67. Carr, "Economic Science or Sectarian Dogmatism," pp. 1–2.

68. Edward Ellis Carr, "Echoes of the Explosion," *Christian Socialist*, December 1, 1908, p. 5; Mrs. Edward Ellis Carr, "Takes away the Scare and Prejudice," *Christian Socialist*, September 1, 1907, p. 6; Carr, "The Church and Capitalism," p. 4; Ward, "Greatest Fighter against Socialism in Texas Surrenders," p. 1.

69. Socialist Party, *Proceedings of the National Convention, 1908* (Chicago: n.p., 1908), pp. 191–194, 204–205, 321.

70. Salvatore, *Eugene V. Debs*, pp. 310–312; Harold W. Currie, "The Religious Views of Eugene V. Debs," *Mid-America* 54 (July, 1972): 147–156; Eugene V. Debs, "Prostitution of Religion," *Christian Socialist* 12 (December, 1915): 2; Debs, "Politicians and Preachers," *American Socialist*, June 24, 1916, reprinted in *Writings and Speeches of Eugene V. Debs*, ed. Arthur M. Schlesinger, Jr. (New York: Hermitage Press, 1948), p. 398; Debs, *Walls and Bars* (1927; rpt. Chicago: Charles H. Kerr, 1973), pp. 268–269, 285–286; Debs, "Jesus," in *The Cry for Justice: An Anthology of the Literature of Social Protest*, ed. Upton Sinclair (Philadelphia: John C. Winston, 1912), p. 345. For an interesting analysis of religion and radicalism, see Donald E. Winters, Jr., *The Soul of the Wobblies: The I.W.W., Religion, and American Culture in the Progressive Era, 1905–1917* (Westport: Greenwood Press, 1985).

71. Sarah N. Cleghorn, *Threescore* (New York: Harrison and Robert Haas, 1934), pp. 154–160; William L. O'Neill, ed., *Echoes of Revolt: "The Masses," 1911–1917* (Chicago: Quadrangle Books, 1966), p. 220.

72. James H. Cone, *For My People: Black Theology and the Black Church* (Maryknoll: Orbis Books, 1984), pp. 175–176.

73. Alexander Clark, "Socialism," *A.M.E. Church Review* 3 (July, 1886): 49–54; John R. Lynch, "Should Colored Men Join Labor Organizations?" *A.M.E. Church Review* 3 (October, 1886): 165–167.

74. T. McCants Stewart, "The Afro-American as a Factor in the Labor Problem," *A.M.E. Church Review* 6 (July, 1889): 30–38.

75. James Theodore Holly, "Socialism from the Biblical Point of View," *A.M.E. Church Review* 9 (1892–1893), reprinted in Foner, *Black Socialist Preacher*, pp. 269–281; David W. Dean, "James Theodore Holly," in *Dictionary of American Negro Biography*, ed. Rayford W. Logan and Michael R. Winston (New York: W. W. Norton, 1982), pp. 319–320; Moses, *Golden Age of Black Nationalism*, p. 18.

76. Two studies that refer to Woodbey and Slater are West, *Prophesy Deliverance!* pp. 39–40, 126–127, 172; and John C. Cort, *Christian Socialism: An Informal History* (Maryknoll: Orbis Books, 1988), pp. 256–260.

77. "George Washington Woodbey," *Who's Who of the Colored Race*, vol. 1: *1915*, ed. Frank Lincoln Mather (Detroit: Gale Research, 1915, 1976), pp. 290–291.

78. "Negro Delegate at Convention," *Chicago Socialist*, January 11, 1908, p. 2; Eliot White, "Bread upon the Waters," *Christian Socialist*, April 1, 1910, p. 3.

79. A. W. Ricker summarizes "The Political Economy of Jesus" in another of his articles, "What to Do and How to Do It," *Appeal to Reason*, October 31, 1903, p. 3; Barbara Leslie Epstein, *The Politics of Domesticity: Women, Evangelism, and Temperance in Nineteenth-Century America* (Middletown: Wesleyan University Press, 1981), pp. 122–123; Lawrence Goodwyn, *Democratic Promise: The Populist Moment in America* (New York: Oxford University Press, 1976), pp. 398–399; Elliott Shore, *Talkin' Socialism: J. A. Wayland and the Role of the Press in American Radicalism, 1890–1912* (Lawrence: University Press of Kansas, 1988), pp. 124–125.

80. Ricker, "What to Do and How to Do It," p. 3; "George Washington Woodbey," *Who's Who of the Colored Race*, p. 291; Foner, Introduction to *Black Socialist Preacher*, p. 7.

81. George Washington Woodbey, "Why the Socialists Must Reach the Churches with Their Message," *Christian Socialist* 12 (February, 1915): 5.

82. George Woodbey, *The Bible and Socialism* (1904), in *Black Socialist Preacher*, pp. 88–89, 134–135, 193–197.

83. George Woodbey, *What to Do and How to Do It; or, Socialism vs. Capitalism* (1903), in *Black Socialist Preacher*, pp. 44–47.

84. Woodbey, *The Bible and Socialism*, pp. 92–96.

85. George Woodbey, *The Distribution of Wealth* (1910), in *Black Socialist Preacher*, pp. 236–238; José Porfirio Miranda, *Marx and the Bible* (Maryknoll: Orbis Books, 1974); José Porfirio Miranda, *Communism in the Bible* (Maryknoll: Orbis Books, 1982), p. 2.

86. George Washington Woodbey, "The New Emancipation," *Chicago Daily Socialist* (January 18, 1909), and Woodbey, "Why the Negro Should Vote the Socialist Ticket" (n.d.), both in *Black Socialist Preacher*, pp. 247–250, 251–254.

87. Woodbey, "Why the Negro Should Vote the Socialist Ticket," pp. 251–254.

88. *Proceedings, National Convention of the Socialist Party* (Chicago, 1908), in Foner, *Black Socialist Preacher*, pp. 243–244.

89. Foner, Introduction, *Black Socialist Preacher*, pp. 32, 293–294; George W. Slater, Jr., "How and Why I Became a Socialist," *Chicago Daily Socialist* (September 8, 1908), in *Black Socialist Preacher*, pp. 296–298; *Who's Who of the Colored Race*, vol. 1: *1915*, p. 245; Allan H. Spear, *Black Chicago: The Making of a Negro Ghetto, 1890–1920* (Chicago: University of Chicago Press, 1967), pp. 7, 91; "Able Colored

Orator," *Christian Socialist*, May 23, 1912, p. 5; Slater, "The Negro and Socialism," *Christian Socialist*, July 1, 1913, p. 7.

90. George W. Slater, Jr., "Socialism and Social Service," *Christian Socialist* 12 (February, 1915): 3–4; S. P. Fullinwider, *The Mind and Mood of Black America* (Homewood, Ill.: Dorsey Press, 1969), pp. 36–37; Slater, "Mine Eyes Have Seen It," *Chicago Daily Socialist* (November 9, 1908), in *Black Socialist Preacher*, pp. 319–320.

91. Articles from *Chicago Daily Socialist*, "Abraham Lincoln a Socialist" (October 6, 1908), "Negroes Becoming Socialists" (September 15, 1908), "The Hell of War" (October 28, 1908), all in *Black Socialist Preacher*, pp. 310, 300–301, 315–316; Slater, "The Negro and Socialism," p. 7; Foner, Introduction, *Black Socialist Preacher*, pp. 336–338.

92. Reverdy C. Ransom, "The Negro and Socialism," *A.M.E. Church Review* 13 (1896–1897), in Foner, *Black Socialist Preacher*, p. 286; David Wills, "Reverdy C. Ransom: The Making of an A.M.E. Bishop," in *Black Apostles: Afro-American Clergy Confront the Twentieth Century*, ed. Randall K. Burkett and Richard Newman (Boston: G. K. Hall, 1978), p. 181.

93. Reverdy C. Ransom, *The Pilgrimage of Harriet Ransom's Son* (Nashville: Sunday School Union, n.d.), pp. 1–118.

94. Calvin Sylvester Morris, "Reverdy C. Ransom: A Pioneer Black Social Gospeler" (Ph.D. diss. Boston University, 1982), pp. 15–46, 134–140, 168–170.

95. Willis, "Reverdy C. Ransom," pp. 182–197; Mary M. Fisher, "Reverdy Cassius Ransom," *Dictionary of American Negro Biography*, pp. 512–513; Reverdy C. Ransom, *The Disadvantages and Opportunities of the Colored Youth* (Cleveland: Thomas and Mattill, 1894), pp. 42–52; W. E. Burghardt Du Bois, *The Negro Church* (Atlanta: Atlanta University Press, 1903), p. 85.

96. Ransom, *Pilgrimage*, pp. 113–114; William M. Tattle, "Labor Conflict and Racial Violence: The Black Worker in Chicago, 1894–1919," *Labor History* 10 (Summer, 1969): 408–432; Reverdy C. Ransom, *The Industrial and Social Conditions of the Negro: A Thanksgiving Sermon*, pamphlet (Chicago: Conservator Print, 1896).

97. Ransom, "The Negro and Socialism," pp. 286–289 (adapted from an address Ransom delivered to the Ohio Federation of Labor on July 4, 1896); Morris, "Reverdy C. Ransom," p. 53; Foner, *Organized Labor and the Black Worker*, p. 120.

98. Fisher, "Reverdy Cassius Ransom," pp. 513–514; Wills, "Reverdy C. Ransom," pp. 203–204.

99. Du Bois, *Dusk of Dawn*, pp. 87–92; Ransom, *Pilgrimage*, pp. 162–164; Marable, *W.E.B. Du Bois*, p. 57; August Meier, *Negro Thought in America, 1880–1915* (Ann Arbor: University of Michigan Press, 1963), pp. 178–179, 220; Gayraud S. Wilmore, *Black Religion and Black Radicalism*, 2nd ed. (Maryknoll: Orbis Books, 1983), p. 136.

100. Reverdy C. Ransom, "The Spirit of John Brown," in *The Spirit of Freedom and Justice: Orations and Speeches* (Nashville: A.M.E. Sunday School Union, 1926), pp. 16–25; W.E.B. Du Bois, "A Word," in Ransom, *The Negro: The Hope or the Despair of Christianity* (Boston: Ruth Hill, 1935). Du Bois more fully analyzes Brown's contribution to the struggle for black liberation in *John Brown* (1909; rpt. New York: International, 1987).

101. Reverdy C. Ransom, "Democracy, Disfranchisement, and the Negro," and "Lynching and American Public Opinion," in *The Spirit of Freedom and Justice*, pp. 42–50, 138–141.

102. Ransom, *The Negro*, pp. 4–7; Ransom, "Race Problem in a Christian State," *Spirit of Freedom and Justice*, pp. 128–132; Ransom, *Industrial and Social Conditions of the Negro*.

103. Ransom, "The Coming Vision," *A.M.E. Church Review* 37 (January, 1921): 135–139; Ransom, "The Spiritual Leadership of the Negro Ministry," *A.M.E. Church Review* 41 (January, 1925): 110–113.

104. Karl Marx and Friedrich Engels, *The Communist Manifesto* (New York: Monthly Review Press, 1964), p. 44; J. E. Franklin, *The Relation of Christianity and Socialism*, pamphlet (Philadelphia: American Baptist Publication Society, 1914), pp. 23–24.

105. West, "Marxist Theory and the Specificity of Afro-American Oppression," pp. 18–19; James H. Cone, "Sanctification and Liberation in the Black Religious Experience," in *Sanctification and Liberation*, ed. Theodore Runyon (Nashville: Abingdon Press, 1981), p. 188.

106. Du Bois to Du Bois Williams, October 8, 1946, in *The Correspondence of W. E. B. Du Bois*, vol. 3: *1944–1963*, ed. Herbert Aptheker (Amherst: University of Massachusetts Press, 1978), p. 117.

107. Reverdy C. Ransom, "No Palliation, Compromise, or Excuse for Race Segregation," *A.M.E. Church Review* 31 (January, 1915): 307–309.

Chapter Four

1. Frederick Douglass, "The Meaning of July Fourth for the Negro," in *The Life and Writings of Frederick Douglass*, vol. 2, ed. Philip S. Foner (New York: International, 1950), pp. 192, 198.

2. Charles H. Long, "Civil Rights—Civil Religion: Visible People and Invisible Religion," in *American Civil Religion*, ed. Russell F. Richey and Donald G. Jones (New York: Harper and Row, 1974), p. 214; Leon F. Litwack, "Trouble in Mind: The Bicentennial and the Afro-American Experience," *Journal of American History* 74 (September, 1987): 315–337.

3. Martin Luther King, Jr., "Letter from Birmingham City Jail," in *A Testament of Hope: The Essential Writings of Martin Luther King, Jr.*, ed. James Melvin Washington (San Francisco: Harper and Row, 1986), pp. 292–298; Joel Williamson, *The Crucible of Race* (New York: Oxford University Press, 1984), p. 488.

4. Another approach to the history of southern radicalism and Christian faith would be an analysis of the history of the Highlander Folk School.

5. Howard Kester, "Autobiographical Sketch," [1937?], pp. 1–3, 13, Howard Kester Papers, Southern Historical Collection University of North Carolina, Chapel Hill; Anthony P. Dunbar, *Against the Grain: Southern Radicals and Prophets, 1929–1959* (Charlottesville: University Press of Virginia, 1981), pp. 18–19; C. Vann Woodward, *The Strange Career of Jim Crow* (New York: Oxford University Press, 1957), p. 67; Williamson, *Crucible of Race*, p. 118. For additional statistics on lynching, see the NAACP study: *Thirty Years of Lynching in the United States, 1889–1918* (New York: Arno Press, 1919, 1969).

6. Kester, "Autobiographical Sketch," pp. 3–5; Dunbar, *Against the Grain*, pp. 19–21, 269–270; Robert F. Martin, "A Prophet's Pilgrimage: The Religious Radicalism of Howard Anderson Kester, 1921–1941," *Journal of Southern History* 48 (November, 1982): 513–515.

7. Norman F. Furniss, *The Fundamentalist Controversy, 1918–1931* (New Haven:

Yale University Press, 1954), p. 127; Ernest R. Sandeen, "Toward a Historical Interpretation of the Origins of Fundamentalism," *Church History* 36 (March, 1967): 67–74;
J. Gresham Machen, *Christianity and Liberalism* (Grand Rapids: Wm. B. Eerdmans,
1923), pp. 7–21; Eldred C. Vanderlaan, comp., *Fundamentalism versus Modernism*
(New York: H. W. Wilson, 1925), p. 391; Kester, "Autobiographical Sketch," pp. 5–7.

8. Kester, "Autobiographical Sketch," pp. 6–7; Dunbar, *Against the Grain*, pp.
21–26.

9. George B. Tindall, *The Emergence of the New South, 1913–1945* (Baton Rouge:
Louisiana State University Press, 1967), p. 549; Howard Kester to Alice Harris, July 7,
November 20, 1926, Howard Kester Papers.

10. Kester, "Autobiographical Sketch," pp. 7–8; Cedric Belfrage, *A Faith to Free a
People* (New York: Dryden Press, 1944), p. 43.

11. Bernard K. Johnpoll, *Pacifist's Progress: Norman Thomas and the Decline of
American Socialism* (Chicago: Quadrangle Books, 1970), pp. 10–25; Murray B. Seidler,
Norman Thomas: Respectable Rebel, 2nd ed. (Syracuse: Syracuse University Press,
1967), pp. 1–29; Ray H. Abrams, *Preachers Present Arms*, rev. ed. (Scottdale, Pa.:
Herald Press, 1933), pp. 49–75, 194–207; Leslie Marcy, "The Emergency National
Convention," *International Socialist Review* 17 (May, 1917): 670.

12. Kirby Page, "Socialism According to Thomas," *World Tomorrow* 14 (April,
1931), 119; "Fellowship of Socialist Christians," *World Tomorrow* 15 (February, 1932):
39; "The Fellowship of Socialist Christians," *World Tomorrow*, September 28, 1933,
p. 533; Reinhold Niebuhr, "Ex Cathedra," *World Tomorrow*, May 10, 1934, p. 218.

13. Kester, "Autobiographical Sketch," pp. 8–9; Howard Kester to George F. Jackson, February 9, 1933, Kester Papers.

14. Howard Kester, "Annual Report of Southern Secretary, Annual Conference of
the Fellowship of Reconciliation, October 1933," pp. 1–8, Kester Papers.

15. Brenda Bell and Fran Ansley, "Strike at Davidson-Wilder, 1932–1933," in
Working Lives: The Southern Exposure History of Labor in the South, ed. Marc S. Miller
(New York: Pantheon Books, 1980), pp. 81–96; Howard Kester, "Religion—Priestly
and Prophetic—in the South," *Radical Religion* 1 (Autumn, 1936): 28; Dunbar, *Against
the Grain*, p. 14.

16. Kester, "Annual Report of Southern Secretary, 1933," p. 1; Dunbar, *Against the
Grain*, pp. 51–51; Charles Chatfield, *For Peace and Justice: Pacifism in America, 1914–
1941* (Knoxville: University of Tennessee Press, 1971), pp. 191–197; Kirby Page, "The
Future of the Fellowship," *World Tomorrow*, January 4, 1934, p. 9; Page, "Unemployment—Shall We Nurse It or Cure It?" *Christian Century*, September 26, 1934, p. 1211.
Murray Kempton's amusing biographical portrait of Matthews is his essay "O'er Moor
and Fen," in *Part of Our Time* (New York: Simon and Schuster, 1955). Interesting as
well is Matthews's own uncritical autobiography *Odyssey of a Fellow Traveler* (New
York: Mount Vernon, 1938).

17. Reinhold Niebuhr, "Why I Leave the F.O.R.," *Christian Century* January 3,
1934, pp. 17–19; Niebuhr, "Radical Religion," *Radical Religion* 1 (Autumn, 1935): 5;
John Strachey, *The Coming Struggle for Power* (New York: Covici Friede, 1933), p. 155;
Irving Bernstein, *Turbulent Years: A History of the American Worker, 1933–1941* (Bos-
ton: Houghton Mifflin, 1971), p. 173; Harry F. Ward, "Some Fascist Tendencies in the
United States," *Social Questions Bulletin* 24 (October, 1934): 1–4; Julius Braunthal,

History of the International, vol. 2: *1914–1943* (New York: Frederick A. Praeger, 1967), pp. 372–415.

18. Kester, "Autobiographical Sketch," p. 10; Ward Rodgers to Kester, September 13, 1934, Kester Papers; Kester, interview by Jacquelyn Hall and William Finger, July 22, 1974, Southern Oral History Program, Southern Historical Collection, University of North Carolina, Chapel Hill, p. 34; H. L. Mitchell, *Mean Things Happening in This Land* (Montclair, N.J.: Allanheld, Osmun, 1979), p. 64.

19. Robert Elwood Wenger, "Social Aspects of American Christianity, 1930–1960, as Observed in the Life and Work of Claude Williams" (M.A. thesis, Southern Methodist University, 1962), p. 6; Belfrage, *Faith to Free a People*, pp. 7–27; David E. Harrell, Jr., "Tennessee," in *Religion in the Southern States*, ed. Samuel S. Hill (Macon: Mercer University Press, 1983), pp. 207, 305; Edwin Scott Gaustad, *Historical Atlas of Religion in America* (New York: Harper and Row, 1962), p. 88.

20. Claude Williams to Helen Ridick Wilson, September 10, 1933, Williams to M. L. Gillespie, November 9, 1933, Claude C. Williams Collection, Correspondence and Papers, 1929–1979, Archives of Labor and Urban History, Wayne State University, Detroit.

21. "The Circuit Rider: Claude Williams," in *Hard Times: An Oral History of the Great Depression*, comp. Studs Terkel (New York: Avon Books, 1970), pp. 377–378; Belfrage, *Faith to Free a People*, pp. 29–65.

22. Harry Emerson Fosdick, *The Modern Use of the Bible* (New York: Macmillan, 1924), preface, n.p.; Bill Troy and Claude Williams, "People's Institute of Applied Religion," *Southern Exposure* 4 (Fall, 1976): 47.

23. Mark Naison, "Claude and Joyce Williams: Pilgrims of Justice," *Southern Exposure* 1 (Winter, 1974): 41; Owen Whitfield to Williams, November 11, 1942, Williams Collection.

24. Willard Uphaus, "A Foul Miscarriage of Justice: A Report of the National Religion and Labor Foundation on the Dismissal of the Reverend Claude C. Williams from the Pulpit of the First Presbyterian Church in Paris, Arkansas," Summer, 1934, pp. 1–11, Williams Collection.

25. Claude C. Williams, "Diary of Paris Pastorate," June, 1930–April, 1935, Williams Collection; Belfrage, *Faith to Free a People*, pp. 66–116.

26. Naison, "Claude and Joyce Williams," pp. 41–42.

27. Belfrage, *Faith to Free a People*, pp. 103–139; Williams, "Diary of Paris Pastorate"; Claude C. Williams, "The Proletarian and Labor Temple," [1932?], Williams Collection, pp. 1–6.

28. Claude C. Williams to O. Austin Gardner, September 9, 1946, Williams Collection.

29. Uphaus, "Foul Miscarriage of Justice," pp. 1–17.

30. Ibid.

31. Claude Williams to M. L. Gillespie, January 18, 1933, J. W. Gray to Warren H. Wilson, May 15, 1935, both in Williams Collection.

32. Claude Williams to Warren H. Wilson, June 18, 1934, Williams Collection.

33. Williams, "Diary of Paris Pastorate"; Belfrage, *Faith to Free a People*, pp. 151–191; Naison, "Claude and Joyce Williams," p. 44; "The Circuit Rider," p. 378; mimeographed letter from W. A. Gilbert, state secretary of the Socialist party of Arkan-

sas, to members of the executive committee, n.d., Claude Williams to W. A. Gilbert, November 2, 1935, both in Williams Collection; Dunbar, *Against the Grain*, pp. 133–135.

34. Bruce Palmer, *"Man over Money": The Southern Populist Critique of American Capitalism* (Chapel Hill: University of North Carolina Press, 1980), p. xiv; John McDermott, *The Crisis in the Working Class: Some Arguments for a New Labor Movement* (Boston: South End Press, 1980), pp. 43–44; Charles S. Johnson, Edwin R. Embree, and W. W. Alexander, *The Collapse of Cotton Tenancy* (Chapel Hill: University of North Carolina Press, 1935), pp. 1–8; T. J. Woofter, Jr., *Landlord and Tenant on the Cotton Plantation* (Washington, D.C.: Works Progress Administration, 1936), pp. 91–106; Donald H. Grubbs, *Cry from the Cotton: The Southern Tenant Farmers' Union and the New Deal* (Chapel Hill: University of North Carolina, 1971), p. 8; Jerold S. Auerbach, "Southern Tenant Farmers: Socialist Critics of the New Deal," *Labor History* 7 (Winter, 1966): 5. Caldwell is quoted by Charles M. McConnell in "Farm Tenants and Sharecroppers," *Missionary Review of the World* 60 (June, 1937): 289.

35. Mitchell, *Mean Things Happening*, pp. 27–47; Stuart Jamieson, *Labor Unionism in American Agriculture*, Bureau of Labor Statistics Bulletin 836 (Washington, D.C.: U.S. Government Printing Office, 1945), p. 302; David Eugene Conrad, *The Forgotten Farmer: The Story of the Sharecroppers in the New Deal* (Urbana: University of Illinois Press, 1965), p. 84; Arthur I. Waskow, *From Race Riot to Sit-In, 1919 and the 1960s* (Garden City: Doubleday, 1966), pp. 121–142; Tindall, *Emergence of the New South*, p. 153; "The Real Causes of Two Race Riots," *The Crisis* 19 (December, 1919): 56–62; Howard Kester, *Revolt among the Sharecroppers* (New York: Covici Friede, 1936), p. 56.

36. C. T. Carpenter, "King Cotton's Slaves," *Scribner's Magazine* 98 (October, 1935): pp. 193–199; Conrad, *Forgotten Farmer*, p. 87; Mitchell, *Mean Things Happening*, pp. 42–92; Grubbs, *Cry from the Cotton*, pp. 30–61, 84–86; Jamieson, *Labor Unionism in American Agriculture*, pp. 307–310; J. R. Butler to Marvin Sanford, October 8, 1938, Southern Tenant Farmers' Union Papers, Southern Historical Collection, University of North Carolina, Chapel Hill; "Local Questionnaire Returns: Preliminary Report, June 29, 1937," STFU Papers.

37. H. L. Mitchell, interview by Professor Pollitt, University of North Carolina Law School, February 1, 1974, STFU Papers; Kester, *Revolt among the Sharecroppers*, p. iii.

38. Kester, "Religion—Priestly and Prophetic," pp. 29–31; "Constitution and By-Laws of the Southern Tenant Farmers' Union" (n.d., n.p.), STFU Papers; Reinhold Niebuhr, "Meditations from Mississippi," *Christian Century*, February 10, 1937, p. 184.

39. *Sharecroppers' Voice* 1 (May, 1935): 1, copy in STFU Papers; Kester, *Revolt among the Sharecroppers*, pp. 60–61, 84; *Sharecroppers' Voice* 1 (April, 1935): 4, copy in STFU Papers.

40. John Steinbeck, *The Grapes of Wrath* (New York: Viking Press, 1939, 1958), p. 572; Mitchell, *Mean Things Happening*, pp. 52–54.

41. Kester, "Religion—Priestly and Prophetic," p. 29; Mitchell, *Mean Things Happening*, pp. 66, 73, 171–177; Kester, *Revolt among the Sharecroppers*, p. 64; Grubbs, *Cry from the Cotton*, pp. 67–68; E. B. McKinney to Wiley Harris, July 29, August 11, 1938, STFU Papers; Mark D. Naison, "Black Agrarian Radicalism in the Great Depres-

sion: The Threads of a Lost Tradition," *Journal of Ethnic Studies* 1 (Fall, 1973): 56–61; Claude Williams to Don Henderson, n.d. [?1935–1939], Williams Collection.

42. "Biographical Sketch of Owen H. Whitfield," two pages (1941), Williams Collection; H. L. Mitchell to James Meyer, February 2, 1939, STFU Papers; Louis Cantor, *A Prologue to the Protest Movement: The Missouri Sharecroppers Roadside Demonstration of 1939* (Durham: Duke University Press, 1969), pp. 30–32, 159–163; Cedric Belfrage, "Cotton-Patch Moses," *Harper's Magazine* 97 (November, 1948): 94–103; Mark Naison, "Claude Williams Talks about Owen Whitfield," *Radical Religion* 4/2 (1978): 24–26.

43. "A Letter from the South: What Happened to the Missouri Sharecroppers' Demonstrators," circular, STFU Papers.

44. Grubbs, *Cry from the Cotton*, pp. 75–76; Martin, "Prophet's Pilgrimage," p. 523; Cantor, *Prologue to the Protest Movement*, p. 19; David Burgess, "The Fellowship of Southern Churchmen: Its History and Promise," *Prophetic Religion* 13 (Winter, 1953): 3–4; H. L. Mitchell to L. B. Granger, September 30, 1935, STFU Papers.

45. Howard Kester, "The Struggle against Peonage," address delivered before the Twenty-Sixth Annual Conference of the NAACP, June 6, 1935, p. 11, Kester Papers.

46. Kester, "Religion—Priestly and Prophetic," p. 30; *Sharecroppers Voice* 1 (April, 1935): 3; Kester, *Revolt among the Sharecroppers*, pp. 88, 96; Mitchell, *Mean Things Happening*, pp. 113–117; Kester, "Autobiographical Sketch," p. 11; Kester and Evelyn Smith, *Ceremony of the Land*, pamphlet (Memphis: Southern Tenant Farmers Union, 1937), pp. 3–16, copy in Kester Papers.

47. Kester, "Autobiographical Sketch," pp. 11–12; Howard Kester, "A Statement of Faith Presented to the 'Examiners' before my Ordination for the Ministry, October, 1936," Kester Papers.

48. H. L. Mitchell to Norman Thomas, William Amberson, and Burt [?], September 26, 1937, STFU Papers; Claude Williams to E. B. McKinney, October 1, 1938, McKinney to Donald Henderson, January, 1939, Williams Collection.

49. Belfrage, *Faith to Free a People*, pp. 192–204.

50. Mitchell, *Mean Things Happening*, pp. 87–89; Grubbs, *Cry from the Cotton*, pp. 109–113.

51. Claude Williams to Willard E. Uphaus, March 5, 1936, September 29, 1939, Williams Collection; Winifred L. Chappell, "Williams Active in State for Past Seven Years," *Commonwealth College Fortnightly* 13 (August, 1937): 1, copy in Raymond and Charolette Moskowitz Koch Collection, Papers, 1925–1982, Archives of Labor and Urban Affairs, Wayne State University, Detroit.

52. William H. Cobb and Donald H. Grubbs, "Arkansas' Commonwealth College and the Southern Tenant Farmers' Union," *Arkansas Historical Quarterly* 25 (Winter, 1966): 293–311; William H. Cobb, "Commonwealth College and the Southern Labor Movement, 1931–1940," in *Southern Workers and Their Unions, 1880–1975*, ed. Merle E. Reed, Leslie S. Hough, and Gary M. Fink (Westport: Greenwood Press, 1981), pp. 81–99; Claude Williams, "The Program of Commonwealth College," *Commonwealth College Fortnightly*, November 15, 1937, pp. 1, 4, Koch Collection.

53. "Cotton Preachers Institute Held at Little Rock," *The Commoner* 1 (August, 1938): 1, 4, "Williams Discusses Relationship between Religion and the Labor Movement in Closing Series of Lectures," *Commonwealth College Fortnightly* 14 (January,

1938): 3, both in Koch Collection; Claude Williams to Philip Randolph, March 18, 1940, Williams Collection.

54. Kester, *Revolt among the Sharecroppers*, pp. 50, 85–88; Howard Kester to Richard B. Gregg, July 28, 1937, STFU Papers; Grubbs, *Cry from the Cotton*, pp. 65–66.

55. Philip S. Foner, "Notes to the Original *Talking Union*," *Talking Union* Folkways Record Album No. FH 5285 (New York: Folkways Records and Service, 1955); Mitchell, *Mean Things Happening*, pp. 111–112, 347; M. H. Barnes, "Song," *STFU News* 3 (September, 1937): 1–2.

56. John H. Ward, "Judgement," *Now and Then*, mimeographed publication, March 15, 1935, pp. 11–12, STFU Papers; "Minister Forbidden to Follow His Master's Footsteps," *STFU News* 1 (January, 1936): 4, STFU Papers.

57. H. L. Mitchell to Howard Kester, September 1, 1937, STFU Papers; Claude Williams to Maynard C. Krueger, January 20, 1937, Williams Collection; Ward Rodgers to Howard Kester and H. L. Mitchell, March 16, 1935, STFU Papers; Williams to Mitchell, February 19, 1976, Williams Collection; Grubbs, *Cry from the Cotton*, pp. 162–192; Lowell K. Dyson, "The Southern Tenant Farmers Union and Depression Politics," *Political Science Quarterly* 88 (June, 1973): 233–234; Sue Thrasher and Leah Wise, "The Southern Tenant Farmers' Union," *Southern Exposure* 1 (Winter, 1974): 28–32; Norman Thomas to Leland Mitchell, September 29, 1937, STFU Papers.

58. Williams, interview by Robert Elwood Wenger, July 7, 1962, app. A, in Wenger, "Social Aspects of American Christianity," pp. 139–142; Williams to Mabel Fulks, May 24, 1975, Williams Collection; "Summary Minutes of the National Executive Meeting of the Southern Tenant Farmers' Union," September 16–17, 1938, pp. 1–2, STFU Papers.

59. Martin, "Prophet's Pilgrimage," pp. 529–530; Dunbar, *Against the Grain*, pp. 191–195, 207–211; John A. Hutchison, "Two Decades of Social Christianity," in *Christian Faith and Social Action*, ed. Hutchison (New York: Charles Scribner's Sons, 1953), pp. 1–22; Ronald Stone, *Reinhold Niebuhr: Prophet to Politicians* (Nashville: Abingdon Press, 1972), pp. 131–211; Arthur Schlesinger, Jr., "Reinhold Niebuhr's Role in American Political Thought and Life," in *Reinhold Niebuhr: His Religious, Social, and Political Thought* (New York: Macmillan, 1961), pp. 126–150; Claude Williams to William F. Cochran, March 21, 1941, Williams to Philip Randolph, March 28, 1940, Williams Collection.

60. Naison, "Claude and Joyce Williams," pp. 11–12; Troy and Williams, "People's Institute of Applied Religion," pp. 48–51; Miriam Crist, "Winifred Chappell: 'Everybody on the Left Knew Her,' " *Radical Religion* 5/1 (1980): 25–27; Belfrage, *Faith to Free a People*, pp. 235–236; Alva Taylor, "Rev. Claude—a Modern Prophet among the Share Croppers," in pamphlet titled *People's Institute of Applied Religion* (Evansville: People's Institute of Applied Religion, 1942), p. 4, copy in Williams Collection.

61. Troy and Williams, "People's Institute of Applied Religion," pp. 48–49; *People's Institute of Applied Religion*, mimeographed newsletter (Spring, 1952): 1, *People's Institute of Applied Religion*, pamphlet (Little Rock: People's Institute of Applied Religion, 1941), Claude C. Williams, *The Scriptural Heritage of the People*, pamphlet (Detroit: Detroit Presbytery, 1943), pp. 8, 14, 16, all in Williams Collection.

62. Claude C. Williams, *Religion: Barrier or Bridge to a People's World?* pam-

phlet (Birmingham: People's Institute of Applied Religion, 1947), pp. 48–64, copy in Williams Collection.

63. Ibid.

64. Ibid.

65. Belfrage, *Faith to Free a People*, pp. 231–245; Vernon G. Olson to Claude Williams, May 27, 1940, Williams Collection.

66. Troy and Williams, "People's Institute of Applied Religion," p. 51; Taylor, "Rev. Claude," p. 6; Oscar G. Starreet, Henry D. Jones, and Robert G. Stranger to Mrs. W. M. Ostrander, February 15, 1941, Williams to Jones, April 3, 1942, Williams to the Presbytery of Detroit, August 30, 1953, Williams Collection.

67. David Gartman, *Auto Slavery: The Labor Process in the American Automobile Industry, 1897–1950* (New Brunswick: Rutgers University Press, 1986), pp. 138–141; Melvin G. Holli, ed., *Detroit* (New York: New Viewpoints, 1976), pp. 118–131, 187–189; Robert Shogan and Tom Craig, *The Detroit Race Riot* (Philadelphia: Chilton Books, 1964), pp. 19–23, 26–33; John C. Leggett, *Class, Race, and Labor: Working-Class Consciousness in Detroit* (New York: Oxford University Press, 1968), pp. 51–55; Belfrage, *Faith to Free a People*, p. 277.

68. Williams, *Scriptural Heritage of the People*, pp. 11–12, 15–18.

69. Belfrage, *Faith to Free a People*, pp. 288–291; "People's Institute of Applied Religion, Inc.: A Report of Action and for Action" (c. 1943), pp. 5–6, Williams Collection.

70. Belfrage, *Faith to Free a People*, pp. 248–249, 260–261, 267–270; "Oral History: Blacks in the Labor Movement," the Reverend Charles Hill, interview by Roberta McBride, May 8, 1967, pp. 1–6, Archives of Labor History and Urban Affairs, Wayne State University, Detroit.

71. Belfrage, *Faith to Free a People*, pp. 248–249, 260–261, 267–270; Williams, *Scriptural Heritage of the People*, p. 4.

72. Belfrage, *Faith to Free a People*, pp. 286–287; "People's Institute of Applied Religion, Inc.: A Report," pp. 1–8; *People's Institute of Applied Religion* (Spring, 1952), p. 2; Claude Williams to the Presbytery of Detroit, August 30, 1953, Williams Collection; "Memorial Service: Claude Williams, August 4, 1979, p. 3, Williams Collection.

73. Gunnar Myrdal, quoted in C. Eric Lincoln, *Race, Religion, and the Continuing American Dilemma* (New York: Hill and Wang, 1984).

74. Claude Williams, " 'White Problem': A Positive Religious View," unpublished address (n.d.), Williams, "The Need for Black and White Working Class Unity," address before the Blount County chapter of the National Democratic Party of Alabama, January 26, 1970, both in Williams Collection.

75. Williams, interview by Wenger, pp. 120–162; Howard Kester, "Friends of the Soil" (1940), pp. 4, 36, Kester Papers.

76. "People's Institute of Applied Religion, Inc.: A Report," p. 3; D. C. Williams, "Startled" (n.d.), Williams Collection.

Chapter Five

1. William Appleman Williams, *The Great Evasion* (Chicago: Quadrangle Books, 1964), pp. 12–13; Warren R. Copeland, *Economic Justice* (Nashville: Abingdon Press, 1988), p. 83.

2. Karl Marx, "On the Jewish Question," in *Early Writings*, ed. T. B. Bottomore (New York: McGraw-Hill, 1964), pp. 24–25; Karl Marx, *Der Volksstaat* (October 2, 1872), in *On Revolution*, Karl Marx Library, vol. 1, ed. Saul K. Padover (New York: McGraw-Hill, 1971), p. 64.

3. Sara M. Evans and Harry C. Boyte, *Free Spaces: The Sources of Democratic Change in America* (New York: Harper and Row, 1986), pp. 184–189; Norman Birnbaum, *The Radical Renewal: The Politics of Ideas in Modern America* (New York: Pantheon Books, 1988), pp. 178–185.

4. John Macmurray, *Challenges to the Churches: Religion and Democracy* (London: Kegan Paul, Trench, Trubner, 1941), pp. 9, 43–44, 63.

5. John Macquarrie, *Twentieth Century Religious Thought* (New York: Harper and Row, 1963), pp. 340, 344; Arthur Schlesinger, Jr., "Reinhold Niebuhr's Role in American Political Thought and Life," in *Reinhold Niebuhr: His Religious, Social, and Political Thought* (New York: Macmillan, 1961), p. 149; William L. O'Neill, *A Better World* (New York: Simon and Schuster, 1982), p. 348; Beverly Wildung Harrison, *Making the Connections: Essays in Feminist Social Ethics*, ed. Carol S. Robb (Boston: Beacon Press, 1985), p. 8.

6. Franz J. Hinkelammert, *The Ideological Weapons of Death: A Theological Critique of Capitalism* (Maryknoll: Orbis Books, 1986), p. viii.

7. Gérard Fourez, *Liberation Ethics* (Philadelphia: Temple University Press, 1982), pp. 205–215.

8. J. King Gordon, "A Christian Socialist in the 1930s," in *The Social Gospel in Canada*, ed. Richard Allen (Ottawa: National Museums of Canada, 1975), pp. 125–126; Robert H. Craig, "An Introduction to the Life and Thought of Harry F. Ward," *Union Seminary Review* 24 (Summer, 1969): 336.

9. Richard Wrightman Fox, *Reinhold Niebuhr: A Biography* (San Francisco: Harper and Row, 1987), p. 7.

10. Fox, *Reinhold Niebuhr*, p. 41; Reinhold Niebuhr, "Lessons of the Detroit Experience," *Christian Century*, April 21, 1965, p. 488; Niebuhr, *Leaves from the Notebook of a Tamed Cynic* (Chicago: Willett, Clark, and Colby, 1929), p. 111; Niebuhr, *Love and Justice: Selections from the Shorter Writings of Reinhold Niebuhr*, ed. D. B. Robertson (Cleveland: World, 1957), pp. 98–108; Niebuhr, "Christianity and Contemporary Politics," *Christian Century*, April 17, 1924, pp. 498–499.

11. Niebuhr, *Leaves from the Notebook*, pp. 85, 89–90, 94–95.

12. Ronald Stone, *Reinhold Niebuhr: Prophet to Politicians* (Nashville: Abingdon Press, 1972), pp. 54–91, 168–314; Paul Merkley, *Reinhold Niebuhr: A Political Account* (Montreal: McGill-Queen's University Press, 1975), pp. 63–125, 166–200; Christopher Lasch, *The New Radicalism in America, 1889–1963* (New York: Alfred A. Knopf, 1965), pp. 299–303; Louis Althusser, *For Marx* (New York: Vintage Books, 1970), pp. 12–14. Another approach to Niebuhr is to realize that for all his critique of the pitfalls of liberalism, he never really overcame the limits of liberal categories in dealing with the individual and society. See Ruth L. Smith, "Reinhold Niebuhr and History: The Elusive Liberal Critique," *Horizons* 15 (Fall, 1988): 283–298.

13. Broadus Mitchell, *Depression Decade: From New Era through New Deal* (New York: Reinhart, 1947), p. 451; David R. Roediger and Philip S. Foner, *Our Own Time: A History of American Labor and the Working Day* (London: Verso, 1989), p. 234;

William E. Leuchtenberg, "The Great Depression," in *The Comparative Approach to American History*, ed. C. Vann Woodward (New York: Basic Books, 1968), p. 297; Thomas Wolfe, *You Can't Go Home Again* (New York: Charles Scribner's Sons, 1940), pp. 369–370.

14. "More Important Than Prohibition," *World Tomorrow* 14 (January, 1931): 7; "The Socialist Party," *World Tomorrow* 15 (May, 1932): 132; Bernard K. Johnpoll, *Pacifist's Progress: Norman Thomas and the Decline of American of Socialism* (Chicago: Quadrangle Books, 1970), pp. 84–86; Murray B. Seidler, *Norman Thomas: Respectable Rebel*, 2nd ed. (Syracuse: Syracuse University Press, 1967), pp. 1–29; "The Future of Norman Thomas," *Christian Century*, November 23, 1932, p. 1431; Kirby Page, "Socialism according to Thomas," *World Tomorrow* 14 (April, 1931): 119.

15. John A. Hutchison, "Two Decades of Social Christianity," in *Christian Faith and Social Action*, ed. Hutchison (New York: Charles Scribner's Sons, 1953), p. 2; "Fellowship of Socialist Christians," *World Tomorrow* 15 (February, 1932): 39; Correspondence of Walter Warner, September 21, 1934, Fellowship of Socialist Christians Papers, Union Theological Seminary, New York; "The Fellowship of Socialist Christians," *World Tomorrow*, September 28, 1933, p. 533; "Membership Letter," December 15, 1935, Fellowship of Socialist Christians Papers.

16. "Thomas for President," *World Tomorrow* 15 (July, 1932): 195; "The Fellowship of Socialist Christians," *Radical Religion* 2 (Winter, 1936): 2; Reinhold Niebuhr, "The Revolutionary Moment," *American Socialist Quarterly* 4 (June, 1935): 8–13; Niebuhr, "Our Romantic Radicals," *Christian Century*, April 10, 1935, p. 474; Niebuhr, "Radical Religion," *Radical Religion* 1 (Autumn, 1935): 3–5; Niebuhr, "The Idea of Progress and Socialism," *Radical Religion* 1 (Spring, 1936): 28; "Paul Blanshard, Ex-Socialist," *World Tomorrow*, September 28, 1933, p. 532.

17. John C. Bennett, *Social Salvation* (New York: Charles Scribner's Sons, 1935), p. 3.

18. Reinhold Niebuhr, *Moral Man and Immoral Society* (New York: Charles Scribner's Sons, 1932), pp. xi–xxv, 15, 18, 21, 44, 144, 149, 163, 166.

19. Niebuhr, *Moral Man and Immoral Society*, pp. 198–199; J. King Gordon, "The Twilight of This Age" (a review of *Reflections on the End of an Era*), *World Tomorrow*, March 1, 1934, p. 115. For a more detailed analysis of Niebuhr's European Socialist orientation, see Donald Meter, *The Protestant Search for Political Realism, 1919–1941* (Berkeley: University of California Press, 1961); and Stone, *Reinhold Niebuhr*.

20. Reinhold Niebuhr, *Reflections on the End of an Era* (New York: Charles Scribner's Sons, 1934), pp. 31–32, 78–79, 161, 168–169, 187–189, 210.

21. James Gilbert, *Designing the Industrial State* (Chicago: Quadrangle Books, 1972), p. 257; Karl Marx, "Critique of the Gotha Program," in *The Marx-Engels Reader*, ed. Robert C. Tucker (New York: W. W. Norton, 1972), p. 388; Harrison, *Making the Connections*, p. 61; Reeve Vanneman and Lynn Weber Cannon, *The American Perception of Class* (Philadelphia: Temple University Press, 1987), pp. 1–16, 283–310; Alan Wolfe, *The Seamy Side of Democracy: Repression in America* (New York: David McKay, 1972), pp. 82–85.

22. George Hammar, *Christian Realism in Contemporary American Theology* (Uppsala: A.-b. Lundequistska, 1940), p. 183; Reinhold Niebuhr, "Marx, Barth, and Israel's Prophets," *Christian Century* 52 (January, 1935): 138–140; Niebuhr, "Is Religion

Counter-Revolutionary?" *Radical Religion* 1 (Autumn, 1935): 14–20; Niebuhr, "The Ethic of Jesus and the Social Problem," *Religion in Life* 1 (Spring, 1932): 198–200; Niebuhr, *An Interpretation of Christian Ethics* (1935; New York: Living Age Books, 1956), p. 169.

23. Reinhold Niebuhr, "Christian Politics and Communist Religion," in *Christianity and the Social Revolution*, ed. John Lewis (London: Victor Gollancz, 1935), pp. 460–471; Niebuhr, *Christianity and Power Politics* (New York: Charles Scribner's Sons, 1940), p. 156; Niebuhr, "Russia and Karl Marx," *The Nation*, May 7, 1938, p. 531; Niebuhr, *Beyond Tragedy* (New York: Charles Scribner's Sons, 1937), p. 130.

24. Reinhold Niebuhr, "Our Mad World," *Radical Religion* 3 (Spring, 1938): p. 2; Niebuhr, "Russia and Karl Marx," p. 530; Leon Trotsky, *Stalin* (New York: Stein and Day, 1967), pp. 365–421; Niebuhr, "The Hitler-Stalin Pact," *Radical Religion* 4 (Fall, 1939): 3. For insights into Trotskyite and left-wing Communist opposition to Stalin, see the works of Victor Serge, particularly *From Lenin to Stalin* (New York: Pioneer, 1937) and *Memories of a Revolutionary, 1901–1941* (London: Oxford University Press, 1963).

25. Reinhold Niebuhr, "Ten Years That Shook My World," *Christian Century*, April 26, 1939, p. 543; Niebuhr, *Christianity and Power Politics*, pp. 137, 154, 169; Gordon, "A Christian Socialist in the 1930s," p. 137.

26. Reinhold Niebuhr, "A Protest against a Dilemma's Two Horns," *World Politics* 2 (April, 1950): 341, 343–344.

27. Lasch, *New Radicalism in America*, pp. 300–302; June Bingham, *Courage to Change: An Introduction to the Life and Thought of Reinhold Niebuhr* (New York: Charles Scribner's Sons, 1961), p. 368; Alexander Bloom, *Prodigal Sons: The New York Intellectuals and Their World* (New York: Oxford University Press, 1986), pp. 189–190; Niebuhr, *The Irony of American History* (New York: Charles Scribner's Sons, 1952), p. 1, 163–166; Niebuhr, *Pious and Secular America* (New York: Charles Scribner's Sons, 1958), pp. 43–44; Niebuhr, *Christian Realism and Political Problems* (New York: Charles Scribner's Sons, 1953), pp. 34–37; Fox, *Reinhold Niebuhr*, pp. 255–256. For an interesting analysis of the extent to which attitudes toward the Soviet Union had less to do with the actuality of Soviet aggression and more with domestic political patterns, see Alan Wolfe *The Rise and Fall of the 'Soviet Threat': Domestic Sources of the Cold War Consensus* (Washington, D.C.: Institute for Foreign Policy, 1979).

28. Niebuhr, *Irony of American History*, pp. 95–103; David Milton, *The Politics of U.S. Labor* (New York: Monthly Review Press, 1982), pp. 159–162; "Once upon a Shop Floor: An Interview with David Montgomery," *Radical History Review* 23 (Spring, 1980): 40–41; Lasch, *New Radicalism in America*, p. 301.

29. Fox, *Reinhold Niebuhr*, p. 252; J. B. Matthews, "Red Propaganda Has Influenced 7,000 U.S. Protestant Clergymen," *Look*, November 17, 1953, pp. 33–35; Reinhold Niebuhr, "To Suspect Innocent Ones of Guilt Does Not Make Guilty Men Innocent," *Look* November 27, 1953, p. 37; Niebuhr, "Editorial Notes," *Christianity and Crisis*, March 16, 1953, p. 26.

30. Niebuhr, *Irony of American History*, pp. 112–113; Niebuhr, *Faith and Politics*, ed. Ronald Stone (New York: George Braziller, 1968), pp. 215–218; Niebuhr, "Well-Tempered Evangelism," *New Republic*, June 26, 1961, quoted in Merkley, *Reinhold Niebuhr*, p. 196; Charles West, *Communism and the Theologians* (London: SCM Press, 1958), pp. 168–169.

31. Craig, "Introduction to the Life and Thought of Ward," pp. 331–332; Eugene P. Link, *Labor-Religion Prophet: The Times and Life of Harry F. Ward* (Boulder, Colo.: Westview Press, 1984), pp. 2–5. Biographical material is also drawn from personal interviews with Ward's son, Lynd Ward, December 1, 1967, March 15, 1968, and February 16, 1969, as well as a paper by Carl E. Hester, "The Thought and Career of Harry F. Ward," 1961, Union Theological Seminary, New York, which was based on a personal interview with Harry F. Ward in the spring of 1961. Maldwyn Edwards, *Methodism and England* (London: Epworth Press, 1943), p. 59; Harry F. Ward, *Which Way Religion?* (New York: Macmillan, 1931), p. 37.

32. Craig, "Introduction to the Life and Thought of Ward," pp. 332–335; Ward, "Why I Have Found Life Worth Living," *Christian Century*, March 1, 1928, p. 282. Years later Ward acknowledged that Gray was "my first and has been my continuous teacher in economics." Harry F. Ward, *Our Economic Morality and the Ethic of Jesus* (New York: Macmillan, 1929), p. vii. For an example of the type of analysis Gray applied to economic and religious issues, see Gray, *The Economic Order: What Is It? What Is It Worth* (New York: George H. Doran Company, 1923). Ward wrote to George Albert Coe, "In thinking of my activities you should remember that you have been one of the two chief influences in the shaping of my mind." See Ward to Coe, January 6, 1946, George A. Coe Papers, Archives and Manuscripts, Yale Divinity School.

33. Charles J. Bushnell, *The Social Problems at the Chicago Stock Yards* (Chicago: University of Chicago Press, 1902), p. 60; Edith Abbott, *The Tenements of Chicago, 1908–1935* (Chicago: University of Chicago Press, 1936), pp. 130–133.

34. Craig, "Introduction to the Life and Thought of Ward," pp. 334–335; Eugene Link, "Dr. Harry F. Ward Centennial," *Social Questions Bulletin* 63 (October, 1973): 26; Link, *Labor-Religion Prophet*, pp. 16–23; Ward, "Why I Have Found Life Worth Living," p. 282; Ward, "Some Things I Have Learned While Teaching," *Alumni Bulletin* (Union Theological Seminary) 16 (June, 1941): pp. 3, 7; Mary Jo Deegan, *Jane Adams and the Men of the Chicago School, 1892–1918* (New Brunswick, N.J.: Transaction Books, 1990), pp. 71–99.

35. David Brody, *The Butcher Workmen: A Study of Unionization* (Cambridge: Harvard University Press, 1964), p. 7; Art Shields, "One Man's Quest," *Worker* January 14, 1945, copy in private papers of Corliss Lamont, New York, N.Y.; Ward, *The Gospel for a Working World* (New York: Missionary Education Movement of the United States and Canada, 1918), pp. xiii–xiv.

36. Ward, *Gospel for a Working World*, pp. 148–155; Ward, "What Has the Church for the Workingman?" *Locomotive Engineers Journal* 21 (January, 1923): 27–28; Ward, *Which Way Religion?* pp. 39–42, 118–132.

37. Harry F. Ward, "The Experience of God in Social Struggle," lecture notes (September 30, 1921), Harry F. Ward Papers, Union Theological Seminary, New York.

38. Robert H. Craig, "The Underside of History: American Methodism, Capitalism, and Popular Struggle," *Methodist History* 27 (January, 1989): 86–87; Donald K. Gorrell, "The Methodist Federation for Social Service and the Social Creed," *Methodist History* 13 (January, 1975): 4–7; William McGuire King, "The Emergence of Social Gospel Radicalism: The Methodist Case," *Church History* 50 (December, 1981): 436–449; George D. McClain, "Pioneering Social Gospel Radicalism: An Overview History of the Methodist Federation for Social Action," *Radical Religion* 5/1 (1980): 11–12.

39. Harry F. Ward, "Christianity, an Ethical Religion," *Union Review* 2 (May, 1941): 7–9; Ward, *The New Social Order* (New York: Macmillan, 1919), pp. 19, 131–182; Ward, "Twenty Years of the Social Creed," *Christian Century*, April 19, 1928, pp. 502–504; Ward, *Which Way Religion?* pp. 23–33, 90–114. See also Ward, *Social Evangelism* (New York: Missionary Education Movement of the United States and Canada, 1915).

40. George Albert Coe, "Religion as a Factor in Individual and Social Development," *Biblical World* 23 (January, 1904): 4; Coe, *The Religion of a Mature Mind* (Chicago: Fleming Revell, 1902), pp. 168–172; Coe, "My Own Little Theatre," in *Religion in Transition*, ed. Vergilius Ferm (New York: Macmillan, 1937), p. 110; George Herbert Mead, *Selected Writings*, ed. Andrew J. Reck (Chicago: University of Chicago Press, 1964), p. xxxi.

41. Marx, "On the Jewish Question," pp. 24–25; Ward, *Our Economic Morality*, pp. 181–182; Ward, *Democracy and Social Change* (New York: Modern Age Books, 1940), pp. 26–45.

42. Craig, "Introduction to the Life and Thought of Ward," pp. 336–350; Upton Sinclair, *The Goose-Step: A Study of American Education*, rev. ed. (Pasadena: the author, 1923), pp. 191, 428, 430; Editorial, *Christian Register*, February 26, 1920, pp. 202–203, copy in Ward Papers; "A Prophet Was among Us," *Social Questions Bulletin* 57 (January, 1967): 1–4; Ward, "Why I Have Found Life Worth Living," p. 281.

43. Ward, *Democracy and Social Change*, pp. 36, 50–56, 292.

44. Ward, *New Social Order*, pp. 43–120; Alan Wolfe, *Whose Keeper? Social Science and Moral Obligations* (Berkeley: University of California Press, 1989), pp. 210–211.

45. Ward, *Democracy and Social Change*, pp. 60–62, 95–114; Ward, "Kingdom of Gold," *World Tomorrow* 9 (December, 1926): 247–248; Ward, *New Social Order*, pp. 13–18, 43–47; Joshua Cohen and Joel Roger, *On Democracy* (New York: Penguin Books, 1983), pp. 50–74.

46. Ward, *Our Economic Morality and the Ethic of Jesus*, pp. 9, 18–19, 269, 309, 320–323; Ward, "The Bible and the Proletarian Movement," *Journal of Religion* 3 (May, 1921): 278–281.

47. Ward, *New Social Order*, pp. 137–152; Ward, "The Function of Faith in the Modern World," in Harry Emerson Fosdick et al. *What Religion Means to Me* (Garden City: Doubleday, Doran, 1929), p. 46.

48. Harry F. Ward, "The Moral Valuation of Our Economic Order," *Journal of Religion* 3 (July, 1921): 416–417; Ward, "Perils of Competition for Private Gain," *World Tomorrow* 12 (January, 1929): 21–24; Ward, "The Strategy for a New Economic Order," *World Tomorrow* 12 (August, 1929): 328–331; Ward, *Which Way Religion?* pp. 206–211.

49. Ward, *Our Economic Morality and the Ethic of Jesus*, pp. 1–30, 209; Ward, "The Future of the Profit Motive," *Christian Century*, March 31, 1943, p. 390; Ward, *Democracy and Social Change*, pp. 209, 219.

50. Harry F. Ward, "We Were Friends," *Religious Education* 47 (March, 1952): 90–91. The correspondence of Ward and George Albert Coe can be found in the Coe Papers.

51. Ward, *Democracy and Social Change*, pp. 153–181.

52. Ibid.

53. Samuel Bowles and Herbert Gintis, *Democracy and Capitalism: Property, Com-*

munity, and the Contradictions of Modern Social Thought (New York: Basic Books, 1986), p. 132; Harry F. Ward, "Class Struggle," lecture notes (n.d., probably late 1930s), Ward Papers.

54. Stephen F. Cohen, *Rethinking the Soviet Experience: Politics and History since 1917* (New York: Oxford University Press, 1985), pp. 4–8; Stephen F. Cohen, *Sovieticus: American Perceptions and Soviet Realities* (New York: W. W. Norton, 1985), pp. 19–33.

55. Paul Robeson, *Here I Stand* (New York: Othello Associates, 1958), pp. 1–2, 38–40, quoted in Martin Bauml Duberman, *Paul Robeson* (New York: Alfred A. Knopf, 1988), p. 458.

56. Cornel West, *Prophesy Deliverance!* (Philadelphia: Westminster Press, 1982), p. 136; Alexander Cockburn, "Exchange: Stalin's Victims," *The Nation*, August 7–14, 1989, p. 184.

57. Philip S. Foner, *The Bolshevik Revolution* (New York: International, 1967), p. 27; John Reed, *Ten Days That Shook the World* (1919; New York: Vintage Books, 1960), p. lii; Eugene V. Debs, "The Day of the People," *Class Struggle* 3 (February, 1919): 4; James Weinstein, *The Decline of Socialism in America, 1912–1925* (New York: Vintage Books, 1969), pp. 206–209; Meno Lovenstein, *American Opinion of Soviet Russia* (Washington, D.C.: American Council on Public Affairs, 1941), pp. 44, 48–49.

58. Craig, "Introduction to the Life and Thought of Ward," pp. 340–342; Harry F. Ward, "The Russian Question," *Social Service Bulletin* (January–February, 1919): 1–4; Ward, *Social Unrest in the United States*, pamphlet (New York: Methodist Federation for Social Service, 1919), pp. 10–15; Ward, *The Opportunity for Religion in the Present World Situation* (New York: Woman's Press, 1919), pp. 8–9.

59. *Christian Advocate*, February 20, 1919, p. 240; *New York Tribune*, March 18, 1919, p. 9; "Methodists and Professor Ward," *Congregationalist and Advance*, April 10, 1919, p. 460.

60. Craig, "Introduction to the Life and Thought of Ward," pp. 344–345; Harry F. Ward, Introduction to Pat Sloan, *Russia without Illusions* (New York: Modern Age Books, 1939), pp. vii–x; "Ward on Russia," *Social Service Bulletin*, November 15, 1924, pp. 1–2; Ward, "Will Russia Return to Capitalism?" *The Nation*, July 8, 1925, pp. 64–67; Milton John Huber, Jr., "A History of the Methodist Federation for Social Action" (Ph.D. diss. Boston University, 1949), pp. 173–174.

61. Peter G. Filene, *Americans and the Soviet Experiment, 1917–1933* (Cambridge: Harvard University Press, 1967), pp. 187–202, 241–262; Frederick Lewis Allen, *Only Yesterday* (New York: Harper and Brothers, 1931); Sheila Fitzpatrick, *The Russian Revolution* (New York: Oxford University Press, 1982), pp. 118–129; Louis Fischer, "Will the Five-Year Plan Succeed?" *The Nation*, February 3, 1931, pp. 119–120, quoted in Richard H. Pells, *Radical Visions and American Dreams: Culture and Social Thought in the Depression Years* (New York: Harper and Row, 1973), p. 65; Harry F. Ward, *In Place of Profit: Social Incentives in the Soviet Union* (New York: Charles Scribner's Sons, 1933), pp. vii, 3.

62. Craig, "An Introduction to the Life and Thought of Ward," pp. 347–348; Ward, *In Place of Profit*, pp. 2, 93, 213, 382–383, 450, 456–458; Harry F. Ward, "Working for Themselves," *Social Service Bulletin* 22 (May, 1932): 4; Ward, *Democracy and Social Change*, pp. 81–87, 151.

63. Harry F. Ward, "Preaching and the Industrial Order," in *Preaching and the Social Crisis*, ed. G. B. Oxnam (New York: Abingdon Press, 1933), pp. 61–62; Ward, "Development of Fascism in the United States," *Annals of the American Academy* 180 (July, 1935): 57; Ward, *The Story of American-Soviet Relations, 1917–1959*, pamphlet (New York: National Council of American-Soviet Friendship, 1959), pp. 11–27; Ward, *Democracy and Social Change*, pp. 116–117; Stephen F. Cohen, *Rethinking the Soviet Experience*, pp. 74–78; Pasternak, quoted in Roy A. Medvedev, "New Pages from the Political Biography of Stalin," in *Stalinism: Essays in Historical Interpretation*, ed. Robert C. Tucker (New York: W. W. Norton, 1977), pp. 208, 212.

64. "Beyond Summitry," *The Nation*, June 18, 1990, p. 844. Some of these reflections on Ward's attitudes toward the Soviet Union are informed by a personal interview with Lynd Ward, February 16, 1969.

65. Harry F. Ward, "Christians and Communists," *Christian Century*, December 25, 1935, pp. 1651–1653; Ward, *Which Way Religion?* pp. 200–202.

66. Richard Falk, *The Promise of World Order: Essays in Normative International Relations* (Philadelphia: Temple University Press, 1987), pp. 220–248; Gordon C. Zahn, *War, Conscience, and Dissent* (New York: Hawthorn Books, 1967), p. 306.

67. Dave Dellinger, Introduction to *Liberation* 12 (September–October, 1967): 3–4; George McTurnan Kahin and John W. Lewis, *The United States in Vietnam* (New York: Dial Press, 1967), p. 241; James Finn, *Protest: Pacifism and Politics* (New York: Random House, 1967), p. 195; Barbara Deming, "It's a Good Life," *Liberation* 12 (September–October, 1967): 60.

68. A. J. Muste, "Sketches for an Autobiography," in *The Essays of A. J. Muste*, ed. Nat Hentoff (Indianapolis: Bobbs-Merrill, 1967), pp. 15–28; Jo Ann Ooiman Robinson, *Abraham Went Out: A Biography of A. J. Muste* (Philadelphia: Temple University Press, 1981), pp. 4–5; Henry S. Lucas, *Netherlanders in America* (Ann Arbor: University of Michigan Press, 1955), pp. 265–272, 511–515.

69. Muste, "Sketches for an Autobiography," pp. 41–43; William George Batz, "Revolution and Peace: The Christian Pacifism of A. J. Muste (1885–1967)" (Ph.D. diss., University of Minnesota, 1974), pp. 7–10.

70. Muste, "Sketches for an Autobiography," pp. 43–44; Judith O'Sullivan and Rosemary Gallick, *Workers and Allies: Female Participation in the American Union Movement, 1824–1976* (Washington, D.C.: Smithsonian Institution Press, 1975), p. 17.

71. Muste, "Sketches for an Autobiography," pp. 45–47; A. J. Muste, Letter to the Editor, *Survey*, March 10, 1917, p. 675, in Batz, "Revolution and Peace," p. 15.

72. Muste, "Sketches for an Autobiography," pp. 51–55; Robinson, *Abraham Went Out*, pp. 21–22.

73. Muste, "Sketches for an Autobiography," pp. 55–77.

74. Muste, "Sketches for an Autobiography," pp. 55–77; Jeremy Brecher, *Strike!* (Boston: South End Press, 1972), p. 115.

75. J. B. S. Hardman, ed., *American Labor Dynamics in Light of Post-War Development* (1928; New York: Russell and Russell, 1968), p. 210; Muste, "Sketches for an Autobiography," pp. 78–79, 92–106; Arthur Gleason, *Workers' Education: American Experiments (with a Few Foreign Examples)* (New York: Bureau of Industrial Research, 1921), pp. 55–57; Arthur Levine, "Brookwood Remembered," *Change* 13 (November–December, 1981): 39–42, Lewis quoted p. 39.

76. Muste, "Sketches for an Autobiography," pp. 127–132.

77. A. J. Muste, "Labor's Left-Wing Vanguard," *World Tomorrow*, September 28, 1932, p. 306; Roy Rosenzweig, "Radicals and the Jobless: The Musteites and the Unemployed Leagues, 1932–1936," *Labor History* 16 (Winter, 1975): 53–54.

78. Muste, "Sketches for an Autobiography," pp. 133–138.

79. Ibid., 155–157; Rosenzweig, "Radicals and the Jobless," pp. 56–59, 75.

80. Roy Rosenzweig, "Organizing the Unemployed: The Early Years of the Great Depression, 1929–1933," *Radical America* 10 (July–August, 1976): 49–52.

81. Rosenzweig, "Radicals and the Jobless," pp. 67–68; Irving Bernstein, *Turbulent Years: A History of the American Worker, 1933–1941* (Boston: Houghton Mifflin, 1971), pp. 219–229.

82. Bernstein, *Turbulent Years*, pp. 219–229.

83. Muste, "Sketches for an Autobiography," pp. 162–170; A. J. Muste, "An American Revolutionary Party," *Modern Monthly* 7 (January, 1934): 713–718.

84. Constance Ashton Myers, *The Prophet's Army: Trotskyists in America, 1928–1941* (Westport: Greenwood Press, 1977), pp. 86–93, 116–122; Nat Hentoff, *Peace Agitator: The Story of A. J. Muste* (New York: Macmillan, 1963), pp. 85–96.

85. A. J. Muste, "My Experience in the Labor and Radical Struggles of the Thirties," in *As We Saw the Thirties*, ed. Rita James Simon (Urbana: University of Illinois Press, 1967), pp. 138–147.

86. Charles Chatfield, *For Peace and Justice: Pacifism in America, 1914–1941* (Knoxville: University of Tennessee Press, 1971), p. 3; Hentoff, *Peace Agitator*, pp. 97–98; A. J. Muste, "The True International," in *Essays of Muste*, pp. 208–209; Muste, "My Experience in Labor and Radical Struggles," pp. 147–148; Muste, "Return to Pacifism," in *Essays of Muste*, pp. 195–202.

87. Jo Ann Ooiman Robinson, "The Pharos of the East Side, 1937–1940: Labor Temple under the Direction of A. J. Muste," *Journal of Presbyterian History* 48 (Spring, 1970): 18–29; Muste, "True International," pp. 207–214.

88. Batz, "Revolution and Peace," pp. 27–40; Penina Migdal Glazer, "From the Old Left to the New: Radical Criticism in the 1940s," *American Quarterly* 24 (December, 1972): 584–603; Muste, "Sketches for an Autobiography," pp. 135–136; Muste, "The Fall of Man," in *Essays of Muste*, p. 449.

89. A. J. Muste, "Theology of Despair: An Open Letter to Reinhold Niebuhr," *Fellowship* 14 (September, 1948): 4–5; Muste, "The Doctrine of Perfection, I," *Fellowship* 16 (March, 1950): 7–12; Muste, *Not by Might* (New York: Harper and Brothers, 1947), pp. 156–157; Juan Luis Segundo, *The Liberation of Theology* (Maryknoll: Orbis Books, 1976), p. 150.

90. Muste, *Not by Might*, pp. 52–53 (Silone quoted p. 53), 110; A. J. Muste, *Non-violence in an Aggressive World* (New York: Harper and Brothers, 1940), pp. 32–35.

91. Muste, *Non-violence in an Aggressive World*, pp. 21–22, 42–44; A. J. Muste, "Pacifism and the Problem of Power," *Fellowship* 16 (January, 1950): 9–10; Muste, *Not by Might*, pp. 108–109; Muste, "Niebuhr on the Brink of War," *Liberation* 1 (February 1957): 9.

92. Paul Ricoeur, quoted in, José Míguez Bonino, *Doing Theology in a Revolutionary Situation* (Philadelphia: Fortress Press, 1975), p. 114; Muste, "Sketches for an Autobiography," pp. 136–137.

93. Muste, "Theology of Despair," pp. 4–7; Muste, "Niebuhr on the Brink of War," p. 10; "Fall of Man," pp. 445–448; Muste, *Not by Might*, pp. 91–93.

94. Muste, "Pacifism and the Problem of Power," pp. 11–13; Richard J. Barnet, "Reflections: Rethinking National Strategy," *New Yorker*, March 21, 1988, pp. 104, 107–110, 113–114.

95. Muste, *Not by Might*, pp. 70–77 (Weil quoted on 71).

96. Muste, *Non-violence in an Aggressive World*, p. 129; Finn, *Protest*, pp. 199–200. For an analysis of violence similar to Muste's, see Robert McAfee Brown, *Religion and Violence*, 2nd ed. (Philadelphia: Westminster Press, 1987).

97. Muste, *Not by Might*, pp. 80–85; Finn, *Protest*, p. 199.

98. A. J. Muste, "Pacifism and Class War," in *Essays of Muste*, pp. 179–185.

99. Hentoff, *Peace Agitator*, pp. 133–136, 190–191.

100. A. J. Muste, "The World Task of Pacifism," in *Essays of Muste*, pp. 223–226.

101. Muste, *Not by Might*, pp. 209–213; Muste, "Sketches for an Autobiography," pp. 87–88.

102. A. J. Muste, "What the Bible Teaches about Freedom," *Essays of Muste*, pp. 279–295.

103. Hentoff, *Peace Agitator*, p. 18; Aldon D. Morris, *The Origins of the Civil Rights Movement* (New York: Free Press, 1984), pp. 157–158; James Farmer, *Lay Bare the Heart: An Autobiography of the Civil Rights Movement* (New York: Arbor House, 1985), pp. 88–94; Howell Raines, *My Soul Is Rested: Movement Days in the Deep South Remembered* (New York: Viking Penguin, 1983), pp. 27–34; August Meier and Elliot Rudwick, *CORE: A Study in the Civil Rights Movement, 1942–1968* (New York: Oxford University Press, 1973), pp. 4–39.

104. Morris, *Origins of the Civil Rights Movement*, pp. 57, 62, 77, 83, 159–166, 218–219; David J. Garrow, *Bearing the Cross: Martin Luther King, Jr., and the Southern Christian Leadership Conference* (New York: William Morrow, 1986), pp. 66–73; Taylor Branch, *Parting the Waters: America in the King Years, 1954–63* (New York: Simon and Schuster, 1988), pp. 173–174, 178–180, 259–260.

105. Henry Hampton and Steve Fayer, *Voices of Freedom: An Oral History of the Civil Rights Movement from the 1950s through the 1980s* (New York: Bantam Books, 1990), pp. 33, 53–55; Raines, *My Soul Is Rested*, pp. 75–93.

106. Hampton and Fayer, *Voices of Freedom*, pp. 73–96; Raines, *My Soul Is Rested*, pp. 109–129; Manning Marable, *Race, Reform, and Rebellion: The Second Reconstruction in Black America, 1945–1982* (Jackson: University Press of Mississippi, 1984), pp. 1, 66, 208–209.

107. A. J. Muste, "Rifle Squads or the Beloved Community," *Essays of Muste*, p. 435; Muste, "The Civil Rights Movement and the American Establishment," *Essays of Muste*, pp. 459–461. King's critique of the Vietnam War was most vividly expressed in an address he gave at Riverside Church in New York City on April 4, 1967, "Declaration of Independence from the War in Vietnam," reprinted in *The Vietnam War: Christian Perspectives*, ed. Michael P. Hamilton (Grand Rapids, Mich.: William B. Eerdmans, 1967), pp. 115–130.

108. Muste, "What the Bible Teaches about Freedom," pp. 279–287.

109. William D. Miller, *Dorothy Day: A Biography* (San Francisco: Harper and Row, 1982), pp. ix–x; Virgil Elizondo, "Transmission of the Faith in the USA," in *The Transmission of the Faith to the Next Generation*, ed. Norbert Greinacher and Elizondo

(Edinburgh; T. and T. Clark, 1984), pp. 103–104; David O'Brien, "The Pilgrimage of Dorothy Day," *Commonweal*, December 19, 1980, p. 711. The most detailed biography is Miller's. The most recent is Robert Coles, *Dorothy Day: A Radical Devotion* (Reading, Pa.: Addison-Wesley, 1987). Among more extensive treatments of Day and the Catholic Worker movement are William D. Miller, *A Harsh and Dreadful Love: Dorothy Day and the Catholic Worker Movement* (New York: Liveright, 1971); Mel Piehl, *Breaking Bread: The Catholic Worker and the Origin of Catholic Radicalism in America* (Philadelphia: Temple University Press, 1982); and Nancy C. Roberts, *Dorothy Day and the Catholic Worker* (Albany: State University of New York Press, 1984).

110. Dorothy Day, *The Long Loneliness* (San Francisco: Harper and Row, 1952, 1981), pp. 9–12; Day, *From Union Square to Rome* (Silver Spring, Md.: Preservation of the Faith Press, 1938), pp. 1–17.

111. Miller, *Dorothy Day*, p. 1; Day, *From Union Square to Rome*, pp. 40–60; Day, *Long Loneliness*, pp. 36–50.

112. Henry F. May, *The End of American Innocence: A Study of the First Years of Our Own Time, 1912–1917* (Chicago: Quadrangle Books, 1964), pp. 279–282; Day, *From Union Square to Rome*, pp. 71–89; Day, *Long Loneliness*, pp. 60–72; William L. O'Neill, ed., *Echoes of Revolt: "The Masses," 1911–1917* (Chicago: Quadrangle Books, 1966), p. 6.

113. Robert Justin Goldstein, *Political Repression in Modern America* (Cambridge: Schenkman, 1978), pp. 110–127; Day, *Long Loneliness*, pp. 72–95; Day, *From Union Square to Rome*, pp. 81–97; Crystal Eastman, *On Women and Revolution*, ed. Blanche Wiesen Cook (New York: Oxford University Press, 1978), pp. 23–24.

114. Day, *Long Loneliness*, pp. 97–105; John Higham, *Strangers in the Land: Patterns of American Nativism, 1860–1925*, 2nd ed. (New York: Atheneum, 1971), pp. 227–232; Melvyn Dubofsky, *We Shall Be All: A History of the Industrial Workers of the World* (New York: Quadrange/New York Times Book, 1969), pp. 454–456.

115. Day, *From Union Square to Rome*, pp. 109–110, 127–142.

116. Day, *Long Loneliness*, pp. 113–116, 140–150; Paul Buhle, *Marxism in the USA* (London: Verso, 1987), pp. 172–175.

117. Day, *Long Loneliness*, pp. 151–169.

118. Dorothy Day, *House of Hospitality* (New York: Sheed and Ward, 1939), pp. v, xvii–xx; Marc H. Ellis, *Peter Maurin: Prophet in the Twentieth Century* (New York: Paulist Press, 1981), pp. 21–38; Dorothy Day, *Loaves and Fishes* (1963; San Francisco: Harper and Row, 1983), p. 9.

119. Day, *Long Loneliness*, pp. 171–174; Day, *Loaves and Fishes*, pp. 9–10.

120. Ellis, *Peter Maurin*, pp. 48–49; Peter Maurin, *Easy Essays*, ed. Chuck Smith (West Hamlin: Green Revolution, 1971), p. 24.

121. Day, *House of Hospitality*, pp. xix–xxvii; Day, *Loaves and Fishes*, pp. 28–30, 42–59; Ellis, *Peter Maurin*, pp. 49–50.

122. Day, *House of Hospitality*, pp. xxviii–xxix, xxxiv; Day, *Long Loneliness*, p. 182.

123. "To Our Readers," *Catholic Worker* (May, 1933), in *A Penny a Copy: Readings from the "Catholic Worker,"* ed. Thomas C. Cornell and James H. Forest (New York: Macmillan, 1968), p. 4.

124. Coles, *Dorothy Day*, pp. 14–15, 111; Dorothy Day, *On Pilgrimage: The Sixties* (New York: Curtis Books, 1972), p. 172.

125. Day, *From Union Square to Rome*, pp. 147–148; Dorothy Day, "Room for

Christ," *Catholic Worker* 12 (December, 1945): 2, in Day, *House of Hospitality*, p. 250; Day, "Why Write about Strife and Violence?" *Catholic Worker* (June, 1934), and "Poverty and Precarity," *Catholic Worker* (May, 1952), both in *By Little and by Little: The Selected Writings of Dorothy Day*, ed. Robert Ellsberg (New York: Alfred A. Knopf, 1988), pp. 63, 106.

126. Day, *Loaves and Fishes*, pp. 78–79, 82; Day, "What Do the Simple Folk Do?" *Catholic Worker* 44 (May, 1978): 5, 8; Peter Townsend, *Poverty in the United Kingdom*, quoted in Michael Harrington, *The New American Poverty* (New York: Viking Penguin, 1984), pp. 74–75; Day, *House of Hospitality*, p. 60; Dorothy Day, *On Pilgrimage* (New York: Catholic Worker Books, 1948), in *By Little and by Little*, p. 229.

127. Day, *On Pilgrimage* (*By Little and by Little*), p. 229; Tom Sullivan, "Remembering Dorothy with Love," *Catholic Worker* 46 (December 1980): 9; Day, *On Pilgrimage: The Sixties*, p. 267.

128. Day, *On Pilgrimage: The Sixties*, p. 273; Dorothy Day, "This Money Is Not Ours," *Catholic Worker* (September 1960), in *A Penny a Copy*, pp. 204–205; Day, *Loaves and Fishes*, pp. 80–82.

129. Day, "What Do the Simple Folk Do?" pp. 174–177; Day, *On Pilgrimage: The Sixties*, pp. 168, 196.

130. Dorothy Day, "Our Brothers, the Communists," in *By Little and by Little*, pp. 270–274; Day, *Loaves and Fishes*, p. 70; Elizondo, "Transmission of the Faith in the USA," p. 104; Day, "Why Write about Strife and Violence?" pp. 62–63; Day, "Letter to the Unemployed," *Catholic Worker* (December 1937), in *By Little and by Little*, pp. 83–84; Day, *House of Hospitality*, pp. 250–256; Day, "The Neglected," in *Who Is My Neighbor?* ed. Esther Pike (Greenwich: Seabury Press, 1960), p. 60.

131. Piehl, *Breaking Bread*, pp. 117–119, 136–143; Mary C. Segers, "Equality and Christian Anarchism: The Political and Social Ideas of the Catholic Worker Movement," *Review of Politics* 40 (April 1978): 196–230; Day, *House of Hospitality*, pp. 75, 146; Day, "Our Brothers, the Communists," pp. 270–271; Day, "Elizabeth Gurley Flynn," *Catholic Worker* (November 1951), in *By Little and by Little*, p. 145.

132. Segers, "Equality and Christian Anarchism," p. 229.

133. Coles, *Dorothy Day*, pp. 89–109; "Catholic Worker Positions," *Catholic Worker* 52 (May 1985), quoted in David O'Brien, *Public Catholicism* (New York: Macmillan, 1989), p. 246; Daniel Berrigan, *To Dwell in Peace: An Autobiography* (San Francisco: Harper and Row, 1987), p. 173.

134. Piehl, *Breaking Bread*, pp. 135–143; Michele Teresa Aronica, *Beyond Charismatic Leadership: The New York Catholic Worker Movement* (New Brunswick: Transaction Books, 1987), pp. 54–56; David J. O'Brien, *American Catholics and Social Reform* (New York: Oxford University Press, 1968), pp. 204–205.

135. Day, *Long Loneliness*, p. 222; Day, "Our Brothers, the Communists," p. 272; Day, *On Pilgrimage: The Sixties*, pp. 170–171.

136. Miller, *Dorothy Day*, p. 382; Martin Buber, *Paths in Utopia* (Boston: Beacon Press, 1958), pp. xii, xvi–xvii, xxiv–xxv, 130–136.

137. Miller, *Dorothy Day*, p. 382; Buber, *Paths in Utopia*, pp. xii, xvi–xvii, xxiv–xv, 130–136; Buber, *A Believing Humanism: My Testament, 1902–1965* (New York: Simon and Schuster, 1967), pp. 87–95; Donald L. Berry, *Mutuality: The Vision of Martin Buber* (Albany: State University of New York Press, 1985), pp. 91–97.

138. David O'Brien, *The Renewal of American Catholicism* (New York: Oxford Uni-

versity Press, 1972), p. 222; Marie Augusta Neal, *The Just Demands of the Poor* (New York: Paulist Press, 1987), p. 7.

139. Williams, *Great Evasion*, p. 167.

140. Max Weber, "Politics as a Vocation," in *From Max Weber: Essays in Sociology*, ed. H. H. Gerth and C. Wright Mills (New York: Oxford University Press, 1946), p. 128.

141. Oscar Romero, *Voice of the Voiceless: The Four Pastoral and Other Statements*, Introductory essays by Ignacio Martín Baró and Jon Sobrino (Maryknoll: Orbis Books, 1985).

142. Wendell Berry, *The Unsettling of America: Culture and Agriculture* (San Francisco: Sierra Club Books, 1977), pp. 3–26; Berry, *What Are People For?* (San Francisco: North Point Press, 1990), pp. 95–102.

143. Berry, *What Are People For?* pp. 123–144, 153–169, 197–210.

144. John Gaventa, *Power and Powerlessness: Quiescence and Rebellion in an Appalachian Valley* (Urbana: University of Illinois Press, 1980), p. 260.

145. Evans and Boyte, *Free Spaces*, pp. 183–202; Birnbaum, *Radical Renewal*, pp. 186–190.

146. Harry F. Ward, "Jesus and Marx," unpublished manuscript (n.d.), pp. 4–29, 291, Ward Papers.

Conclusion

1. Vincent Harding, *Hope and History: Why We Must Share the Story of the Movement* (Maryknoll: Orbis Books, 1990), p. 16.

2. Gustavo Gutiérrez, *The Power of the Poor in History* (Maryknoll: Orbis Books, 1983), pp. 21, 202; Bill Schwartz, "The People in History: Communist Party Historians' Group, 1946–56," in *Making Histories: Studies in History-Writing and Politics*, ed. Richard Jones, Gregor McLennan, Bill Schwartz, and David Sutton (Minneapolis: University of Minnesota Press, 1982), pp. 94–96; Robert H. Craig, "Liberative History and Liberation Ethics: A Case Study of American Methodism and Popular Struggle," in *The Annual of the Society of Christian Ethics*, ed. D. M. Yeager (Washington, D.C.: Georgetown University Press, 1987), pp. 134–135.

3. *People's Institute of Applied Religion*, mimeographed newsletter (Spring, 1951): 4, Claude C. Williams Collection, Correspondence and Papers, 1929–1979, Archives of Labor and Urban History, Wayne State University, Detroit.

4. Beverly Wildung Harrison, "Theological Reflection in the Struggle for Liberation: Feminist Perspective," in *Making the Connections: Essays in Feminist Social Ethics*, ed. Carol S. Robb (Boston: Beacon Press, 1985), p. 249; Pablo Richard, "La Biblia y la memoria histórica de los pobres," in *Las iglesias en la practica de la justicia* (San Jose: Departamento Ecuménico de Investigaciones, 1984), p. 41; Craig, "Liberative History and Liberation Ethics," pp. 135–136; Reverdy C. Ransom, *The Negro: The Hope or the Despair of Christianity* (Boston: Ruth Hill, 1935), pp. 6–7.

5. John Howard Yoder, *The Priestly Kingdom: Social Ethics as Gospel* (Notre Dame: University of Notre Dame Press, 1984), p. 95.

6. James Gustafson, "The Relevance of Historical Understanding," in *Toward a Discipline of Social Ethics: Essays in Honor of Walter George Muelder*, ed. Paul Deats, Jr. (Boston: Boston University Press, 1972), pp. 49, 67–68; Craig, "Liberative History and Liberation Ethics," p. 133.

7. Gibson Winter, *Liberating Creation: Foundations of Religious Social Ethics* (New

York: Crossroads, 1981), pp. 131–134; Harrison, "Theological Reflection," p. 249.

8. Christopher Lasch, "What's Wrong with the Right?" *Tikkun* 1/1 (1986): 23; Craig, "Liberative History and Liberation Ethics, pp. 155–156.

9. Michael Harrington, *Taking Sides: The Education of a Militant Mind* (New York: Holt, Rinehart, and Winston, 1985), p. 1.

10. Harrison, "Theological Reflection," p. 249; Gustavo Gutiérrez, "Two Theological Perspectives: Liberation Theology and Progressive Theology," in *The Emergent Gospel: Theology from the Underside of History*, ed. Sergio Torres and Virginia Fabella (Maryknoll: Orbis Books, 1978), p. 244.

11. Karen L. Bloomquist, *The Dream Betrayed: Religious Challenge of the Working Class* (Minneapolis: Fortress Press, 1990), p. 41.

12. Cornel West, *Prophesy Deliverance!* (Philadelphia: Westminster Press, 1982), pp. 113–115; West, "Left Strategies: A View from Afro-America," *Socialist Review* 16/86 (1986): 43–45.

13. Eugene D. Genovese, "On Antonio Gramsci," in *For a New America*, ed. James Weinstein and David W. Eakins (New York: Vintage Books, 1970), p. 301.

14. Linda Phelps, "Patriarchy and Capitalism," in *Building Feminist Theory: Essays from "Quest"*, ed. Carlotte Bunch et al. (New York: Longman, 1981), pp. 162–163; Carol S. Robb, "A Framework for Feminist Ethics," in *Women's Consciousness, Women's Conscience*, ed. Barbara Hilkert Andolsen, Christine E. Gudorf, and Mary D. Pellauer (San Francisco: Harper and Row, 1985), pp. 230–231; Randy Albelda et al., *Mink Coats Don't Trickle Down* (Boston: South End Press, 1988), pp. 41–53.

15. Children's Defense Fund, *A Vision for America's Future* (Washington, D.C.: Children's Defense Fund, 1989), pp. xviii–xix; John C. Bennett, *The Radical Imperative: From Theology to Social Ethics* (Philadelphia: Westminster Press, 1975), p. 164.

16. Michael Harrington, *The New American Poverty* (New York: Viking Penguin, 1984), p. 8.

17. James Cone, *For My People: Black Theology and the Black Church* (Maryknoll: Orbis Books, 1984), p. 184.

18. Robert Blauner, *Racial Oppression in America* (New York: Harper and Row, 1972), p. 146, as quoted in Alphonso Pinkney, *The Myth of Black Progress* (Cambridge: Cambridge University Press, 1984), p. 50.

19. Pinkney, *Myth of Black Progress*, p. 50; Ann Weick, "Other Ways of Seeing: The Female Vision," in *Seeing Female: Social Roles and Personal Lives*, ed. Sharon S. Brehm (New York: Greenwood Press, 1988), p. 188.

20. William K. Tabb, "Introduction: Transformative Theologies and the Commandment to Do Justice," in *Church in Struggle: Liberation Theologies and Social Change in North America* (New York: Monthly Review Press, 1986), pp. xiii–xix; Preface to the issue "Religion and the Left," *Monthly Review* 36 (July–August, 1984): 1–8.

21. Otto Maduro, "Marxist Analysis and the Sociology of Religion: An Introduction," *Social Compass* 22 (1975): 313–314; José Míguez Bonino, *Christians and Marxists* (Grand Rapids, Mich.: William B. Eerdmans, 1976), p. 26; Robert Craig, "Ideology as U.S. Religious History: The Political Economy of Religion," *Radical Religion* 3/1 (1976), pp. 9–10.

22. Gustavo Gutiérrez, *A Theology of Liberation* (Maryknoll: Orbis Books, 1973), p. 202; Dorothee Sölle, "Resurrection and Liberation," in *Border Regions of Faith*, ed. Kenneth Aman (Maryknoll: Orbis Books, 1987), p. 506.

23. Robert McAfee Brown, *Unexpected News: Reading the Bible with Third World Eyes* (Philadelphia: Westminster Press, 1984), pp. 117–118; Vicky Randall, *Women and Politics* (New York: St. Martin's Press, 1982), p. 7, quoted by Joey Sprague, "The Other Side of the Banner: Toward a Feminization of Politics," in *Seeing Female*, p. 167; José Míguez Bonino, *Towards a Christian Political Ethics* (Philadelphia: Fortress Press, 1983), p. 108.

24. David Obey, quoted in J. Peter Euben, "Democracy in America: Bringing It All Back Home," *Tikkun* 5 (November–December, 1990): 13; Raymond Williams, *Keywords* (New York: Oxford University Press, 1976), pp. 84–86.

25. Harding, *Hope and History*, p. 205.

26. Martin Luther King, Jr., "A Time to Break Silence," in *A Testament of Hope: The Essential Writings of Martin Luther King, Jr.*, ed. James Melvin Washington (San Francisco: Harper and Row, 1986), p. 242; Edward W. Said, "Ignorant Armies Clash by Night," *The Nation*, February 11, 1991, p. 163.

27. West, "Left Strategies," p. 42; Clayborne Carson, "Reconstructing the King Legacy: Scholars and National Myths," in *We Shall Overcome: Martin Luther King, Jr., and the Black Freedom Movement* (New York: Pantheon Books, 1990), p. 248.

28. Martin Luther King, Jr., *The Strength to Love* (New York: Harper and Row, 1963), as found in *A Testament of Hope*, p. 501.

Index